Autodesk

Architectural Desktop 2004 Fundamentals

Elise Moss

autodesk
authorized publisher

ISBN: 1-58503-135-6

SDC
PUBLICATIONS

Schroff Development Corporation

www.schroff.com
www.schroff-europe.com

Schroff Development Corporation
P.O. Box 1334
Mission, KS 66222
(913) 262-2664
www.schroff.com

Trademarks

The following are registered trademarks of Autodesk, Inc.: AutoCAD, Architectural Desktop, Inventor, Autodesk, AutoLISP, AutoCAD Design Center, Autodesk Device Interface, pointA and HEIDI.

Microsoft, Windows, NetMeeting, Word, and Excel are either registered trademarks or trademarks of Microsoft Corporation.

All other trademarks are trademarks of their respective holders.

Moss, Elise
Autodesk Architectural Desktop 2004 Fundamentals
Elise Moss
ISBN: 1-58503-135-6

Printed and bound in the United States of America.

Preface

For users familiar with Architectural Desktop 3.3 or earlier releases, the 2004 release marks a serious change to the user interface. No textbook can cover all the features in any software applications. This textbook is meant for beginner users who want to gain a familiarity with the tools and interface of ADT before they start exploring on their own. By the end of the text, the user should feel comfortable enough to create a standard model, and even know how to customize the interface for their own use.

The files used in this text are accessible from the Internet at www.schroff1.com/. They are free and available to students and teachers alike.

We value customer input. Please contact us with any comments, questions, or concerns about this text.

Elise Moss
elise_moss@mossdesigns.com

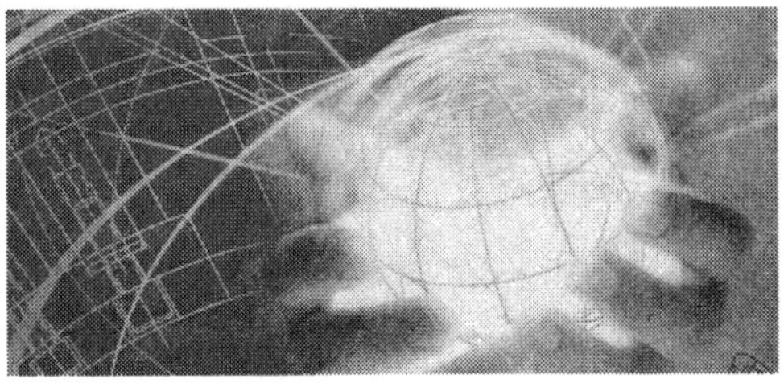

Acknowledgements from Elise Moss

This book would not have been possible without the support of some key Autodesk employees. A special thanks to Lynn Allen, Melrose Ross, Bill Zhang, and Denis Cadu.

Additional thanks to the board and members of the Silicon Valley AutoCAD Power Users, a dedicated group of Autodesk users, for educating me about the needs and wants of CAD users.

My deep appreciation to Reid M. Addis of Addis Computer Consultants, Bob Callori, Lay Chris Fox, Shao-ying Cheng, Roy Salume, Jason Ellisor, and a host of other architects and facilities managers whose insight into the field of architecture and the use of Architectural Desktop has been invaluable.

The effort and support of the editorial and production staff of Schroff Development Corporation is gratefully acknowledged. I especially thank Stephen Schroff for his helpful suggestions regarding the format of this text.

Finally, truly infinite thanks to Ari for his encouragement and his faith.

- Elise Moss

TABLE OF CONTENTS

Preface
Acknowledgements

Lesson 1
Desktop Features
Exercise 1-1: Creating a New Drawing with an AEC Template 1-5
Exercise 1-2: Creating a New Project 1-17
Exercise 1-3: Creating a New Geometric Profile 1-25
Exercise 1-4: Creating a New Wall Style 1-28
Exercise 1-5: Downloading Styles from Autodesk's pointA 1-42
Exercise 1-6: Creating a Fireplace Chimney 1-44
Exercise 1-7: Creating a Display Configuration 1-63

Lesson 2
Site Plans
Exercise 2-1: Creating Custom Line Types 2-2
Exercise 2-2: Creating a Custom Text Style 2-5
Exercise 2-3: Creating New Layers 2-6
Exercise 2-4: Creating a Site Plan 2-10
Exercise 2-5: Creating a Layer User Group 2-22

Quiz 1 Q1-1

Lesson 3
Floor Plans
Exercise 3-1: Creating Exterior Walls 3-1
Exercise 3-2: Convert to Walls 3-3
Exercise 3-3: Wall Cleanup 3-5
Exercise 3-4: Adding Closet Doors 3-11

Exercise 3-5: 3-14
Adding Interior Doors
Exercise 3-6: 3-15
Add Opening
Exercise 3-7: 3-20
Adding Doors
Exercise 3-8: 3-24
Add Window Assemblies
Exercise 3-9: 3-30
Adding a Fireplace

Quiz 2 Q2-1

Lesson 4
Space Planning
Exercise 4-1: 4-1
Creating AEC Content
Exercise 4-2: 4-5
Equipping the Bathrooms
Exercise 4-3: 4-9
Furnishing the Common Areas
Exercise 4-4: 4-14
Adding to the Service Areas
Exercise 4-5 4-17
Creating Layer Settings

Lesson 5
Roofs
Exercise 5-1: 5-4
Creating a Roof using Existing Walls
Exercise 5-2: 5-6
Roof Slabs
Exercise 5-3: 5-8
Creating a Roof Cricket

Quiz 3 Q3-1

Lesson 6
Structural Members
Exercise 6-1: 6-3
Creating Member Styles
Exercise 6-2: 6-7
Adding Structural Members
Exercise 6-3: 6-15
Add Floorboards
Exercise 6-4: 6-19
Add Railing
Exercise 6-5: 6-25
Add Stairs

Lesson 7
Layouts
Exercise 7-1: 7-2
Creating a Custom Titleblock
Exercise 7-2: 7-11
Creating an Elevation Label
Exercise 7-3 7-17
Creating an Elevation Window Tag
Exercise 7-4: 7-21
Creating Elevation Views
Exercise 7-5: 7-26
Annotating Elevation Views
Exercise 7-6: 7-32
Creating Section Views
Exercise 7-7: 7-39
Creating 3D Section Views

Quiz 4 Q4-1

Lesson 8:
Documentation
Exercise 8-1: 8-10
Dimensioning a Floor Plan

Lesson 9:
Schedules
Exercise 9-1: 9-7
Creating a Schedule Table
Exercise 9-2: 9-11
Adding Door & Window Tags
Exercise 9-3: 9-13
Adding a Schedule Table
Exercise 9-4: 9-16
Exporting a Schedule

Lesson 10
Creating a Video
Exercise 10-1: 10-1
Adding a Path
Exercise 10-2: 10-4
Adding a Camera Tool to a Palette
Exercise 10-3: 10-9
Creating a Video

Comprehensive Exam E-1
Index
About the Author

NOTES:

Lesson 1:
Desktop Features

Architectural Desktop enlists object oriented process systems (OOPS). That means that ADT uses intelligent objects to create a building. This is similar to using blocks in AutoCAD. Objects in Architectural Desktop are blocks on steroids. They have intelligence already embedded into them. A wall in ADT is not just a collection of lines. It represents a real wall. It can be constrained, has thickness and material properties, and is automatically included in your building schedule.

The following table describes the key features of ADT:

Feature Type	Description
AEC Camera	Create perspective views from various camera angles. Create avi files.
AEC Profiles	Create AEC objects using polylines to build doors, windows, etc.
Anchors and Layouts	Define a spatial relationship between objects. Create a layout of anchors on a curve or a grid to set a pattern of anchored objects, such as doors or columns.
Annotation	Set up special arrows, leaders, bar scales
Ceiling Grids	Create reflected ceiling plans with grid layouts
Column Grids	Define rectangular and radial building grids with columns and bubbles
Design Center	Customize your AEC block library
Display System	Control views for each AEC object
Doors and Windows	Create custom door and window styles or use standard objects provided with ADT
Elevations and Sections	An elevation is basically a section view of a floor plan.
Layer Manager	Create layer standards based on AIA CAD Standards. Create groups of layers. Manage layers intelligently using Layer Filters.
Masking Blocks	Store a mask using a polyline object and attach to AEC objects to hide graphics
Model Explorer	View a model and manage the content easily. Attach names to mass elements to assist in design
Multi-view blocks	Blocks have embedded defined views to allow you to easily change view

Feature Type	Description
Railings	Create or apply different railing styles to a stair or along a defined path
Roofs	Create and apply various roof styles.
Floorplate slices	Generate the perimeter geometry of a building.
Spaces and Boundaries	Spaces and boundaries can include floor thickness, room height, and wall thickness.
Stairs	Create and apply various stair types
Tags and Schedules	Place tags on objects to generate schedules. Schedules will automatically update when tags are modified, added, or deleted.
Template Files	Use templates to save time. Create a template with standard layers, text styles, linetypes, dimension styles, etc.
Walls	Create wall styles to determine material composition. Define end caps to control opening and end conditions. Define wall interference conditions.

Architectural Desktop sits on top of AutoCAD. It is helpful for users to have a basic understanding of AutoCAD before moving to Architectural Desktop. Users should be familiar with the following:

- AutoCAD toolbars
- zoom and move around the screen
- manage blocks
- draw and modify commands
- model and paper space (layout),
- dimensioning and how to create/modify a dimension style

If you are not familiar with these topics, you can still move forward with learning ADT, but you may find it helpful to have a good AutoCAD textbook as reference in case you get stuck.

> **TIP:** The best way to use Architectural Desktop is start your project with massing tools (outside-in design) or space planning tools (inside-out design) and continue through to construction documentation.

The AEC Project Process Model

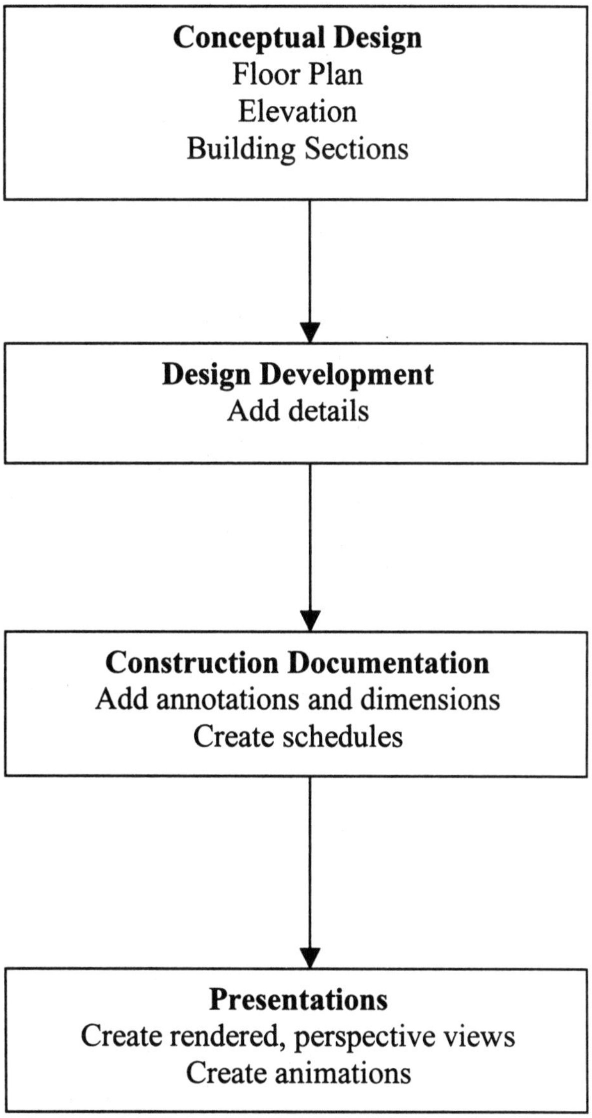

Conceptual Design

In the initial design phase, you can assemble Architectural Desktop mass elements as simple architectural shapes to form an exterior model of your building project. You can also lay out interior areas by arranging general spaces as you would in a bubble diagram. You can manipulate and consolidate three-dimensional mass elements into massing studies.

Later in this phase, you can create building footprints from the massing study by slicing floorplates, and you can begin defining the structure by converting space boundaries into walls. At the completion of the conceptual design phase, you have developed a workable schematic floor plan.

Design Development

As you refine the building project, you can add more detailed information to the schematic design. Use the features in Architectural Desktop to continue developing the design of the building project by organizing, defining, and assigning specific styles and attributes to building components.

Construction Development

After you have fully developed the building design, you can annotate your drawings with reference marks, notes, and dimensions. You can also add tags or labels associated with objects. Information from the objects and tags can be extracted, sorted, and compiled into schedules, reports, tables, and inventories for comprehensive and accurate construction documentation.

Presentations

A major part of any project is presenting it to the customer. At this stage, you develop renderings, animations, and perspective views.

Exercise 1-1:

Creating a New Drawing with an AEC Template

Drawing Name: New
Estimated Time: 15 minutes

This exercise reinforces the following skills:

- ❑ Use of templates
- ❑ Getting user familiar with tools and ADT environment

Menu	File Edit New...
Toolbar	
Command Line	Command: new
Shortcut Key	Ctl + N

1. Start a New Drawing. This can be done using the Menu, the Standard toolbar, or the command line as shown in the table above.

2. We will use a standard default template – Architectural Building Model and View (Imperial- ctb).dwt.

   To select the template, we place our mouse over the template name as shown and select Open.

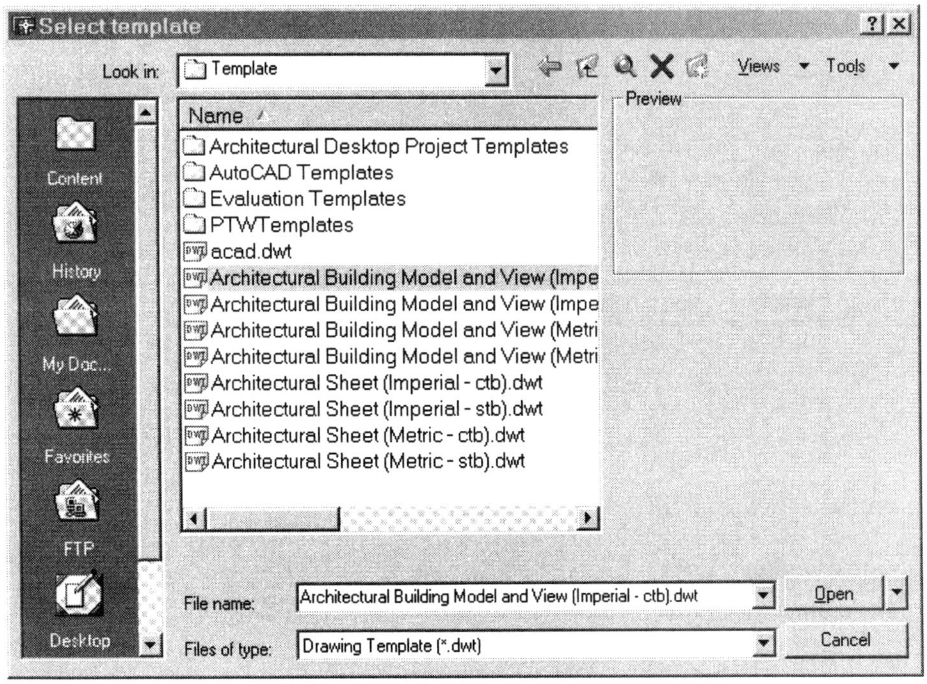

3. 

You have two layout tabs available: Model and Work. Model is where you will create your 3D model and Work is your first layout sheet.

4. Type **Options** at the command line.

5. Select the Files tab.

   Locate the Default Template File Name for QNEW.
   Note that no template is assigned.

   We can assign a template to QNEW and then bypass the template dialog box.

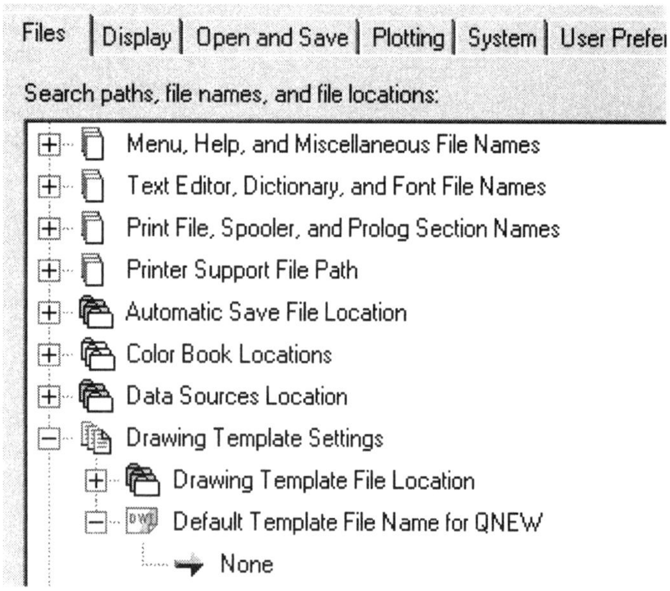

   Highlight **None** and then select **Browse**.

6. Locate the **Architectural Building Model and View (Imperial-ctb).dwt** template. Select **Open**.

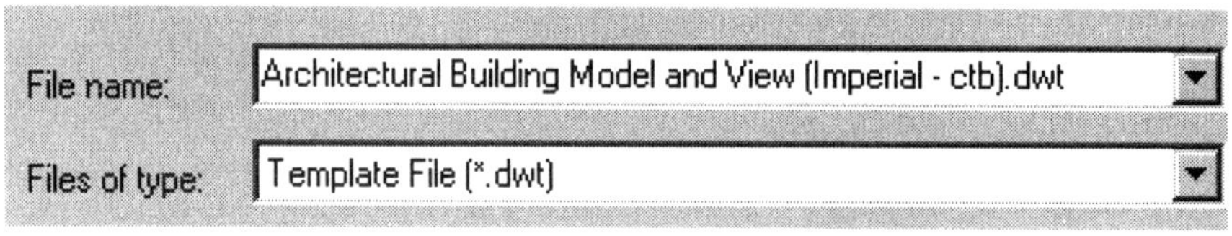

7. The template is now assigned to the **QNEW** command.

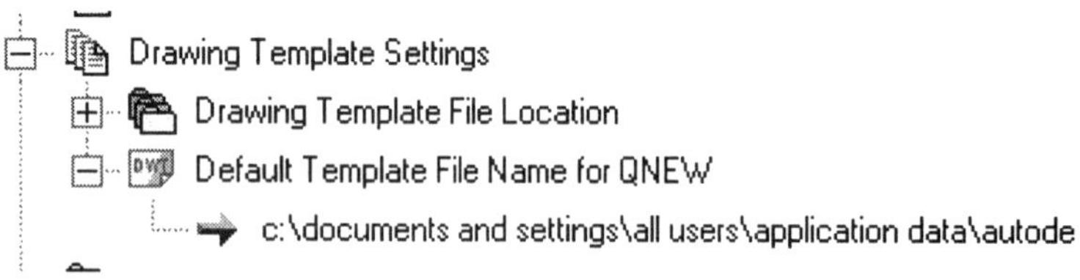

   Press **Apply** and **OK**.

Setting AEC Drawing Options

Menu	Tools→Options
Command line	Options
Context Menu→Options	Place Mouse in the graphics area and right click
Shortcut	Place mouse in the command line and right click

Access the Options dialog box.

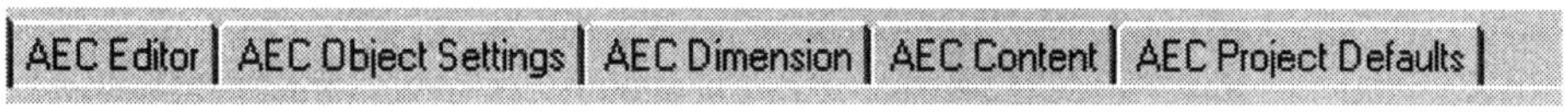

ADT's Options includes six additional AEC specific tabs.
They are AEC Editor, AEC Object Settings, AEC Dimension, AEC Content, and AEC Project Defaults.

AEC Editor

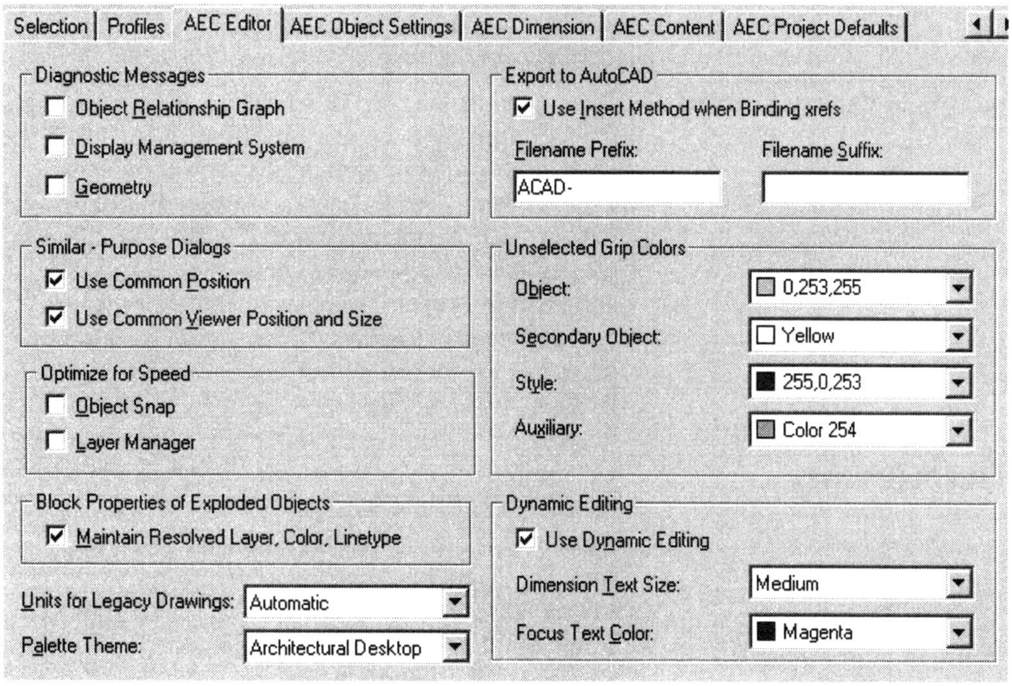

Diagnostic Messages	All diagnostic messages are turned off by default.
Similar-Purpose Dialogs	Options for the position of dialog boxes and viewers
Use Common Position	Sets one common position on the screen for similar dialog boxes, such as door, wall, and window add or modify dialog boxes. Some dialog boxes, such as those for styles and properties, are always displayed in the center of the screen, regardless of this setting.
Use Common Viewer Position and Sizes	Sets one size and position on the screen for the similar-purpose viewers in Architectural Desktop. Viewer position is separately controlled for add, modify, style, and properties dialog boxes.
Optimize for Speed	Options for display representations and layer loading in the Layer Manager dialog
Object Snap	Enable to limit certain display representations to respond only to the Node and Insert object snaps. This setting affects stair, railing, space boundary, multi-view block, masking block, slice, and clip volume result (building section) objects.
Layer Manager	Enable Layer Manager to load layers into the Layer Manager faster.
Block Properties of Exploded Objects	When you explode an AEC object, you create several objects grouped in a block definition. To maintain the layer, color, and linetype of AEC objects when you explode them, select Maintain Resolved Layer, Color, Linetype under Block Properties of Exploded Object. Any objects whose component layer, color, and linetype properties are set to ByBlock take the color of the parent object. If this option is cleared when you explode an object, then properties set to ByBlock remain ByBlock. Clear this option if you want to explode the block definition further.
Units for Legacy Drawings	Determines the units to be used when opening an AutoCAD drawing in ADT. Automatic – uses the current ADT units setting Imperial – uses Imperial units Metric – uses Metric units
Palette Theme	Controls the colors of tool palettes Architectural Desktop Windows
Export to AutoCAD 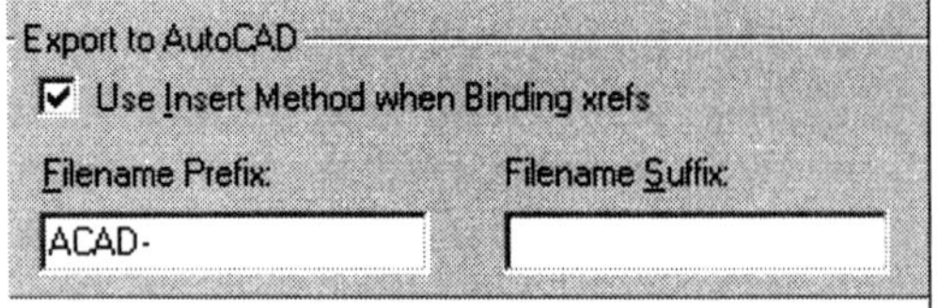	Enable Use Insert Method when binding Xrefs if you want all objects from an xref drawing referenced in the file you export to be automatically exploded into the host drawing. If you enable this option, the drawing names of the xref drawings are discarded when the exported drawing is created. In addition, their layers and styles are incorporated into the host drawing. For example,

	all exploded walls, regardless of their source (host or xref) are located on the same layer. Disable Use Insert Method when binding Xrefs if you want to retain the xref identities, such as layer names, when you export a file to AutoCAD or to a DXF file. For example, the blocks that define walls in the host drawng are located on A-Wall in the exploded drawing. Walls in an attached xref drawing are located on a layer whose name is created from the drawing name and the layer name, such as Drawing1|WallA. Many architects automatically bind and explode their xrefs when sending drawings to customers to protect their intellectual property. Enter a prefix or a suffix to be added to the drawing filename when the drawing is exported to an AutoCAD drawing or a DXF file.
Unselected Grip Colors	Assign the colors for each type of grip
Dynamic Editing	Enable Dynamic Editing if you want temporary dimensions to appear when you use grips to shift objects. You can also set the text size for the temporary dimensions and text color.
Layer Manager	Enable Optimize for Speed to load layers into the Layer Manager faster. After the layers are scanned and loaded into the Layer Manager, the status (in use/not in use) of each layer is indicated by the icon to the left side of the layer name in the Layer Manager. When you select Optimize for Speed, the Layer Manager does not scan the drawing to determine the status of the layers, speeding up the loading time. The icons that are displayed next to the layer name in the Layer Manager do not indicate whether or not the layer is in use.

TIP: Option Settings are applied to your current drawing and saved as the default settings for new drawings. Because ADT operates in a Multiple Document Interface, each drawing stores the Options Settings used when it was created and last saved. Some users get confused because they open an existing drawing and it will not behave according to the current Options Settings.

AEC Object Settings

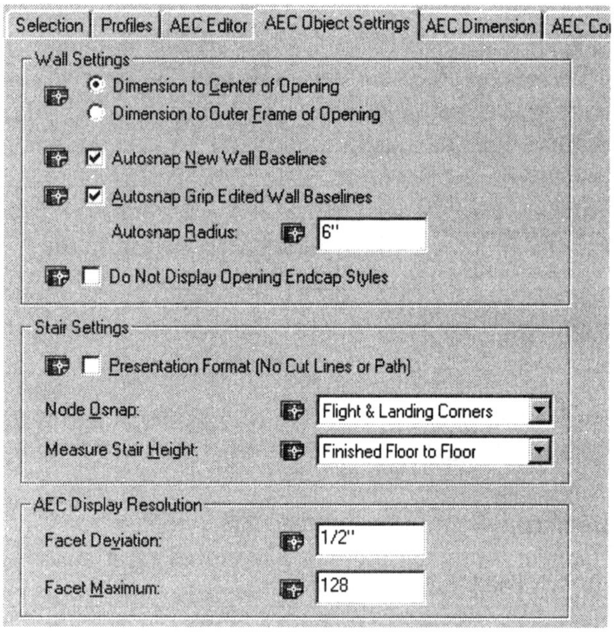

Wall Settings	
Dimension to Center of Opening	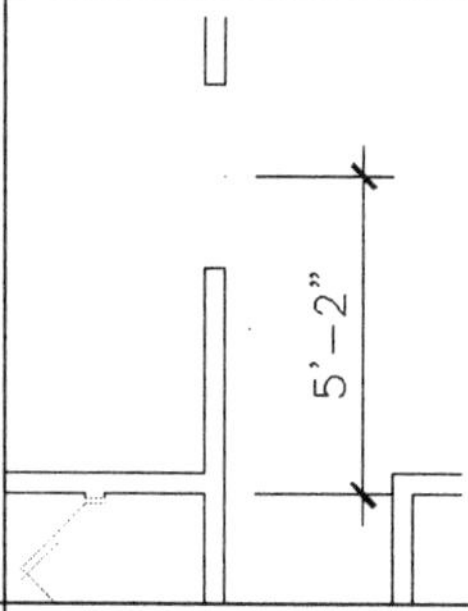
Dimension to Outer Frame of Opening	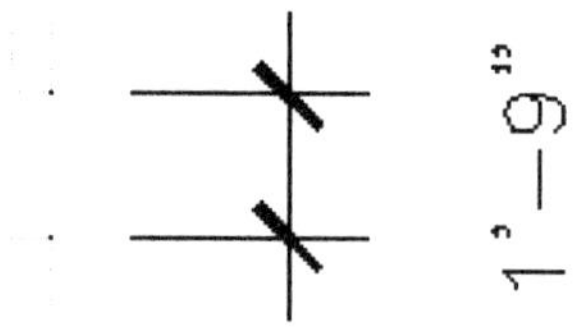
Autosnap New Wall Baselines	Enable Autosnap New Wall Baselines to have the endpoint of a new wall that is drawn within the Autosnap Radius of the baseline of an existing wall automatically snap to that baseline. If you select this option and set your Autosnap Radius to 0, then only walls that touch, clean up with each other.

Autosnap Grip Edited Wall Baselines	Enable Autosnap Grip Edited Wall Baselines to snap the endpoint of a wall that you grip edit within the Autosnap Radius of the baseline of an existing wall. If you select this option and set your Autosnap Radius to 0, then only walls that touch clean up with each other.
Autosnap Radius	Enter a value to set the snap tolerance
Do not display opening end cap styles	Enable Do Not Display Opening Endcap Styles to suppress the display of endcaps applied to openings in walls. Enabling this option boosts drawing performance when the drawing contains many complex endcaps.
Stair Settings	
Presentation Format (No Cut Lines or Path)	If this is enabled, a jagged line and directional arrows will not display
Node Osnap	Determines which snap is enabled when creating stairs: Vertical Alignment Flight and Landing Corners
Measure Stair Height	Rough floor to floor – ignore offsets Finished floor to floor – include top and bottom offsets
AEC Display Resolution	This determines the resolution of arcs and circular elements. Facet Deviation – The default is ½″ Facet Maximum – this can be set from 100 to 10,000. Higher settings use more memory and may affect screen refresh rates

AEC Dimension

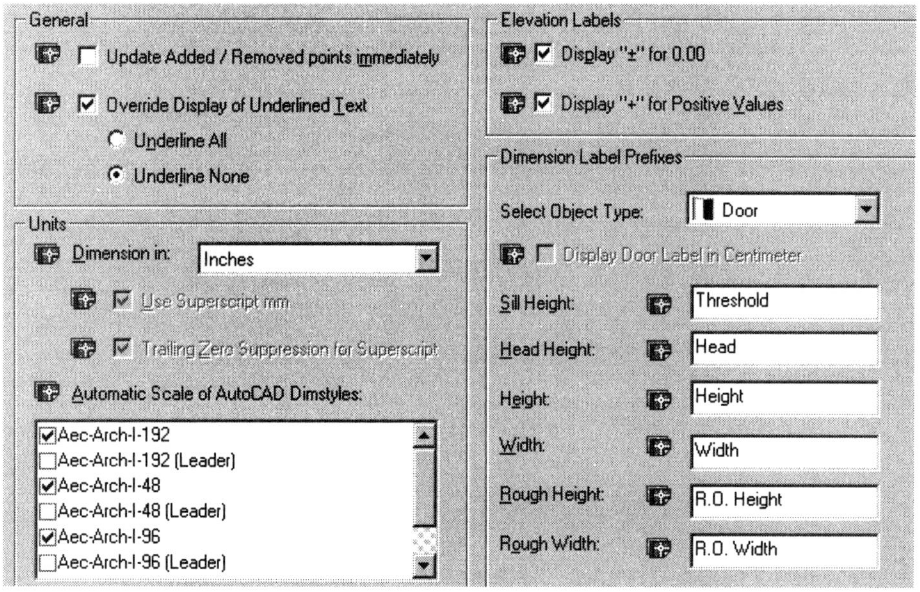

General	
Update Added/Removed points immediately	Enable to update the display every time you add or remove a point from a dimension chain
Override Display of Undefined Text	Enable to automatically underline each manually overridden dimension value
Undefine All	Enable to manually underline overriden dimension values
Undefine None	Enable to not underline any overriden dimension value
Units	
Dimension in:	Select the desired units from the drop-down list
Use Superscript mm	If your units are set to meters or centimeters, enable superscripted text to display the millimeters as superscript. 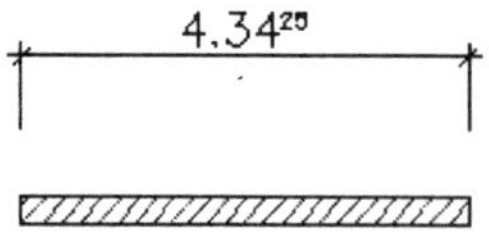
Trailing Zero Suppression for Superscript	To suppress zeros at the end of superscripted numbers, select Trailing Zeros Suppression for Superscript. You can select this option only if you have selected Use Superscript mm and your units are metric. 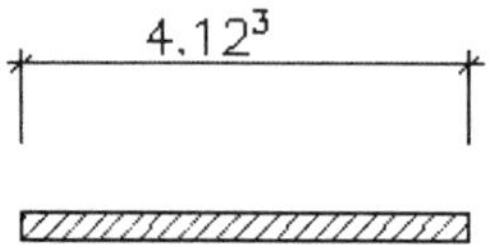

Automatic Scale of AutoCAD Dimstyles	Select the dimstyles you would like to automatically scale when units are reset.
Elevation Labels	Select the unit in which elevation labels are to be displayed. This unit can differ from the drawing unit.
Display +/- for 0.00 Values	
Display + for Positive Values	
Dimension Label Prefixes Dimension Label Prefixes are set based on the object selected from the drop-down. You can set label prefixes for Doors, Windows, Openings, and Stairs. Select the object, and then set the prefix for each designation. The designations will change based on the object selected.	

AEC Content

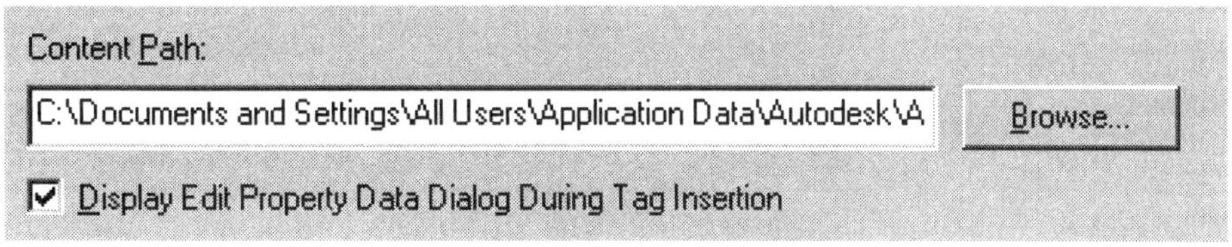

Content Path	Type the path and location of your content files, or click Browse to search for the content files.
Display Edit Schedule Data Dialog During Tag Insertion	To attach schedule data to objects when you insert a schedule tag in the drawing, this should be ENABLED.

TIP: Your Autodesk Architectural Desktop CD-ROM provides two imperial content menus: an Autodesk Architectural Desktop content menu and a CSI MasterFormat content menu. You can also locate FREE AEC Content on Autodesk's pointA.

Using AEC Content

Architectural Desktop uses several pre-defined and user-customizable content including:

- Architectural Display Configurations
- Architectural Profiles of Geometric Shapes
- Wall Styles and Endcap geometry
- Door styles
- Window styles
- Stair styles
- Space styles
- Schedule tables

Standard style content is stored in the AEC templates subdirectory. You can create additional content, import and export styles between drawings.

AEC Project Defaults

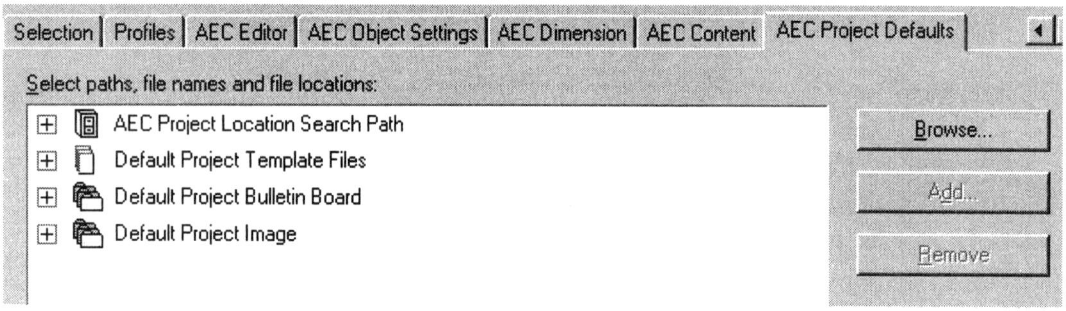

This dialog allows you to specify the folders in which Autodesk® Architectural Desktop searches for projects, palettes, templates, and other project files.

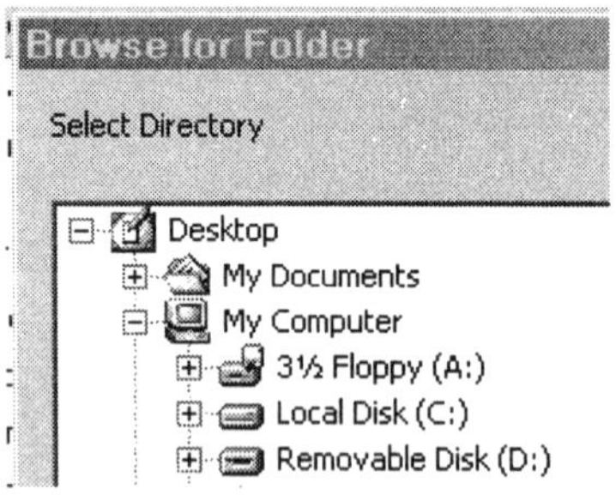

To add a path, simply expand the folder and use the Browse button to locate the desired folder.

You can add more than one path to the AEC Project Location Search Path. All the other folders only allow you to have a single location for template files, the project bulletin board, and the default project image.

> **TIP:** I highly recommend that you store any custom content in a separate directory as far away from AutoCAD Architectural Desktop as possible. This will allow you to back up your custom work easily and prevent accidental erasure if you upgrade your software application.
>
> You should be aware that ADT currently allows the user to specify only ONE path for custom content, so drawings with custom commands will only work if they reside in the specified path.

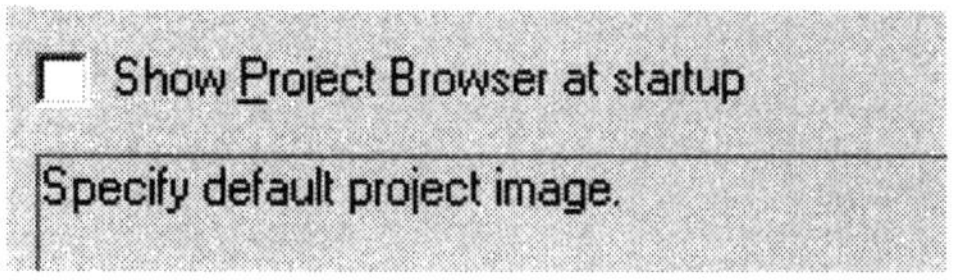

If you enable the Show Project Browser at startup, you will automatically have access to the Project Browser whenever you start ADT.

Accessing the Project Browser

Command line	AECProjectBrowser
Navigation Toolbar	
Files Menu	Project Browser
Shortcut Key	Ctl+5

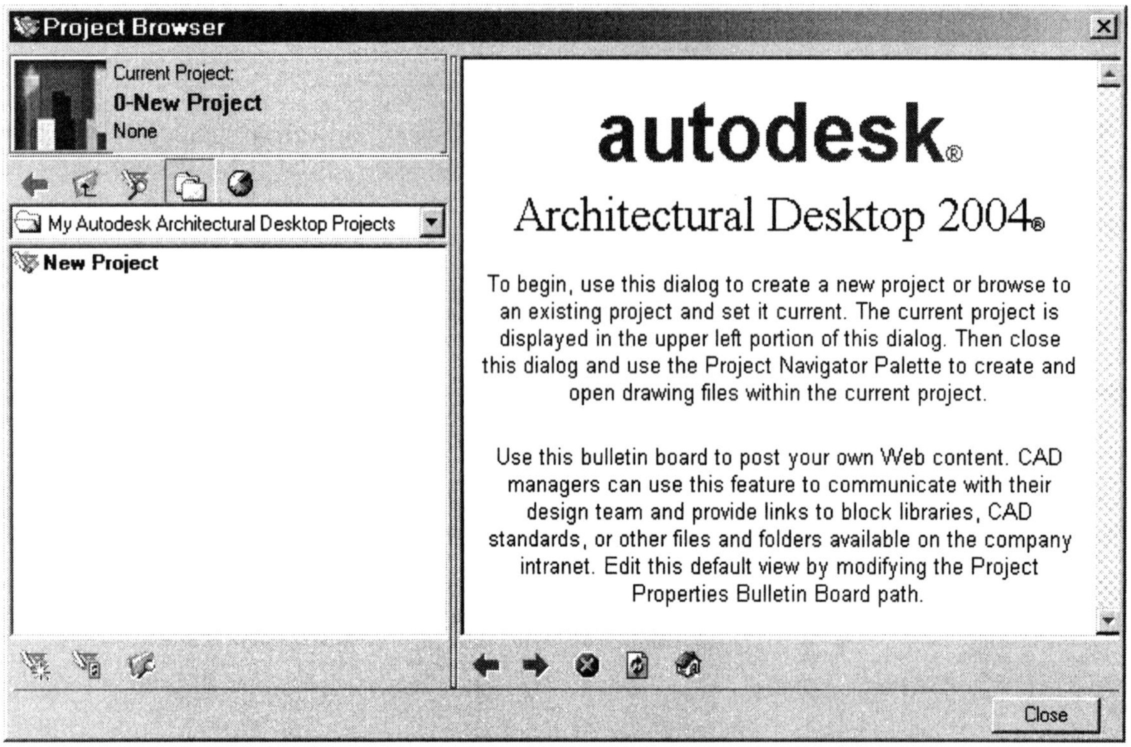

The Project Browser is a new feature in ADT that allows you to manage your project, similar to the old Today window in 2002, but more powerful.

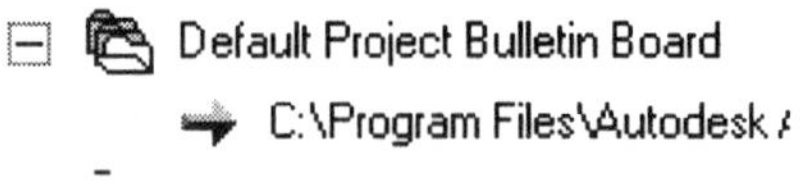

The text you see in the right window is actually an html file. The path to this file is controlled in the path for the Default Project Bulletin Board.

	New Project – creates a new project
	Refresh Project – updates a project
	Project File Navigator

Exercise 1-2:
Creating a New Project

Drawing Name: New
Estimated Time: 15 minutes

This exercise reinforces the following skills:

- Project Navigator

1. Type 'aecprojectbrowser' at the command line.

2. 

   Select the New Project tool.

3. In the Number field, enter **A103**.
   In the Name field, enter **BROWN RESIDENCE**.
   In the Description field, enter **BASEMENT REMODEL**.

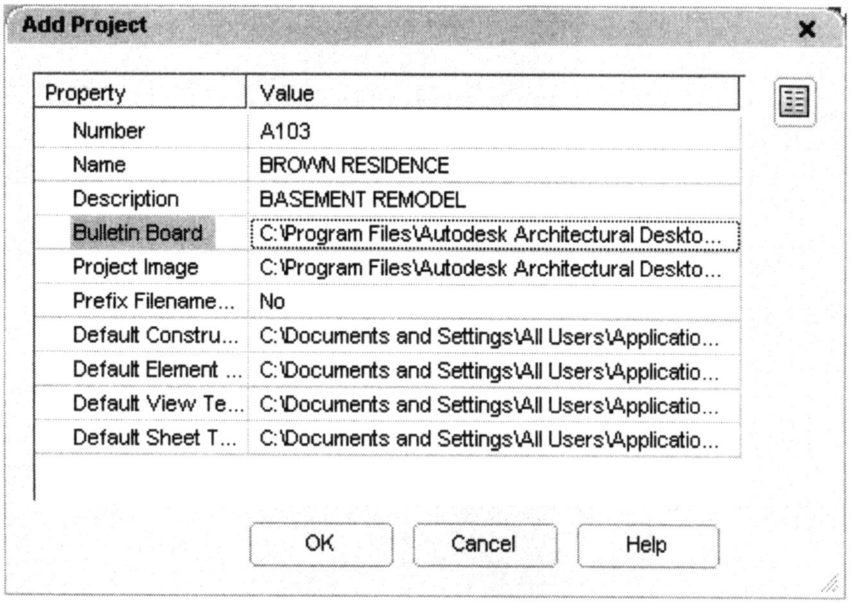

You can also set the default templates you wish to use for a specific project.

4.  Select the Project Details tool.

5. You can enter in contact information and detail information about the project in this area.

6.  Select the **Add Detail** tool.

7. Enter **Plumbing Contractor** in the New Name field.

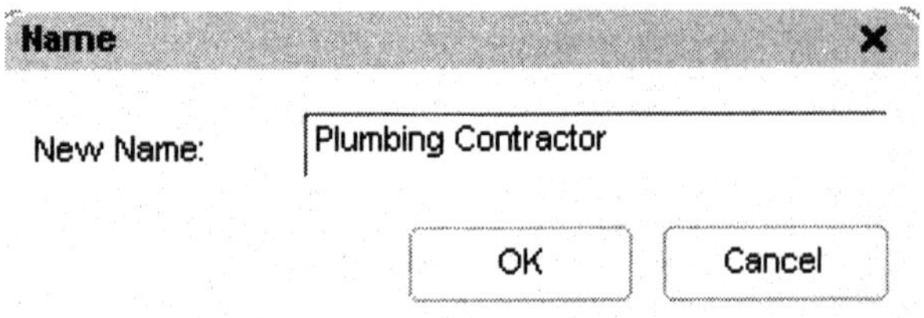

Press **OK**.

8.  Select the **ADD Detail** tool.

9. Enter **Contractor Name** and press ENTER.
Then type **Bob's Plumbing** in the Value field.

10. Use the Add Detail tool to add a phone number and PO Number for Bob's Plumbing.

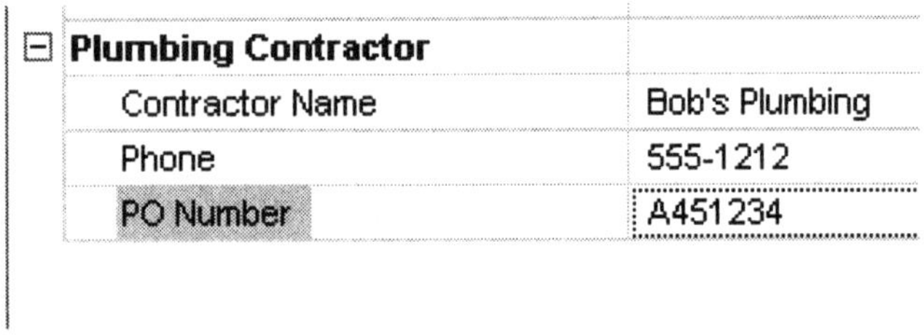

11. Press OK twice and Close to exit the dialog.

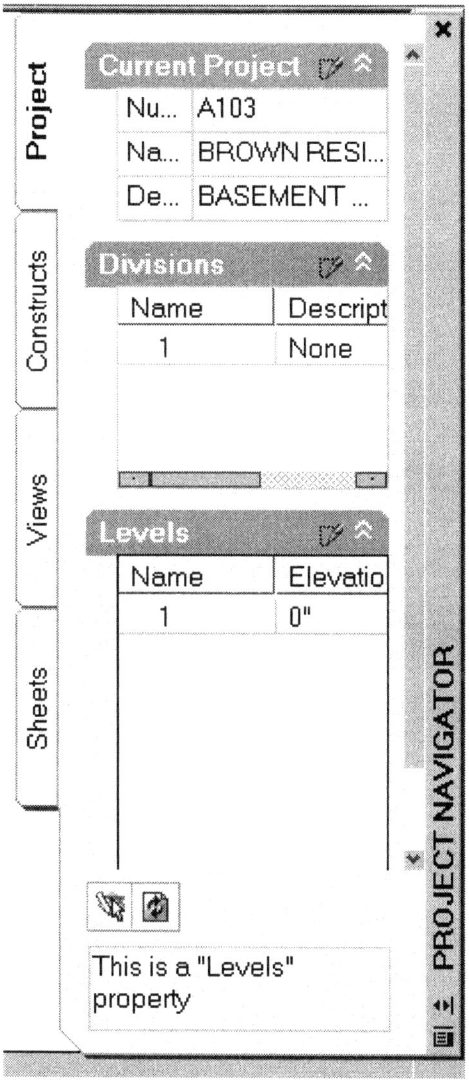

The Project Navigator Pallete is a powerful new tool in ADT2004. You can organize your sheets, your views, your xrefs, etc. all from within this tool palette.

You can set the tool palette to auto-hide to conserve screen space or close it unless you are using it.

You can drag-and-drop from the Project Navigator to the Autodesk® Architectural Desktop drawing area, and to and from Internet Explorer.

Elements in ADT are similar to blocks. They are DWG files that consist of geometry that is used more than once. For example, a desk or a chair. You can convert your existing blocks into elements.

Constructs are the components of the building model. A construct describes one unique portion of a building. A construct can be an elevator shaft, a flight of stairs, an apartment, or an entire floor. The construct needs to be assigned to a level and a division within the project. Spanning constructs, like curtain walls, can be assigned to multiple levels and divisions.

To minimize the Project Manager, pick the left-right arrows located in the lower right of the Project Manager dialog.

Desktop Display Manager

Menu	Format →Display Manager
Command Line	DisplayManager

Access the Display Manager using the Menu.
Go to Format →Display Manager

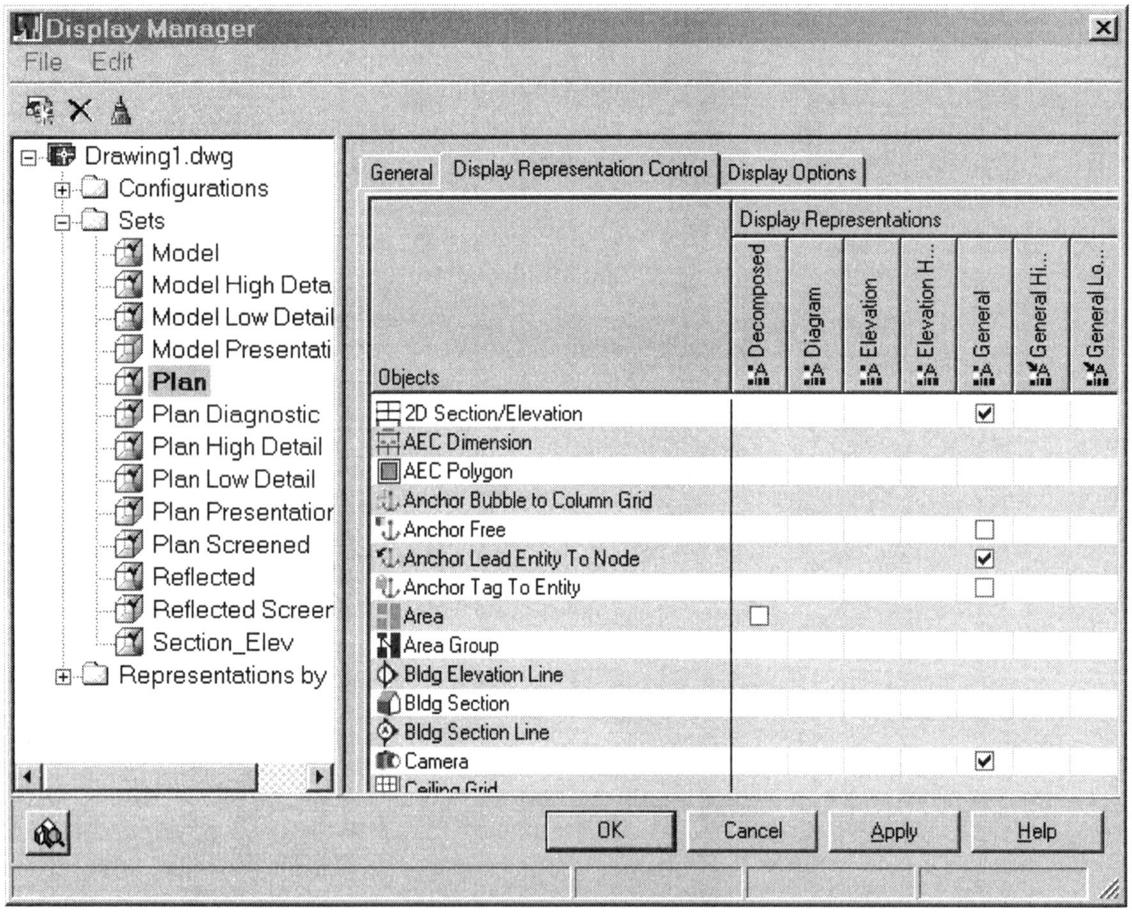

The display system in Autodesk® Architectural Desktop controls how AEC objects are displayed in a designated viewport. By specifying the AEC objects you want to display in a viewport and the direction from which you want to view them, you can produce different architectural displays, such as floor plans, reflected plans, elevations, 3D models, or schematic displays.

Architectural Profiles of Geometric Shapes

You can create mass elements to define the shape and configuration of your preliminary study, or mass model. After you create the mass elements you need, you can change their size as necessary to reflect the building design.

- **Mass element**: A single object that has behaviors based on its shape. For example, you can set the width, depth, and height of a box mass element, and the radius and height of a cylinder mass element.

Mass elements are parametric, which allows each of the shapes to have very specific behavior when it comes to the manipulation of each mass element's shape. For example, if the corner grip point of a box is selected and dragged, then the width and depth are modified. It is easy to change the shape to another form by right-clicking on the element and selecting a new shape from the list.

Through Boolean operations (addition, subtraction, intersection), mass elements can be combined into a mass group. The mass group provides a representation of your building during the concept phase of your project.

- **Mass group**: Takes the shape of the mass elements and is placed on a separate layer from the mass elements.
- **Mass model**: A virtual mass object, shaped from mass elements, that defines the basic structure and proportion of your building. A marker appears as a small box in your drawing to which you attach mass elements.

As you continue developing your mass model, you can combine mass elements into mass groups and create complex building shapes through addition, subtraction, or intersection of mass elements. You can still edit individual mass elements attached to a mass group to further refine the building model.

To study alternative design schemes, you can create a number of mass element references. When you change the original of the referenced mass element, all the instances of the mass element references are updated.

The mass model that you create with mass elements and mass groups is a refinement of your original idea that you carry forward into the next phase of the project, in which you change the mass study into floorplates and then into walls. The walls are used to start the design phase.

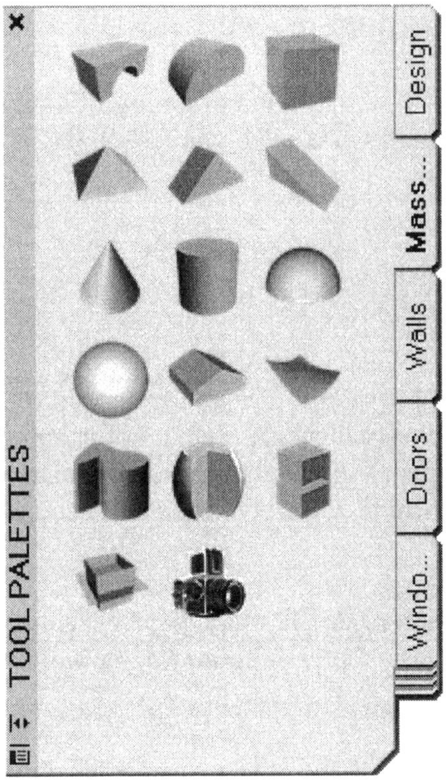

Mass Elements are accessed from the Massing Tool Palette.

To bring up the tool palette, press Ctl+3 and select the Massing tab.

Mass Elements that can be defined include Arches, Gables, Doric Columns, etc.

To create or add a mass element you can simply select it from the tool palette or type **MassElementAdd** on the command line.

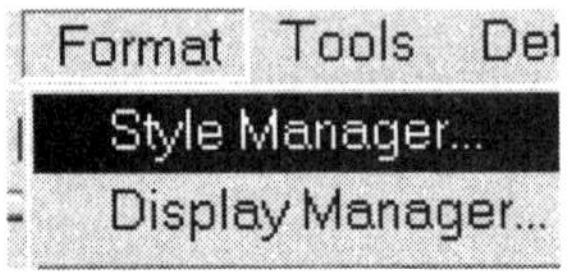

The Style Manager

Menu	Format →Style Manager
Command Line	AecStyleManager

The Style Manager is a Microsoft® Windows Explorer-based utility that provides you with a central location in Autodesk Architectural Desktop where you can view and work with styles in drawings or from Internet and intranet sites.

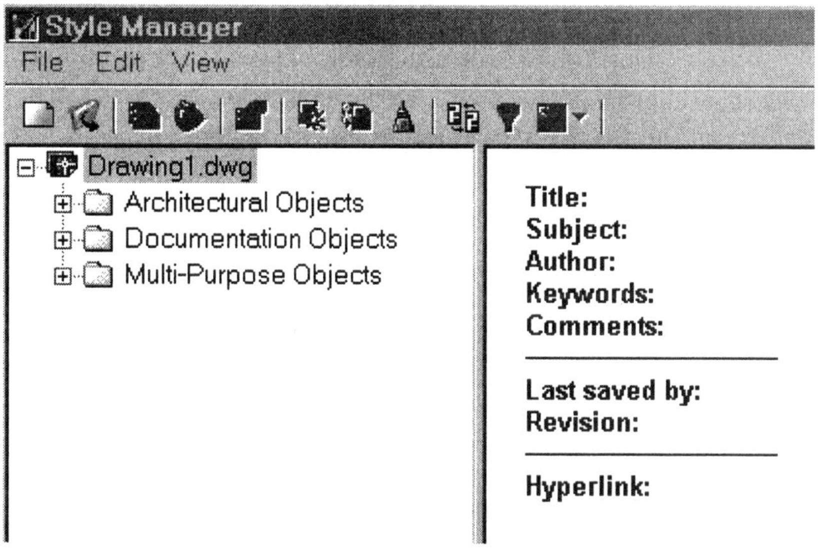

Styles are sets of parameters that you can assign to objects in Autodesk Architectural Desktop to determine their appearance or function. For example, a door style in Autodesk Architectural Desktop determines what door type, such as single or double, bi-fold or hinged, a door in a drawing represents. You can assign one style to more than one object, and you can modify the style to change the all the objects that are assigned that style.

Depending on your design projects, either you or your CAD Manager might want to customize existing styles or create new styles. The Style Manager allows you to easily create, customize, and share styles with other users. With the Style Manager, you can:

- Provide a central point for accessing styles from open drawings and Internet and intranet sites
- Quickly set up new drawings and templates by copying styles from other drawings or templates
- Sort and view the styles in your drawings and templates by drawing or by style type
- Preview an object with a selected style
- Create new styles and edit existing styles
- Delete unused styles from drawings and templates
- Send styles to other Autodesk Architectural Desktop users by email

Objects in Autodesk Architectural Desktop that use styles include 2D sections and elevations, AEC Polygons, curtain walls, curtain wall units, doors, endcaps, railings, roof slab edges, roof slabs, schedule tables, slab edges, slabs, spaces, stairs, structural members, wall modifiers, walls, window assemblies, and windows.

Additionally, layer key styles, schedule data formats, and cleanup group, mask block, multi-view block, profile, and property set definitions are handled by the Style Manager.

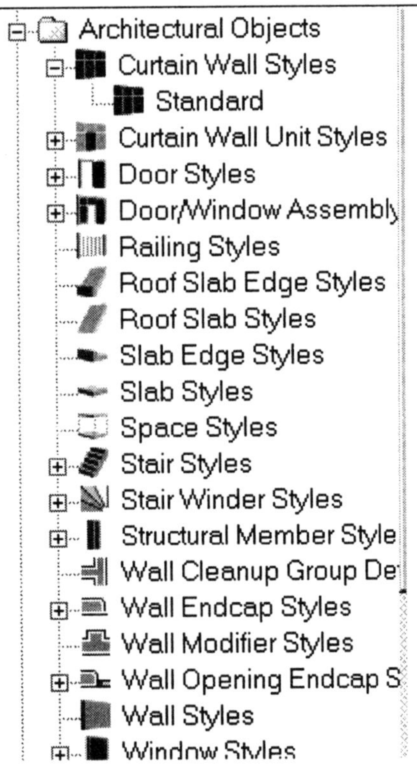

Most of the objects in Autodesk Architectural Desktop have a default Standard style. In addition, Autodesk Architectural Desktop includes a starter set of styles that you can use with your drawings. The Autodesk Architectural Desktop templates contain some of these styles. Any drawing that you start from one of the templates includes these styles.

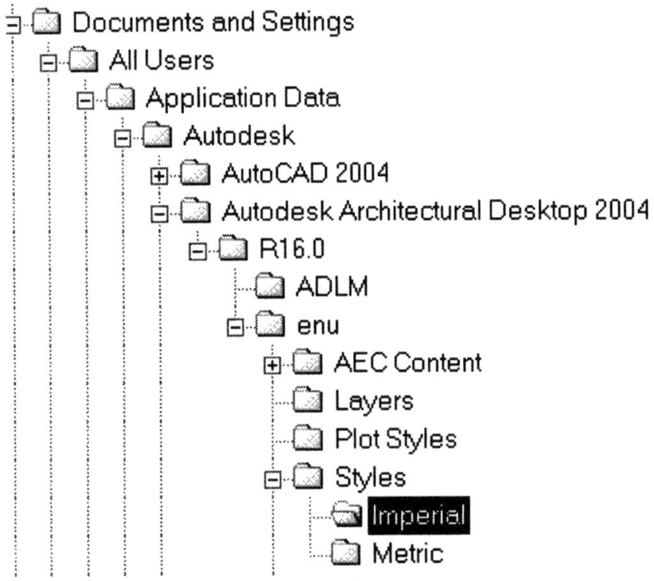

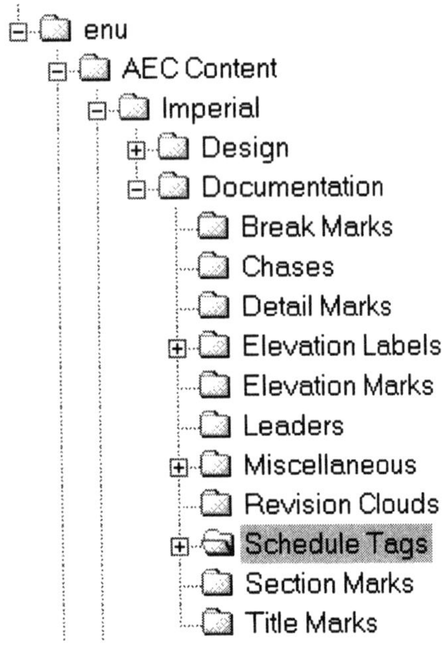

You can also access the styles for doors, endcaps, spaces, stairs, walls, and windows from drawings located in *Documents and Settings\All Users\Application Data\Autodesk\Architectural Desktop 2004\R16\enu\Styles\Imperial or Metric.* Property set definitions and schedule tables are located in the *Documents and Settings\All Users\Application Data\Autodesk\Architectural Desktop 2004\R16\enu\AEC Content\Imperial\Documentation\Schedule Tags* folder.

TIP: I do not recommend modifying ADT's standard styles as this may affect drawings you bring in from outside sources. Instead, copy the existing style to a NEW style and modify it using the desired properties.

Exercise 1-3:
Creating a New Geometric Profile

Drawing Name: New using Imperial.dwt
Estimated Time: 15 minutes

This exercise reinforces the following skills:

- Use of AEC Design Content
- Use of Mass Elements in ADT

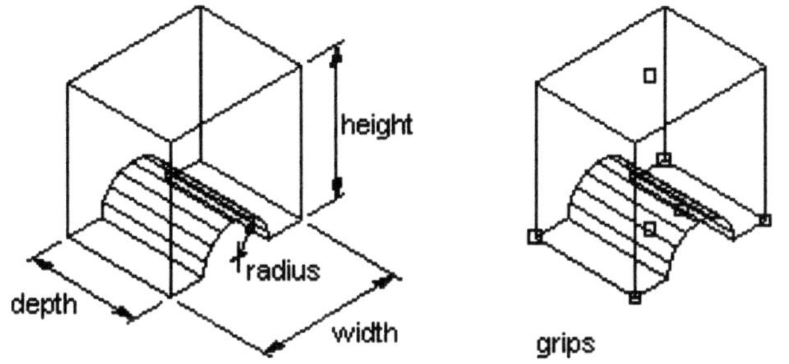

Creating an arch mass element

1. Start a New Drawing.

   Select the QNEW tool from the Standard toolbar.

   Because we assigned a template in Exercise 1-1, a drawing file opens without prompting us to select a template.

2. Select the **Tool Palettes** tool from the Standard toolbar.

3.

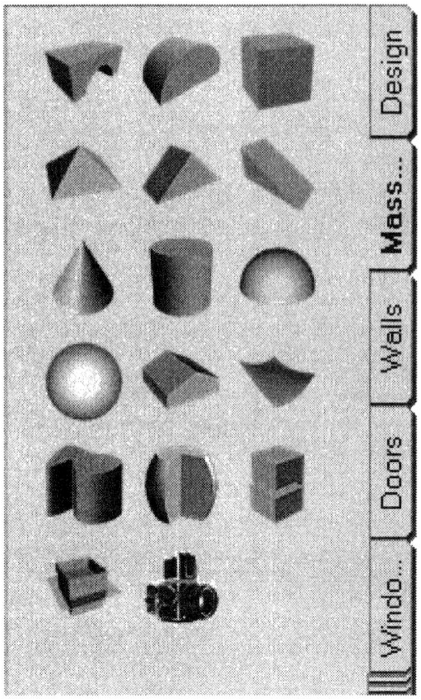

Select the Massing tab on the Tool Palette.

Select the Arch icon.

4.

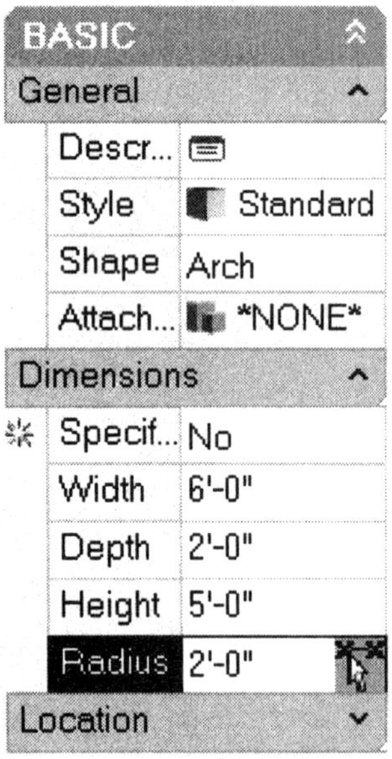

Expand the Dimensions section.

Set Specify on screen to No.
Set the Width to 6′-0″.
Set the Depth to 2′-0″.
Set the Height to 5′-0″.
Set the Radius to 2′-0″.

5. 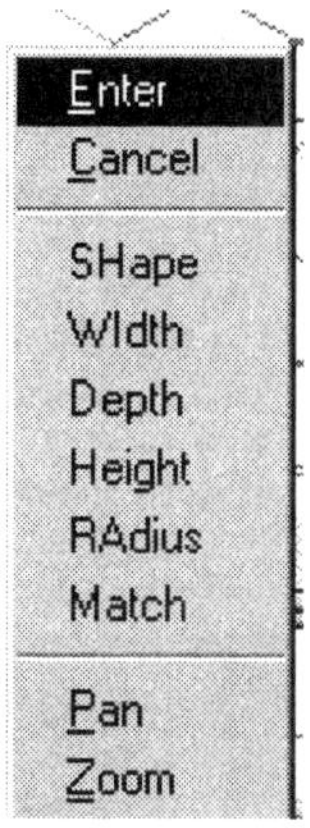

Pick a point any where in the drawing area.

Press ENTER to accept a Rotation Angle of 0 or right click and select ENTER.

Press ENTER to exit the command.

6.  Switch to an isometric view.

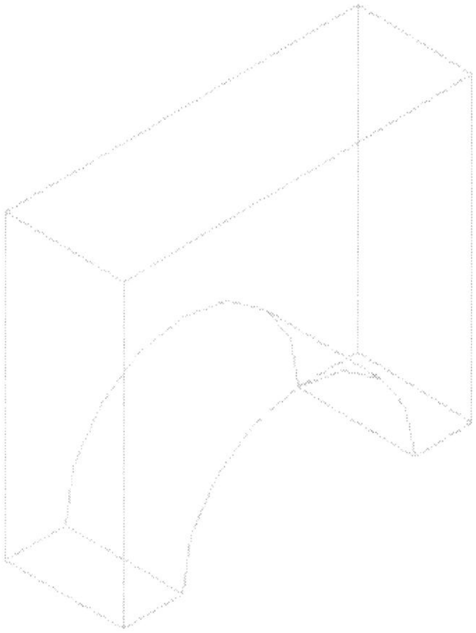

7.  Use the Flat Shaded tool.

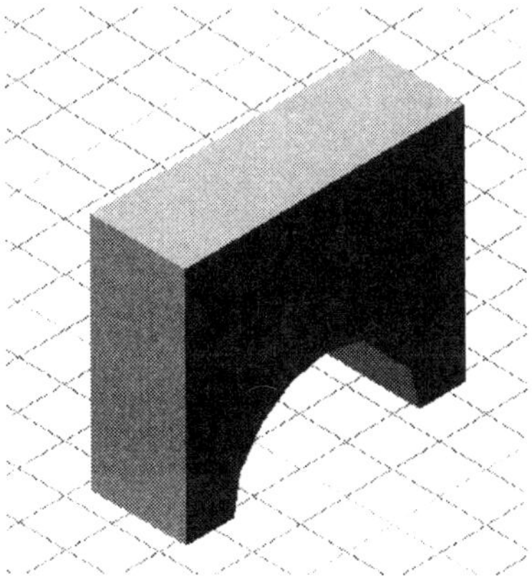

8. To change the arch properties, select the arch so that it is highlighted. Right click and select 'Properties.'

9. 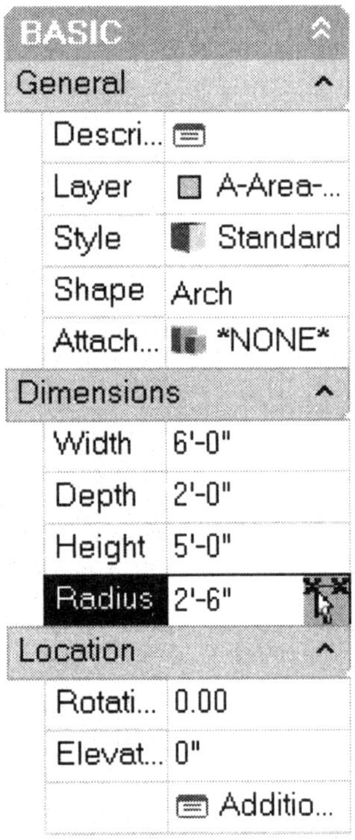

Change the Radius to 2′-6″.

Pick into the graphics window and the arch will update.

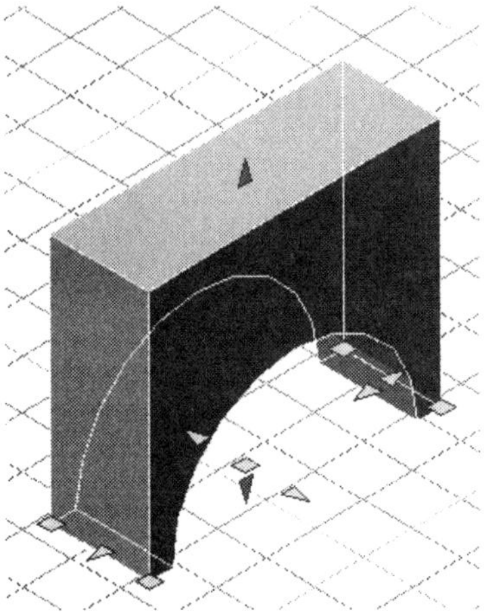

Press ESC to release the grips on the arc.

10. Close the drawing without saving.

Exercise 1-4:

Creating a New Wall Style

Drawing Name: New using Imperial.dwt
Estimated Time: 15 minutes

This exercise reinforces the following skills:

- Use of AEC Design Content
- Use of Wall Styles

1. Start a New Drawing.

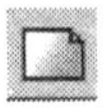 Select the QNEW tool from the Standard toolbar.

2. Type Ctl+3 to activate the Tool Palettes if it is not currently visible.

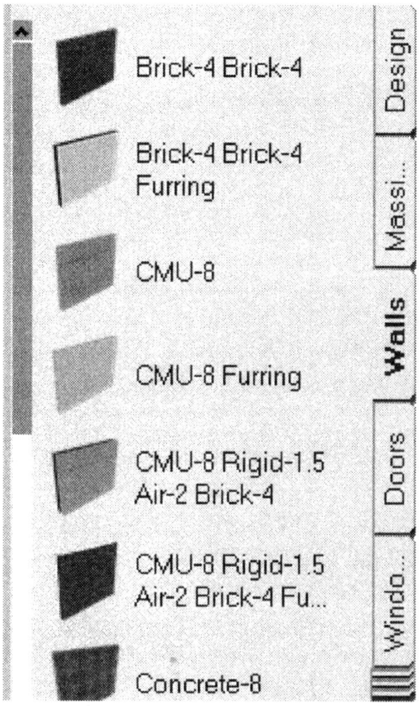

Select the Walls tab.

3. 

Highlight the first wall icon.

Right click and select Wall Styles.

The Style Manager is displayed, with the current drawing expanded in the tree view. The wall styles in the current drawing are displayed under the wall style type. All other style and definition types are filtered out in the tree view.

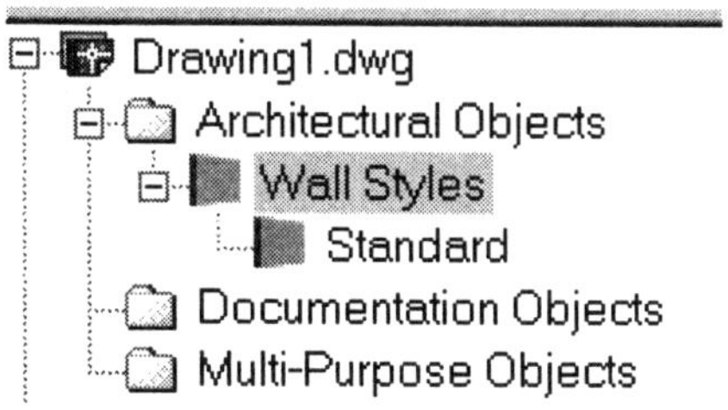

4.  Select the New Style tool.

5. Change the name of the new style by typing 'Brick_Block.'

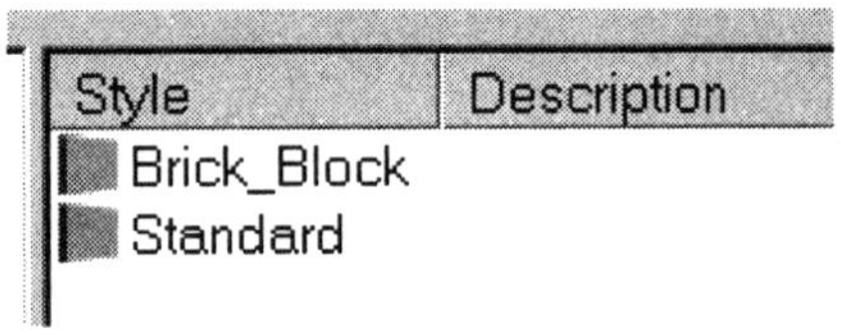

6. Highlight the new style you just created.

   Right click and select 'Edit.'

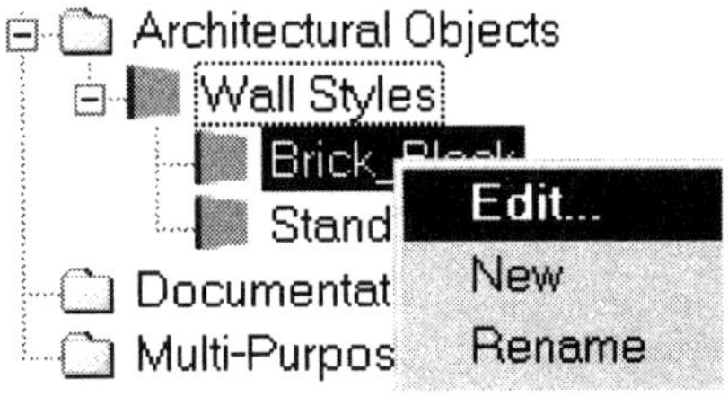

7. The Wall Style Properties dialog appears.

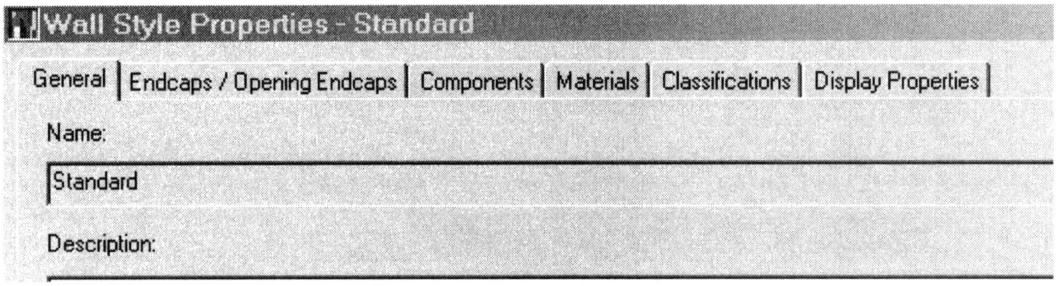

8. In the General tab, type in the description **8″ CMU and 3-1/2″ Brick Wall** in the Description field as shown.

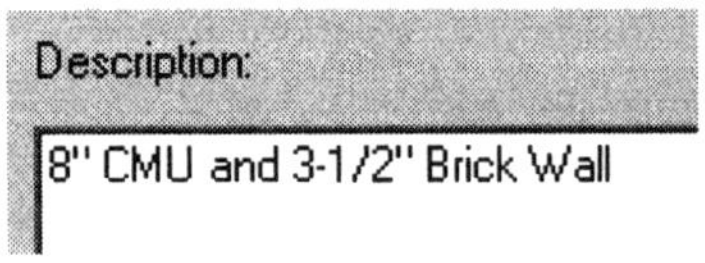

Adding Wall Components

9. Select the Components tab.
   Change the Name to **CMU** by typing in the Name field indicated.
   Press the dropdown arrow next to the Edge Offset Button.
   Set the Edge Offset to 0″.

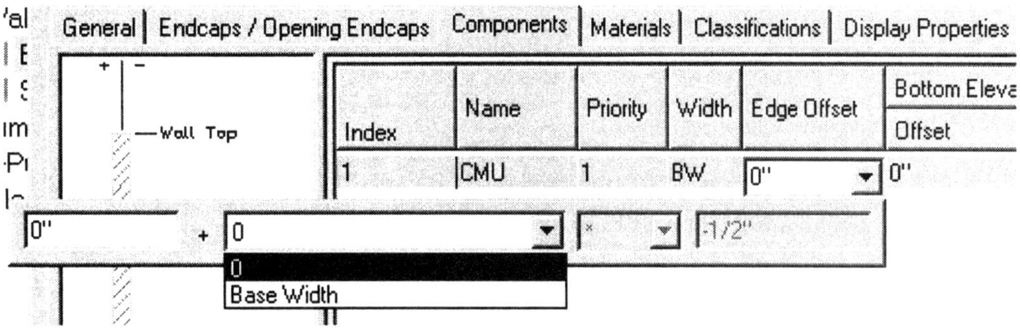

A 0″ edge offset specifies that the outside edge of the CMU is coincident with the wall baseline.

10. Press the Width down arrow button.

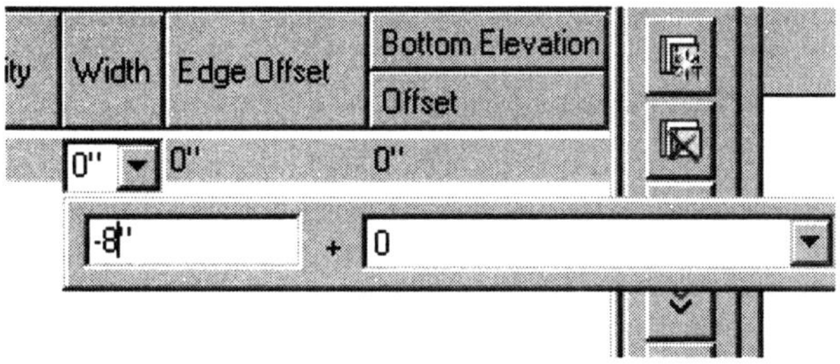

Set the value to -8″.

This specifies that the CMU has a fixed width of 8″ in the negative direction from the wall baseline (to the inside).

11. You now have one component defined for your wall named CMU with the properties shown.

Next, we'll add wall insulation.

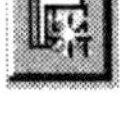

Press the Add Component button on the right side of the dialog box.

12. In the Name field, type **Insulation**.

    Set the Priority to 1. (The lower the priority number, the higher the priority when creating intersections.)

    Set the Edge Offset with a value of **0″**.

    Set the Component Width as shown, with a value of 1.5″ and the Base Width set to 0.

    This specifies that the insulation has a fixed width of 1.5″ offset in a positive direction from the wall baseline (to the outside).

Index	Name	Priority	Width	Edge Offset	Bottom Elevation Offset
1	CMU	1	-8"	0"	0"
2	Insulation	1	1 1/2"	0"	0"

13. 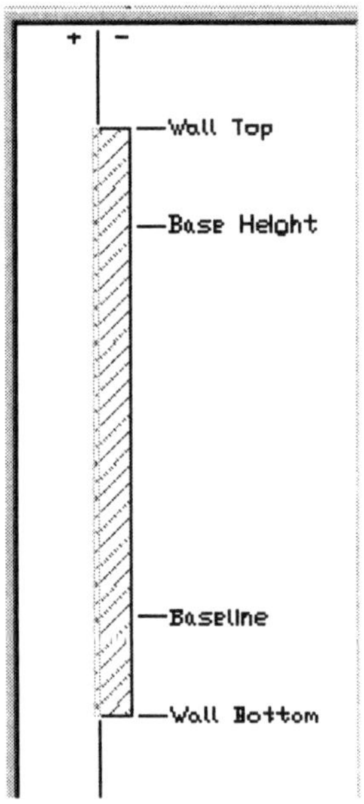

Note that the preview changes to show the insulation component.

14. Now, we add an air space component to our wall.

Press the Add Component button.

15. Rename the new component **Air Space.**

    Set the Edge Offset to **0″**.

    This specifies that the inside edge of the air space is coincident with the outside edge of the insulation.

    The width should be set to **1**″.

    This specifies that the air gap will have a fixed width of 1″ offset in the positive direction from the wall baseline (to the outside).

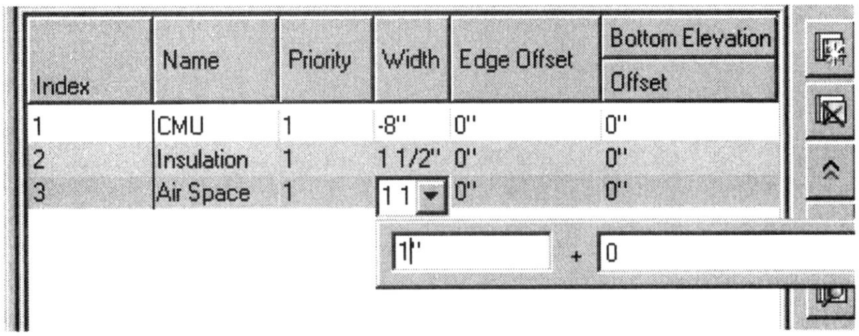

Index	Name	Priority	Width	Edge Offset	Bottom Elevation Offset
1	CMU	1	-8"	0"	0"
2	Insulation	1	1 1/2"	0"	0"
3	Air Space	1	1 1	0"	0"

16. Use the Add Component tool to add the fourth component.

    The Name should be **Brick**.
    The Priority set to **1.**
    The Edge Offset set to **2.5″.**
    The Width set to **3.5″.**

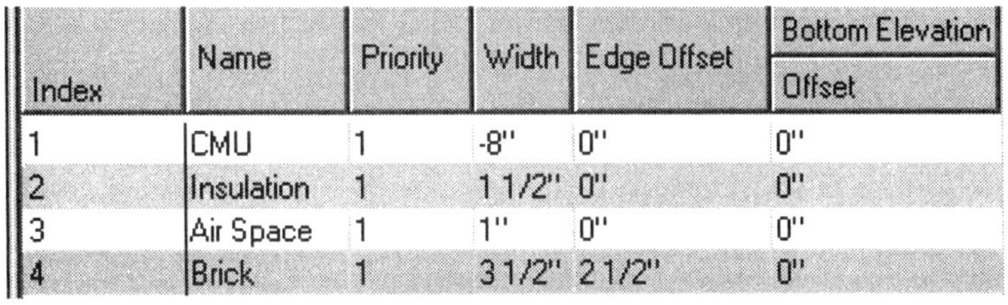

Index	Name	Priority	Width	Edge Offset	Bottom Elevation Offset
1	CMU	1	-8"	0"	0"
2	Insulation	1	1 1/2"	0"	0"
3	Air Space	1	1"	0"	0"
4	Brick	1	3 1/2"	2 1/2"	0"

17. 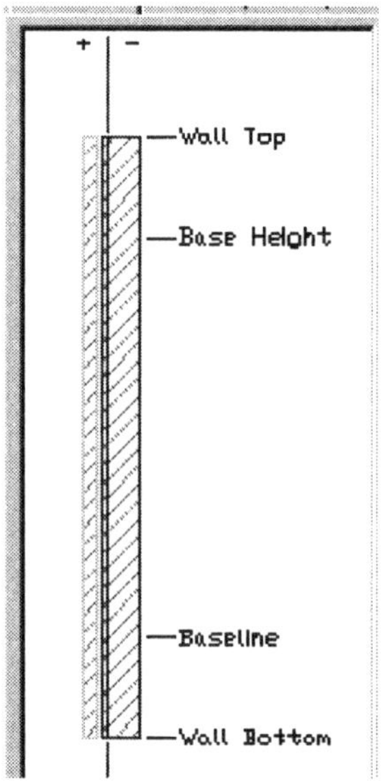

Note how your wall style previews.

Assigning Materials

18. Select the Materials tab.

Highlight the CMU component.

 Select the Add New Material tool.

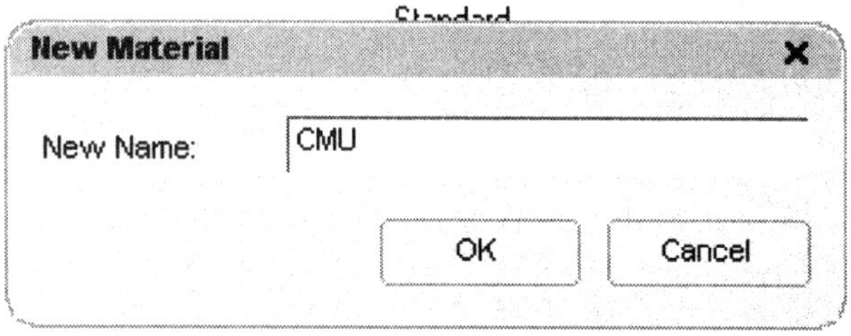

Enter **CMU** in the New Name field and press **OK**.

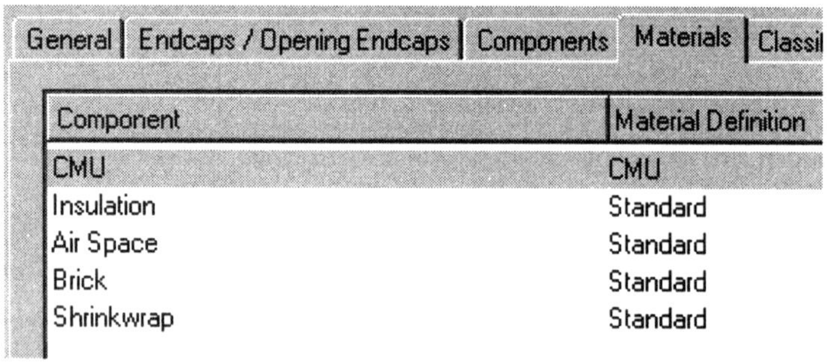

19. Use the Add New Material tool to assign new materials to each component.

Component	Material Definition
CMU	CMU
Insulation	Insulation
Air Space	Air Space
Brick	Brick
Shrinkwrap	Standard

Defining Display Properties

20. Highlight the **CMU** Component.

Select the Edit Material tool.

Select the Display Properties tab.

Highlight the General Medium Detail Display Property.

Click on the Style Override rectangle.

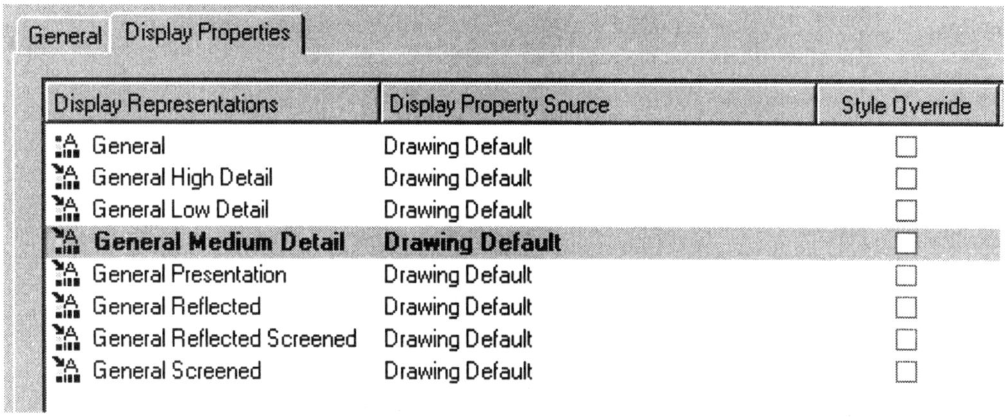

21. Select the Layer/Color/Linetype tab.

    Set the Layer for all the Display Components to A-Wall.

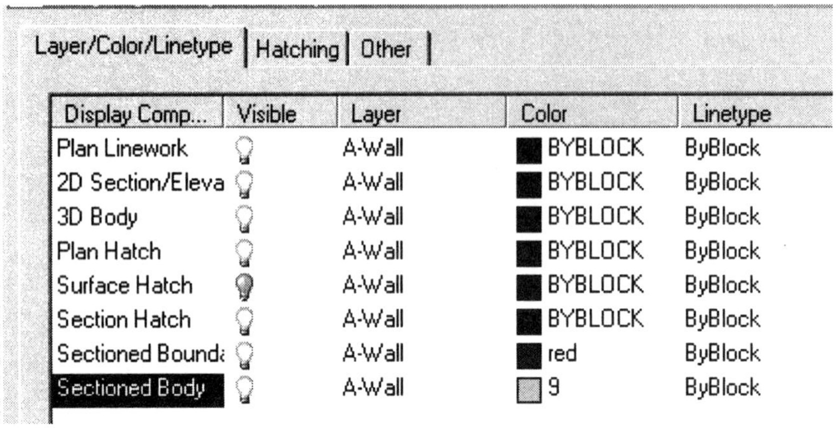

22. Select the Hatching tab.

    Highlight Plan Hatch and select Pattern.

    Under Type, select **Predefined**.

    Under Pattern Name, select **CMU_Running**.

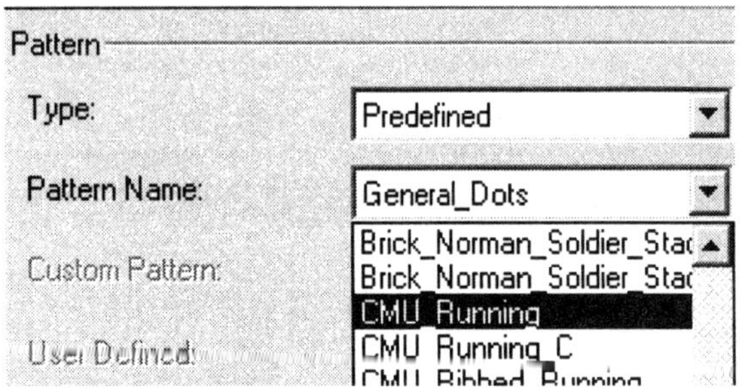

Assign the CMU_Running Pattern to all the Display Components.

Set the Angles to 0.

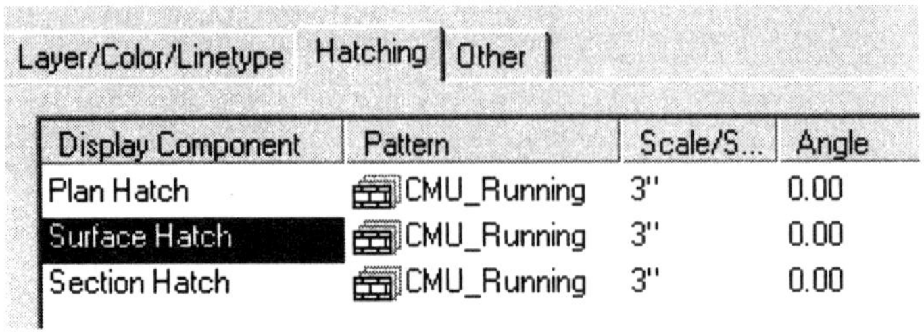

Press **OK** twice to return to the Materials tab of the Wall Properties dialog.

23. 

Highlight **Insulation** and select the **Edit Material** tool.

Select the Hatching tab.

Select all the Display Components so they all are highlighted.

Set the Plan Hatch to the INSUL pattern under Predefined type.

Set the Angle to 0.00.

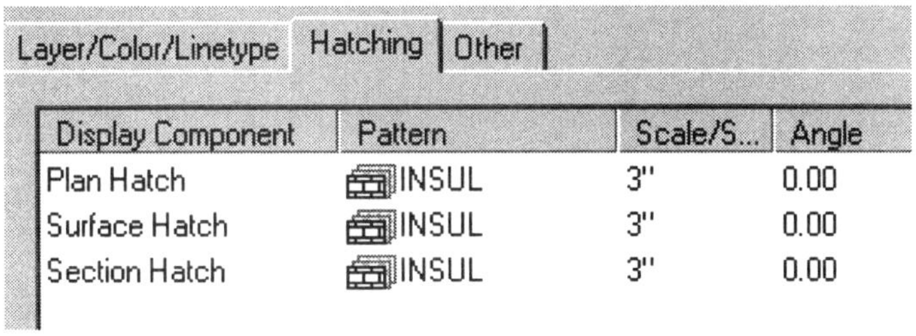

24. 

Highlight **Brick** and select the **Edit Material** tool.

Select all the Display Components so they are highlighted.

Set the **Plan Linework** Display Component to Layer **A-Wall**.

All the other display components will be assigned to the new layer as well.

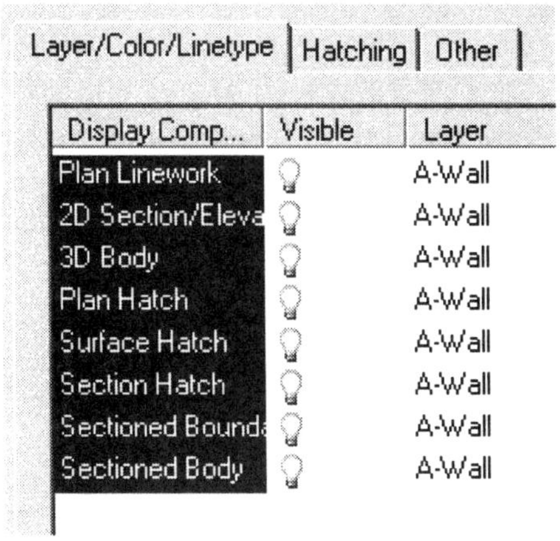

25. Select the Hatching tab.

Set the Type to **Predefined.**

Select the **Browse** button.

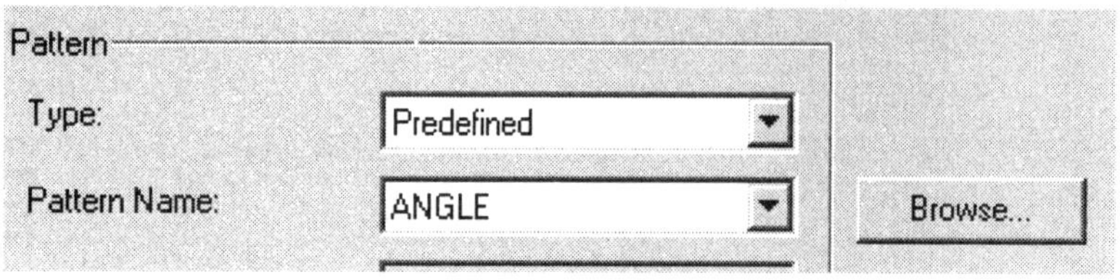

26. Select the **Brick_BrickStone** pattern.

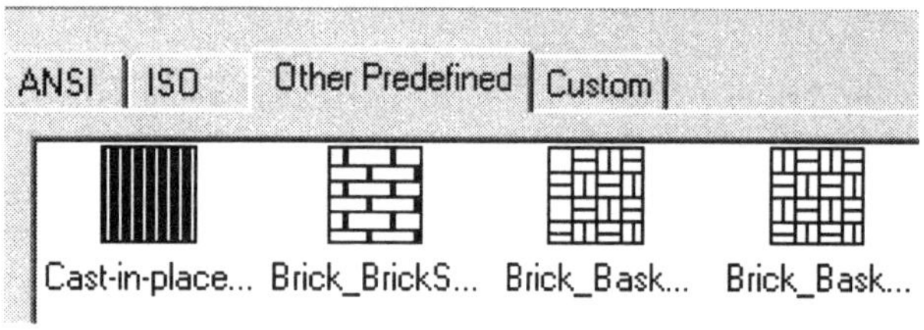

27. Set the Angle to 0 for all hatches.

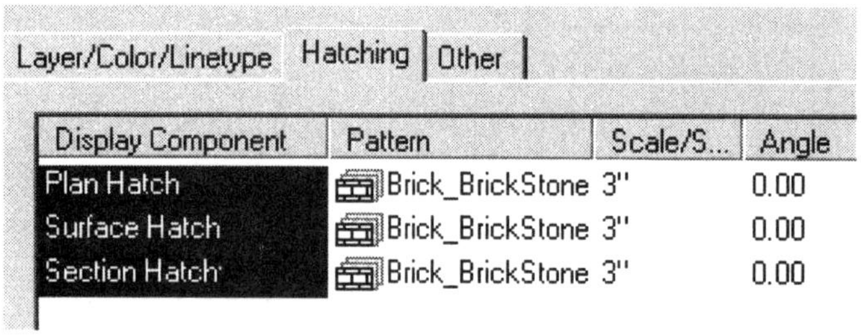

Press **OK** twice.

28. 

Press OK to exit the Edit dialog.
You can preview how the changes you made to the material display will appear when you create your wall.

Copying a Tool

29. 

Highlight the **Brick-4 Brick-4** tool on your tool palette.

Right click and select **Copy**.

30. 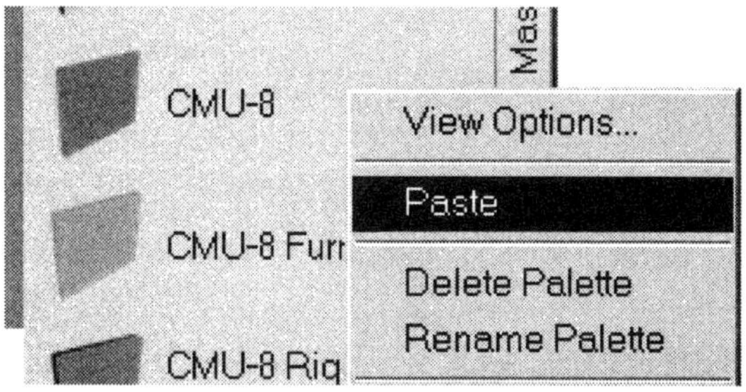

Pick in the grey palette area.

Right click and select **Paste**.

31. 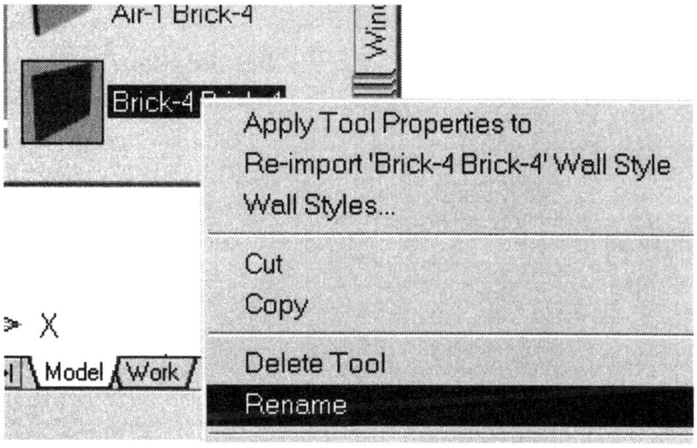

Highlight the Copied tool.

Right click and select **Rename**.

32. 

Change the name to **8″ CMU- 3.5″ Brick.**

33. 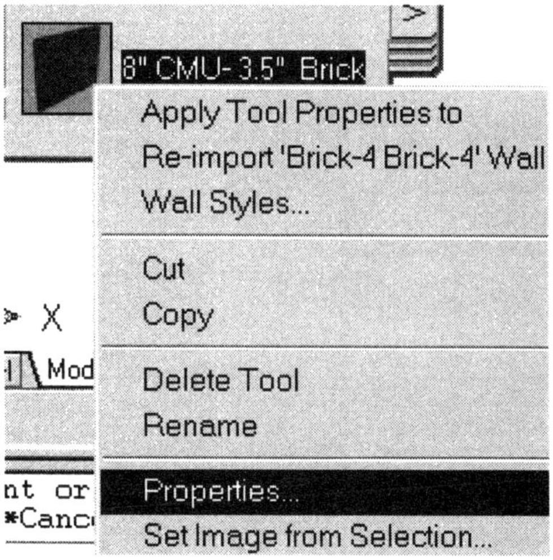

Highlight **8″ CMU- 3.5″ Brick** tool.

Right click and select **Properties.**

34. Select the Description field.

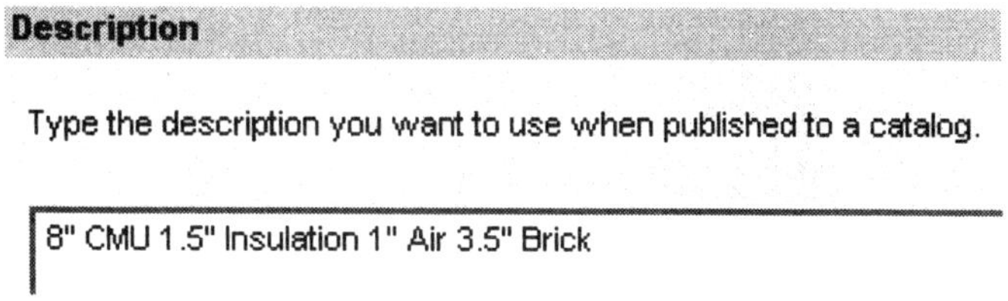

Enter in the description:

8″ CMU 1.5″ Insulation 1″ Air 3.5″ Brick.

Press **OK**.

35.

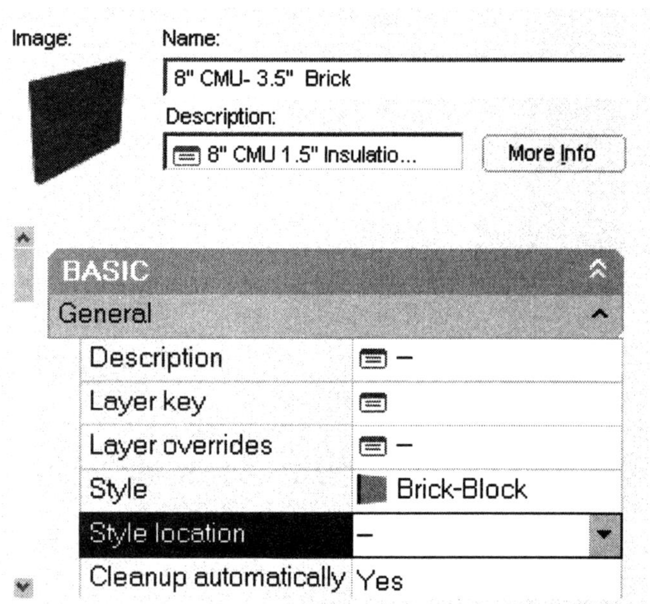

Set the **Style** to **Brick-Block.**

Set the **Style Location** to **--.**

Specifying a Tool icon

36.

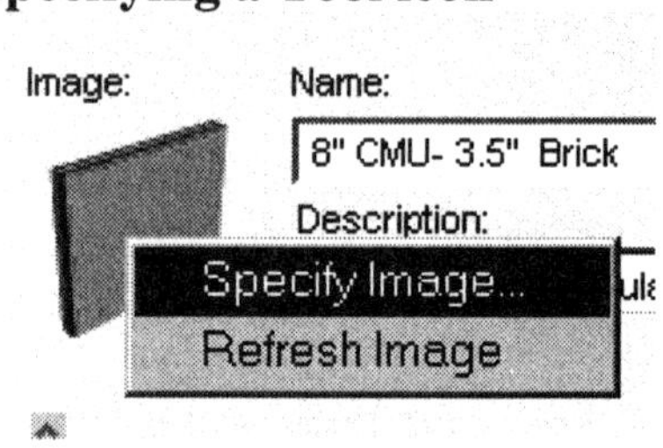

Highlight the image icon in the dialog. Right click and select **Specify Image.**

37. Locate the file called **aecwall-CMU-8-Rigid-Air Brick-4.png**.

The image is reset.

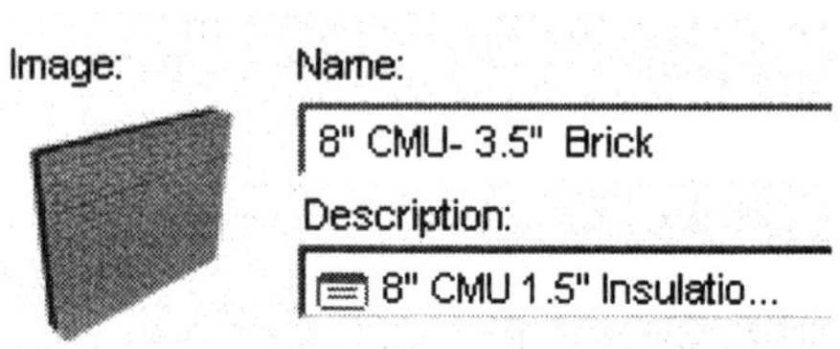

Press OK.

Organizing your Palette

38. 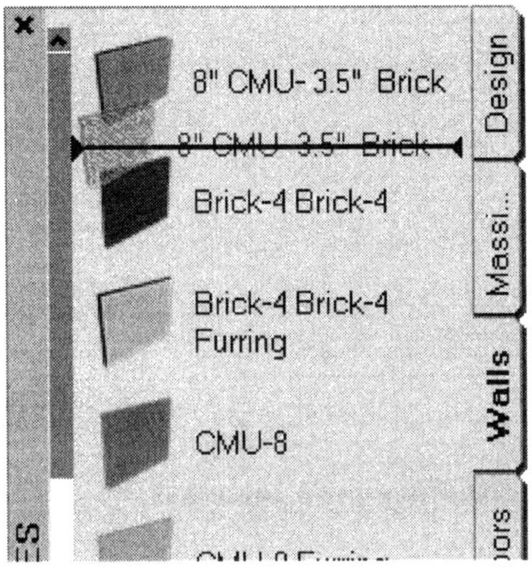

Drag the new tool to the top of your palette.

39. Select the new tool and draw a wall.

40 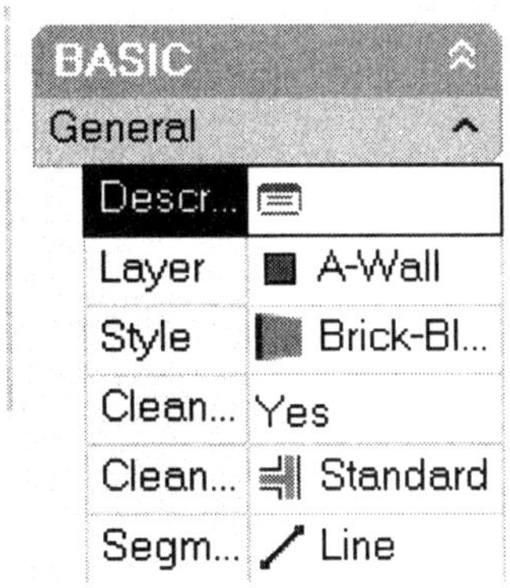

Select the wall you drew.

Right click and select **Properties**.

Note that the wall is placed on the A-Wall Layer and uses the Brick-Block Style you defined.

41. Save your file as **Styles1.dwg**.

> **TIP:** The wall style you created will not be available in any new drawings unless you copy it over to the default template.

Exercise 1-5:

Downloading Styles from Autodesk's pointA

Drawing Name: Styles1.dwg
Estimated Time: 15 minutes

This exercise reinforces the following skills:

- Use of AEC Design Content
- Use of Wall Styles

NOTE: **This exercise requires access to the Internet. idrop capability should also have been installed.**

1.  Open the **Styles1.dwg** created in Exercise 1-4.

2.  Select the Design Center tool from the Standard toolbar.

   You can also press **Ctl+2** on your keyboard.

3. Select the **DC Online** tab.

   Scroll down to the 3D Architectural heading.

   Select **More>.**

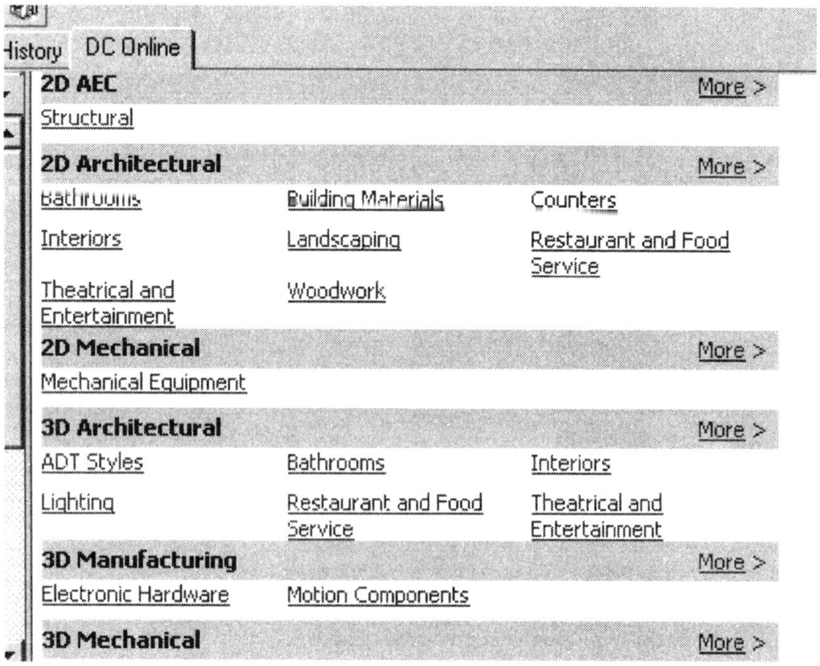

4. 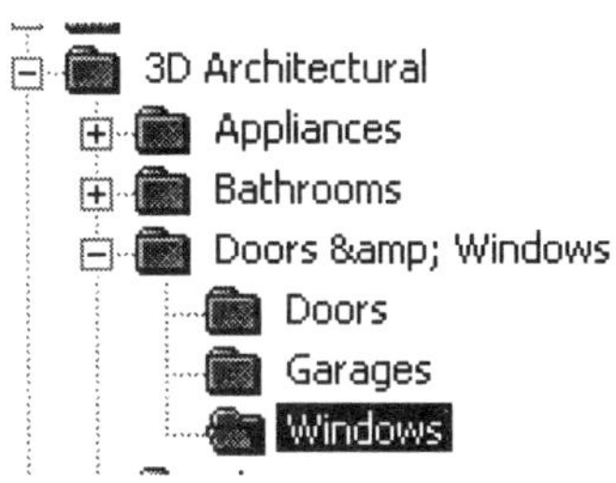

Browse to the Windows folder under 3D Architectural.

5. 

Click on a window.

Your cursor changes to an idrop.

In order to access idrop capabilities, you need to download the idrop software. This is available for free from Autodesk's website.

You will know idrop is properly installed, if you see an eyedropper when you mouse over an idrop-enabled object.

6. 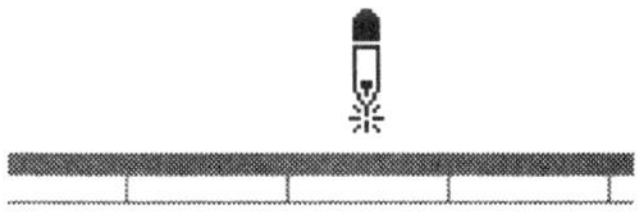

Place your cursor next to the wall you drew in the previous exercise.

7. Pick to place the window into the wall.

8. If you mouse over the window, a hyperlink is displayed.

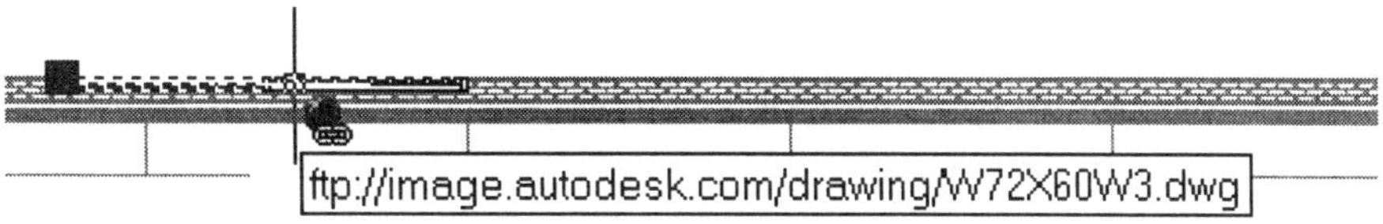

9. Save the file as **Styles2.dwg**.

Exercise 1-6:
Creating a Fireplace/Chimney

Drawing Name: New
Estimated Time: 30 minutes

Although ADT 2004 has some fireplace blocks as part of the content, you may prefer to learn how to create your own. Since most residences now have at least one fireplace, it is a good idea to know how to create one. We use the Mass Elements tools included within ADT to assist us in this process.

1.  Start a new drawing using the **QNEW** tool.

2. Type **Ctl-3** to launch the Palette Toolbar.

3. Select the Massing tab.

 Select the **Box** tool.

4. 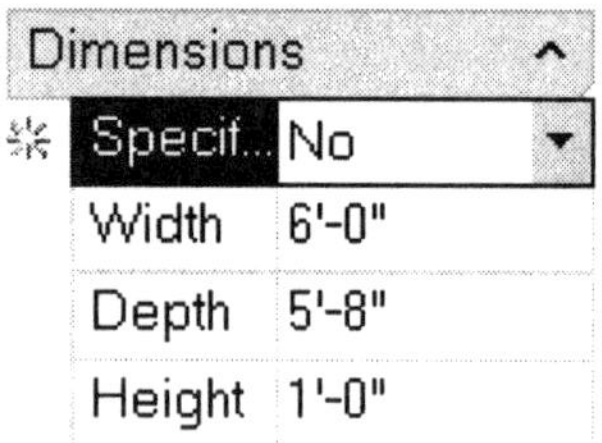

In the Dimensions area:
Set the **Width** to 6′-0″.
Set the **Depth** to 5′-8″.
Set the **Height** to 1′-0″.

5. Place at 0,0 with a rotation of 0.

```
Command: MassElementAdd
Insert point or [SHape/WIdth/Depth/Height/Match]:
Insert point or [SHape/WIdth/Depth/Height/Match]:
Insert point or [SHape/WIdth/Depth/Height/Match]: 0,0
Rotation or [SHape/WIdth/Depth/Height/Match/Undo] <0.00>:
Insert point or [SHape/WIdth/Depth/Height/Match/Undo]: *Cancel*
```

 Set the view to **SW Isometric**.

 Set the display to **Flat Shaded**.

6.

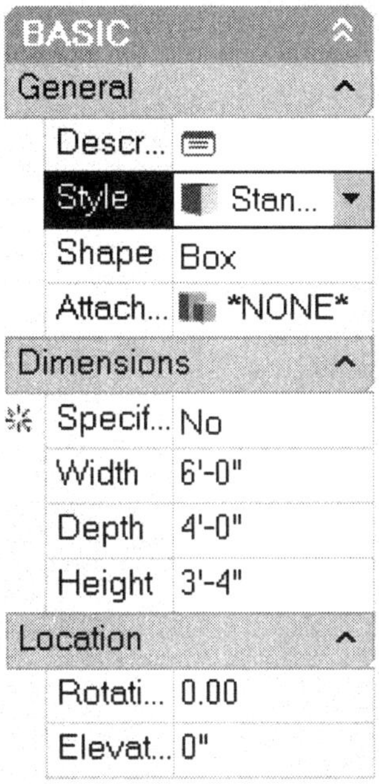

Create a second box.
Set the **Width** to 6′.
Set the **Depth** to 4′.
Set the **Height** to 3′-4″.

Place the second box next to the first box.

7. You can then use the MOVE tool to place the second box on top of the first box.

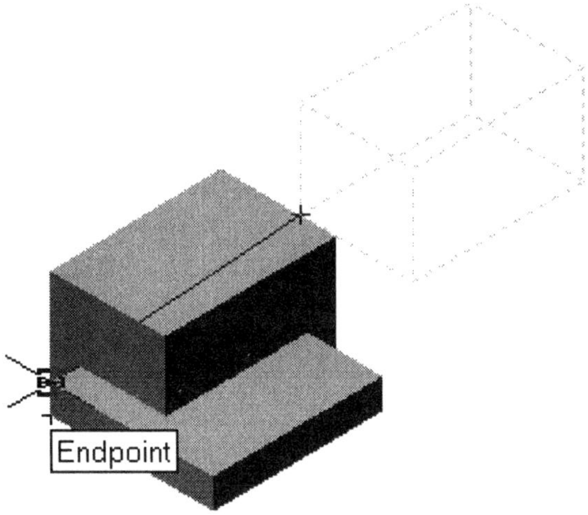

Use the Endpoints to align the two corners of the boxes.

8.

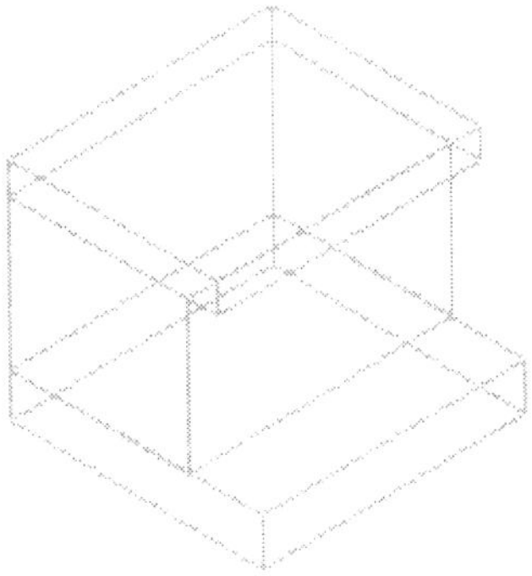

Create a third box.

Set Width to 6′.
Set Depth to 4′-8″.
Set Height to 8″.

Place on top of the stack.

9. 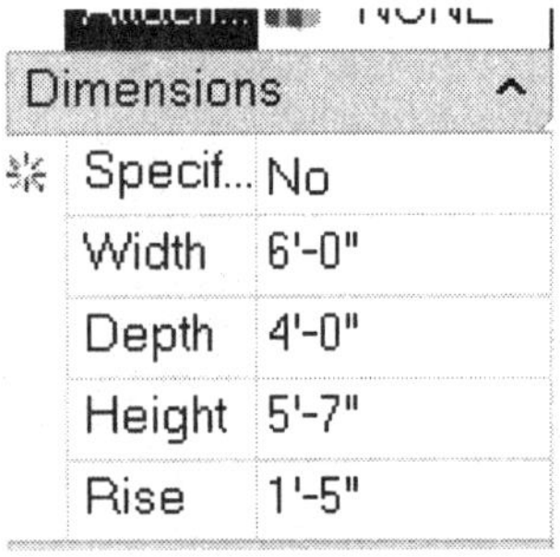

Select Gable for the next Mass Element.

Set the Width to 6′.
Set the Depth to 4′.
Set the Rise to 1′-5″.
Set the Height to 5′-7″.

Stack the Gable on top as shown.

> **TIP:** If you see shadows or 'ghosts' when creating your mass elements, use REGEN to refresh your screen.

10. 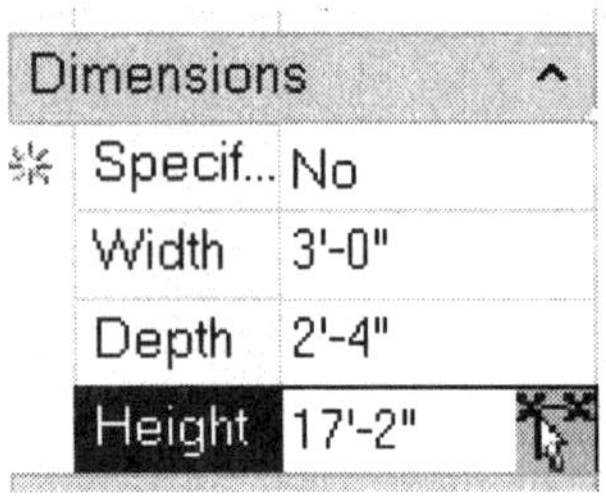

Create another box.

Set the Width to 3′-0″.
Set the Depth to 2′-4″.
Set the Height to 17′-2″.

11. 

Place the tall box as shown.
To locate it properly, use the MOVE tool. Select the midpoint of the rear back wall of the box and then select the rear vertex of the gable.
Then move using the rear vertex of the gable for the first point and **@0,0,-2′** as the second point to lower the tall box appropriately. This will shift the box down appropriately.

Command: _move
Select objects: 1 found (select tall box)
Select objects:
Specify base point or displacement: _endp of (Select rear vertex)

Specify second point of displacement or <use first point as displacement>: @0,0,-2′.

12.

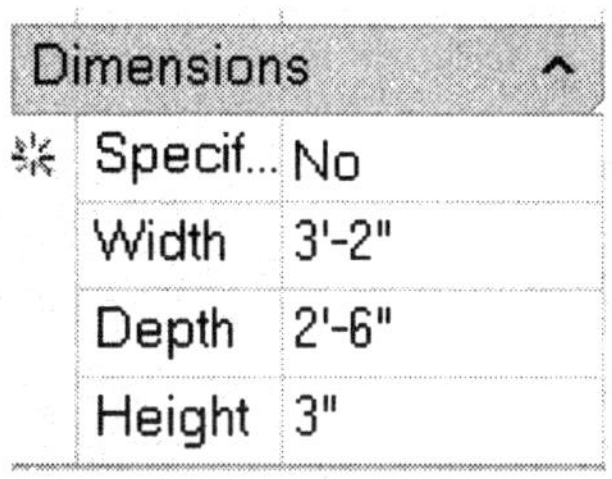

Create another box.
Set the Width to 3′-2″.
Set the Depth to 2′-6″.
Set the Height to 3″.

13.

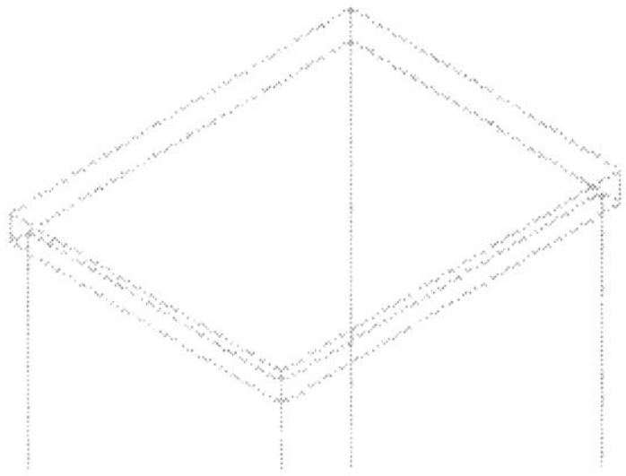

Place the box so there is a 1″ overhang on each side. You can do this by using the MOVE command. Place the box so two corners of the boxes are even. Then MOVE again. When prompted for displacement, type –1″,-1″.

14.

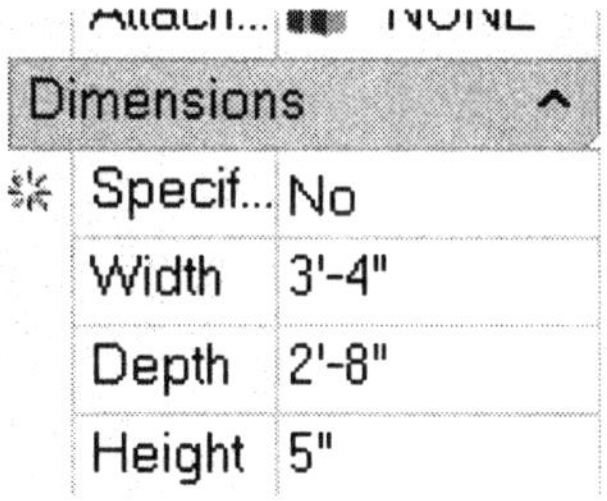

Create another box.
Set the Width to 3′-4″.
Set the Depth to 2′-8″.
Set the Height to 5″.

15.

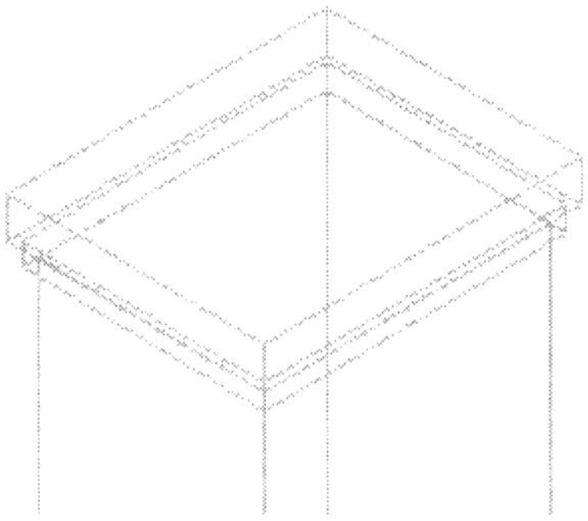

Place this box so it overhangs the previous box 1″ on each side.

16.

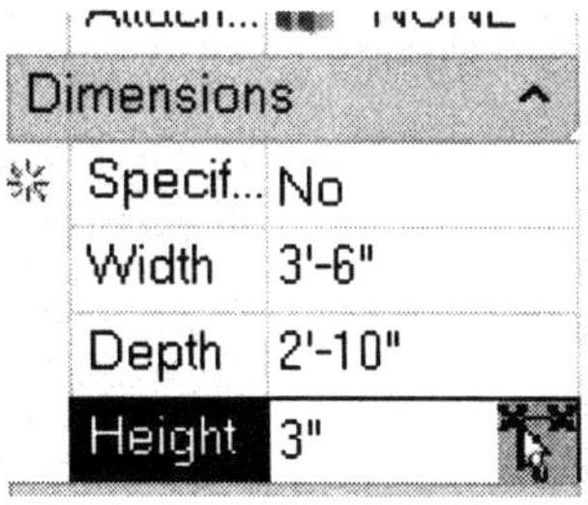

Create another box.
Set the Width to 3′-6″.
Set the Depth to 2′-10″.
Set the Height to 3″.

17.

Place this box so it overhangs the previous box 1″ on each side.

18.

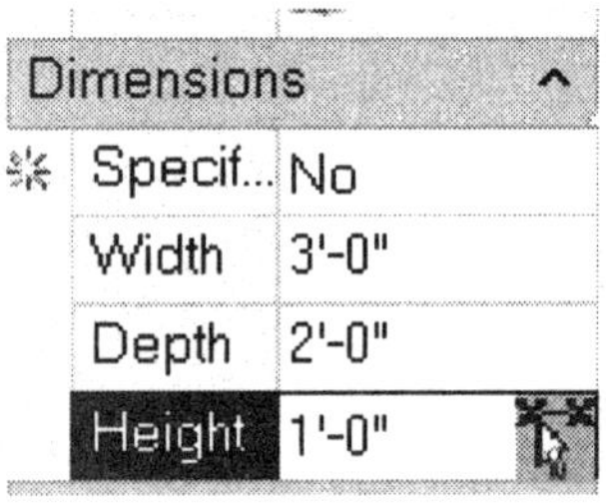

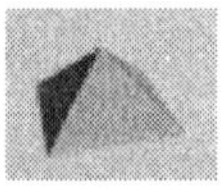

Top your chimney with a pyramid.
Set the Width to 3′.
Set the Depth to 2′.
Set the Height to 1′.

19.

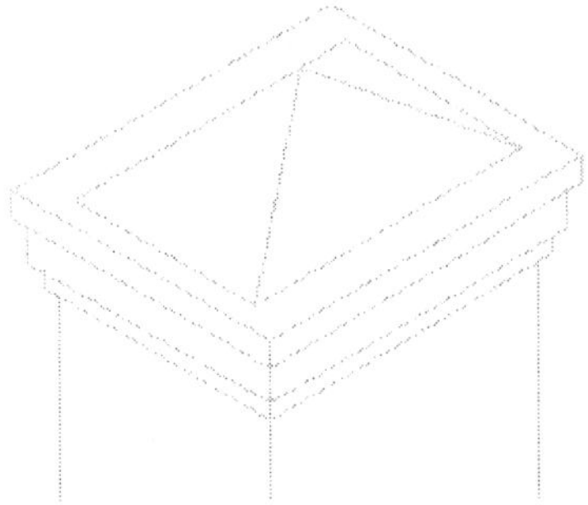

Center the pyramid on top of the chimney.

We've created the base part of our model. We will be adding additional mass elements that will be subtracted from this part to create the openings for the fireplace.

First, we define our Mass Group.

20.

Select the **Add Mass Group** tool.

```
Command: _AecMassGroupAdd
Location: 0,0,0

Rotation angle <0.00>:
```

When prompted for the location, type 0,0,0.

When prompted for the angle, press ENTER.

21.

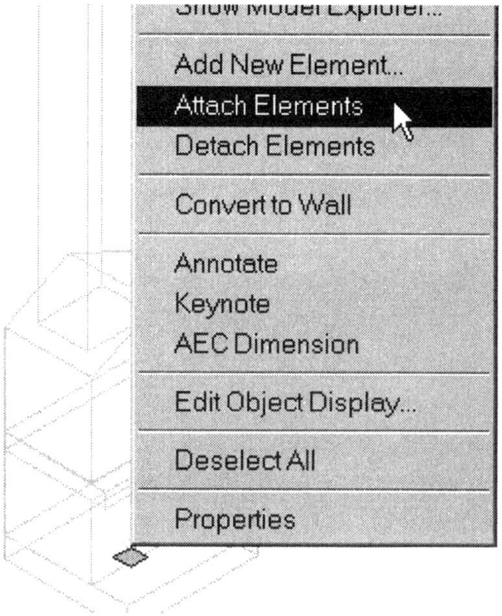

Switch to Wireframe display mode.

Select the Mass Group icon – it looks like a small cube.

Right click and select **Attach Elements.**

Select all the mass elements you just created.

When prompted for the Mass Element Group, type **L f**or last.

Then select all the elements you just created.

22.

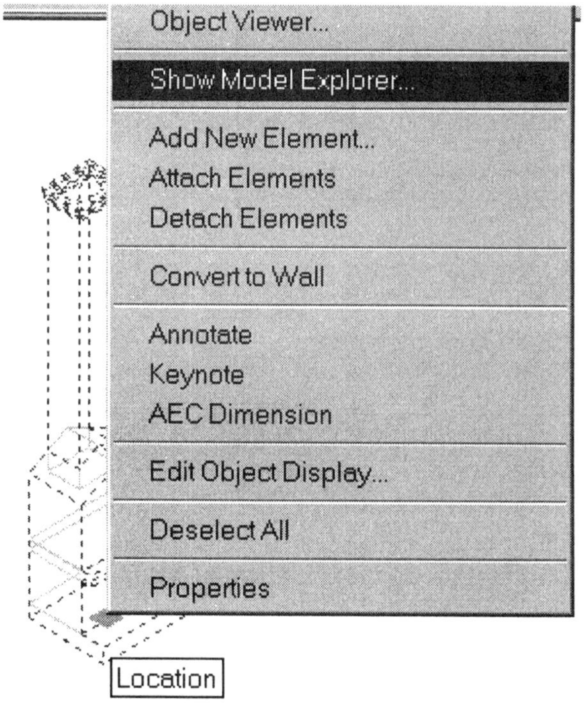

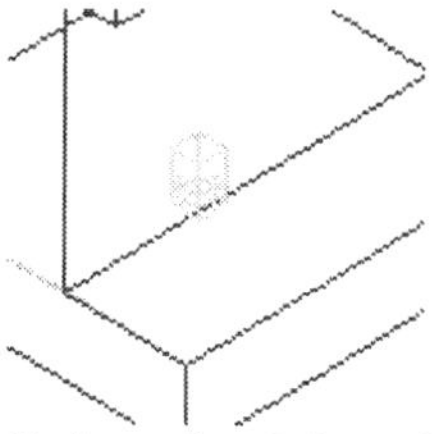

Select the Mass Group icon.

Right click and select **Show Model Explorer.**

23.

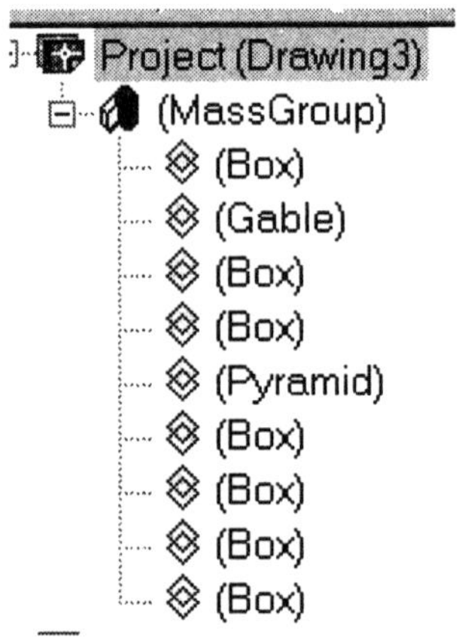

A window opens to reveal your Mass Elements group that you have created.

Expanding the Mass Group reveals a feature tree showing all the Mass Elements.

24. If you right-click in the window, a context sensitive menu will appear providing you with different viewing options.

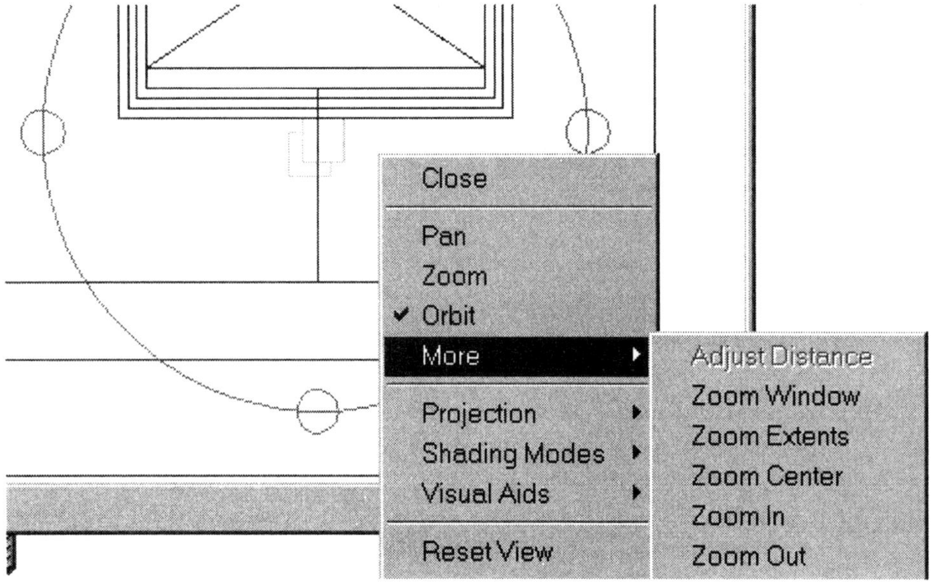

Close the Explorer dialog.

24.

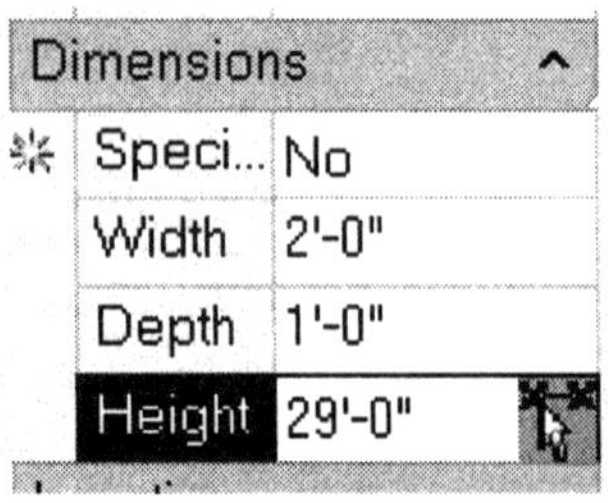

Create a tall box with Width set to 2′, Depth set to 1′ and Height set to 29′. This will be used to create the flue opening for the chimney.

25.

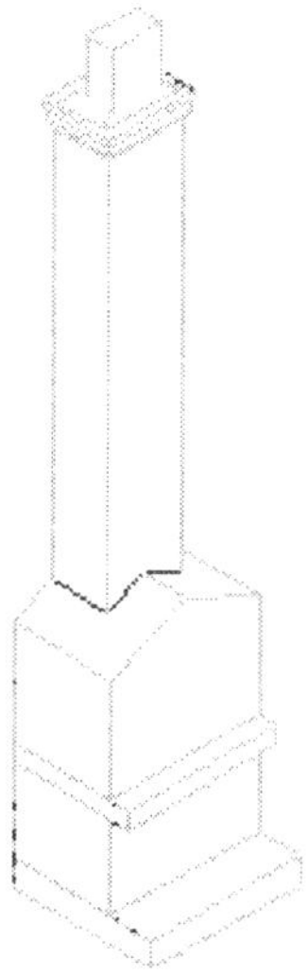

Center the opening inside the chimney.

26.

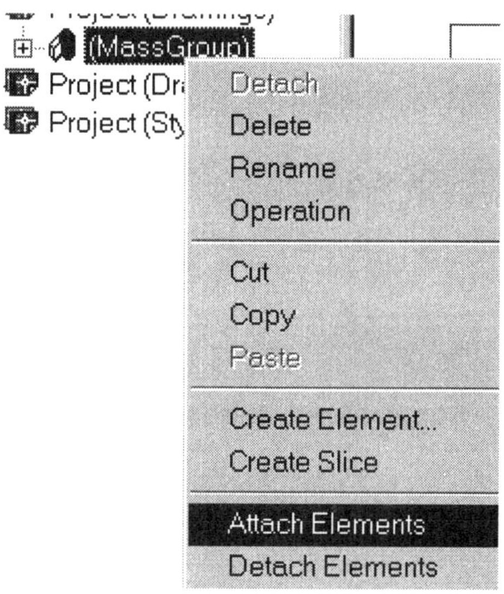

Bring up the Mass Element Explorer. Type **MODELEXPLORER** on the command line.

Highlight the Mass Group. Select 'Attach Elements.' Select the tall flue opening we just created.

27. Place your cursor in the command line.
Right click and select **Recent Commands>MODELEXPLORER** to launch the Model Explorer.

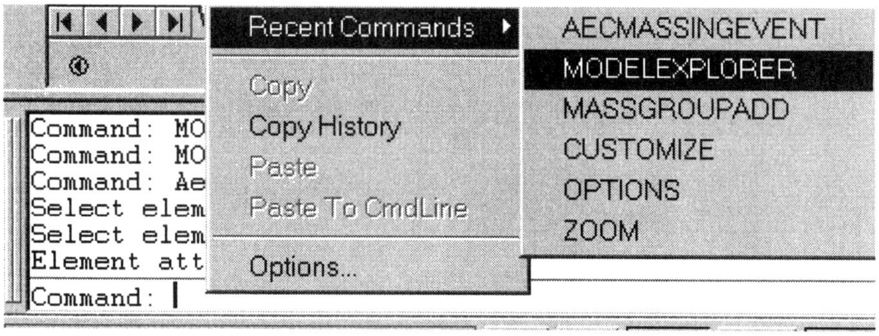

27. 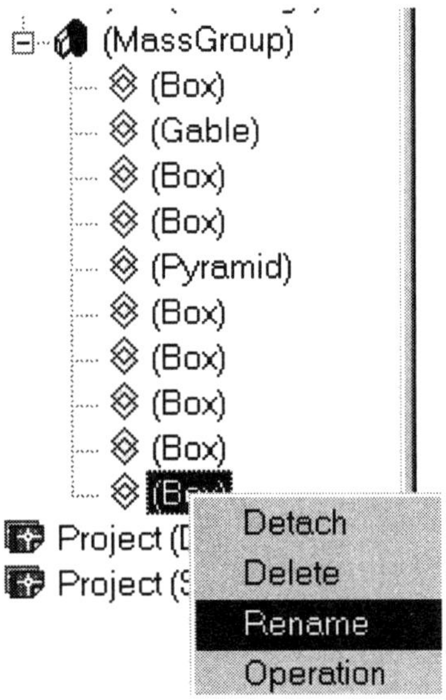

To help us with identifying the various mass elements, we can rename them.

Highlight the last box in the list, right click and select 'Rename.'

Type in 'flue-opening' as our new name.

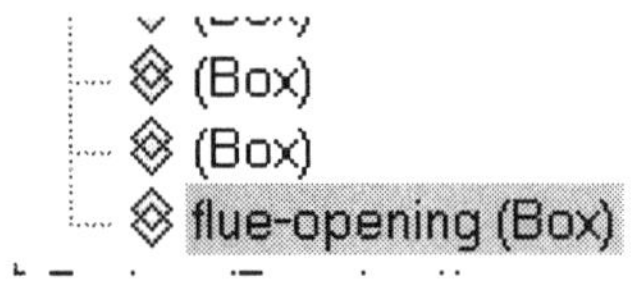

 Switch to a Top View.

28. Draw this polyline on the XY plane.

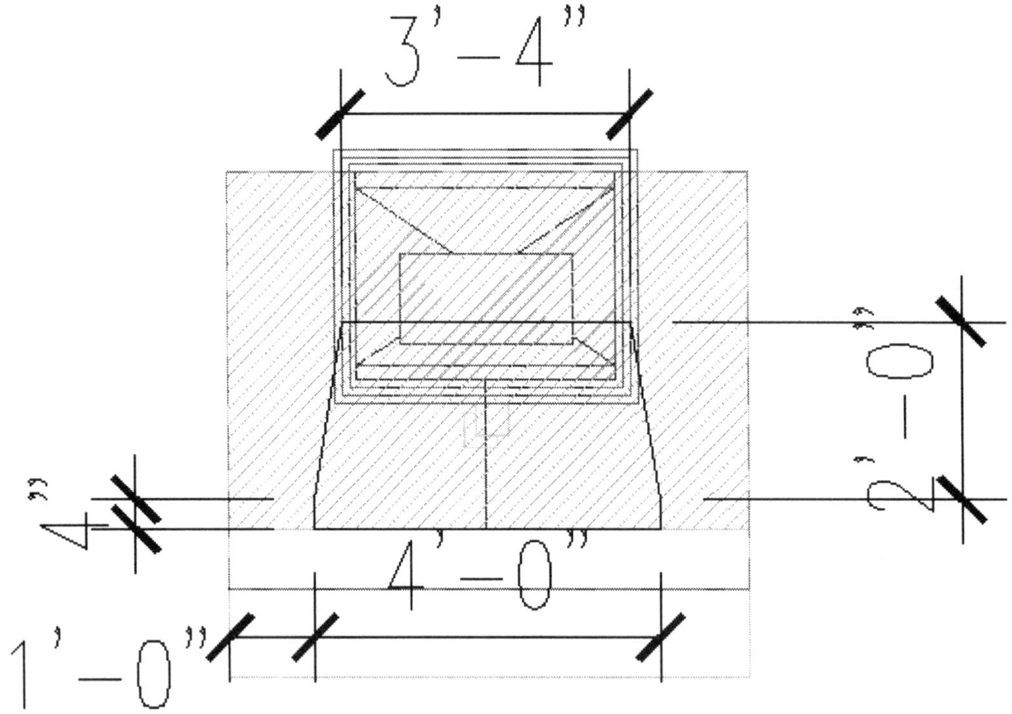

Below is one method to create the polyline:

Command: _pline
Specify start point: 1′ (Start your polyline 1′ in from the intersect point on the left.)

Current line-width is 0′-0″
Specify next point or [Arc/Halfwidth/Length/Undo/Width]: 4″ (go up vertically)

Specify next point or [Arc/Close/Halfwidth/Length/Undo/Width]: @4″,2′

Specify next point or [Arc/Close/Halfwidth/Length/Undo/Width]: 3′4″ (move to the right)

Specify next point or [Arc/Close/Halfwidth/Length/Undo/Width]: @4″,-2′

Specify next point or [Arc/Close/Halfwidth/Length/Undo/Width]: 4″ (go down vertically)

Specify next point or [Arc/Close/Halfwidth/Length/Undo/Width]: C

29.

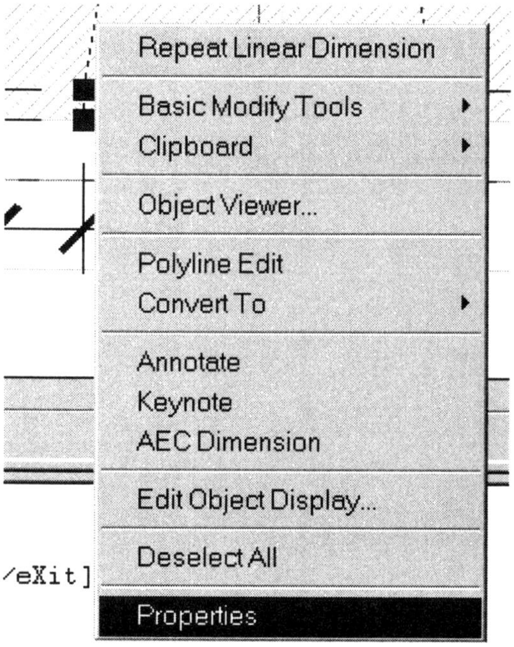

Locate the polyline so it is at 1′ elevation as shown.

Select the polyline, right click and select **Properties**.

Elevation	1'-0"

Set the Elevation to 1′-0″.

30.

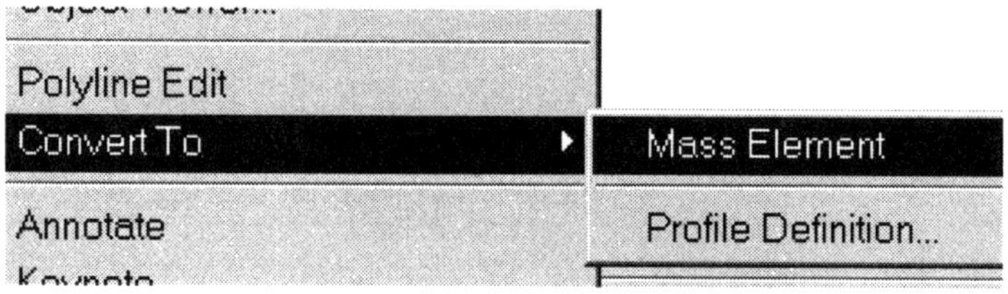

Select the polyline.

Right click and select **Convert To>Mass Element**

31. When prompted to erase the selected linework, press **Y**. When prompted to specify extrusion height, type **2′6″**.

```
Command: ExtrudeLinework
Erase selected linework? [Yes/No] <No>: Y
Specify extrusion height <1'-0">: 2'6"
(1) new mass element(s) created.
```

32. 

Go back to your Mass Group Explorer.

An icon for the Mass Group Explorer is minimized at the bottom of your screen. Either select the icon or right click and select **Maximize**.

33. 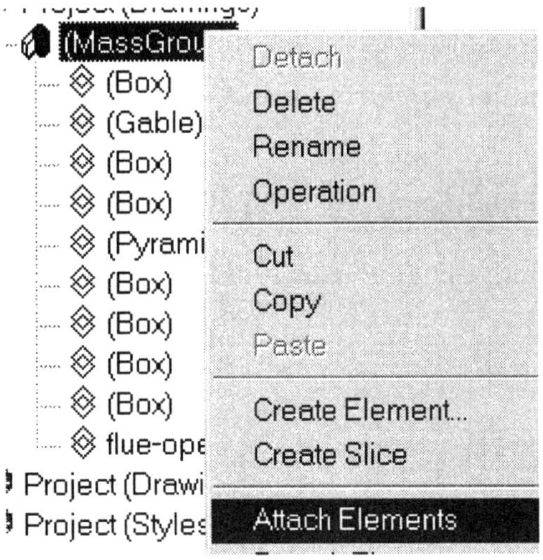

Select the Mass Group.
Right click and select **Attach Elements**.

Select the polyline extrusion.

The extrusion is now listed in the Model Explorer.

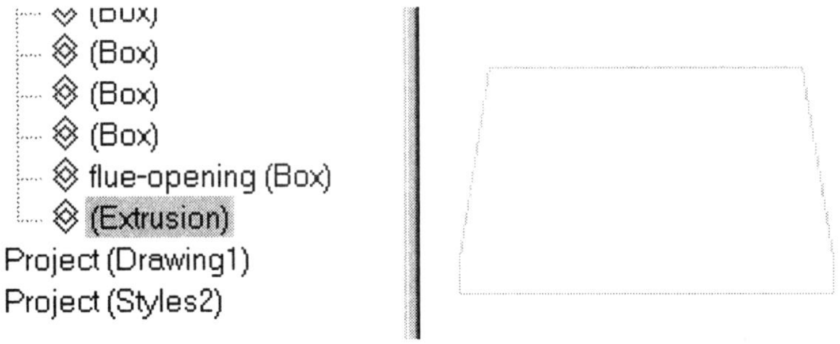

34. 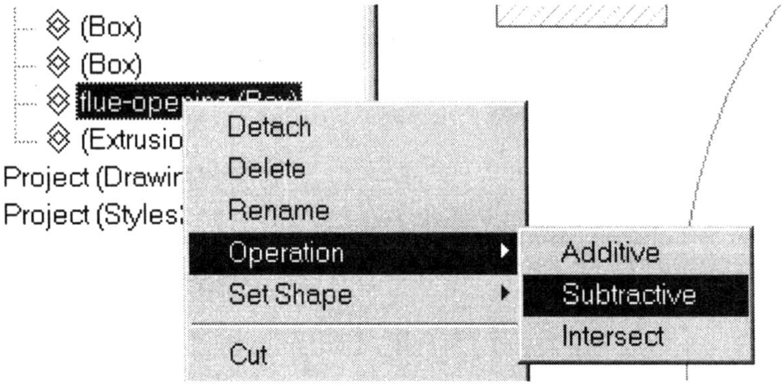

Highlight the flue-opening.

Right click and select **Operation>Subtractive**.

35. Highlight the Extrusion.

Right click and select **Operation>Subtractive**.

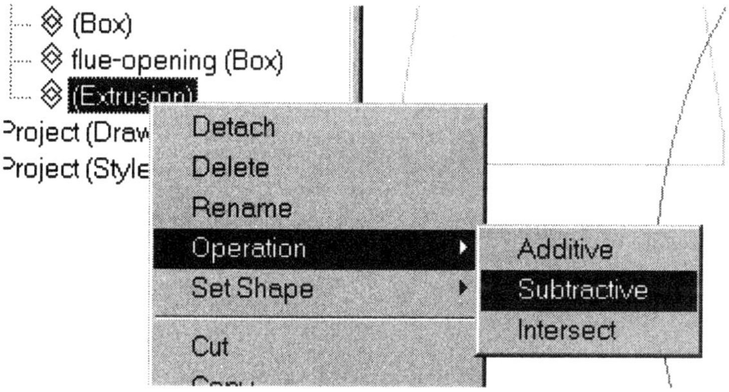

36.

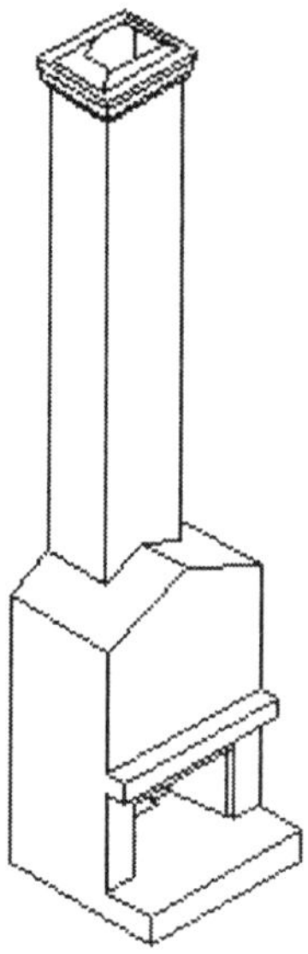

 Set the view display in the Model Explorer to Hidden Line.

Our completed fireplace with chimney.

 To save an image of the chimney, select the **Save** tool.

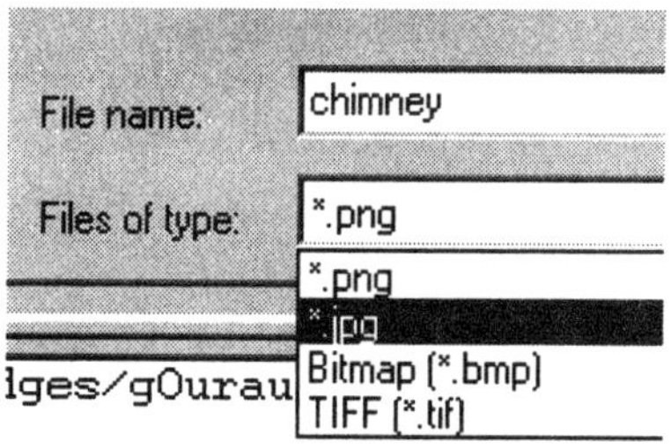

Browse to the folder of your choice and name the image **Chimney.jpg.**

37.

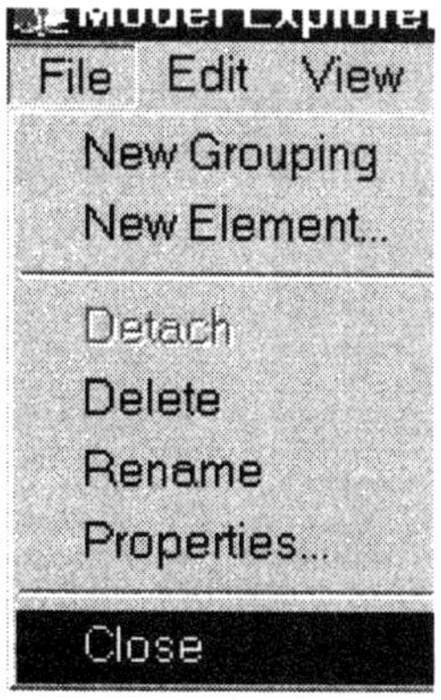

Go to **File→Close** to close the Model Explorer.

38. We will create a display configuration in Exercise 1-7 to view the chimney properly inside ADT.

Save the file as **Fireplace with Chimney.dwg**.

Layer Manager

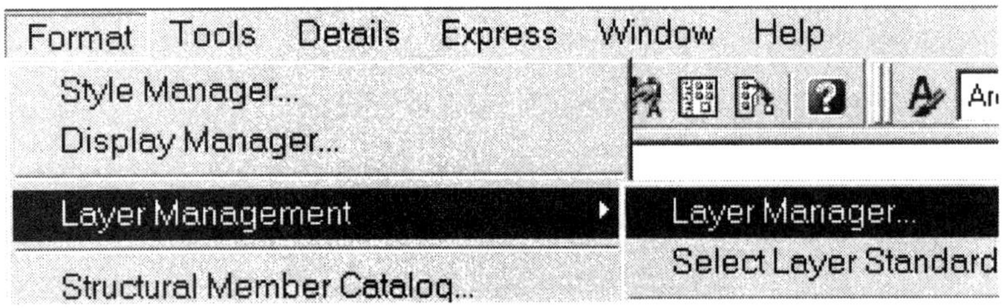

Back in the days of vellum and pencil, drafters would use separate sheets to organize their drawings. So one sheet might have the floor plan, one sheet the site plan, etc. The layers of paper would be placed on top of each other and the transparent quality of the vellum would allow the drafter to see the details on the lower sheets. Different colored pencils would be used to make it easier for the drafter to locate and identify elements of a drawing, such as dimensions, electrical outlets, water lines, etc.

When drafting moved to Computer Aided Design, the concept of sheets was transferred to the use of Layers. Drafters could assign a Layer Name, color, linetype, etc. and then place different elements on the appropriate layer.

ADT is unique in that it has a Layer Management system to allow the user to implement AIA standards easily.

Layer Manager

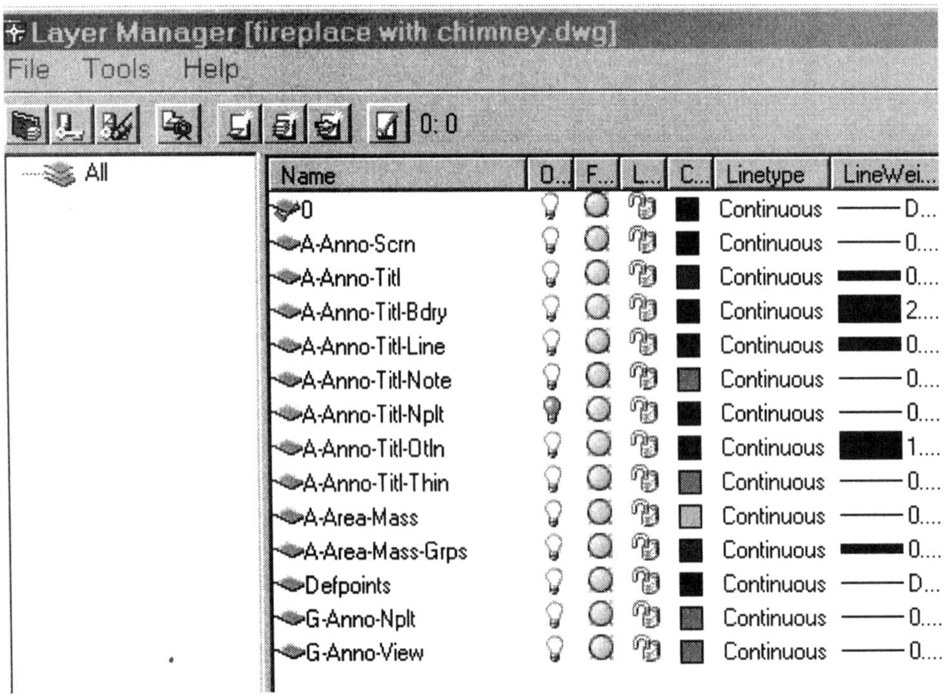

The Layer Manager helps you organize, sort, and group layers, as well as save and coordinate layering schemes. You can also use layering standards with the Layer Manager to better organize the layers in your drawings.

When you open the Layer Manager, all the layers in the current drawing are displayed in the right panel. You can work with individual layers to:

- Change layer properties by clicking AutoCAD layer property icons
- Make a layer the current layer
- Create, rename, and delete layers

If you are working with drawings that contain large numbers of layers, you can improve the speed at which the Layer Manager loads layers when you open it by selecting the Layer Manager/Optimize for Speed option in your AEC Editor options.

The Layer Manager has a tool bar as shown.

	*Layer Standards* You can import Layer Standards from an existing drawing or Export Layer Standards using the current drawing. 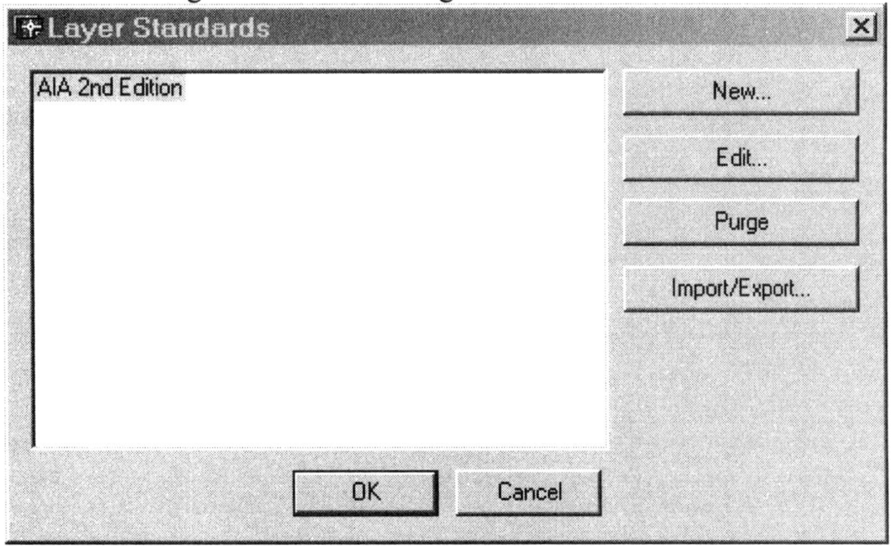
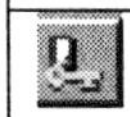	*Layer Key Styles* – Brings up the Style Manager. A layer key is a map between the AEC object that you draw on screen and a defined layer. When you create an object, the layer key that is associated with the object automatically places that object on the layer to which the layer key is mapped. Using layer keys to automatically place objects on predefined layers is called *layer keying*.

TIP: The layer key styles in Autodesk Architectural Desktop, Release 3 and above replace the use of LY files. If you have LY files from S8 or Release 1 of AutoCAD Architectural Desktop that you want to use, then you can create a new layer key style from an LY file. On the command line enter **-AecLYImport** to import legacy LY files.

Layer Key Overrides

You can apply overrides to any layer keys within a layer key style that is based on a layer standard. The structure of the layer name of each layer that each layer key maps an object to is determined by the descriptive fields in the layer standard definition. You can override the information in each field according to the values set in the layer standard definition. You can allow overrides on all the layer keys within a layer key style, or you can select individual layer keys that you want to override. You can also choose to allow all of the descriptive fields that make up the layer name to be overridden, or you can specify which descriptive fields you want to override.

Snapshots

A layer snapshot is a specific set of layers and view information that you can save, edit, and restore in your drawing. By saving layer and view information in a snapshot, you can quickly recall specific layer and view configurations from complex data sets. For example, a facilities manager might create snapshots of individual floor plans and furniture, cable, and HVAC layouts to separate this information from a complete building layout.

New Layer

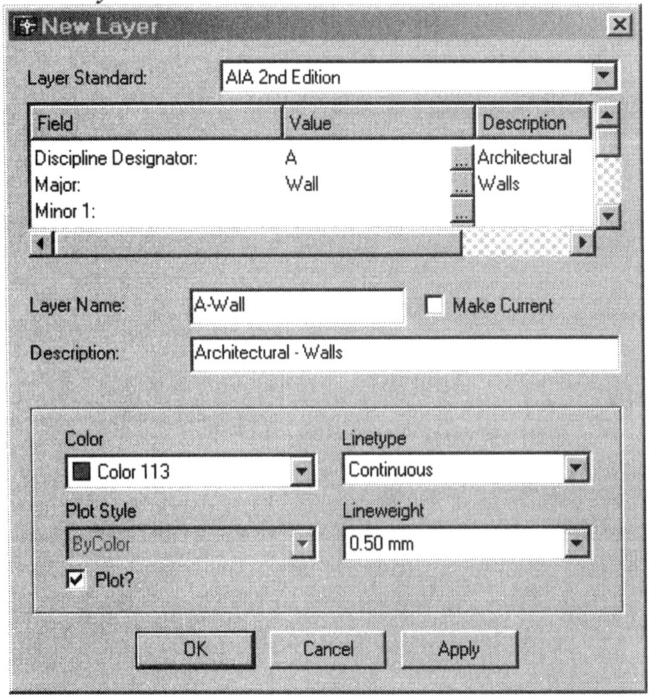

New Filter Group

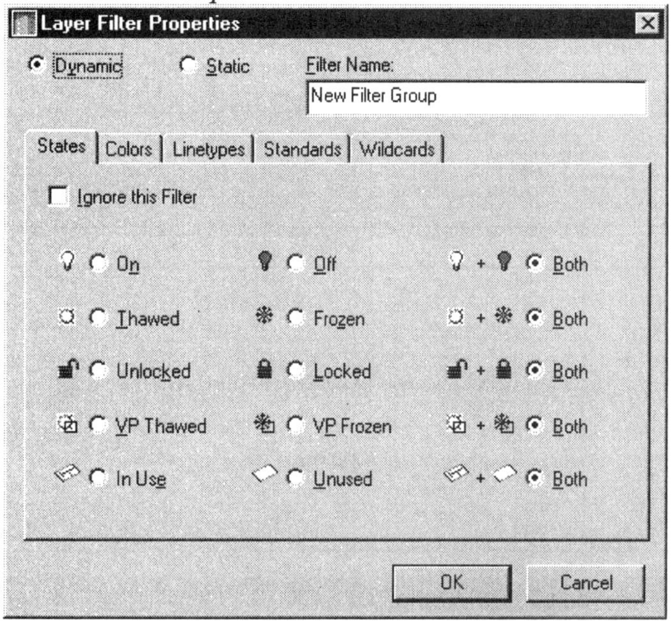

Controls the display of layer names in the Object Properties toolbar. Set the drop down to only display layers that are ON, layers with specific colors, etc.

New User Group

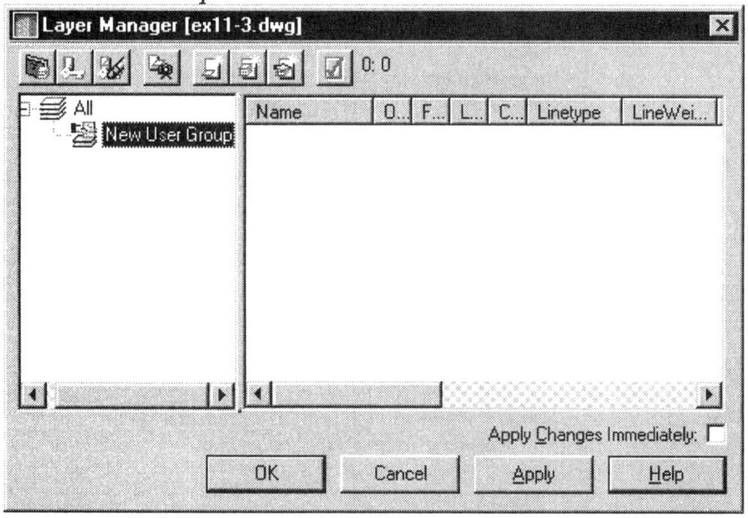

Allows you to group layers for easier control.

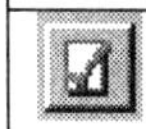

Make selected layer current

Highlight a layer name in the list and press this button to set current.

The following are the default layer keys used by Autodesk Architectural Desktop when you create AEC objects.

Default layer keys for creating AEC objects			
Layer Key	**Description**	**Layer Key**	**Description**
ANNDTOBJ	Detail marks	CONTROL	Control systems
ANNELOBJ	Elevation objects	CWLAYOUT	Curtain walls
ANNOBJ	Notes, leaders, etc.	CWUNIT	Curtain wall units
ANNREV	Revisions	DIMLINE	Dimensions
ANNSXKEY	Section marks	DIMMAN	Dimensions (AutoCAD points)
ANNSXOBJ	Section marks	DOOR	Doors
ANNSYMOBJ	Annotation marks	DOORNO	Door tags
APPL	Appliances	DRAINAGE	Drainage
AREA	Areas	ELEC	Electric
AREAGRP	Area groups	ELECNO	Electrical tags
AREAGRPNO	Area group tags	ELEV	Elevations
AREANO	Area tags	ELEVAT	Elevators
CAMERA	Cameras	ELEVHIDE	Elevations (2D)
CASE	Casework	EQUIP	Equipment
CASENO	Casework tags	EQUIPNO	Equipment tags
CEILGRID	Ceiling grids	FINCEIL	Ceiling tags
CEILOBJ	Ceiling objects	FINFLOOR	Finish tags
CHASE	Chases	FIRE	Fire system equip.
COLUMN	Columns	FURN	Furniture
COMMUN	Communication	FURNNO	Furniture tags

Layer Key	Description	Layer Key	Description
GRIDBUB	Plan grid bubbles	SITE	Site
GRIDLINE	Column grids	SLAB	Slabs
LAYGRID	Layout grids	SPACEBDRY	Space boundaries
LIGHTCLG	Ceiling lighting	SPACEOBJ	Space objects
LIGHTW	Wall lighting	STAIR	Stairs
MASSELEM	Massing elements	STAIRH	Stair handrails
MASSGRPS	Massing groups	STRUCTBEAM	Structural beams
MASSSLCE	Massing slices	STRUCTBEAMIDEN	Structural beam tags
OPENING	Wall openings	STRUCTBRACE	Structural braces
PEOPLE	People	STRUCTBRACEIDEN	Structural brace tags
PFIXT	Plumbing fixtures	STRUCTCOLS	Structural columns
PLANTS	Plants - outdoor	STRUCTCOLSIDEN	Structural column tags
PLANTSI	Plants - indoor	SWITCH	Electrical switches
POLYGON	AEC Polygons	TITTEXT	Border and title block
POWER	Electrical power	TOILACC	Arch. specialties
PRK-SYM	Parking symbols	TOILNO	Toilet tags
ROOF	Rooflines	UTIL	Site utilities
ROOFSLAB	Roof slabs	VEHICLES	Vehicles
ROOMNO	Room tags	WALL	Walls
SCHEDOBJ	Schedule tables	WALLFIRE	Fire wall patterning
SEATNO	Seating tags	WALLNO	Wall tags
SECT	Miscellaneous sections	WIND	Windows
SECTHIDE	Sections (2D)	WINDASSEM	Window assemblies
		WINDNO	Window tags

Set Current Display Configuration

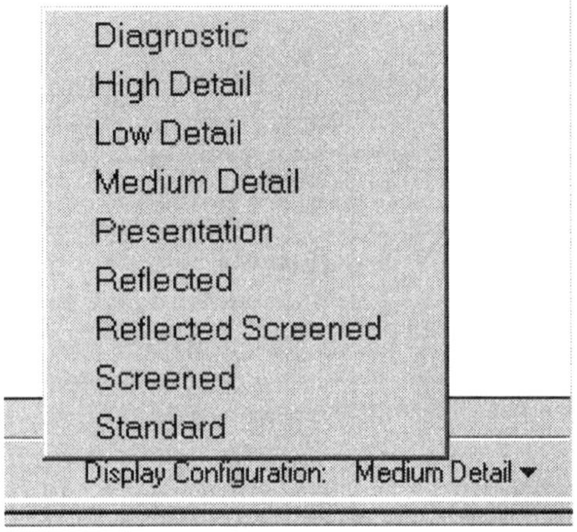

The display system in Autodesk® Architectural Desktop controls how AEC objects are displayed in a designated viewport. By specifying the AEC objects you want to display in a viewport and the direction from which you want to view them, you can produce different architectural displays, such as floor plans, reflected plans, elevations, 3D models, or schematic displays.

Autodesk Architectural Desktop, Release 3 includes templates with predefined display systems applied to viewports. You can use the display systems and viewports supplied by the templates, or you can modify the display system settings to suit your own office standards. If you want to create your own display systems, you can start a drawing from scratch or from a template that does not contain pre-defined display systems.

Display Manager

Menu	Format→Display Manager
Command Line	DisplayManager

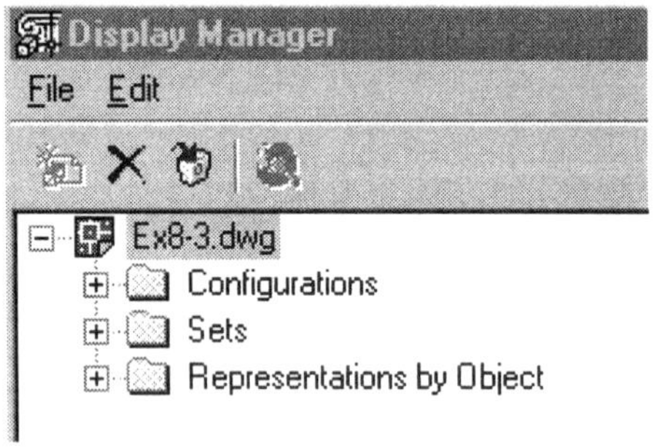

The display system in Autodesk® Architectural Desktop controls how AEC objects are displayed in a designated viewport. By specifying the AEC objects you want to display in a viewport and the direction from which you want to view them, you can produce different architectural displays, such as floor plans, reflected plans, elevations, 3D models, or schematic displays.

The current viewport and all viewports that have the same display configuration assigned to it are drawn with the new display representations.

Exercise 1-7:
Creating a Display Configuration

Drawing Name: Fireplace with Chimney.dwg
Estimated Time: 15 minutes

This exercise reinforces the following skills:

- Display Configuration
- Display Manager

1.  Open the **Fireplace with Chimney.dwg** file.

To view the chimney properly, you need to set up a mass group display configuration.

2. 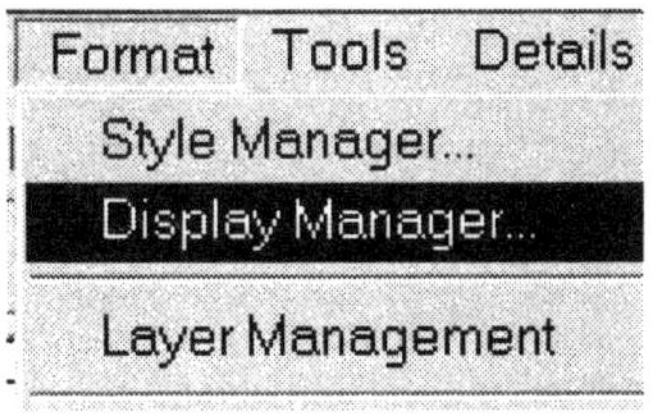

Go to **Format→Display Manager**.

3. 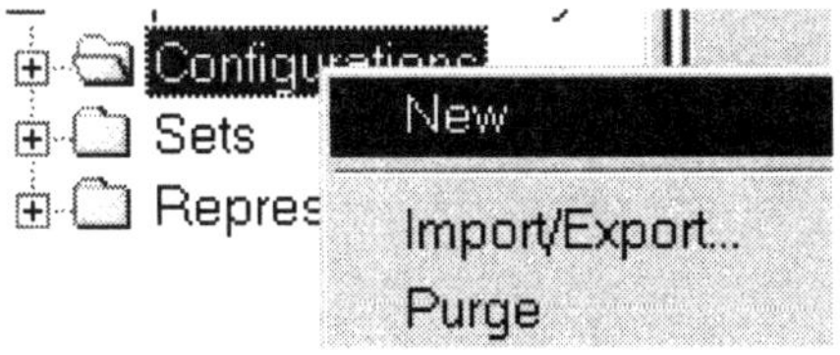

Highlight **Configurations**.
Right click and select **New.**

4. 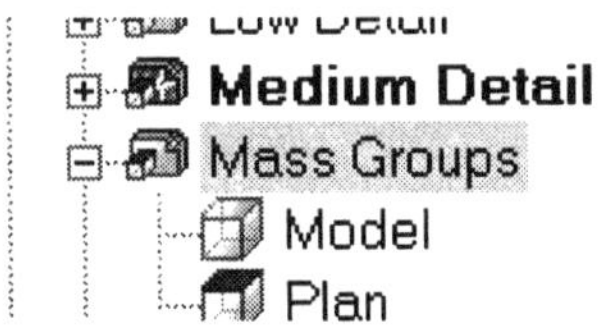

Name the configuration **Mass Groups.**

5. 

Highlight **Mass Groups**.
Right click and select **Set to Current Viewport.**

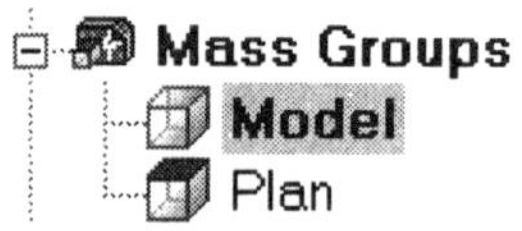

Model is now bolded.

6. 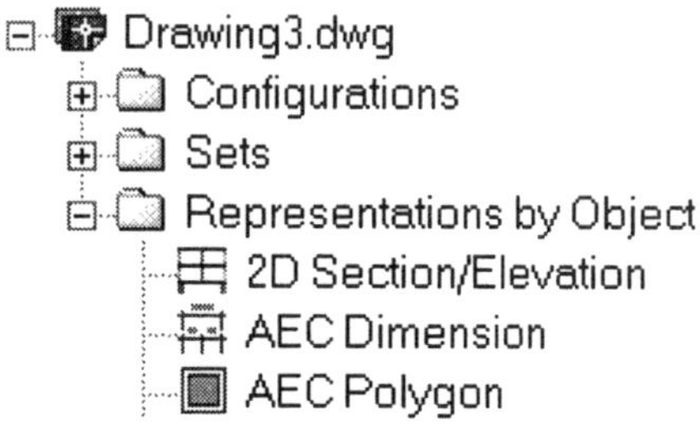

Expand the **Representations by Object** folder.

7. Highlight **Mass Element** in the list.

Uncheck all rectangles that are checked.

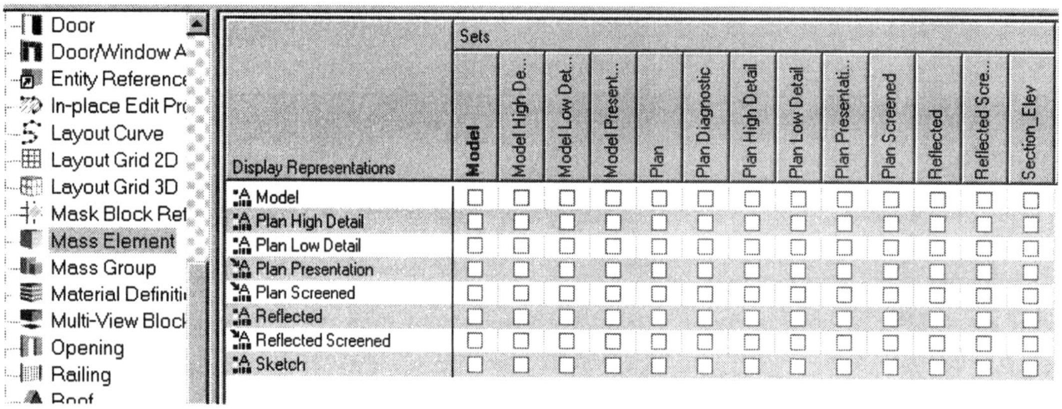

Press **OK.**

8. 

You now see the Mass Group, but not the individual Mass Elements that comprise the group.

9. Save the file as **Fireplace with Chimney.dwg.**

Lesson 2:
Site Plans

Most architectural projects start with a site plan. The site plan indicates the property lines, the house location, a North symbol, any streets surrounding the property, topographical features, location of sewer, gas, and/or electrical lines (assuming they are below ground – above ground connections are not shown), and topographical features.

When laying out the floor plan for the house, many architects take into consideration the path of sun (to optimize natural light), street access (to locate the driveway), and any noise factors.

Architectural Desktop allows the user to simulate the natural path of the sun based on the longitude and latitude coordinates of the site, so you can test how natural light will affect various house orientations.

A plot plan must include the following features:

- Length and bearing of each property line
- Location, outline, and size of buildings on the site
- Contour of the land
- Elevation of property corners and contour lines
- North symbol
- Trees, shrubs, streams, and other topological items
- Streets, sidewalks, driveways, and patios
- Location of utilities
- Easements and drainages (if any)
- Well, septic, sewage line, and underground cables
- Fences and retaining walls
- Lot number and/or address of the site
- Scale of the drawing

The plot plan is drawn using information provided by the county/city and/or a licensed surveyor.

It used to be that you would draw to a scale, such as 1/8″ = 1′, but with Architectural Desktop, you draw full-size and then set up your layout to the proper scale. This ensures that all items you draw will fit together properly.

Exercise 2-1:
Creating Custom Line Types

Drawing Name: New
Estimated Time: 15 minutes

This exercise reinforces the following skills:

- Creation of linetypes
- Customization

Architectural drafting requires a variety of custom linetypes in order to display specific features. The standard linetypes provided with Architectural Desktop are insufficient from an architectural point of view. You may find custom linetypes on Autodesk's pointA website, www.cadalog.com, or any number of websites on the Internet. However, the ability to create linetypes as needed is an excellent skill for an architectural drafter.

It's a good idea to store any custom linetypes in a separate file. The standard file for storing linetypes is acad.lin. If you store any custom linetypes in acad.lin file, you will lose them the next time you upgrade your software.

1. 

AutoCAD2004 includes Express Tools.

The tools are installed separately from AutoCAD. To install the tools, close all applications, including AutoCAD. Turn off any virus checking software, such as Nortion. Use your AutoCAD installation CD and select the option to install the Express Tools.

Once the Express Tools are installed, you can start this exercise.

2.  Start a new drawing using QNEW.

3.

Draw a property line.
This property line was created as follows:
Set ORTHO ON.
Draw a horizontal line 12 units long
Use SNAP FROM to start the next line @3,0 distance from the previous line.
The short line is 6 units long.
Use SNAP FROM to start the next line @3,0 distance from the previous line.
The second short line is 6 units long.
Use SNAP FROM to start the next line @3,0 distance from the previous line.
Draw a second horizontal line 12 units long.

4. 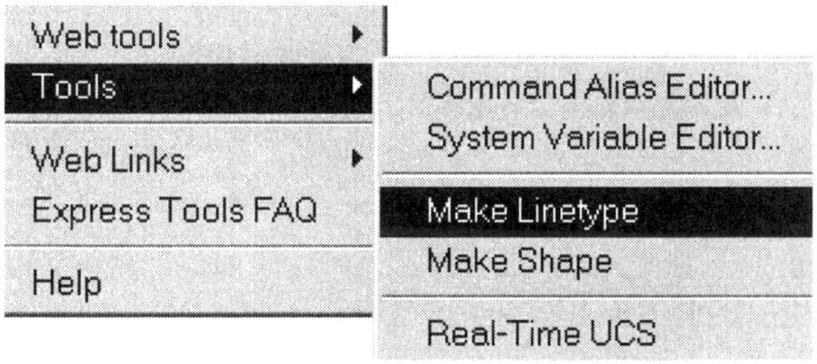

Go to Express→Tools→Make Linetype

5. Create a file name called custom-arch.lin and press 'Save.'

TIP: Place all your custom linetypes in a single drawing file and then use the AutoCAD Design Center to help you locate and load the desired linetype.

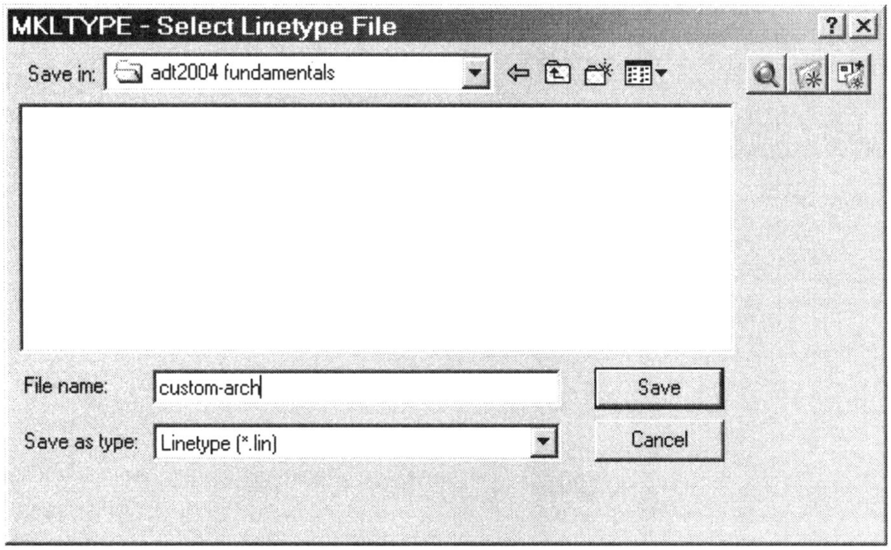

6. When prompted for the linetype name, type: property-line.
   When prompted for the linetype description, type: property-line
   Specify starting point for line definition; select the far left point of the line type.
   Specify ending point for line definition; select the far right point of the line type.
   When prompted to select the objects, start at the long line on the left and pick the line segments in order.

7. Under the linetype drop-down, locate the property-line just created and make it active.

   Draw some lines to see if they look OK. Make sure you make them long enough to see the dashes.

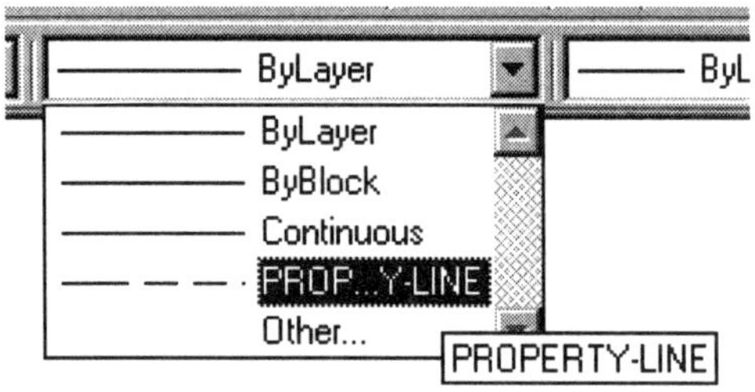

8. Locate the custom-arch.lin file you created.

   Open it using NotePad.

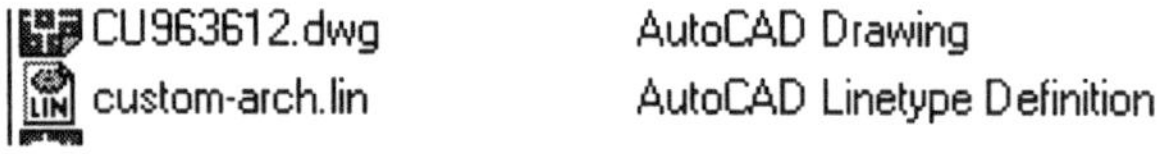

9. 

   You see a description of the property-line.

10. Save as *ex2-1.dwg*.

Exercise 2-2:

Creating a Custom Text Style

Drawing Name: ex2-1.dwg
Estimated Time: 15 minutes

This exercise reinforces the following skills:

- Text Styles
- Customization

Most architects use custom text styles. You may find custom text styles on Autodesk's pointA website, www.cadalog.com, or any number of websites on the Internet. However, the ability to create text styles as needed is an excellent skill for an architectural drafter.

1.  Open *ex2-1.dwg*.

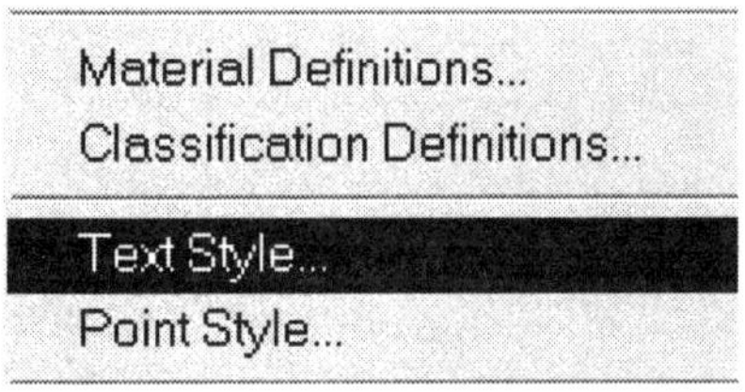

Select Format→Text Style.

You can also type TEXTSTYLE on the command line.

3. Press the New button.

4. Type **Architectural** for the new style name.

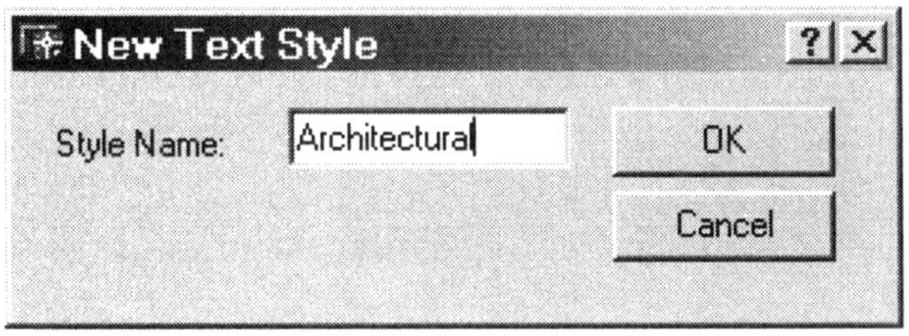

5. 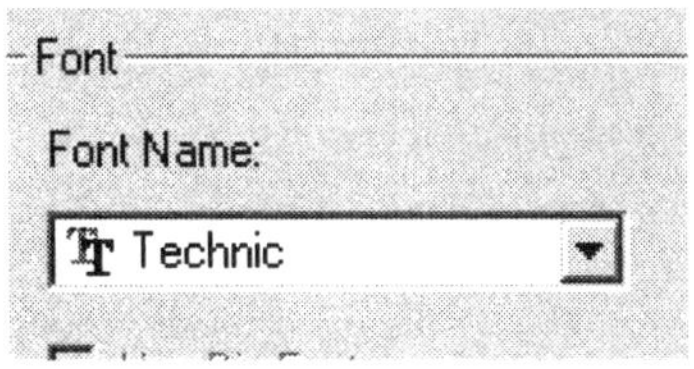

Select **Technic** for the font name.
Technic is a standard font included with Windows.
Press **Apply**.
Then **Close**.

6. 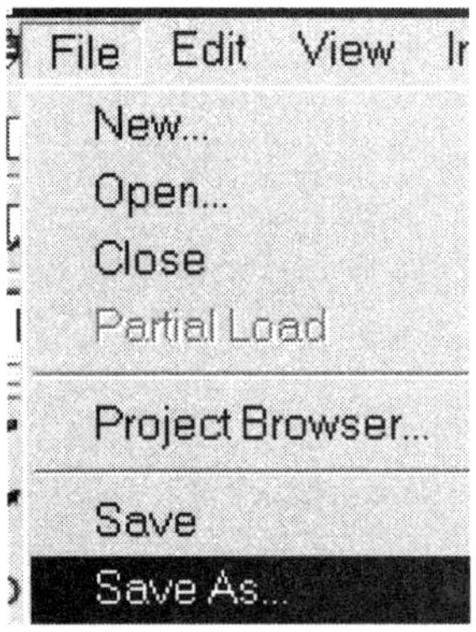

Save the file as 'fonts.dwg' in your custom subdirectory.

Use this drawing to store all your custom text styles. You can then use the Design Center to load any custom fonts from this drawing.

Exercise 2-3:

Creating New Layers

Drawing Name: New
Estimated Time: 15 minutes

This exercise reinforces the following skills:

- Use of toolbars
- Layer Manager
- Creating New Layers
- Loading Linetypes

1.  Start a new drawing using QNEW.

2. First, we need to load the property-line linetype we defined in Exercise 2-1.

 Launch the Design Center.

3. 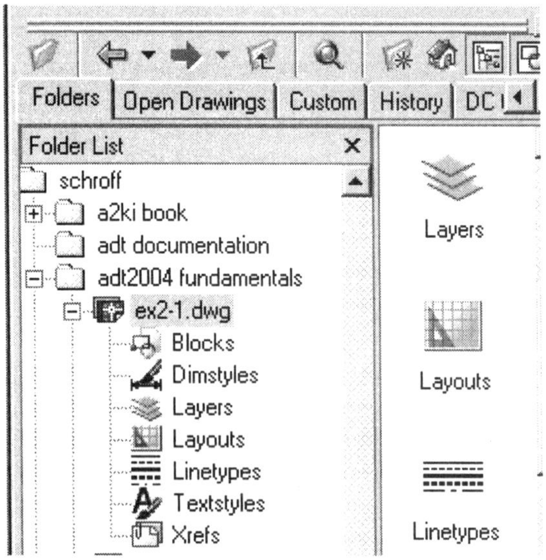

Select the **Folders** tab.

Browse to the folder where you saved the Ex2-1.dwg file.

4.

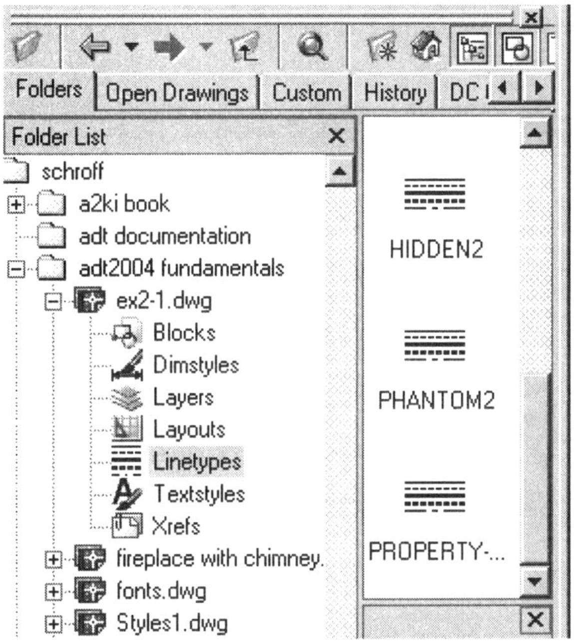

Open the Linetypes folder.

Scroll to the **Property-line** linetype definition.

5. Highlight the PROPERTY-LINE linetype.
Drag and drop into your active window.

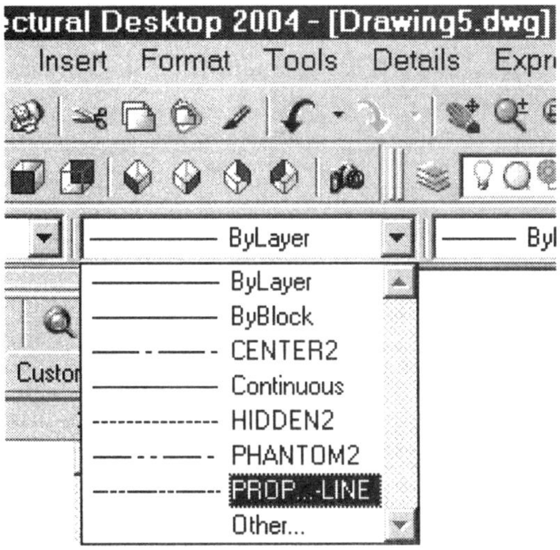

You now should see the property-line linetype in the linetype drop-down list.

Close the Design Center.

6. Activate the **Layer Manager.**
Go to Format→Layer Management→Layer Manager.

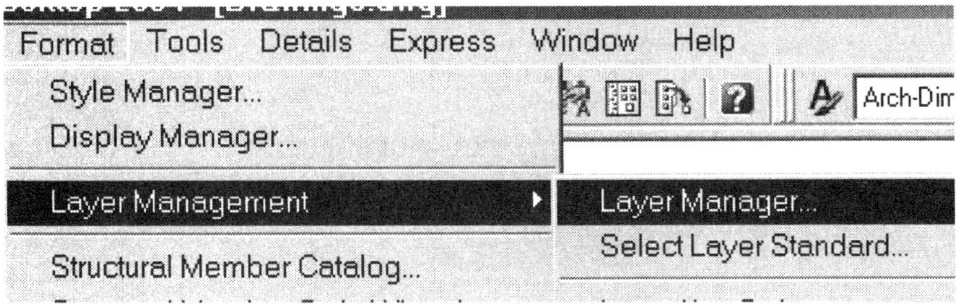

7. Note that several layers have already been created. The template automatically sets your Layer Standards to AIA.

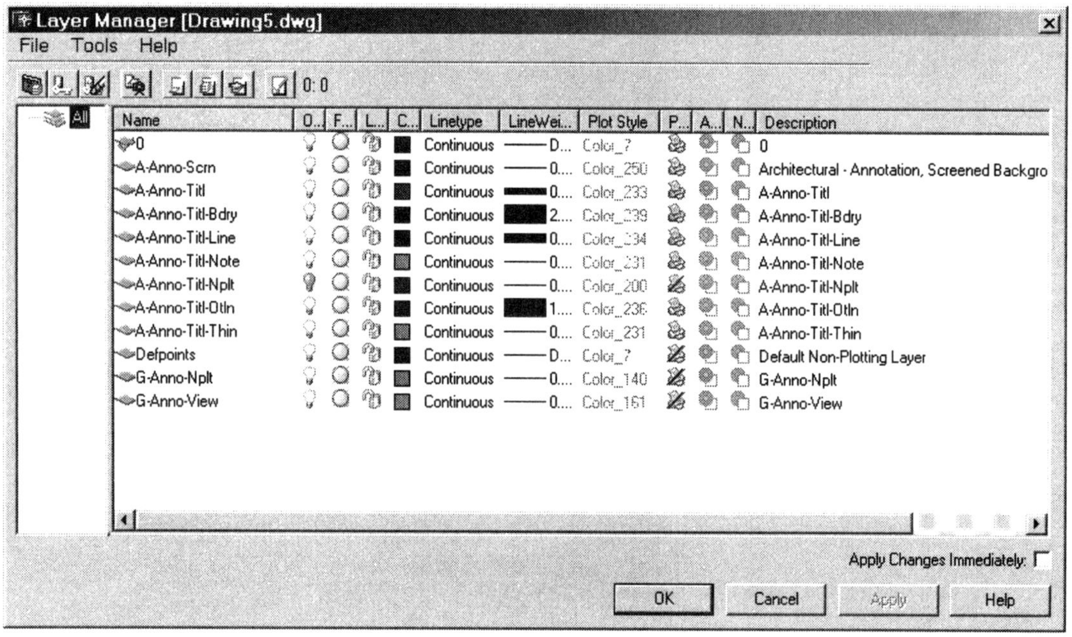

Select the 'New Layer' tool.

8.

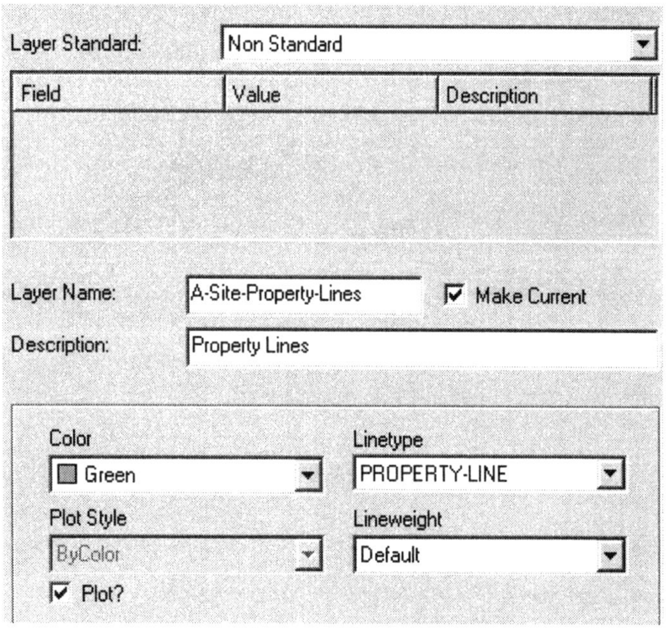

Name the layer **A-Site-Property-Lines**.

Enable **Make Current.**

Type in the **Description Property Line**.

Set the Color to **Green**.

Under Linetype, select **PROPERTY-LINE**.

Press **Apply** and **OK**.

You will get an error message if the linetype is NOT first loaded in the drawing and it will cause your system to crash. Use Format→Linetype to load.

9.

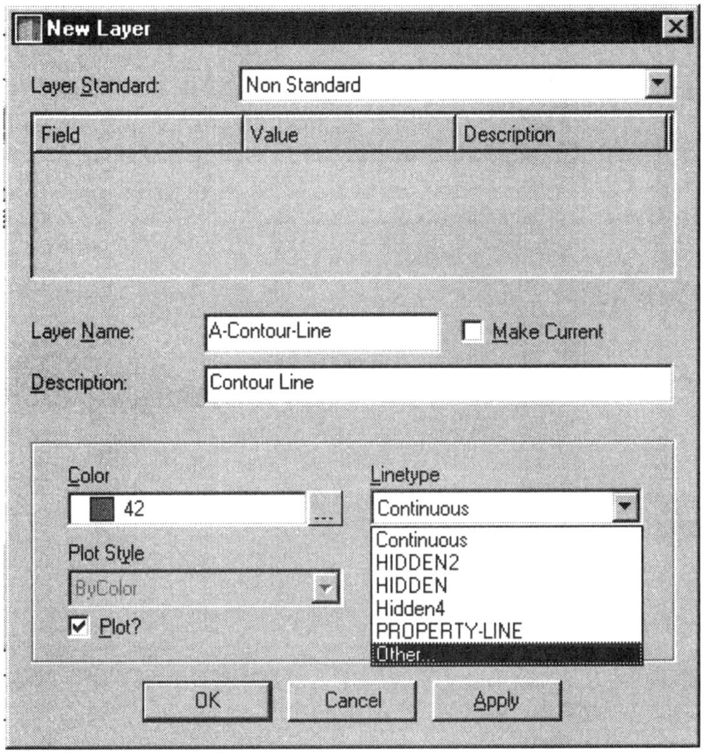

Create a new layer called **A-Contour-Line.**

Set the color to **42**.

Under Linetype, select **Other.**

10. Enable the 'Show Linetypes in File' and set the file to 'acad.lin.' Select the Linetype called **DASHEDX2**.

Press **OK.**

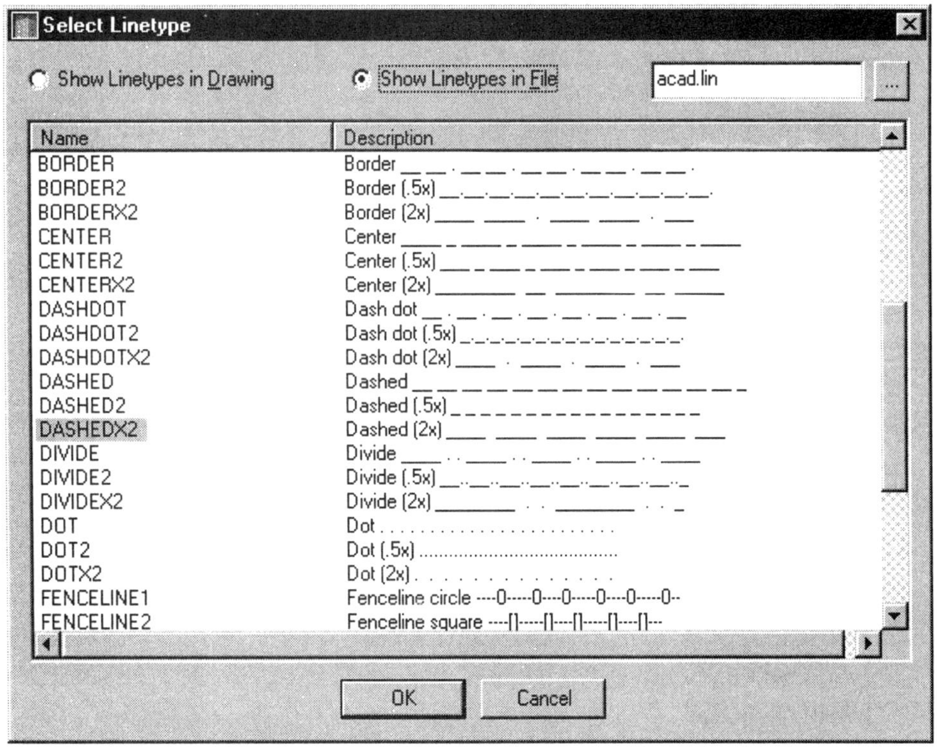

Press 'Apply' and 'OK.'

11. 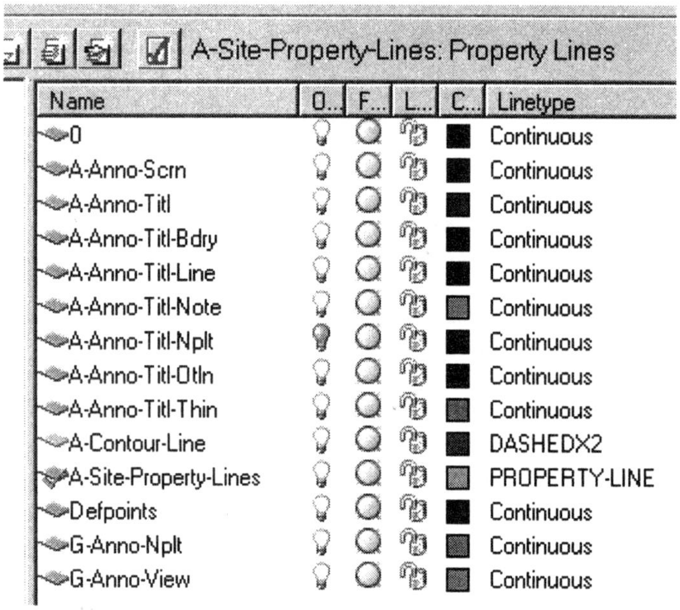

Note that the new layers are listed in the dialog and the Property Lines layer is current.

Press **OK** to close the Layer Manager.

12. Save as *Ex2-3.dwg.*

Exercise 2-4:

Creating a Site Plan

Drawing Name: Ex2-3.dwg
Estimated Time: 15 minutes

This exercise reinforces the following skills:

- Use of toolbars
- Documentation Tools
- Elevation Marks
- Surveyor's Angles

1.  Open *ex2-3.dwg.*

2. Go to **Format→Drawing Setup**.

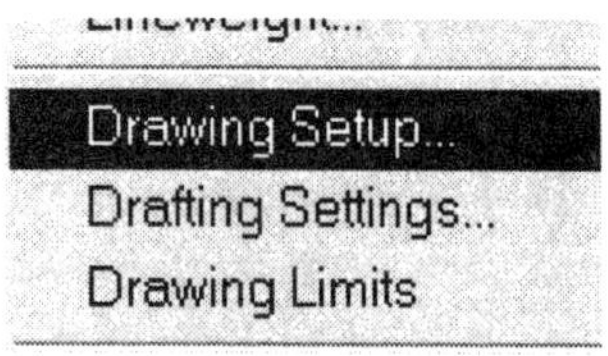

3. Select the **Units** tab.
   Set up the Length Type to **Engineering**.
   Set the Precision to **0′-0.00″**.
   Set the Angle Type to **Surveyor**.
   Set the Precision to **N 0d00′ E.**
   Press **OK**.

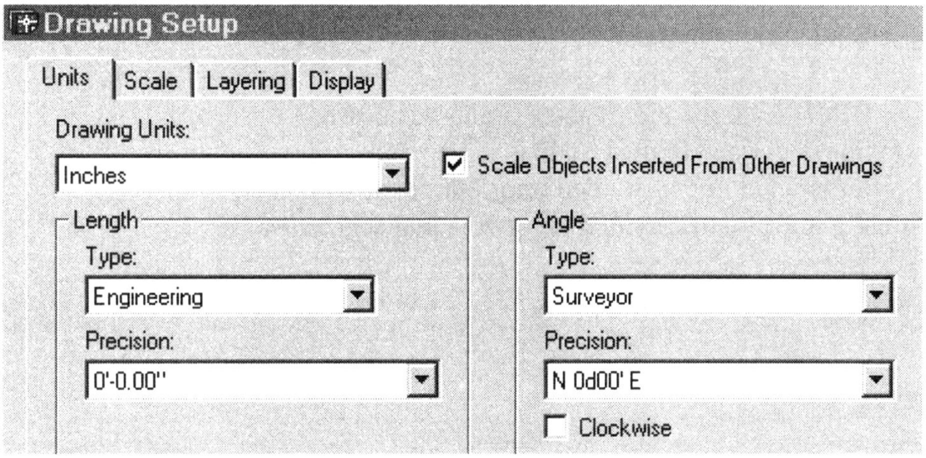

4. Draw the property line shown on the **A-Site-Property-Lines** layer.

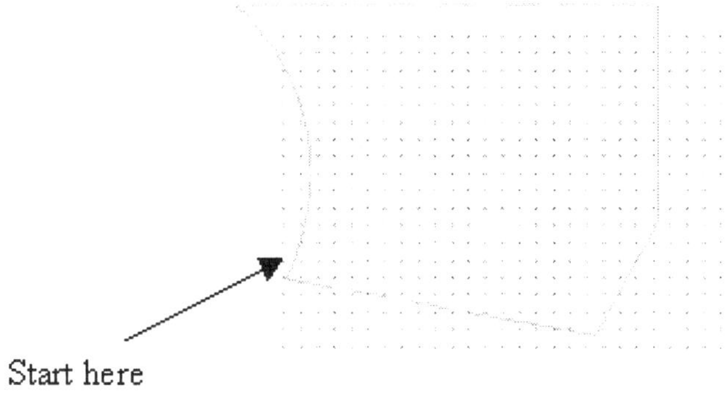


```
Command: l
LINE Specify first point: 1',50'

Specify next point or [Undo]: @187'<s80de

Specify next point or [Undo]: @75'<n30de

Specify next point or [Close/Undo]: @126'<n

Specify next point or [Close/Undo]: @250'<180
```

This command sequence uses Surveyor's Units.

Draw an arc using Start, End, Radius to close the figure.

Select the bottom point as the Start point.
Select the top point at the End point.

The radius is 132′.

(Make sure you use the apostrophe to indicate feet, or your measurements will all be in inches.)

5. Set the **A-Contour-Line layer** current.

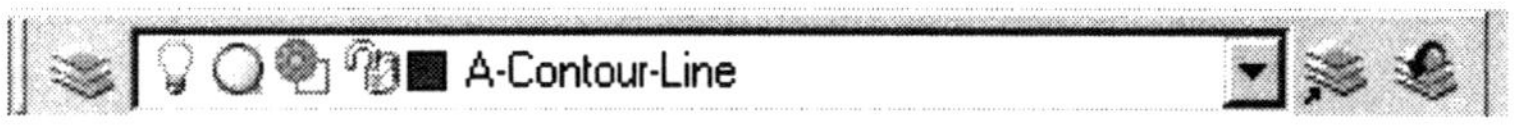

Use the **DIVIDE** command to place points as shown.
The top line is divided into five equal segments.
The bottom-angled line is divided into four equal segments.
The small angled line is divided into two equal segments.

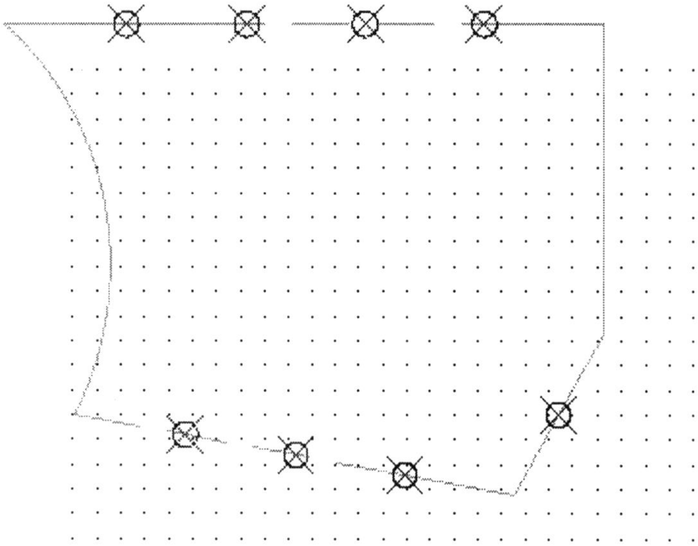

6. 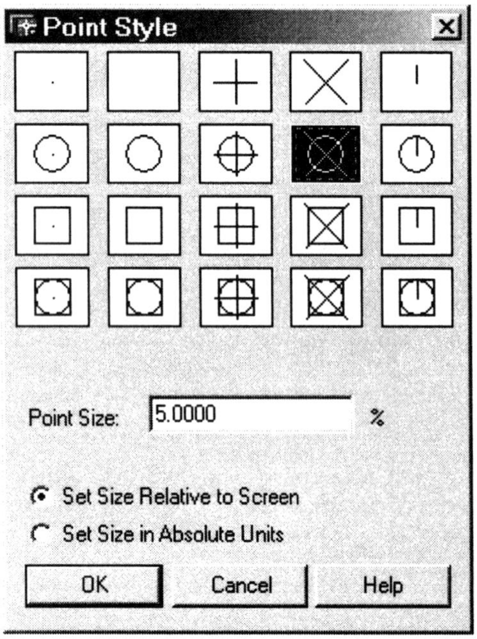

Go to **Format→Point Style** to set the points so they are visible.

Select the Point Style indicated.

Press **OK**.

7. Draw contour lines using **Pline** and **NODE** Osnaps as shown.

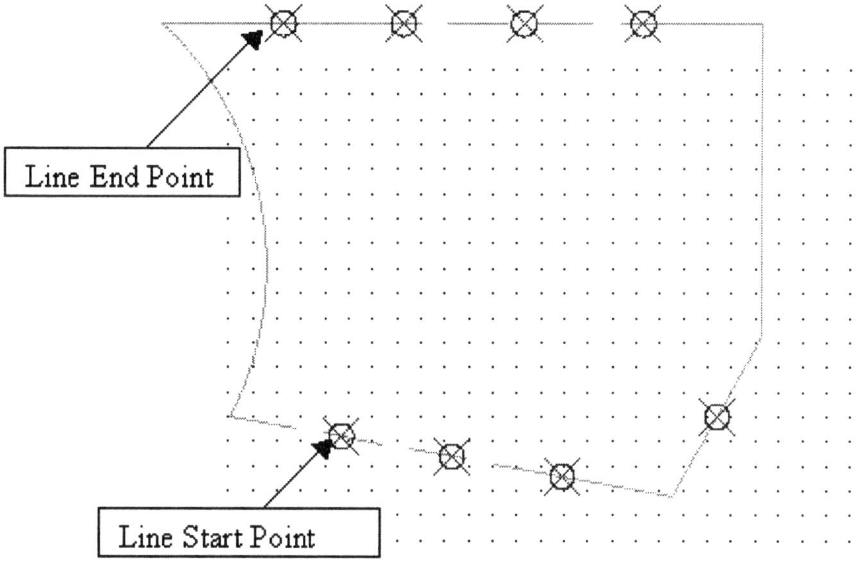

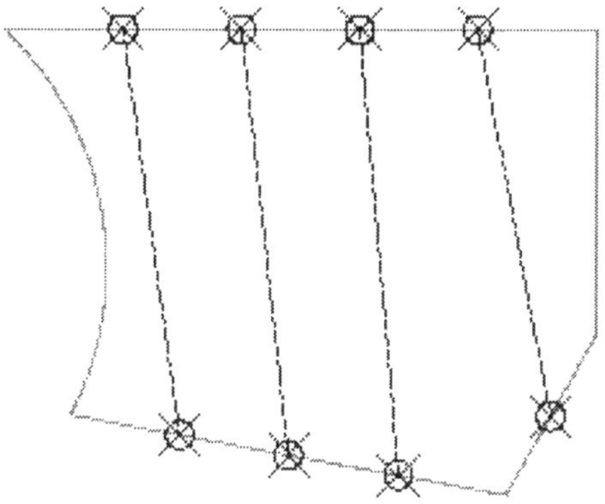

8. Go to **Tools→Quick Select**.

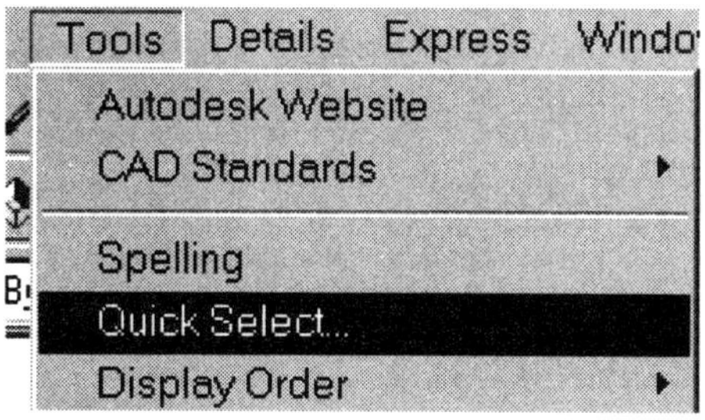

9.

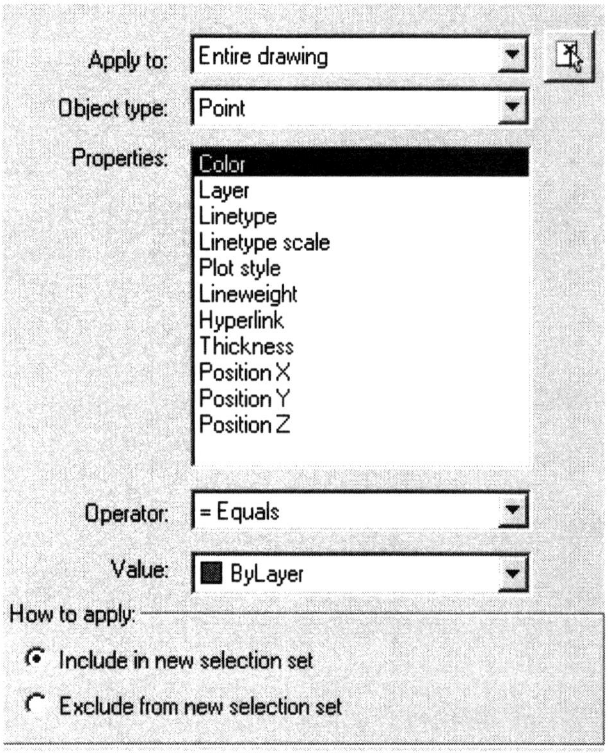

Set the Object Type to **Point**.
Set the Color = Equals **ByLayer**.

Press **OK**.

10.

All the points are selected.

Right click and select **Basic Modify Tools→Erase.**

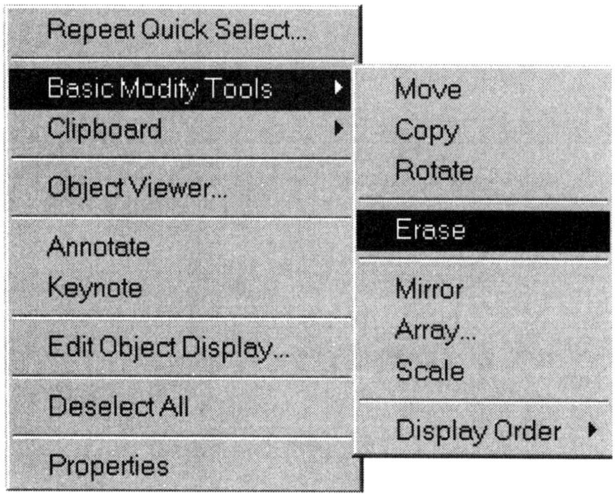

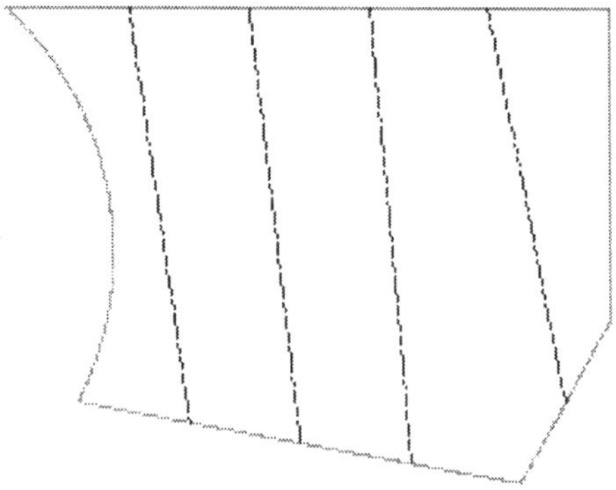

11.

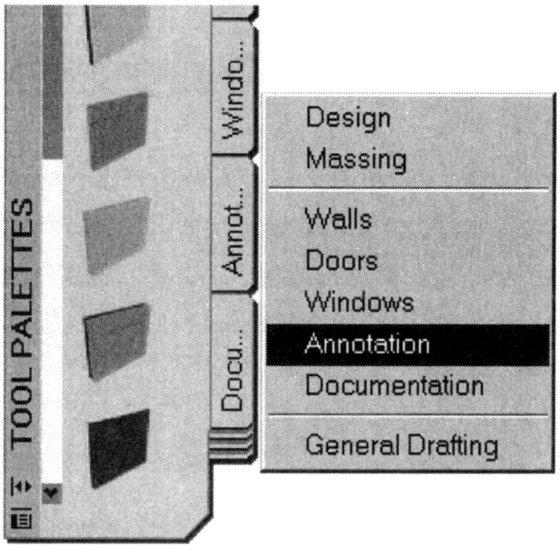

Type **Ctl+3** to bring up the Tool Palette.

Pick on the tabs and right click. Select **Annotation**.

12.

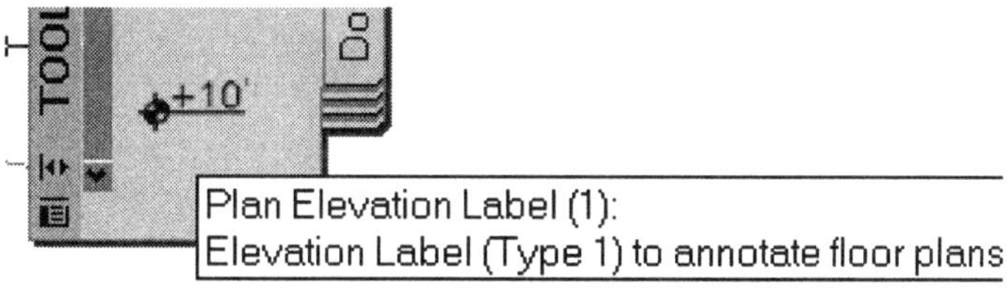

If you scroll down, you'll see an Elevation Label, but it's not the type we need for a site plan.

Instead we'll have to add an elevation label from the Design Center and add it to the Tool Palette.

13. Type **Ctl+2** to launch the Design Center.
Select the Custom tab.
Browse to *Imperial/Elevation Labels/2D Section.*

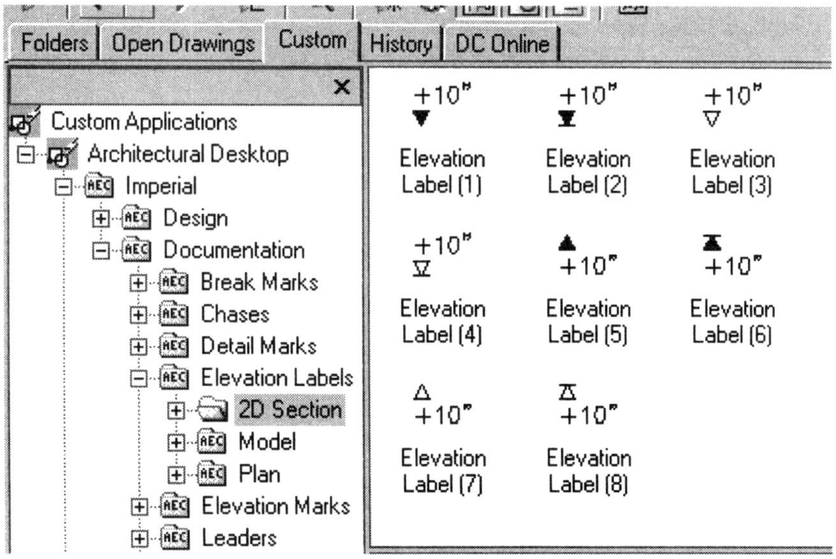

Locate the **Elevation Label (1)** file.

14.

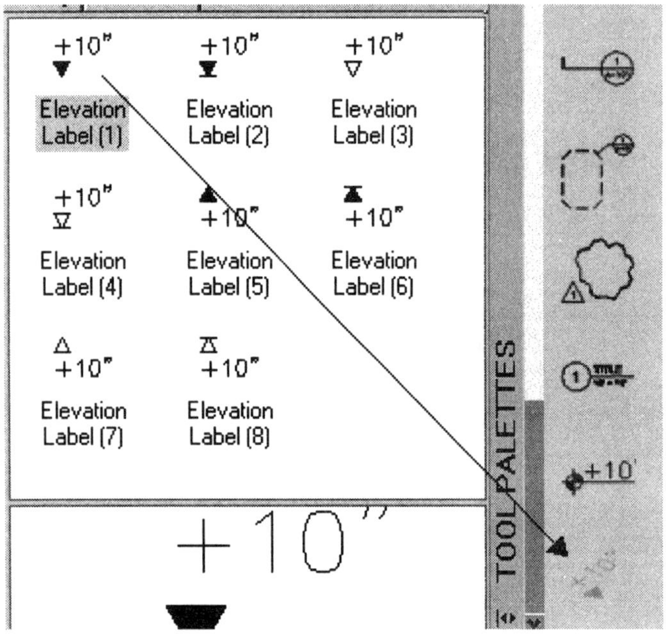

Highlight the elevation label.

Drag and drop onto the Tool Palette.

Close the Design Center.

15. Select the Elevation Label on the Tool Palette.
Select the Endpoint shown.

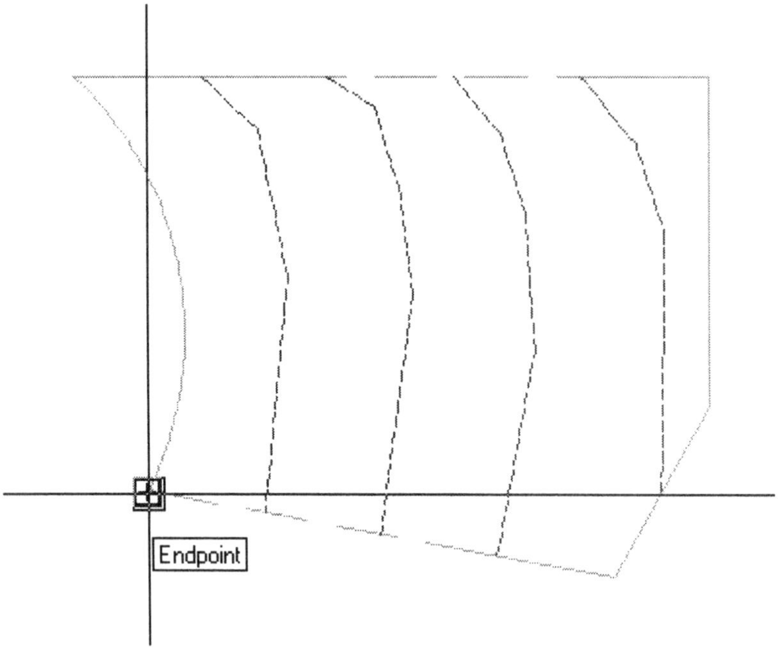

16. Set the Elevation to **0.00″**.
Set the Prefix to **EL**.
Press **OK**.

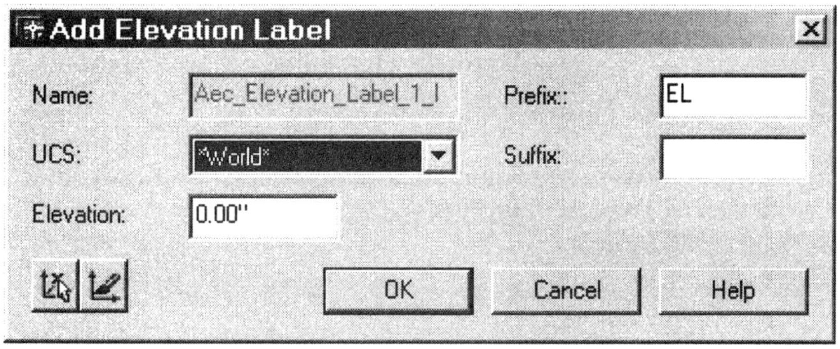

17. 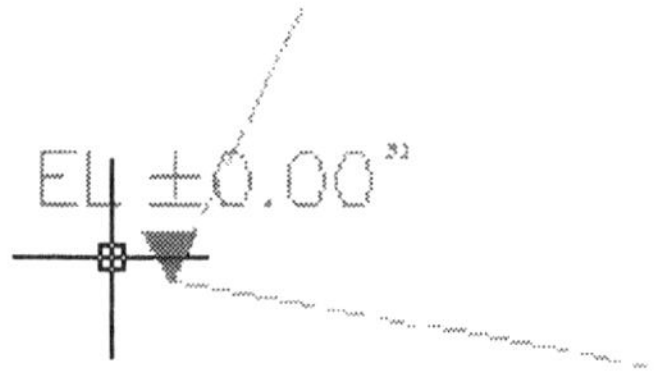

Zoom into see the elevation label.

The Elevation Label is automatically placed on the A-Anno-Dims layer.

18. 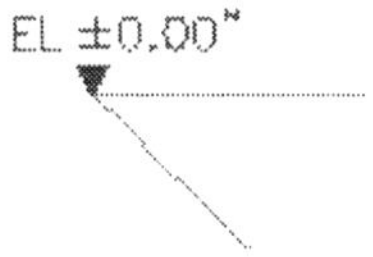

Locate an elevation label on the upper left vertex as shown.

19. 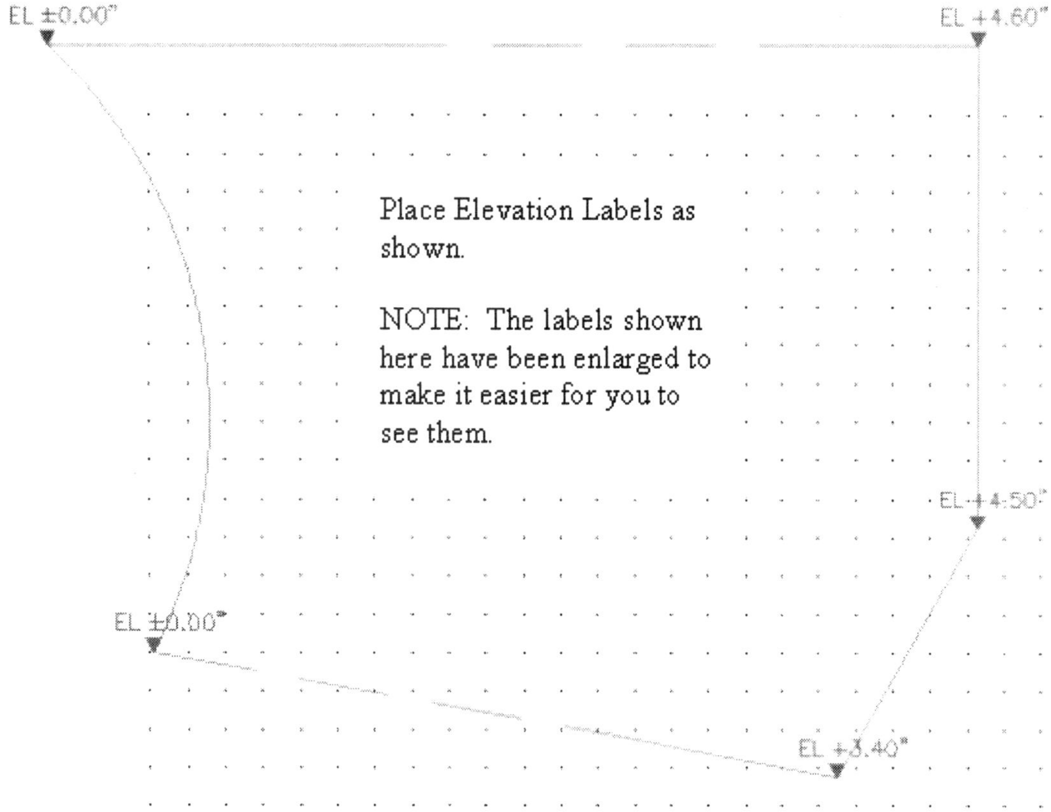

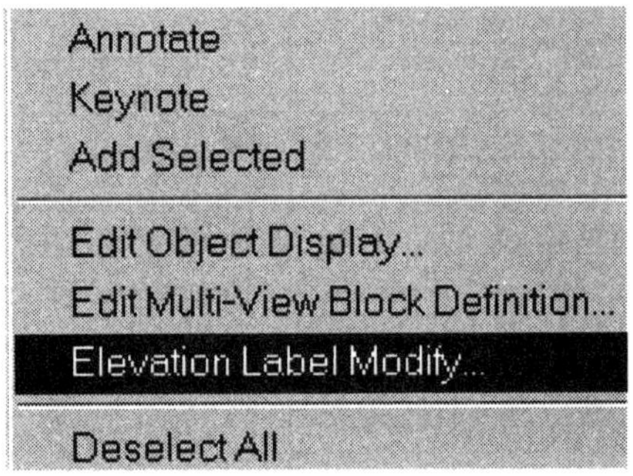

To modify the value of the elevation label, select the label.

Right click and select **Elevation Label Modify**.

20. Type **Ctl+2** to launch the Design Center.

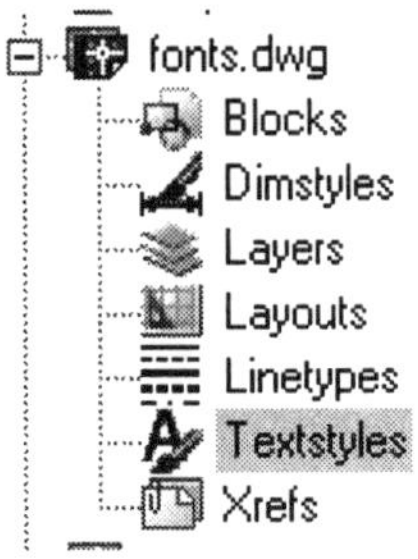

Select the Folders tab.
Browse to the *fonts.dwg* created in Exercise 2-2.

21. 

Drag and drop the **Architectural** text style into the drawing.

Close the Design Center.

22. Set the A-Anno-Dims Layer current.

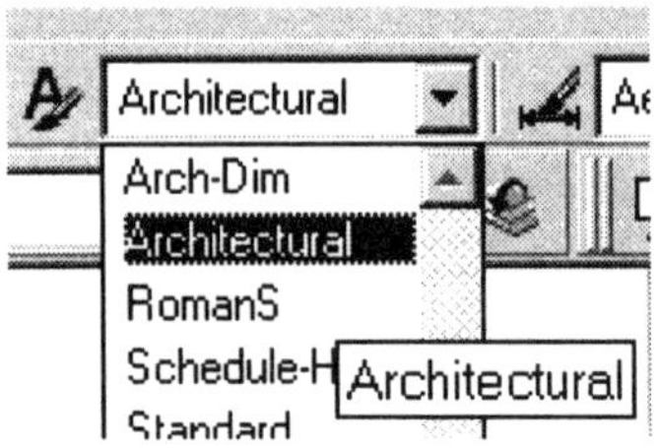

Set **Architectural** as the current text style.
Use the **TEXT** command to create the text.
Set the text to 5′ high so you can see it.
Set the rotation angle to –10 degrees
Use %%d to create the degree symbol.

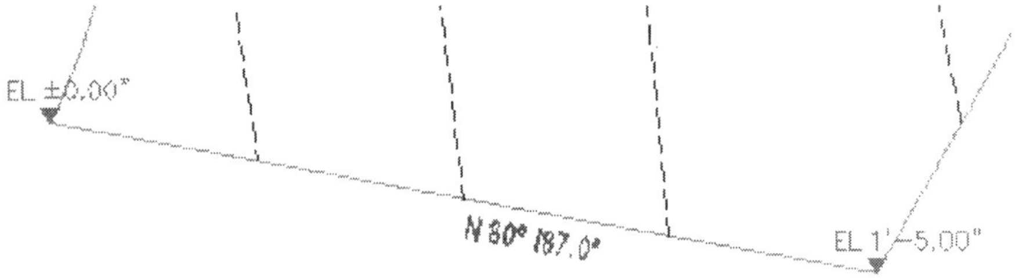

23.

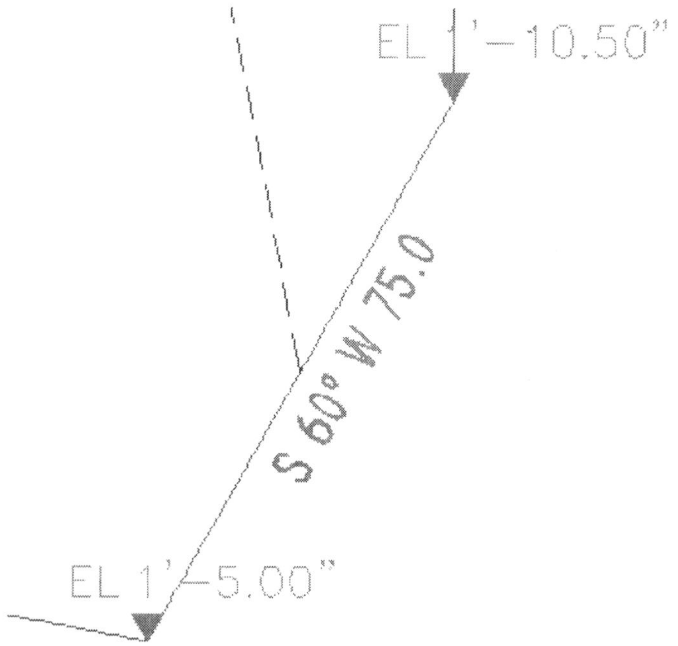

To create the S60… note, use the **TEXT** command. Height is 5′, rotation angle is 60 degrees.

24.

Create the **Due South 126.0′** note using height of 5′, rotation angle of 90 degrees.

25. Add the text shown.

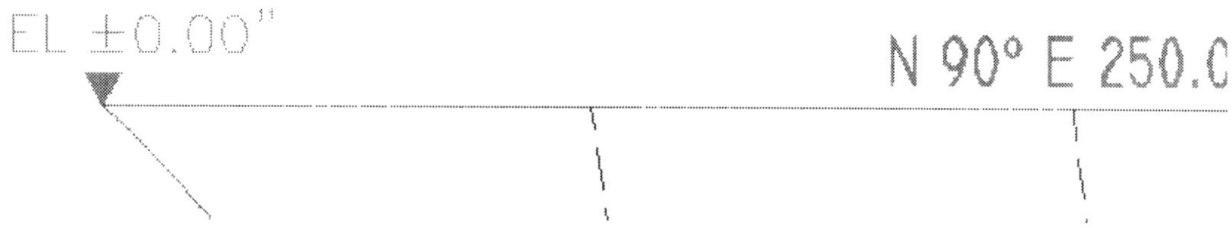

26.

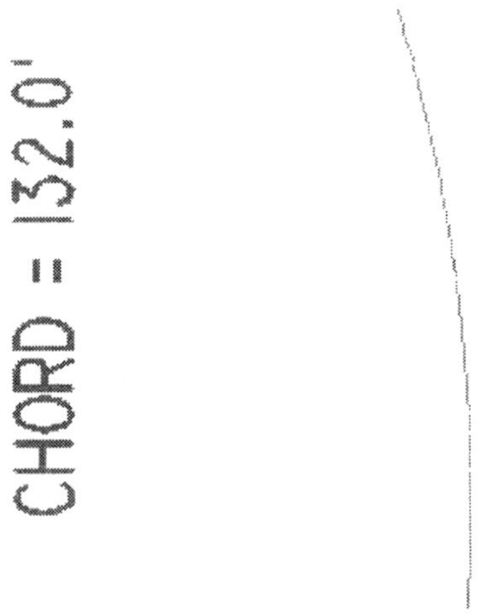

Add the Chord note shown.
Rotation angle is 90 degrees.

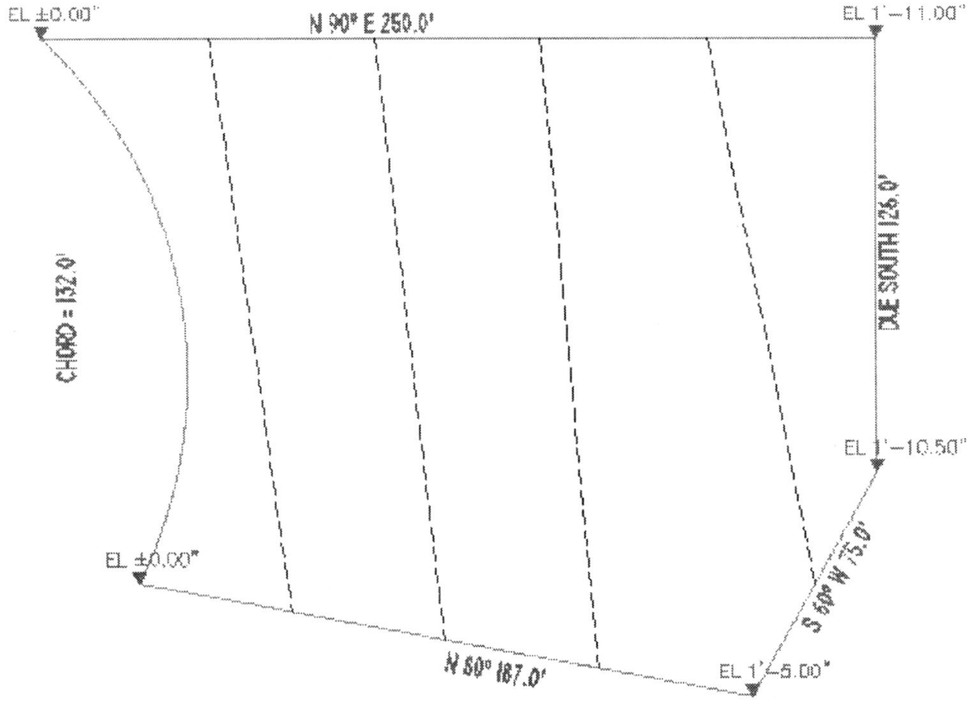

27. 

Select the Design Center tool.

Select the Custom tab.

Browse to *Imperial/Documentation/ Miscellaneous/North Arrows.*

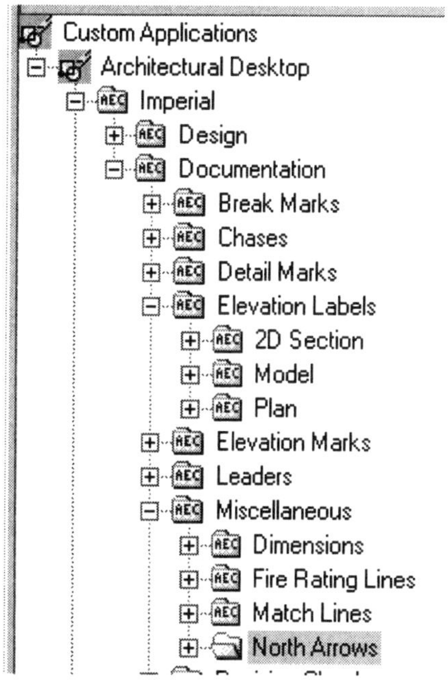

28. 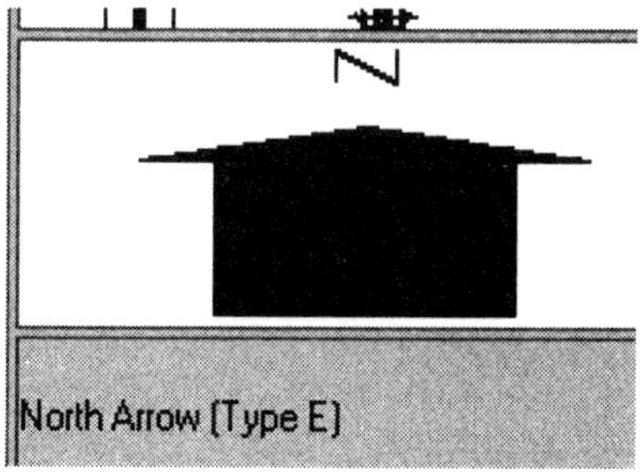

Locate **North Arrow (Type E).**

Drag and drop into the active window.

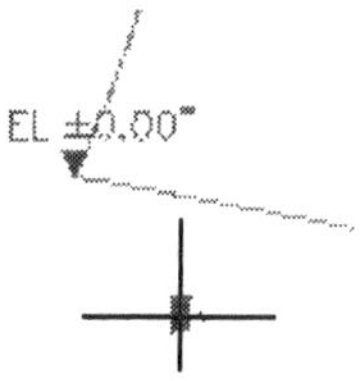

Set the rotation to 90.

Place as shown.

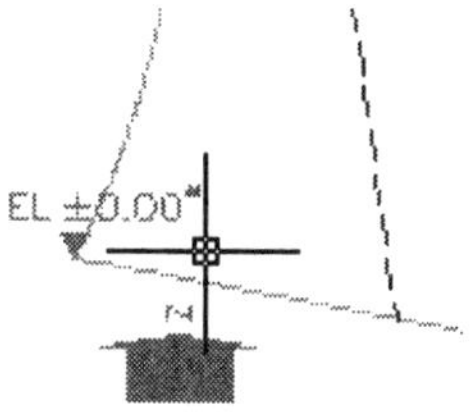

29. Save the file as *ex2-4.dwg.*

Exercise 2-5:

Creating a Layer User Group

Drawing Name: Ex 2-4.dwg
Estimated Time: 15 minutes

This exercise reinforces the following skills:

- Use of toolbars
- Layer Manager
- Layer User Group

A Layer User Group allows you to group your layers, so you can quickly freeze/thaw them, turn them ON/OFF, etc.

TIP: The difference between FREEZING a Layer and turning it OFF is that entities on FROZEN Layers are not included in REGENS. Speed up your processing time by FREEZING layers.

We can create a group of layers that are just used for the site plan and then freeze them when we don't need to see them.

1.  Open *ex2-4.dwg*.

2. Go to Format→Layer Management→Layer Manager.

3.  Select the 'New User Group' tool.

4. 

Name the user group **Site Plan.**

5. 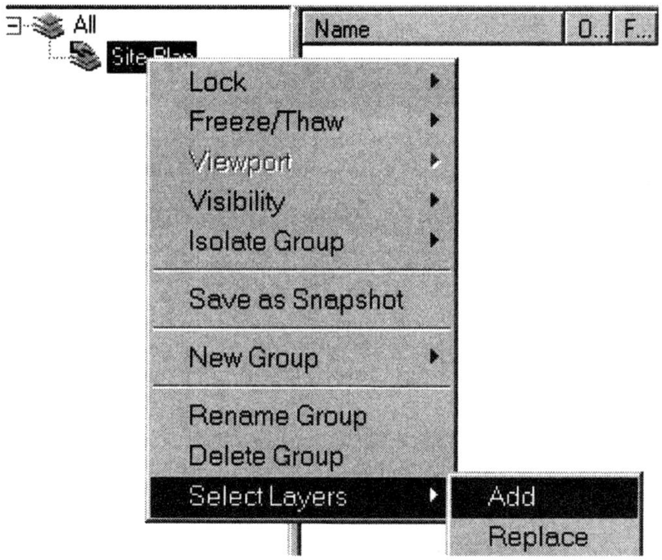

Highlight the Site Plan group.
Right click and select **Select Layers→Add.**

6. Type **ALL** on the command line.
This selects all the items in the drawing.
The layers are now listed in the Layer Manager under the Site Plan group.

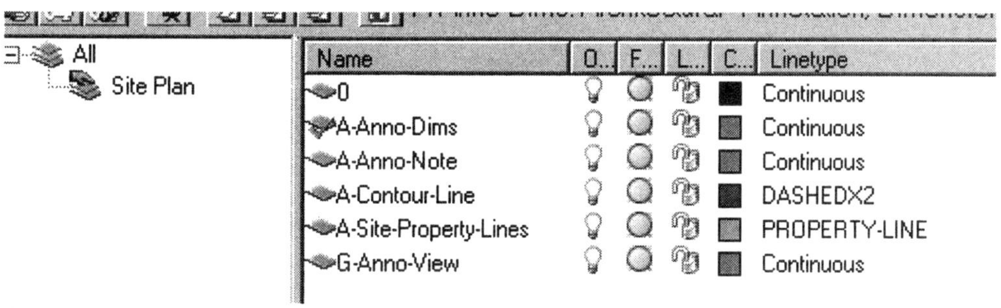

Press **Apply.**

Close the Layer Manager.

7. We can use this group to quickly freeze, turn off, etc. the layers in the Site Plan group.

Save the drawing as *ex2-5.dwg.*

NOTES:

Quiz 1

True or False

1. Doors, windows, and walls are inserted into the drawing as objects.
2. The Architectural Toolbars are loaded from the ADT Menu Group.
3. To set the template used by the QNEW tool, use Options.

4. If you start a New Drawing using 'QNew' tool shown above, the Start-Up dialog will appear unless you assign a template.
5. Mass elements are used to create Mass Models.
6. The Layer Manager is used to organize, sort, and group layers.
7. Layer Standards are set using the Layer Manager.
8. You must load a custom linetype before you can assign it to a layer.

Multiple Choice
Select the Best Answer.

9. If you start a drawing using one of the standard templates, ADT will automatically create ___________ layouts.

    A. A work layout plus Model Space
    B. Four layouts, plus Model Space
    C. Ten layouts, plus Model Space
    D. Eleven layouts, plus Model Space

10. ADT Options are set through:

    A. Options
    B. Desktop
    C. User Settings
    D. Template

11. The Display Manager controls:

    A. How AEC objects are displayed in the graphics window
    B. The number of viewports
    C. The number of layout tabs
    D. Layers

12. Mass Elements are created using the _____ Tool Palette.

    A. Massing
    B. Concept
    C. General Drafting
    D. Documentation

13. Wall Styles are created by:

    A. Highlighting a Wall on the Wall tab of the Tool Palette, right click and select Wall Styles
    B. Type **WallStyle** on the command line
    C. Go to Format→Style Manager
    D. All of the Above

14. To create a New Layer, use:

    A. Type **LayerManager** at the command line
    B. Type **Layer** at the command line
    C. Use **Format→Layer Management→Layer Manager**
    D. All of the Above

15. You can change the way AEC objects are displayed by using:

    A. Edit Object Display
    B. Edit Display Properties
    C. Edit Entity Properties
    D. Edit AEC Properties

ANSWERS:

1) T; 2) T; 3) T; 4) T; 5) T; 6) T; 7) T; 8) T; 9) A; 10) A; 11) A; 12) A; 13) D; 14) D; 15) A

Lesson 3
Floor Plans

The floor plan is central to any architectural drawing. We start by placing the exterior walls, then the interior walls, then doors, and finally windows.

Exercise 3-1:
Creating Exterior Walls

Drawing Name: New
Estimated Time: 15 minutes

This exercise reinforces the following skills:

- Create Walls

TIP: Walls are automatically created on the layer assigned by palette properties.

Tool Palette	Walls
Command Line	WallAdd

TIP: If you draw a wall and the materials composing the wall are on the wrong side, you can reverse the direction of the wall. Simply select the wall, right click and select the Reverse option from the menu.

TIP: You can convert lines, arcs, circles, or polylines to walls. If you have created a floor plan in AutoCAD and want to convert it to 3D, open the floor plan drawing inside of ADT. Use the Convert to Walls tool to transform your floor plan into walls.

1.  Start a new drawing using QNEW.

2.  Launch the Tool Palette.

Select the **Walls** tab.

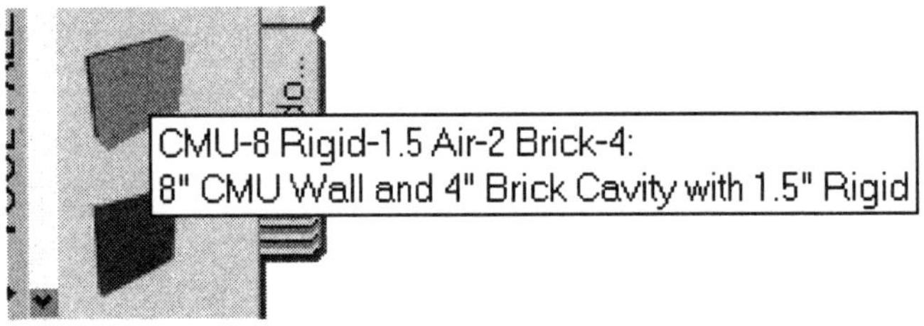

Select the **CMU-8 RIGID-1.5 Air-2 Brick-4:** wall style.

3. 

Toggle **ORTHO** ON.

Start the wall at 0,0.
Create a rectangle 60′ tall and 30′ wide.

4. Select the **Work** tab.

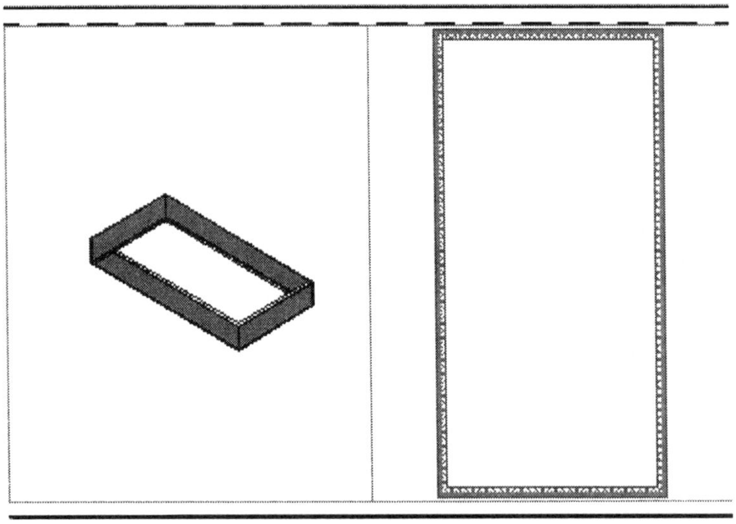

5. You see that the walls you placed are really 3-dimensional.
Save your drawing as *Ex3-1.dwg.*

Exercise 3-2:

Convert to Walls

Drawing Name: ex3-1.dwg
Estimated Time: 60 minutes

This exercise reinforces the following skills:

- Convert to Walls
- Creating Interior Walls

1.  Open *ex3-1.dwg.*

2.

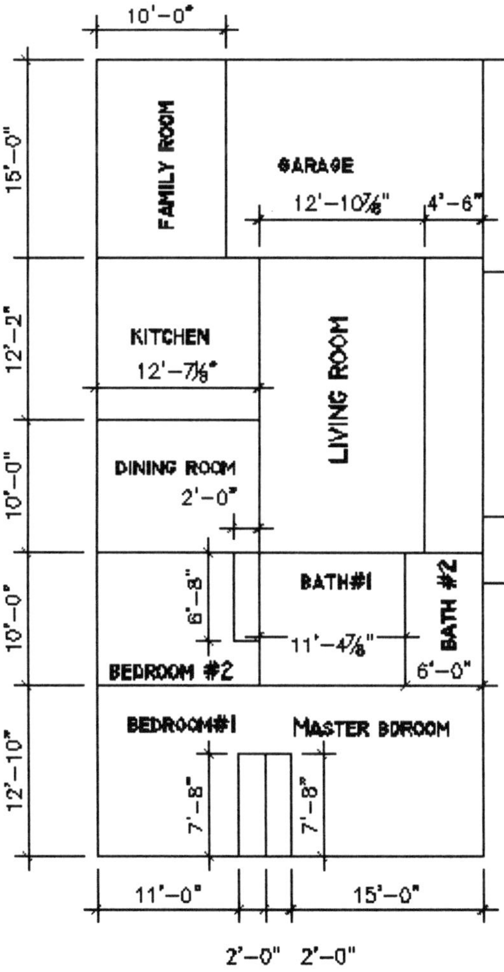

Create the layout shown using lines or polylines. (It may be helpful to turn off the A-Walls layer while you are working and create your lines on layer 0).

Do not add the dimensions or the text to your drawing. They are there to help you place the lines only.

Don't draw using rectangles if you are going to use the CONVERT method or you will get duplication of lines over lines, which will affect the wall creation.

If you do not want to spend time creating the floor plan, you can download the drawing 'floor plan.dwg' from www.schroff1.com.

3. 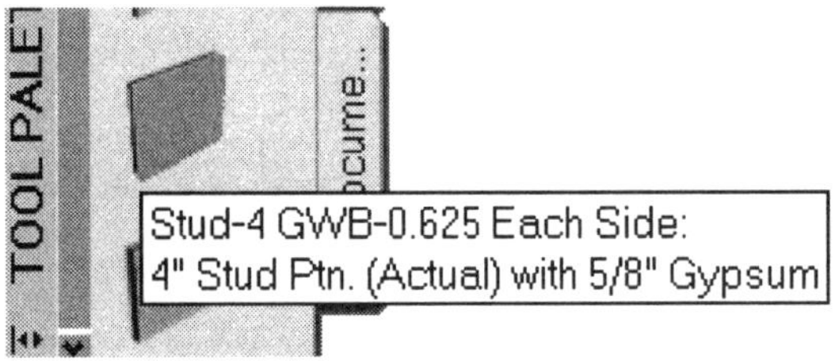

Locate the **Stud-4 GWB-0.625 Each Side:** wall style.

4. Highlight the wall tool.
Right click and select **Apply Tool Properties to→Linework.**

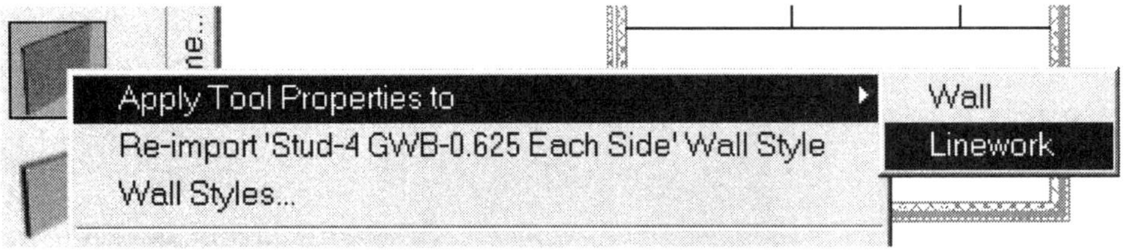

5. Select all the interior polylines you just created.

```
Erase layout geometry? [Yes/No] <N>: Y

15 new wall(s) created.
Command: Regenerating model.
```

You are prompted if you want to erase the layout geometry. Type **Y** for Yes.

6. Your walls appear. Some walls may not be aligned with others, and wall cleanup error symbols may appear as well.

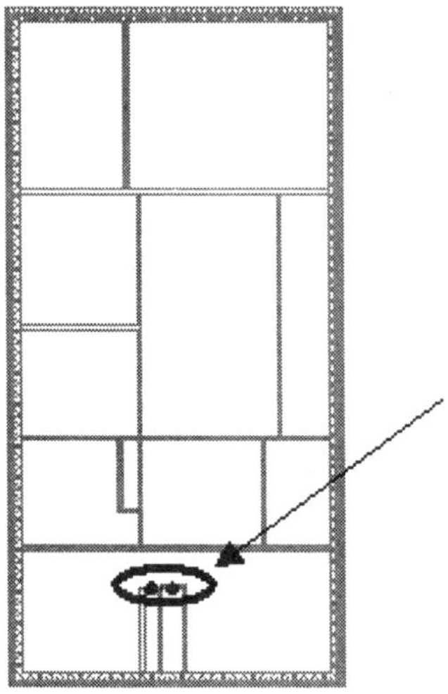

7. Switch to the Work tab so you can see how your house looks in 3D.

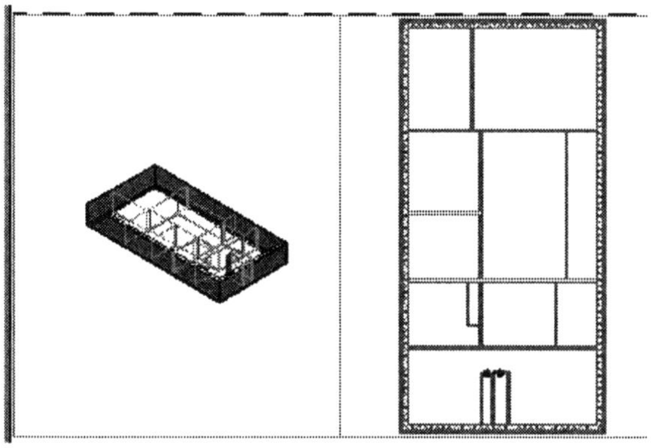

8. Save the file as *ex3-2.dwg.*

Exercise 3-3:
Wall Cleanup

Drawing Name: ex3-2.dwg
Estimated Time: 15 minutes

This exercise reinforces the following skills:

- Modifying Walls
- Wall Tools

If your walls are all clean, you can skip this exercise.

1.  Open *ex3-2.dwg.*

2. 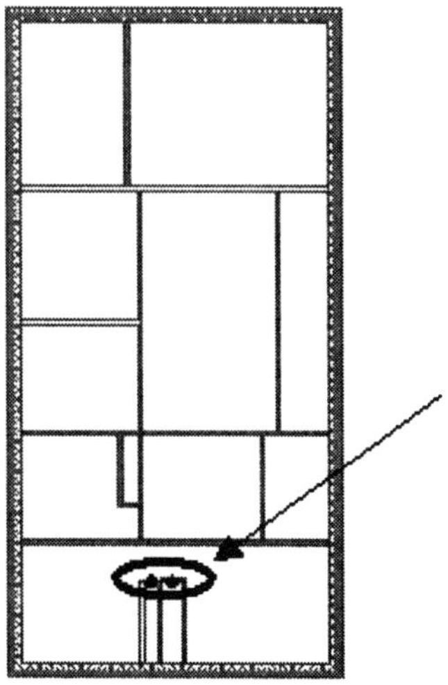

Select the Model Tab.

Zoom into the area indicated.

3. Our closet walls are not even. This is because the lines we converted to walls were drawn in different directions.

When you see a red circle like the ones shown, this is considered a 'defect condition.'

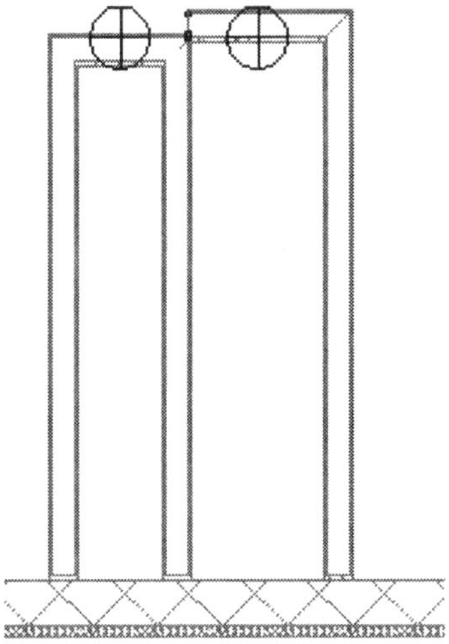

4.

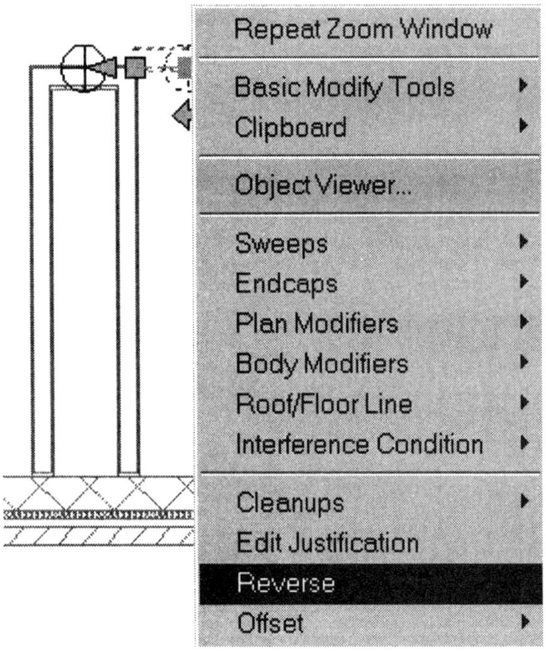

Select one of the walls.
Right click and select **Reverse**.

5.

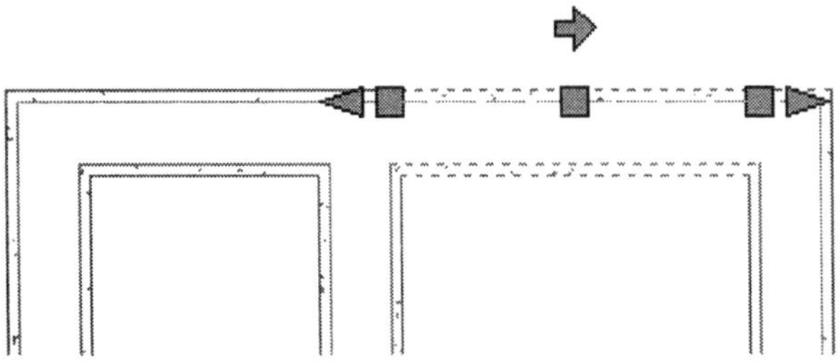

Use the middle blue group to line up the walls.

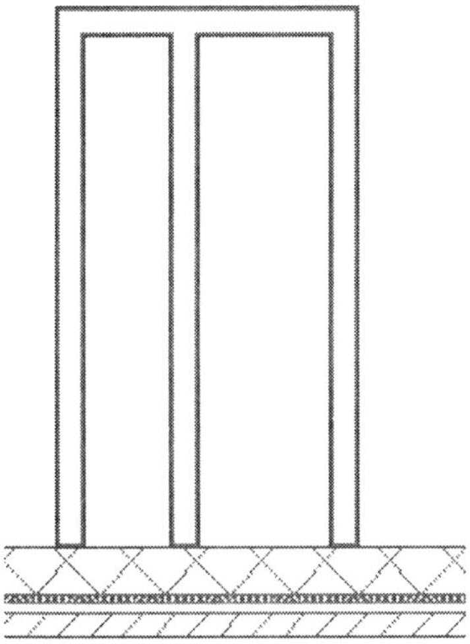

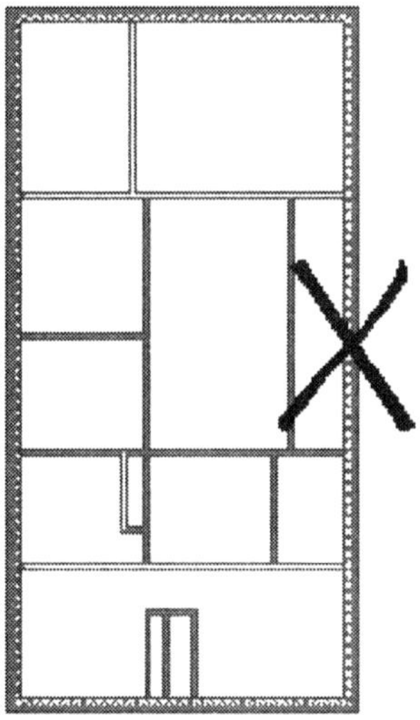

Next, we delete the wall indicated.

6.

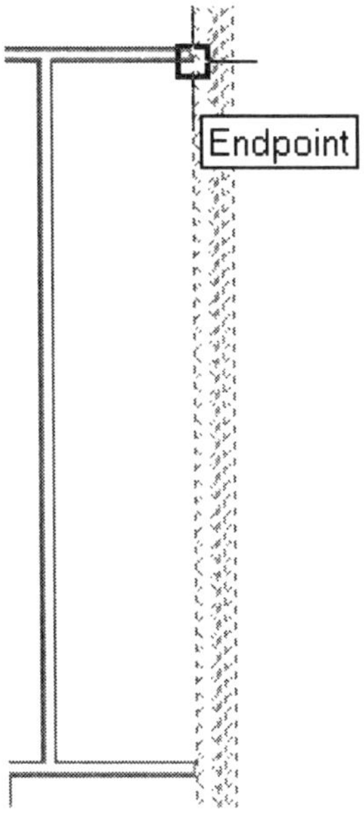

 Select the **Break** tool.

Select the point indicated for the Break.

7.

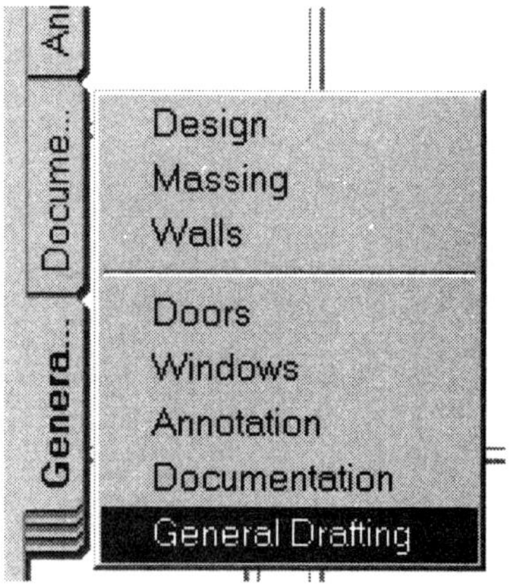

Select the **General Drafting** tab on the Tool Palette.

8.

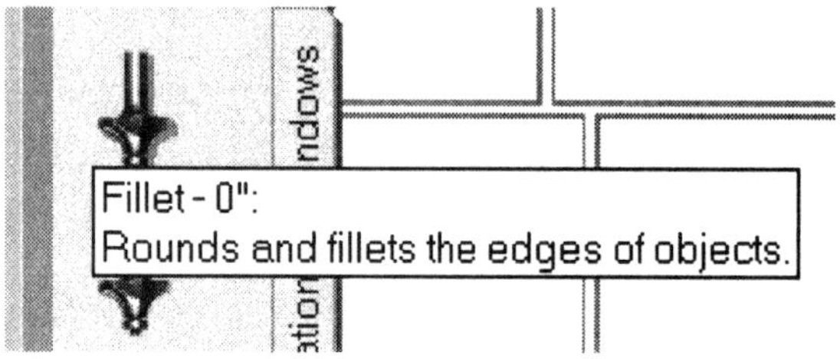

Select the **Fillet-0″** tool.

9.

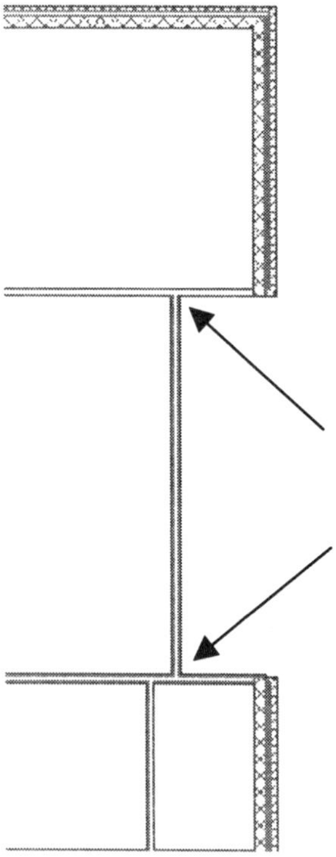

Select the walls so they trim as shown.

Use the **Break t**ool to break the walls at the points indicated.

10. 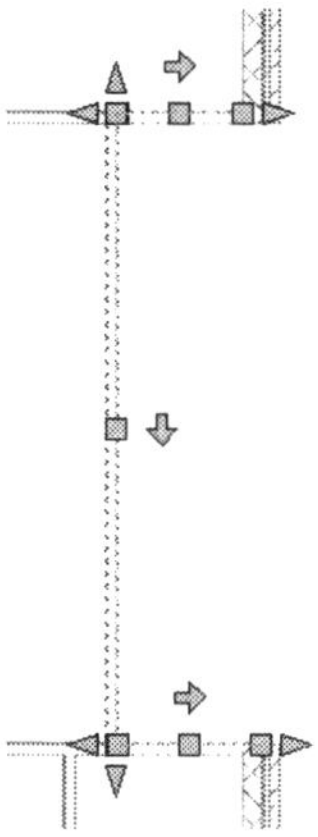

Select the three walls highlighted.

Select the **Properties** tool.

11. 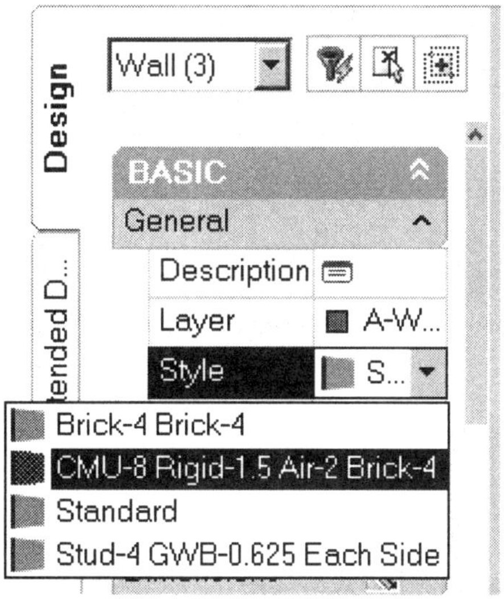

Select the **CMU-8…** Wall Style from the drop-down.

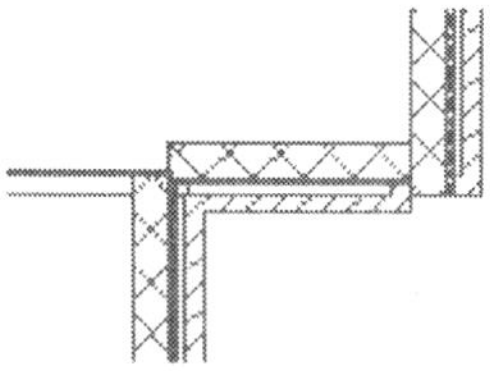

One of the corners needs to be cleaned up.

Select the horizontal wall.
Right click and select **Cleanups→Apply 'L' Cleanup.**

12. 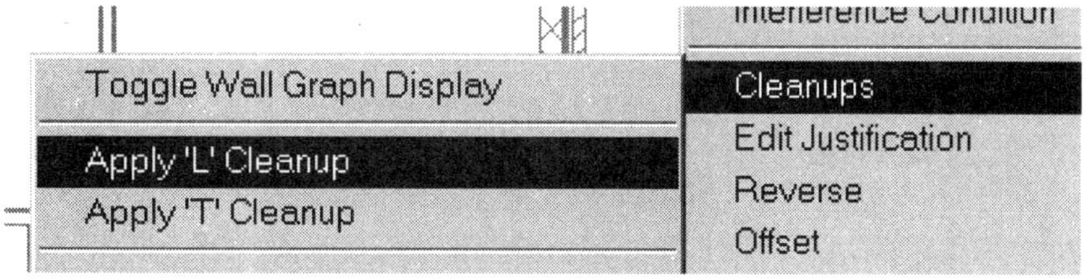

13. 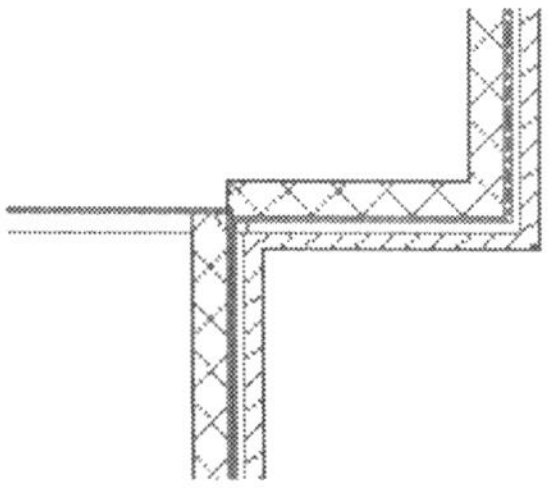

Select the vertical wall.

The walls clean up.

14. Use the **Reverse** tool to clean up any wall defects.
    You can also select the wall and then select the middle blue arrow to reverse the wall direction.

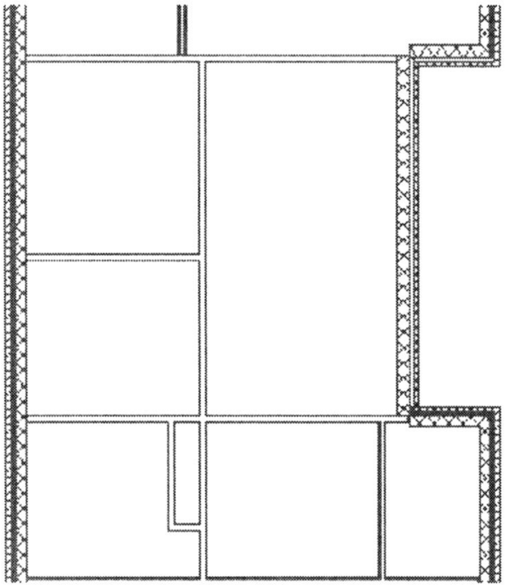

15. Save as *ex3-3.dwg.*

TIP: To create a freestanding door, press the ENTER key when prompted to pick a wall. You can then use the grips on the door entity to move and place the door wherever you like.

To move a door along a wall, use Door->Reposition->Along Wall. Use the OSNAP From option to locate a door a specific distance from an adjoining wall.

Exercise 3-4:
Adding Closet Doors

Drawing Name: Ex3-3.dwg
Estimated Time: 30 minutes

This exercise reinforces the following skills:

- Adding Doors

1.  Open *ex3-3.dwg.*

2. 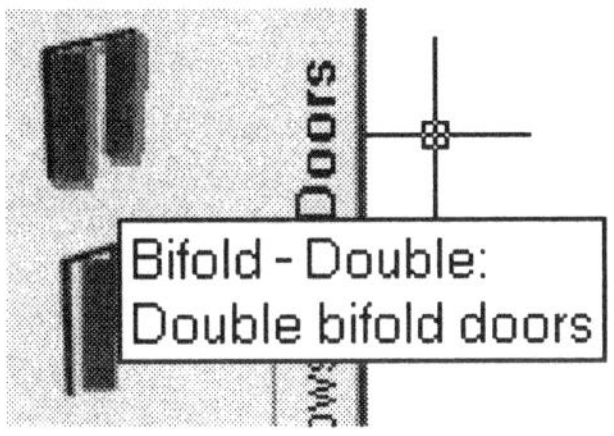

Locate the **Bifold-Double** door on the Doors tab of the Tool Palette.

3. 

Highlight the **Bifold-Double** door. Right click and select **Properties.**

4. 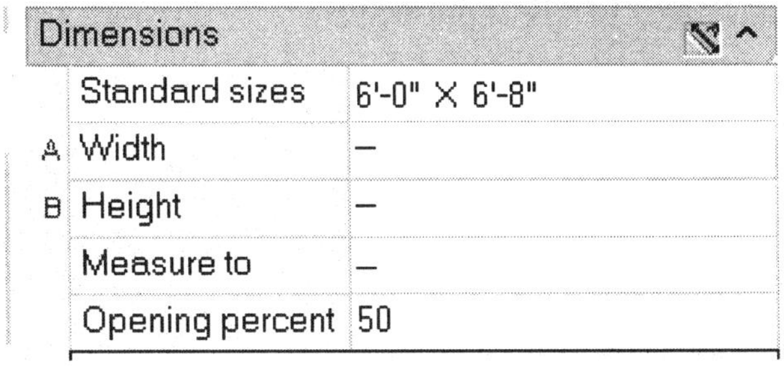

Expand the **Dimensions** section. Set the Standard sizes to **6′-0″ x 6′-8″.** Set the Opening percentage to **50**.

A 25% opening will show a door swing at a 45-degree angle.

The value of the Opening percentage determines the angle of the arc swing. A 50% value indicates the door will appear half-open at a 90-degree angle.

5. 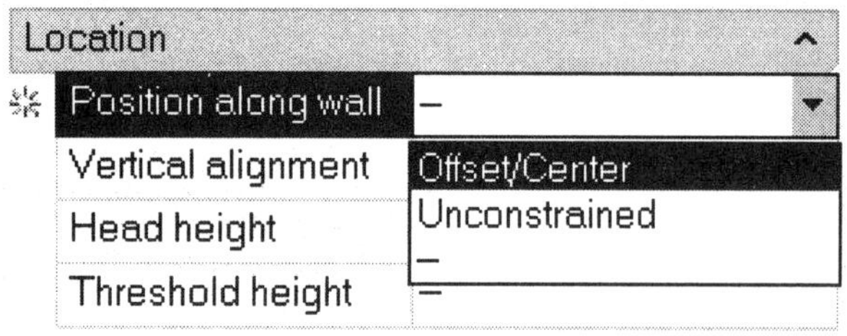

Expand the **Location** section.

Set Position along wall to **Offset/Center.**

Set the Automatic offset to **1′-2 1/2″.**

(This will center the closet doors along the wall.)

Press **OK** to close the Properties dialog.

TIP: Note the vertical alignment field. It defaults to a threshold height of 0″ for doors and a head height of 6′8″ for windows. You will need to adjust these defaults in multi-story buildings.

6. Place the Bifold Double doors at the two closets.

The orientation of the door swing is determined by the wall side selected. In both cases, you want to select the outside face of the wall.

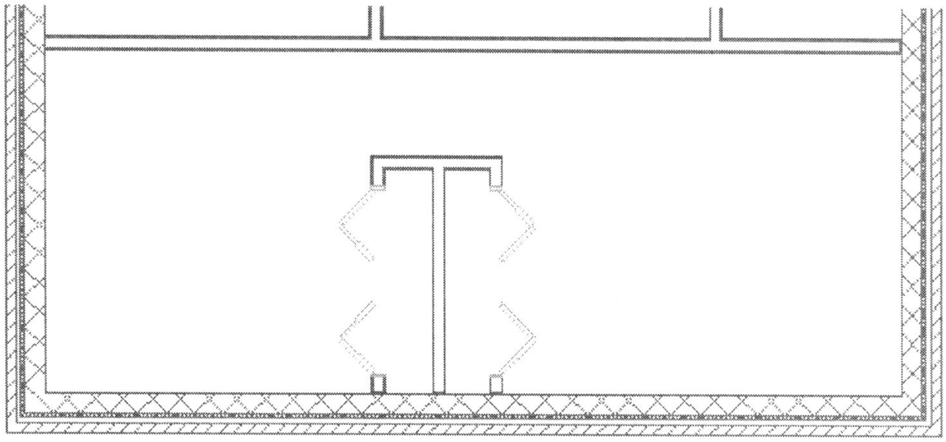

7.

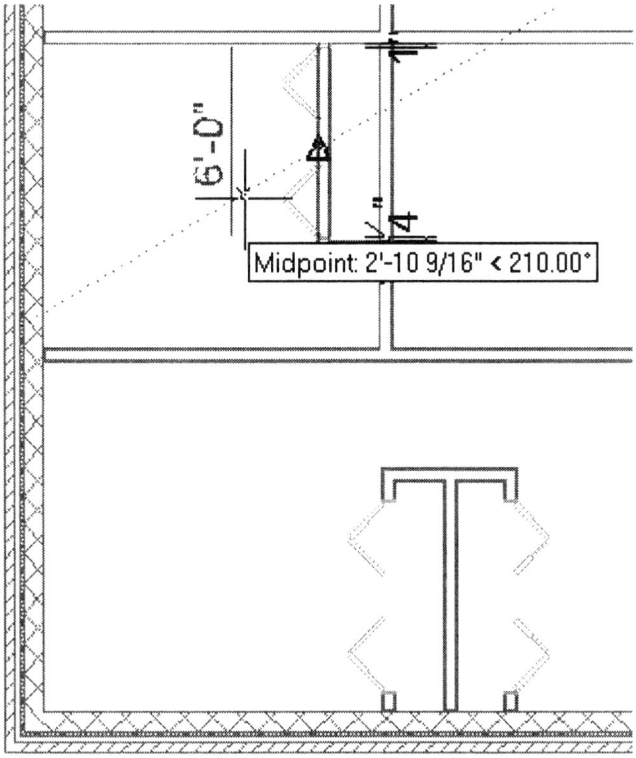

Place a Bi-fold Double door in the wall shown.

The door will be too wide for the wall.

Select the door.
Right click and select **Properties**.

8.

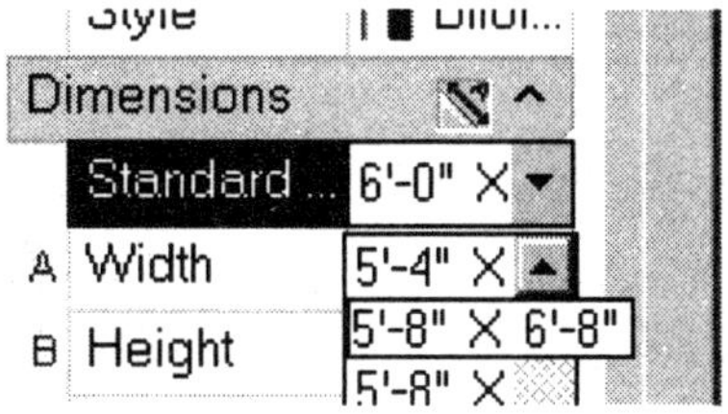

Change the Standard size to **5′-8″ x 6′-8″**.

Close the Properties dialog.

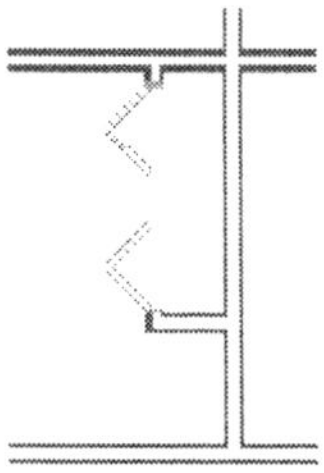

The door is updated.

9. Save as *ex3-4.dwg.*

Exercise 3-5:
Adding Interior Doors

Drawing Name: Lesson 4.dwg
Estimated Time: 30 minutes

This exercise reinforces the following skills:

- Adding Doors

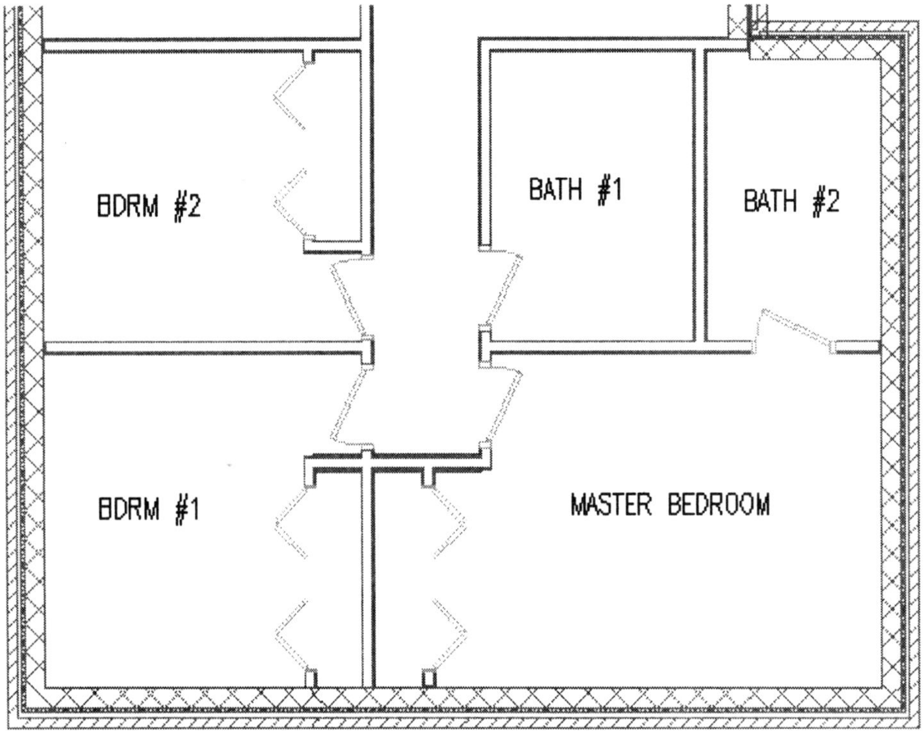

We will add single hinge doors in the areas shown.

You will need to do some wall cleanup to get the rooms to look proper.

Use AddWall, Extend, and Trim.

Try to keep the walls so they line up to keep the floor plan looking clean.

1.  Open *ex3-4.dwg.*

2.  Locate the **Single Hinged** door on the Doors tab of the Tool Palette. Right click and select **Properties**.

3. 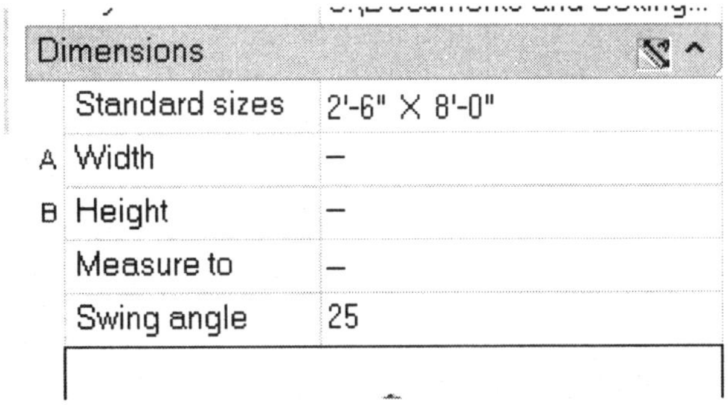

Expand the Dimensions section.
Set the Standard sizes to **2′-6″ x 8′-0″.**
Set the Swing angle to **25.**

4. 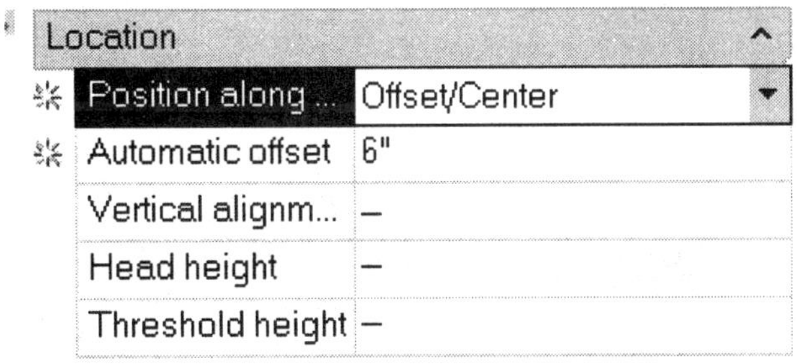

Set the Position along wall to **Offset/Center**.
Set the Automatic offset to **6″**.

Press **OK**.

5. Save the file *ex3-5.dwg.*

Exercise 3-6:

Add Opening

Drawing Name: ex3-5.dwg
Estimated Time: 30 minutes

This exercise reinforces the following skills:

- Adding Openings
- Opening Properties
- Copying Tools
- Set Image from Selection

Openings can be any size and elevation. They can be applied to a wall or be freestanding. Openings are placed on Layer A-Wall-Open. The Add Opening Properties allow the user to either select a Pre-defined shape for the opening or use a custom shape.

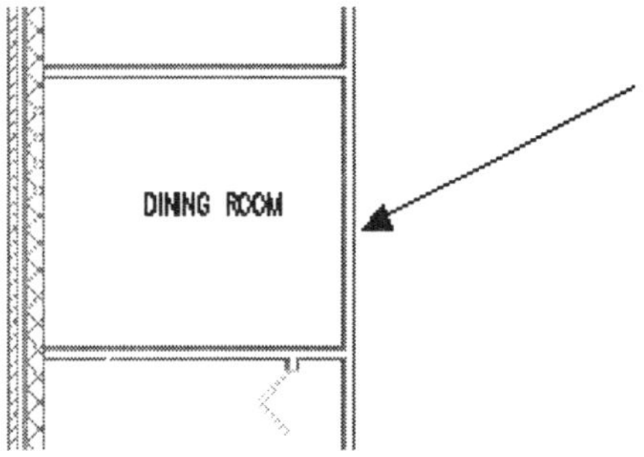

Add opening to the midpoint of this wall.

1.  Open *ex3-5.dwg.*

2. 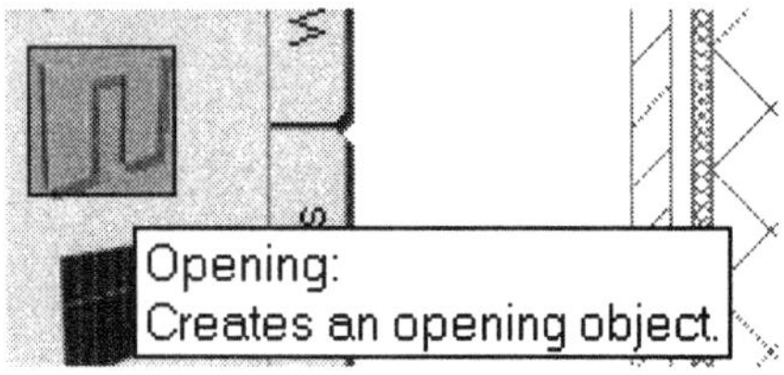

Locate the **Opening** on the Design tab of the Tool Palette.

Copy a Tool

3. 

Right click and select **Copy**.

4. 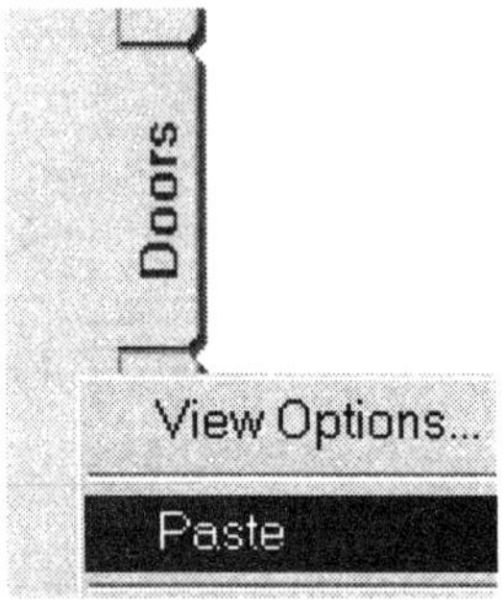

Select the **Doors** tab.
Right click and select **Paste**.

5. 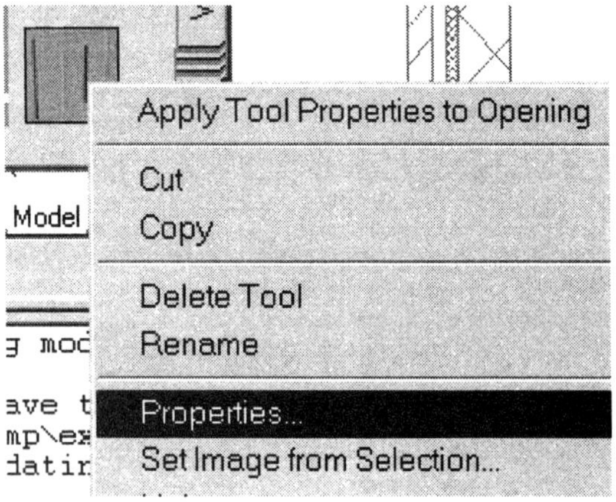

Highlight the copied tool.
Right click and select **Properties.**

6. 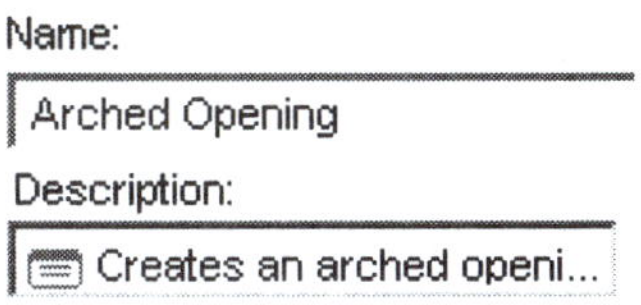

Change the Name to **Arched Opening.**
Change the Description to
Creates an arched opening object.

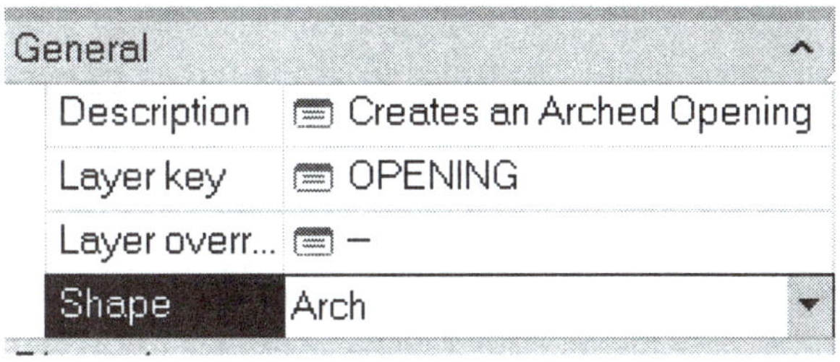

Expand the General section.
Set the Description to
Creates an Arched Opening.
Set the Layer key to
OPENING.
Set the Shape to **Arch.**

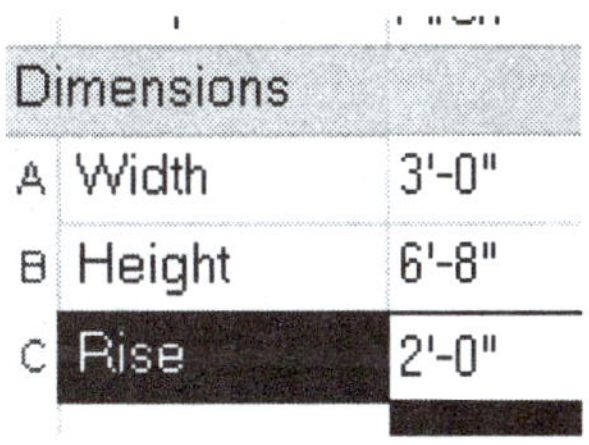

Expand the Dimensions section.
Set the Width to **3′-0″**.
Set the Height to **6′-8″**.
Set the Rise to **2′-0″**.

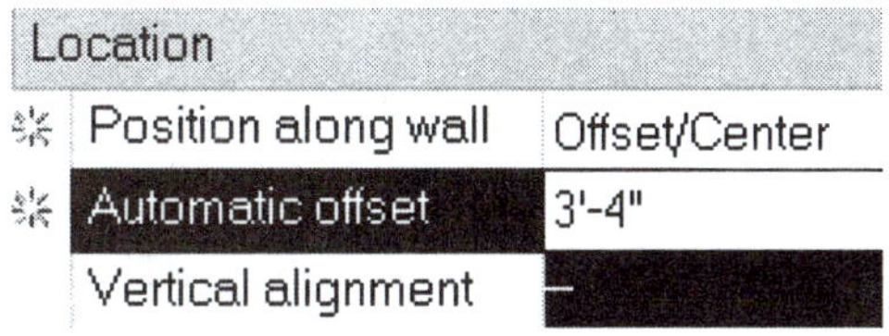

Expand the Location section.
Set the Position along wall to
Offset/Center.
Set the Automatic offset to
3′-4″.

Press **OK**.

7. 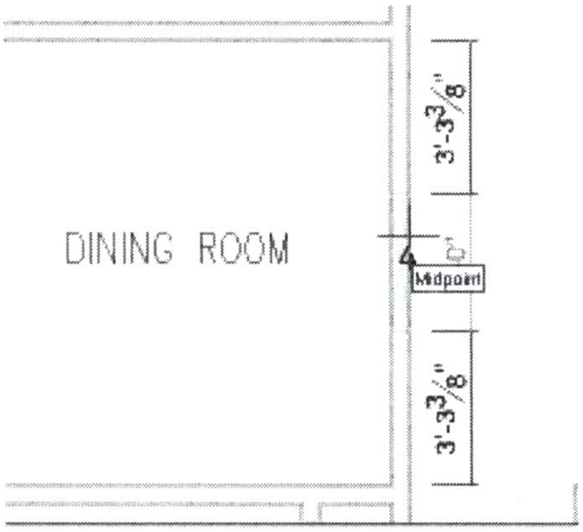

Place the arched opening in the dining room wall.

8. Use View→3D orbit to view the arched opening.

Create an Image for a Tool

9. 

Select the Arched Opening icon.
Right click and select
Set Image from Selection…
Pick the arched opening you created.

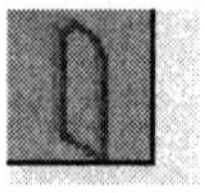

The icon updates to show an arched opening.

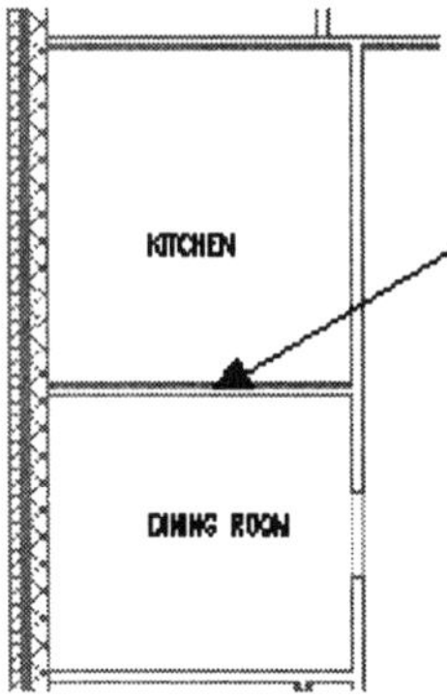

Next we place a rectangular opening in the location indicated.

10. 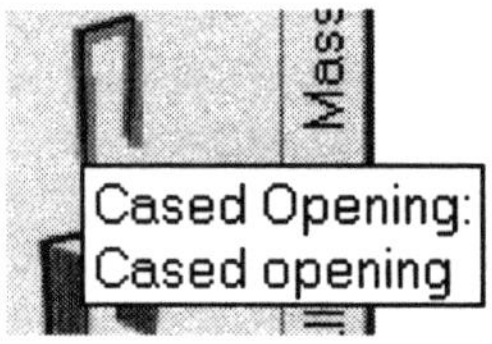

Select the **Cased Opening** tool.

11. 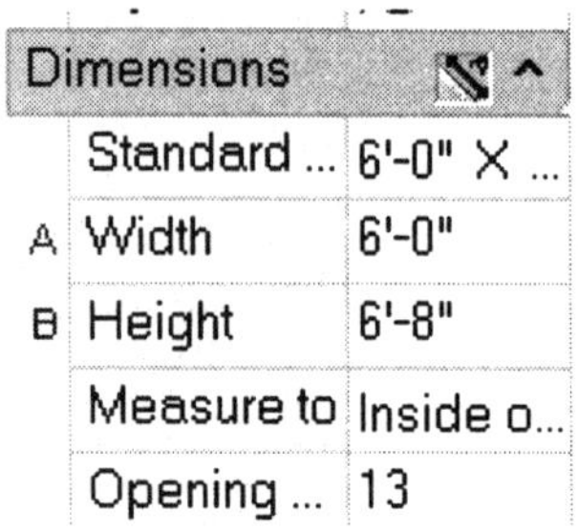

Expand the Dimensions section.
Set the Width to **6′-0″**.
Set the Height to **6′-8″.**

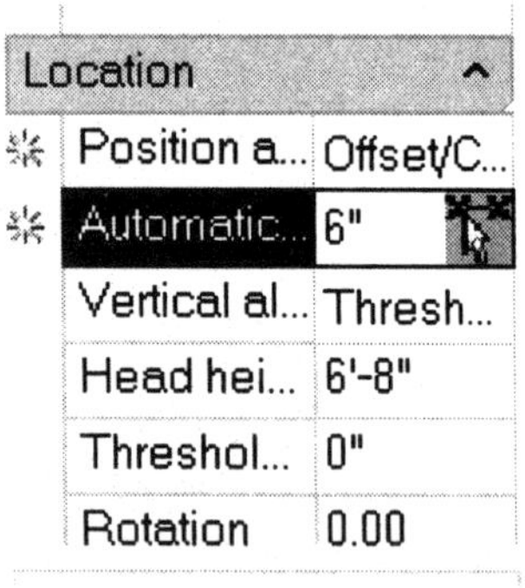

Expand the Location section.
Set the Position along wall to **Offset/Center.**
Set the Automatic offset to **6″.**

12. 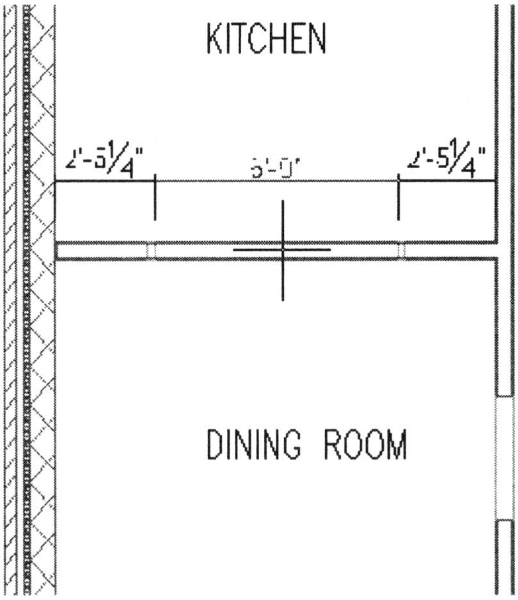

Place the opening in the wall between the kitchen and the dining room.

13. 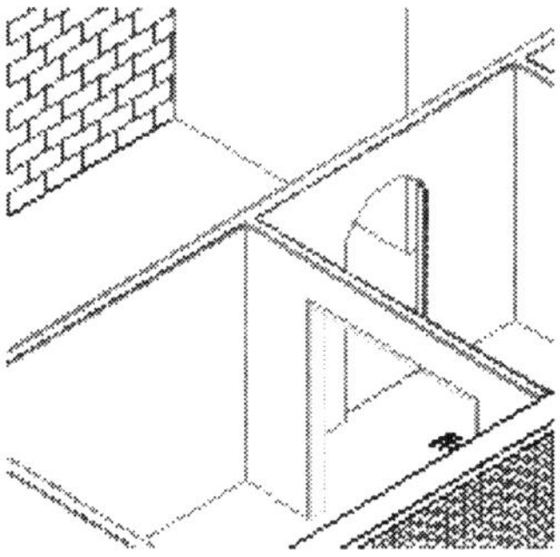

Select the Work tab to view the openings.

Select the Model tab.

14. 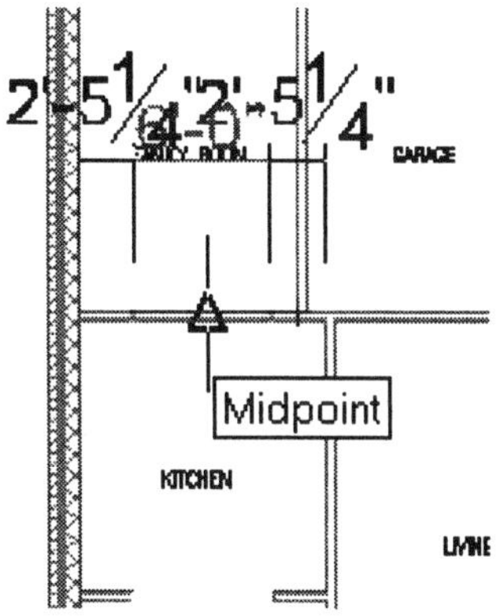

Place a rectangular opening between the kitchen and the family room.

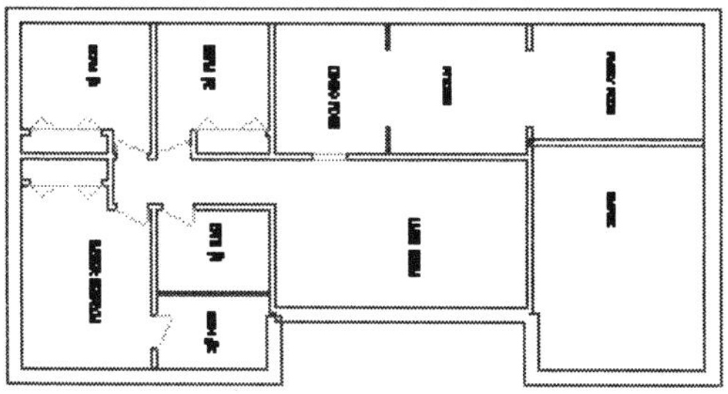

This is our floor plan so far.

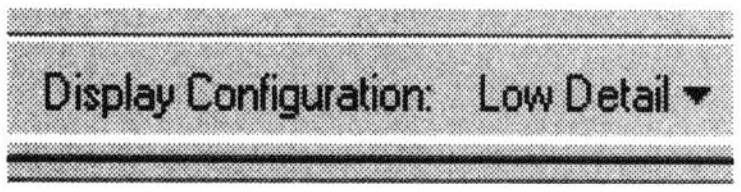

The view is set to Low Detail and rotated 90 degrees.

15. Save the file as *ex3-6.dwg.*

Exercise 3-7:

Adding Doors

Drawing Name: ex3-6.dwg
Estimated Time: 30 minutes

This exercise reinforces the following skills:

- Adding Doors

1.  Open *ex3-6.dwg.*

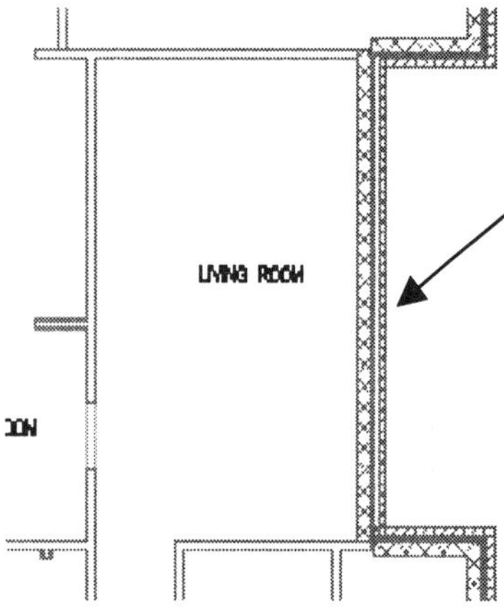

We will add an entry door on the wall indicated.

2. 

Select the **Hinged-Double-Exterior** door.

3. 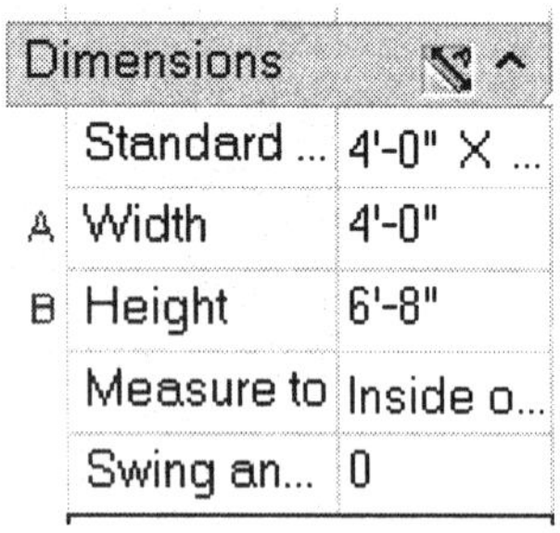

Expand the Dimensions section.
Set the Standard size to **4′-0″ x 6′-8″**.
Set the Swing angle to **0.**

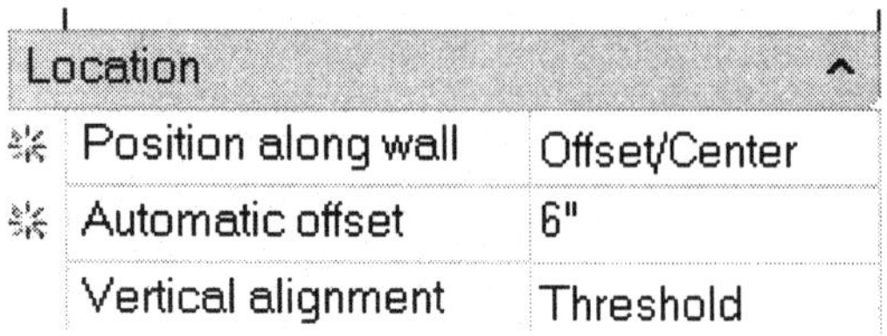

Expand the Location section.
Set the Position along wall to **Offset/Center.**
Set the Automatic offset to **6″.**

4.

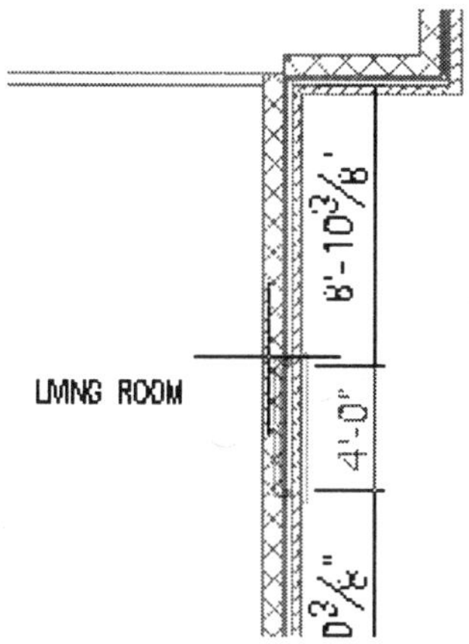

Place the door so it is centered in the wall.

5.

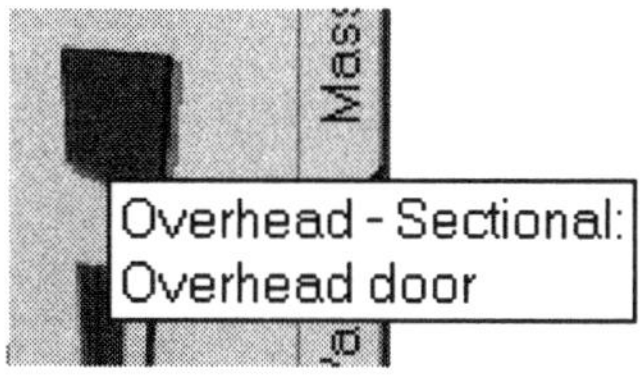

Select the **Overhead-Sectional** door.

6..

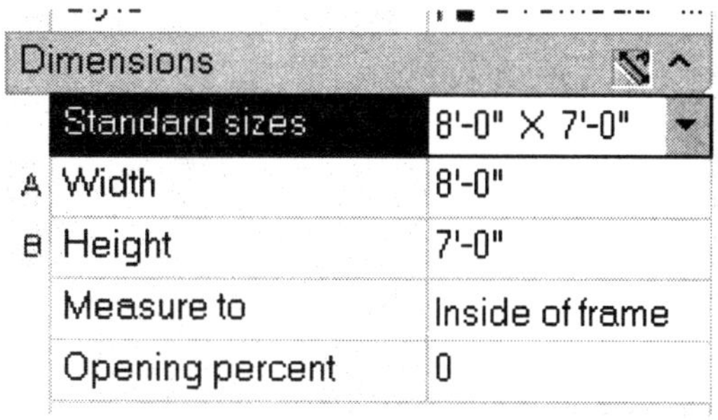

Expand the Dimensions section.
Set the Standard size to **8′-0″ x 7′-0″**.
Set the Swing angle to **0.**

7.

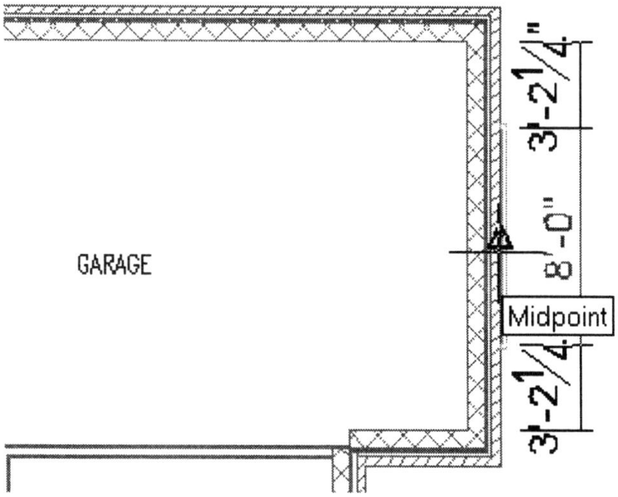

Place the door in the garage wall.

8.

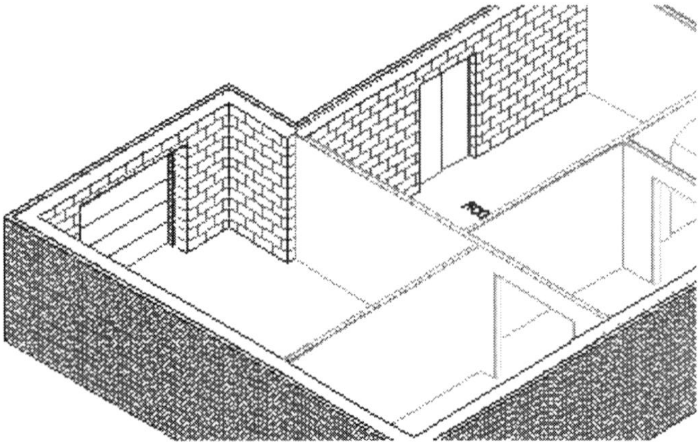

Switch to the Work tab to view the garage door and front entry door.

Switch back to the Model tab.

Next we add a sliding door to the family room wall indicated.

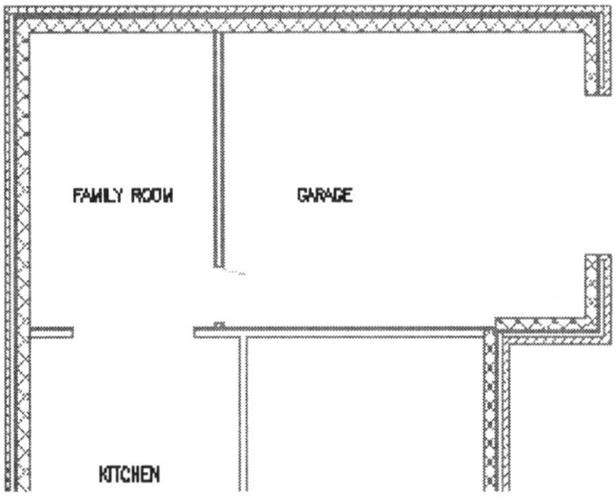

9.

Select a **Sliding Door –Double Full Lite** to add to the family room.

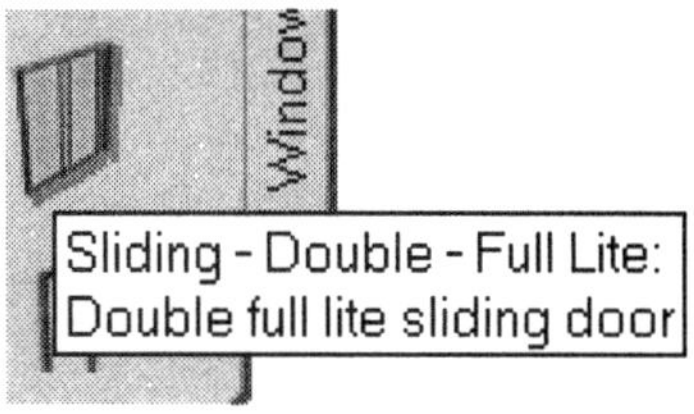

10.

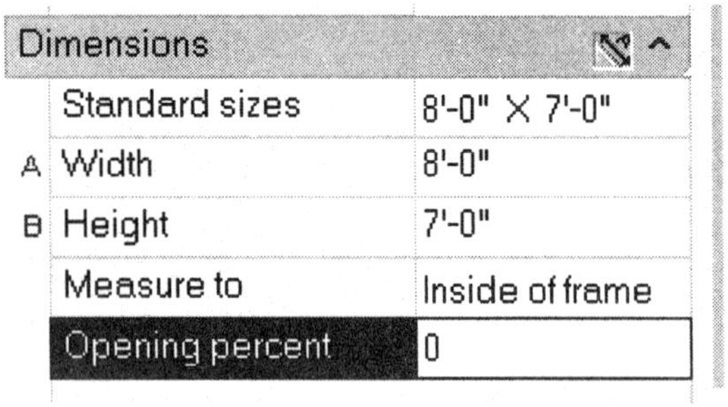

Set the Standard Size to **8′-0″ x 7′-0″.**
Set the Opening percent to **0.**

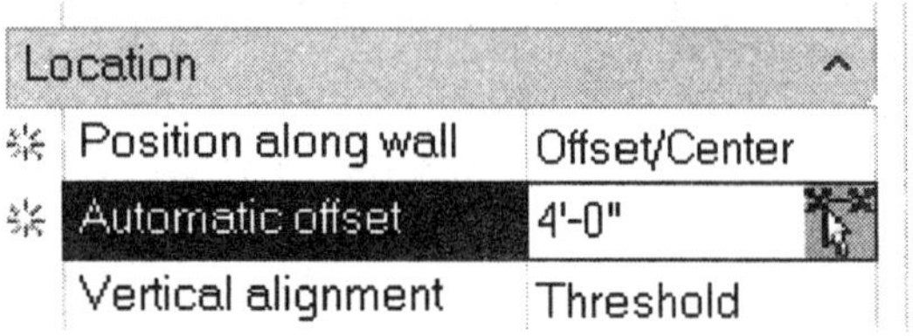

Expand the Location section.
Set the Position along wall to **Offset/Center.**
Set the Automatic offset to **4′-0″.**

11. 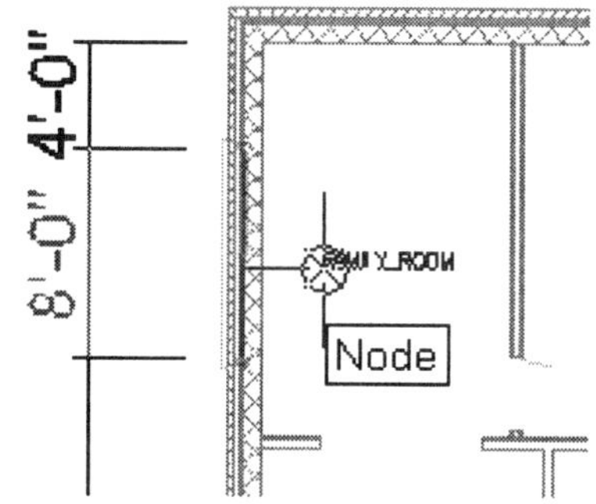

Place the sliding door.

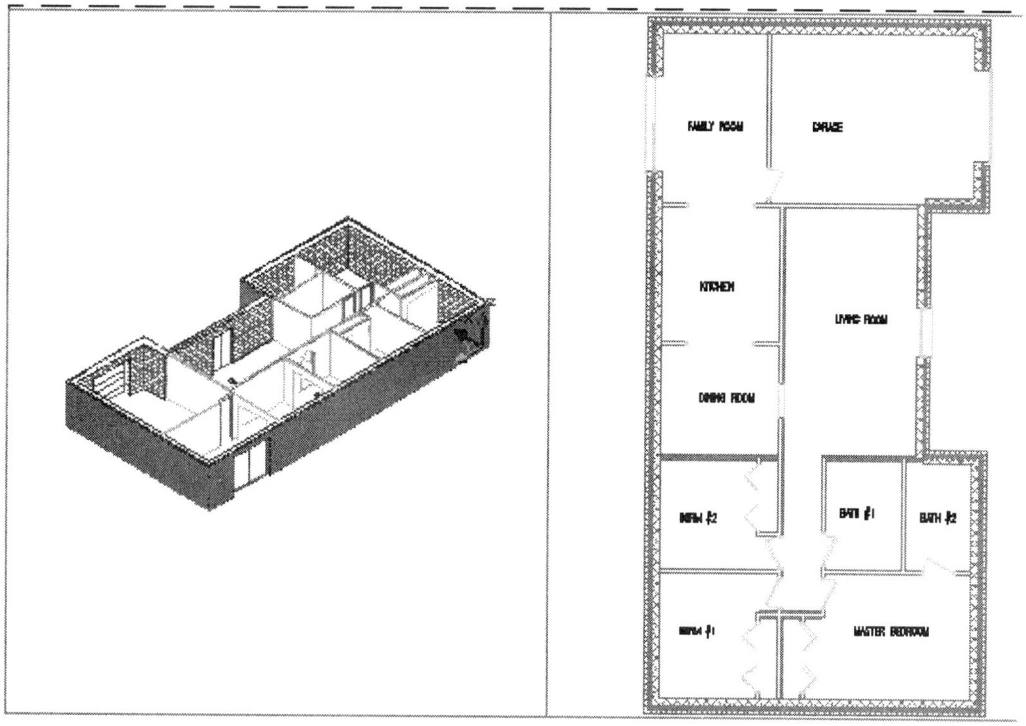

Select the Work tab to view your model.

12. Save the file as *ex3-7.dwg.*

Exercise 3-8:
Add Window Assemblies

Drawing Name: Lesson 3-7.dwg
Estimated Time: 30 minutes

This exercise reinforces the following skills:

- ❑ Add Windows

1.	 Open *ex3-7.dwg.* Select the Model tab.
2.	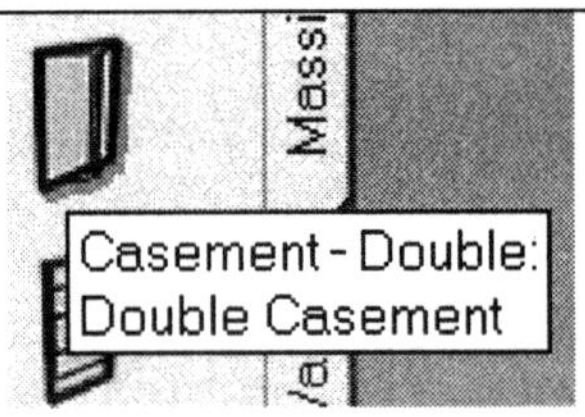 Select the Windows tab of the Tool Palette. Select the **Casement-Double** window.
3.	Expand the Dimensions section. Set the size to **2′-10″ x 3′-0″**. 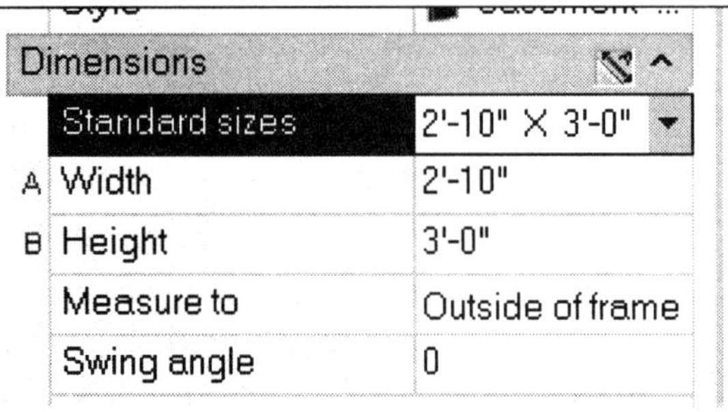 Expand the Location section. Set the Position along wall to **Offset/Center.** Set the Offset to **10′-0″**. Note the vertical alignment controls shifts to head height, at 4′8″. 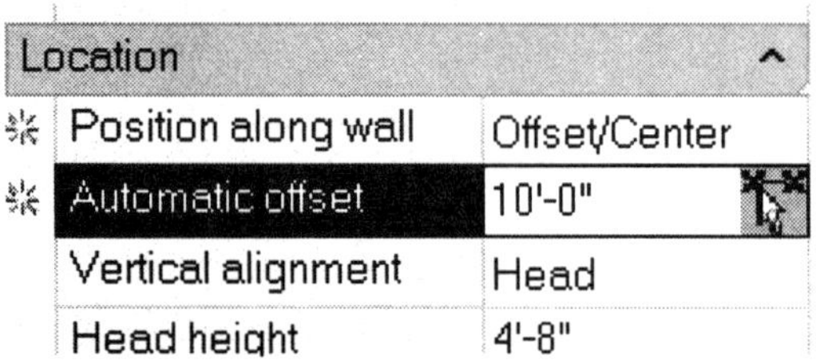
4.	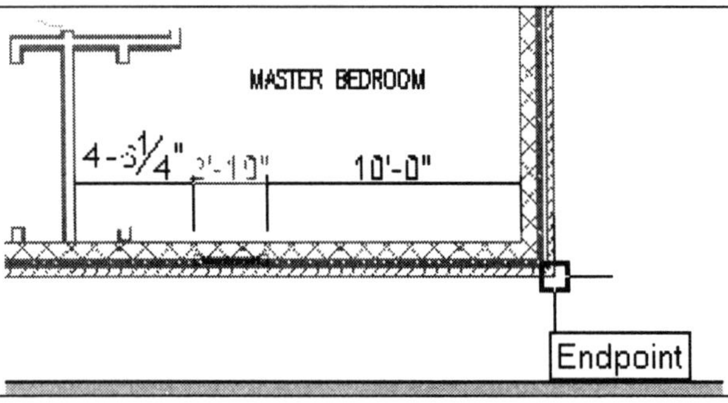 Select the wall shown and the endpoint indicated. The endpoint is where the offset is calculated from.

5. Select the **Casement-Double** window again.
Expand the Location section.
Set the Position along wall to **Offset/Center.**
Set the Offset to 6′**-2″**.

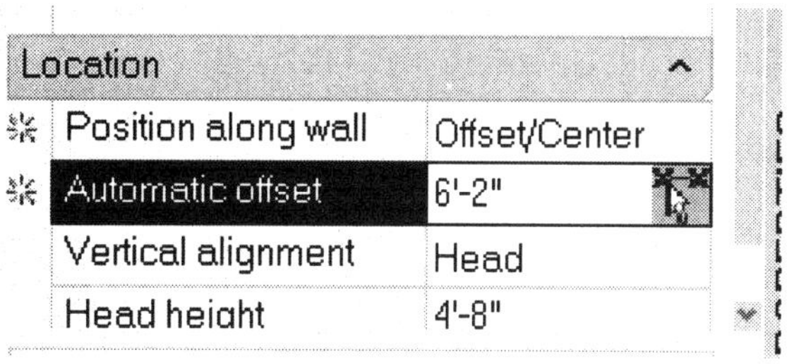

6.

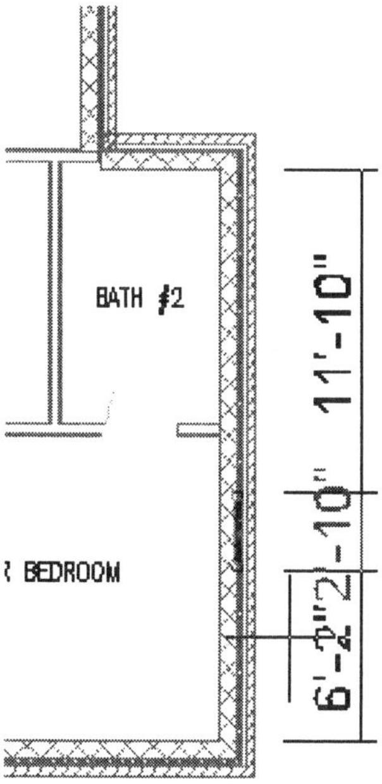

Place the window on the vertical master bedroom wall.

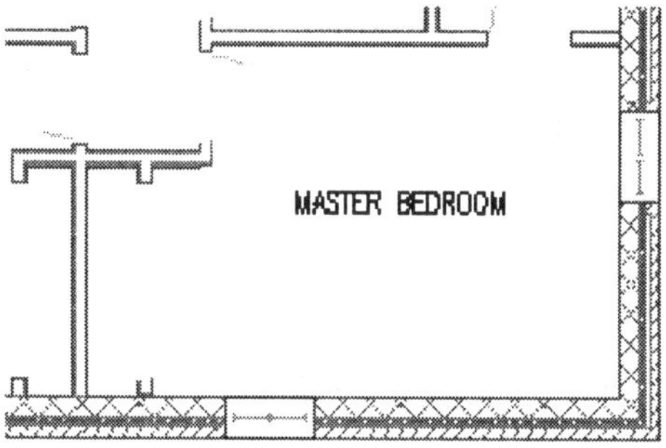

Remember – if you don't like the position of any of the Windows, you can reposition them.
Just select the window, right click, and select 'Reposition Along Wall.'

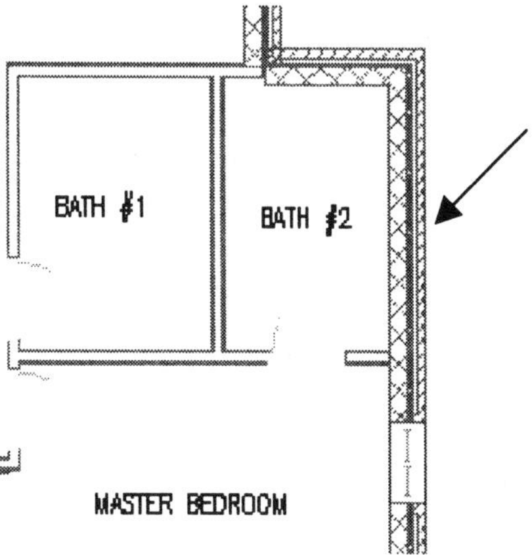

Place a window in Bathroom #2.

7. 

Select the **Casement: Single Casement** window.

8. 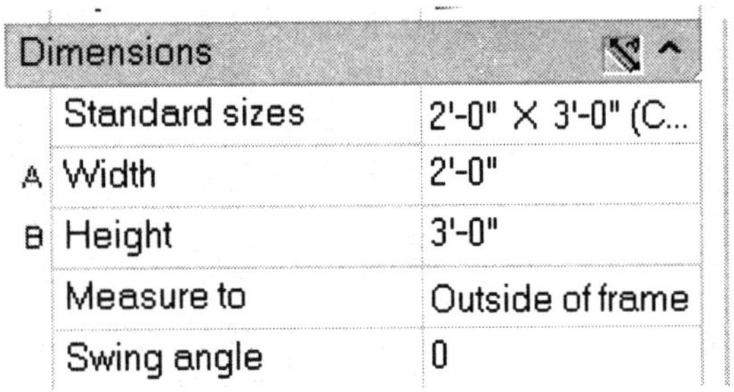

Expand the Dimensions section.
Set the size to **2′-0″ x 3′-0″**.

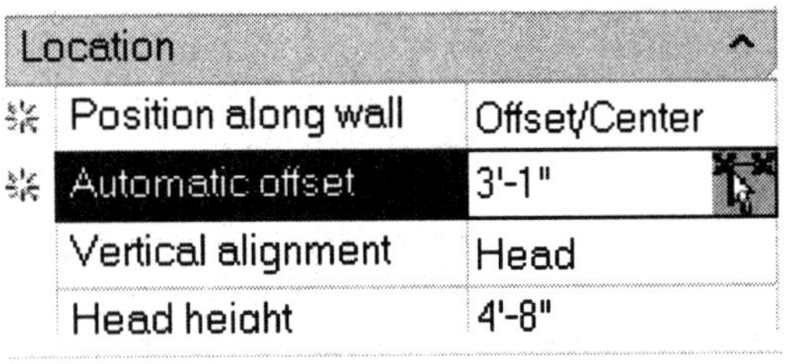

Expand the Location section.
Set the Position along wall to **Offset/Center.**
Set the Offset to **3′-1″**.

9. 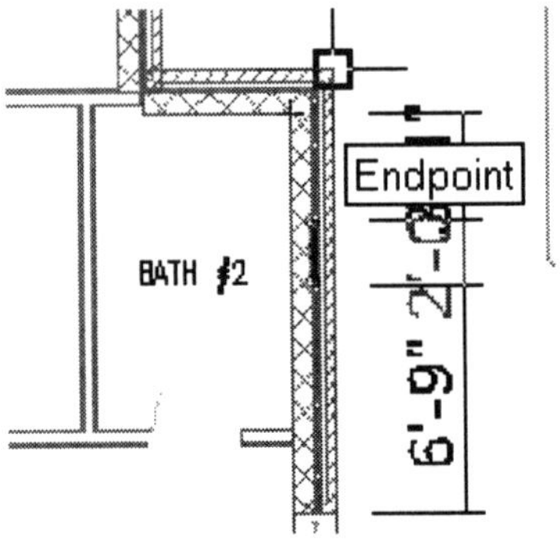

Place the window in the wall indicated.

10. Place a 2′-10″ x 3′-0″ Double Casement window in Bedroom #1 using a 4′-8″ offset.

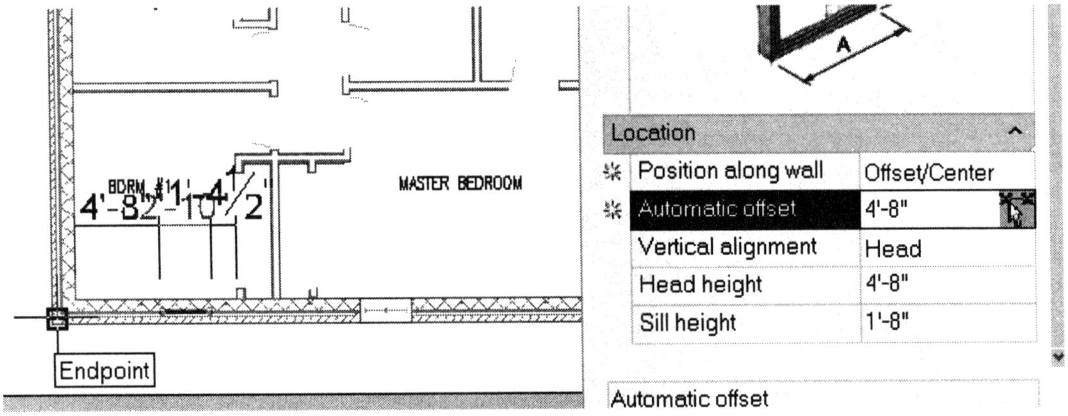

11.

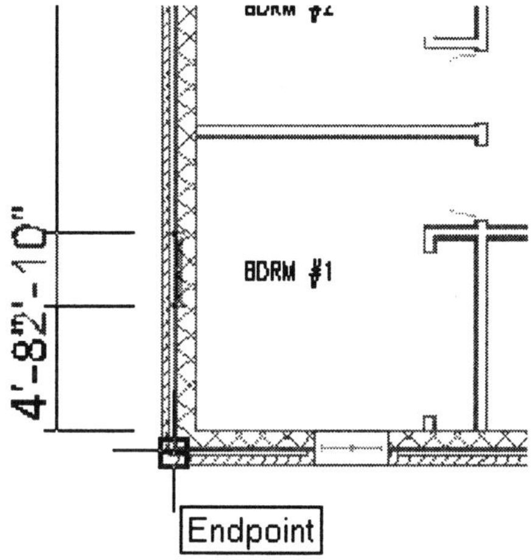

Place a 2′-10″ x 3′-0″ Double Casement window in Bedroom #1 using a 4′-8″ offset on the left vertical wall.

12.

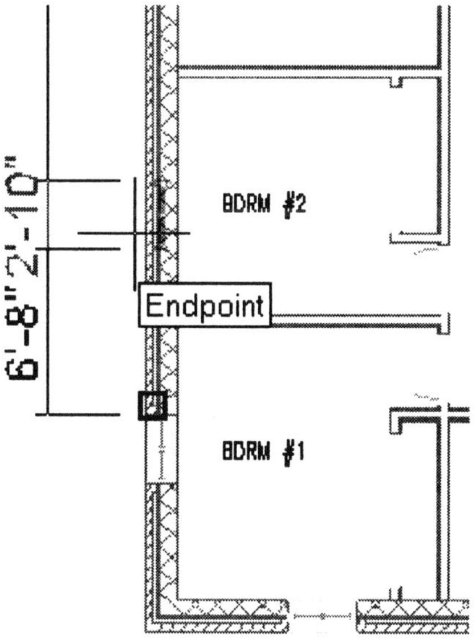

Place a 2′-10″ x 3′-0″ Double Casement window in Bedroom #2 using a 6′-8″ offset on the left vertical wall.

13.

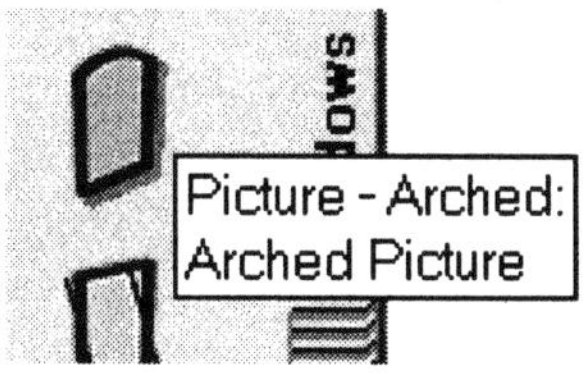

Locate the **Picture- Arched** to place in the left dining room wall.

14.

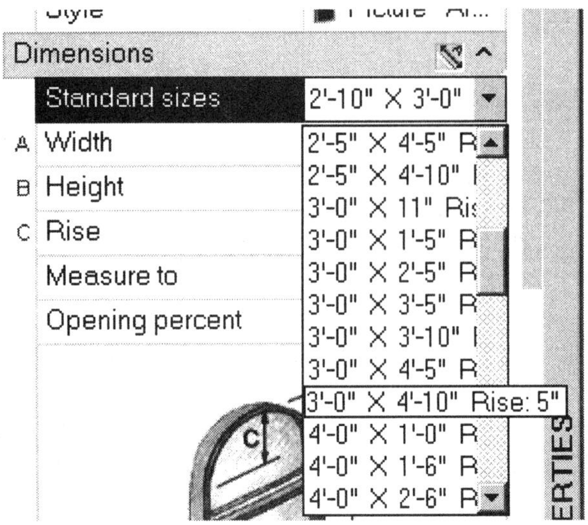

Expand the Dimensions section.
Set the size to **2′-10″ x 4′-10″ Rise 5″**.

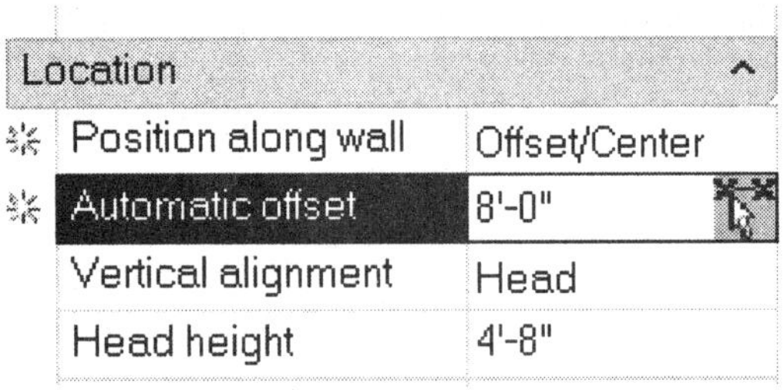

Expand the Location section.
Set the Position along wall to **Offset/Center.**
Set the Offset to **8′-0″**.

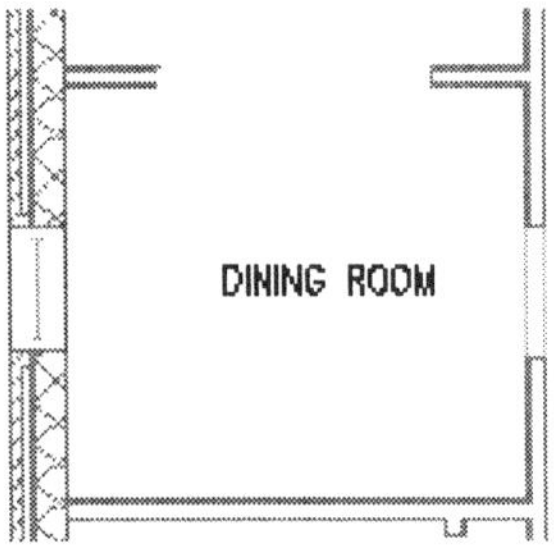

Place the window.

15.

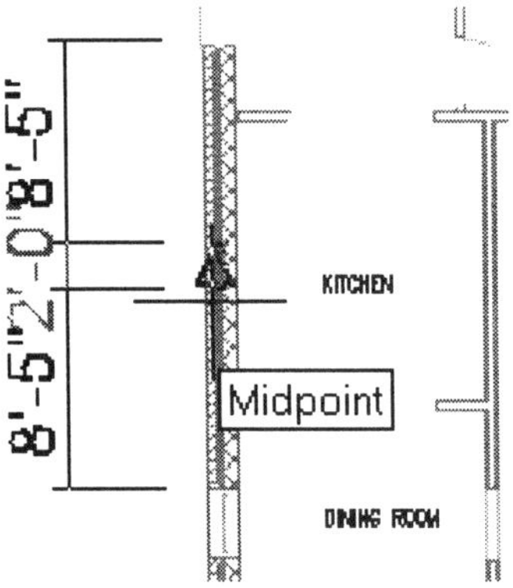

Add a 2′-0″ x 3′-0″ **Casement: Single** window using a **5′-2″** offset.

16.

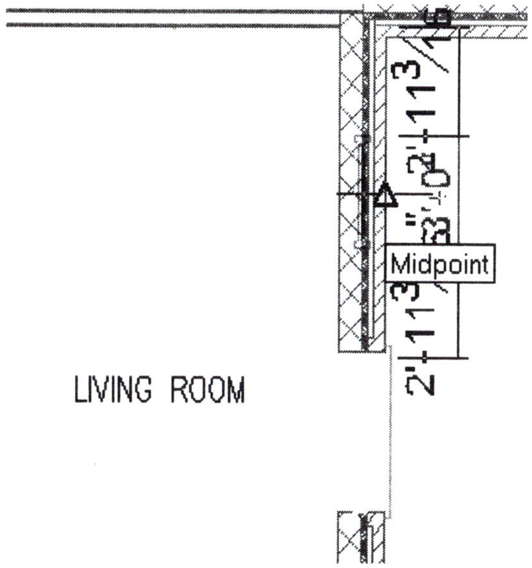

Place an **3′-0″ x 4.5″ Rise 5″ Arched Picture** window with an offset of 0″ on each side of the entry door in the right living room wall.

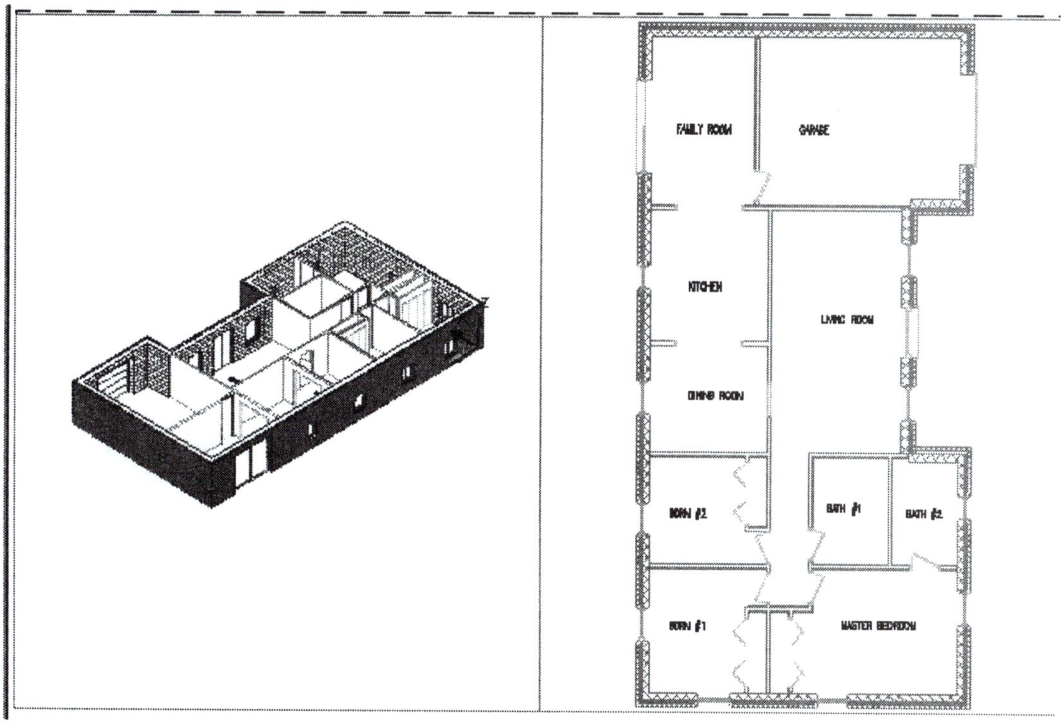

Your floor plan should look similar to the one shown here.

17. Save as *ex3-8.dwg*.

Exercise 3-9:

Adding a Fireplace

Drawing Name: Lesson 3-8.dwg
Estimated Time: 30 minutes

This exercise reinforces the following skills:

- Adding Complex Geometry
- Adding Openings

In this exercise, we add a fireplace to the family room. You can download the fireplace from the publisher's website or use the fireplace created in Lesson 1.

1.  Open *ex3-8.dwg.*
   Select the Model tab.

2.  Select the Design Center tool.

3. 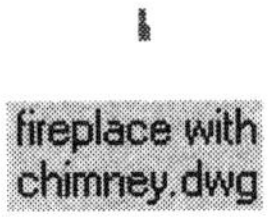

   Select the Folders tab.
   Locate the **fireplace with chimney.dwg** file.
   Drag and drop into your active window.
   When prompted for the scale, set the scale to ½ size.
   Close the Design Center.

   Explode the fireplace with chimney block, so you can control the display of the mass elements and mass groups.

4. 

   Set the Display Configuration to Low Detail to make it easier to locate the fireplace.

5. 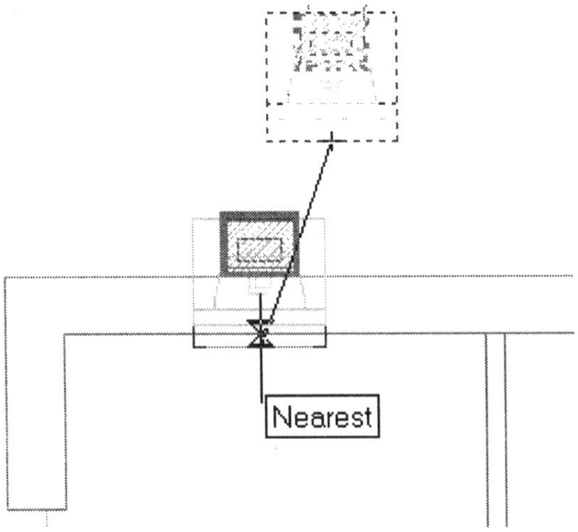

   Move the fireplace so it aligned with the wall.

   We need to add an opening for the flue.

6.

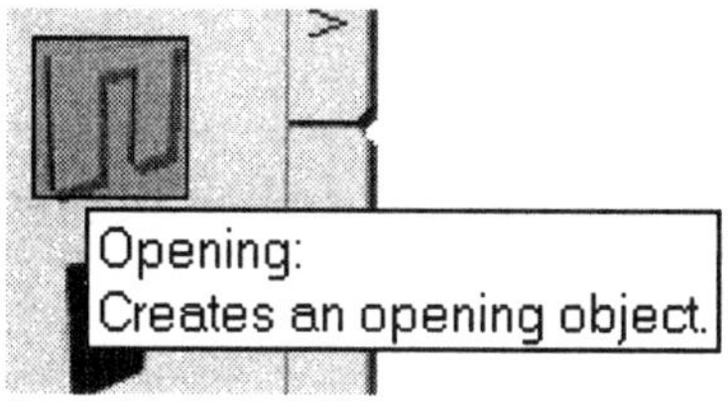

Select the Opening tool on the Design tab.

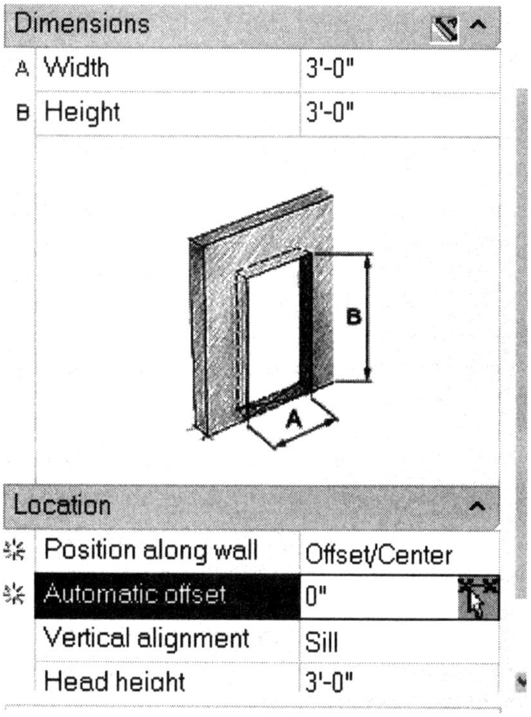

Set the Width to **3′-0″**.
Set the Height to **3′-0″**.
Set Position along wall to **Offset/Center.**
Set the Automatic offset to **0″.**

7.

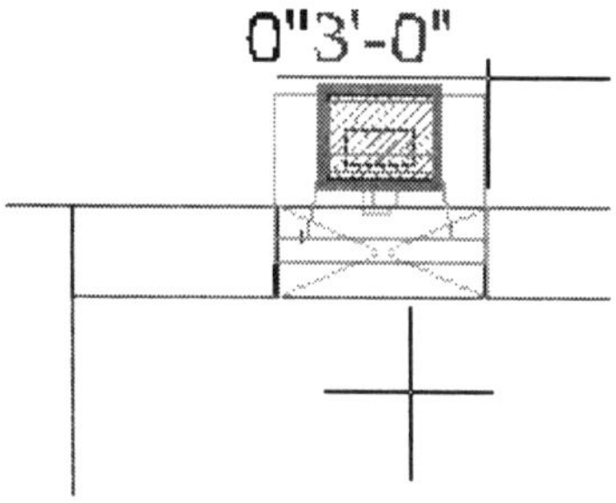

Place the opening so it is centered on the fireplace.

8. 

Activate the Mass Groups display configuration to turn off the display of mass elements.

Use 3D orbit to view your fireplace and ensure that the opening and fireplace are aligned.

9. Save as *ex3-9.dwg.*

Quiz 2

True or False

1. The two types of Layer Filter Groups are Dynamic and Stationary.
2. You can create Layer Filter Groups using the Layer Style Manager Dialog.
3. A Snapshot saves the layer settings.
4. Once a door or window is placed, it can not be moved or modified.
5. Openings can be any size and any elevation.
6. The Offset value when placing a door/window/opening determines how far the door/window/opening is placed from a selected point.
7. Door, window and opening dimensions can be applied using the Design Center.

Multiple Choice

8. Select the entity type that can NOT be converted to a wall:

    A. Line
    B. Polyline
    C. Circle
    D. Spline

9. Doors are automatically placed on this layer:

    A. A-OPENING
    B. A-DOOR
    C. A-WINDOW
    D. A-WALL-OPENING

10. A HOT grip is indicated by this color:

    A. GREEN
    B. BLUE
    C. RED
    D. YELLOW

11. Openings are placed on this layer:

    A. A-OPENING
    B. A-DOOR
    C. A-WINDOW
    D. A-WALL-OPENING

12. To assign an image to a tool on the tool palette using existing geometry, use

    A. Assign image
    B. Set Image from selection
    C. Insert
    D. Import

ANSWERS:

1) F; 2) T 3) T; 4) F; 5) T; 6) T; 7) F; 8) C; 9) B; 10) C; 11) A; 12) B

Lesson 4
Space Planning

A residential structure is divided into three basic areas:

- Bedrooms: Used for Sleeping and Privacy
- Common Areas: Used for gathering and entertainment, such as family rooms and living rooms, and dining area
- Service Areas: Used to perform functions, such as the kitchen, laundry room, garage, and storage areas

When drawing your floor plan, you need to verify that enough space is provided to allow placement of items, such as beds, tables, entertainment equipment, cars, stoves, bathtubs, lavatories, etc.

ADT comes with Design Content to allow designers to place furniture to test their space. Additional architectural content is provided at no charge from the Schroff Development Corporation's website at www.schroff1.com for readers of this textbook.

Exercise 4-1:
Creating AEC Content

Drawing Name: ex3-9.dwg
Estimated Time: 15 minutes

This lesson reinforces the following skills:

- Design Center
- AEC Content
- Customization

1.  Open *ex3-9.dwg*.
   Select the Model tab.

2.  Launch the Design Center.

3.

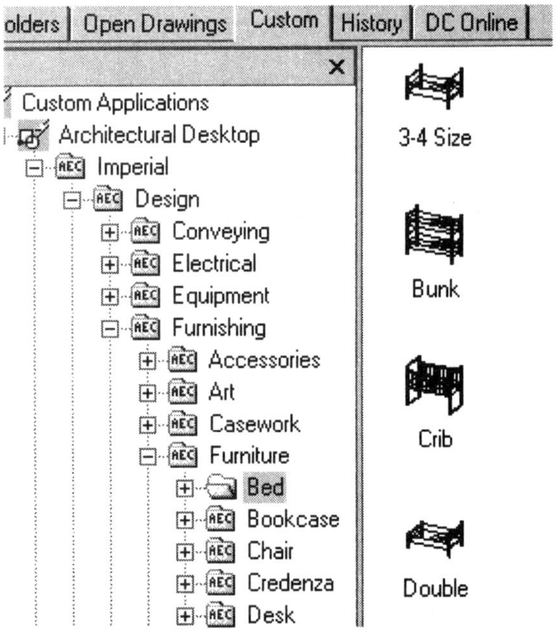

Select the Custom tab.
Browse to *Architectural Desktop/Imperial/Furnishing/Furniture/Bed.*

4.

Select the *Kingbed.dwg* file.
Right click and select **Insert**.

5.

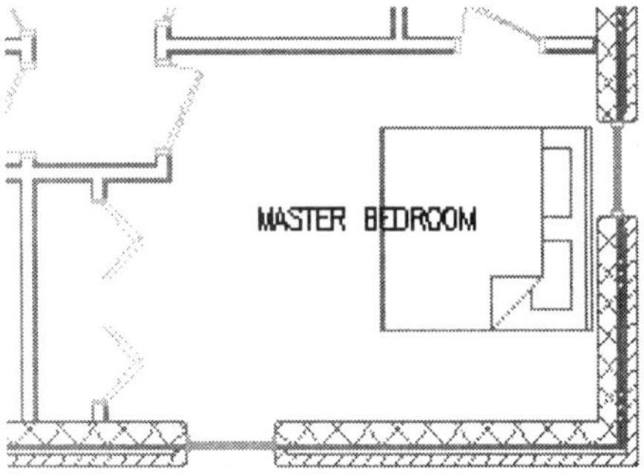

Place the bed in the master bedroom.

6.

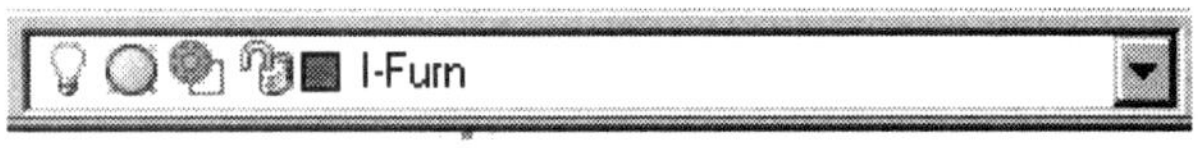

Select the bed.

Note that the bed was automatically placed on the I-Furn layer.

7.

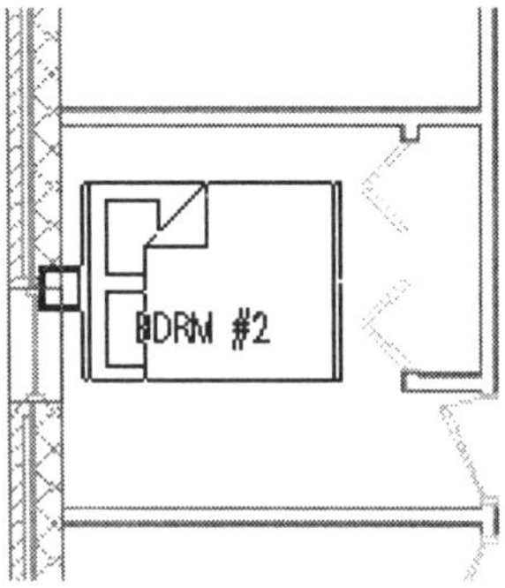

Locate the *Queen.dwg.*

Drag and drop it into Bedroom #2 as shown.

8.

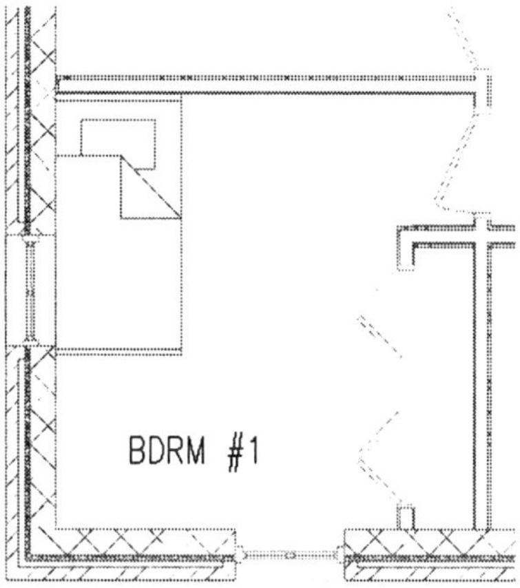

Locate the *Twin.dwg* and place it in Bedroom#1.

9.

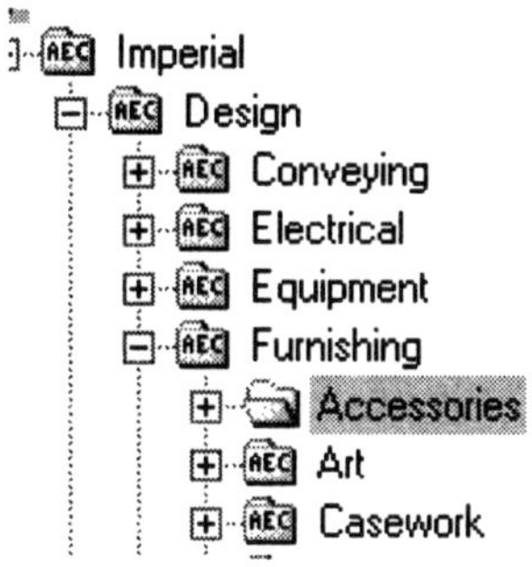

Browse to the *Accessories* folder in the Design Center.

10.

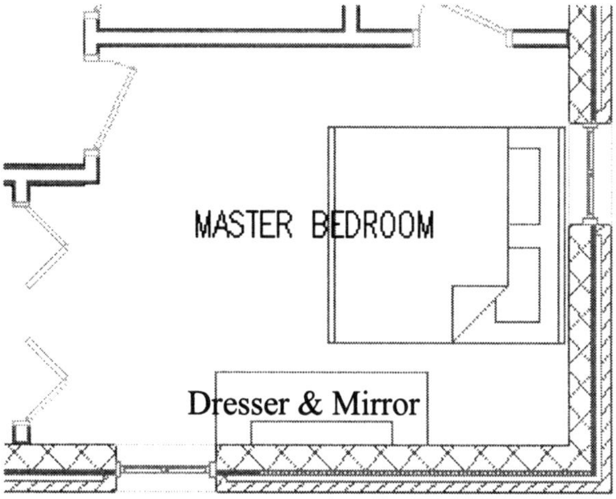

Place a Dresser & Mirror in the master bedroom.

11.

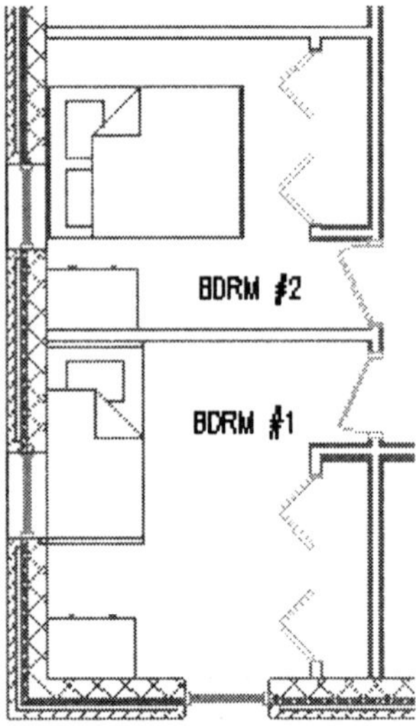

Add a dresser to each of the smaller bedrooms.

12.

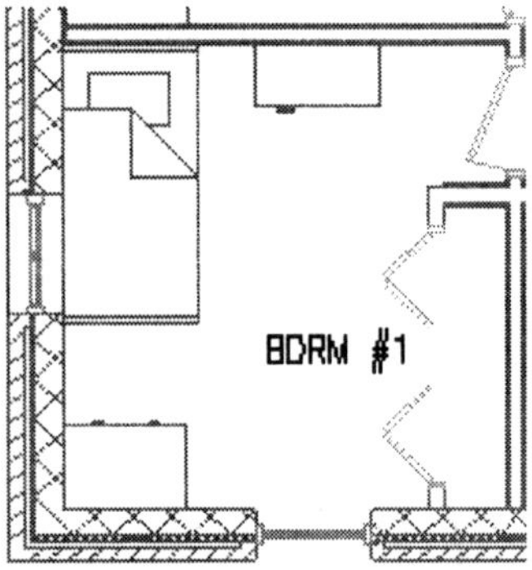

Locate the *36x18 Left.dwg* file under the *Desk* folder.
Place into Bedroom #1.

13.

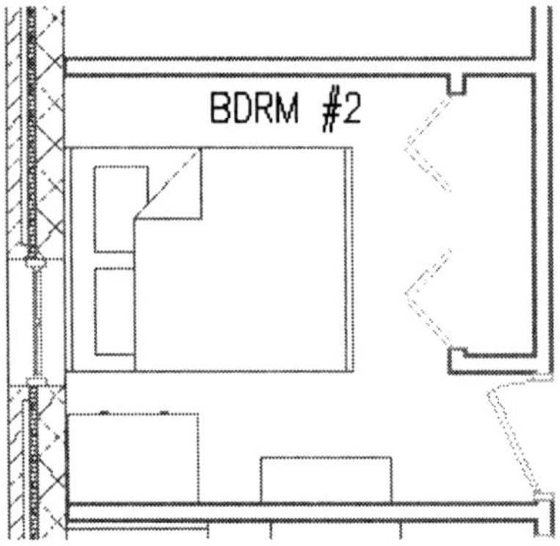

Locate the *6 Shelves,dwg* bookcase in the *Bookcase* folder.
Place in Bedroom #2.

14.

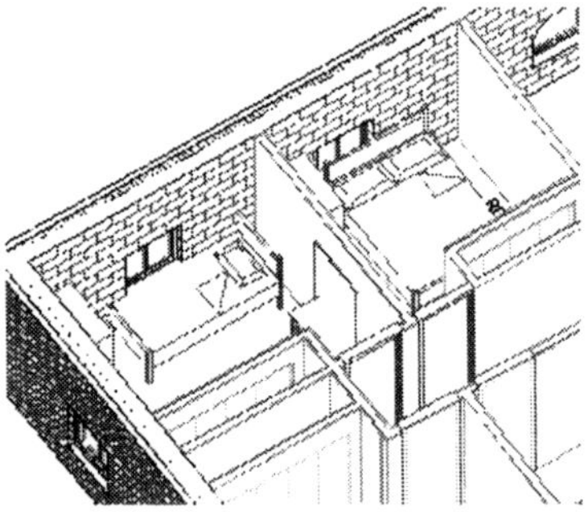

Switch to a 3D view and use 3D Orbit to view the furniture placement.

15. Save as *ex4-1.dwg*.

Exercise 4-2:

Equipping the Bathrooms

Drawing Name: Ex4-1.dwg
Estimated Time: 30 minutes

This lesson reinforces the following skills:

- Design Center
- Tool Palette
- Customization

1. 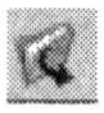 Open *ex4-1.dwg.*
   Select the Model tab.
   Switch to a top view.

2.  Launch the Design Center.

3.  Launch the Tool Palette

Creating a Tool Palette

4. 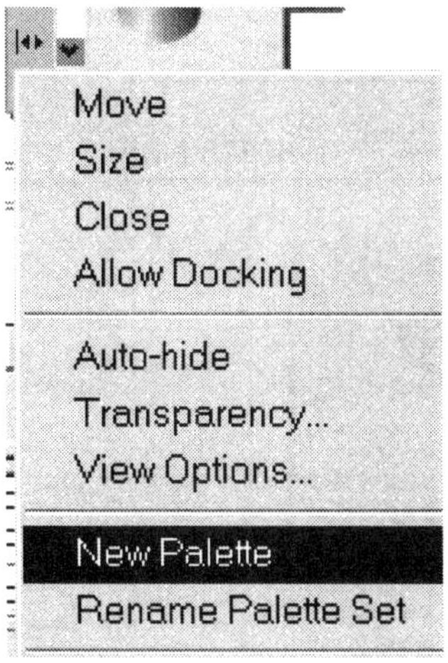

   Select the bottom of the Tool Palette below the expand/contract arrows.
   Right click and select **New Palette.**

5. 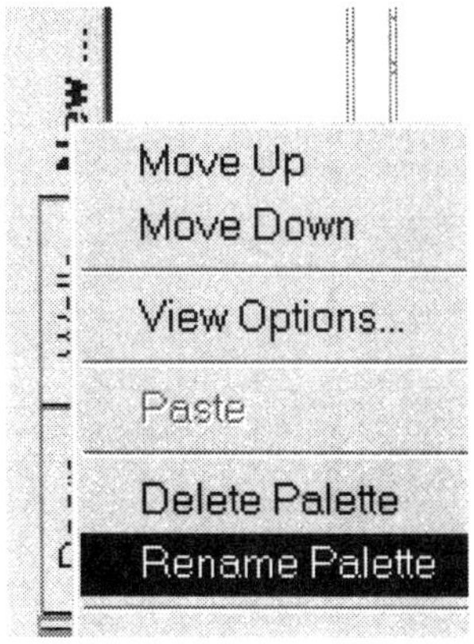

   Pick the new palette tab.
   Right click and select **Rename Palette.**

6. 

Type **Plumbing**.

7. 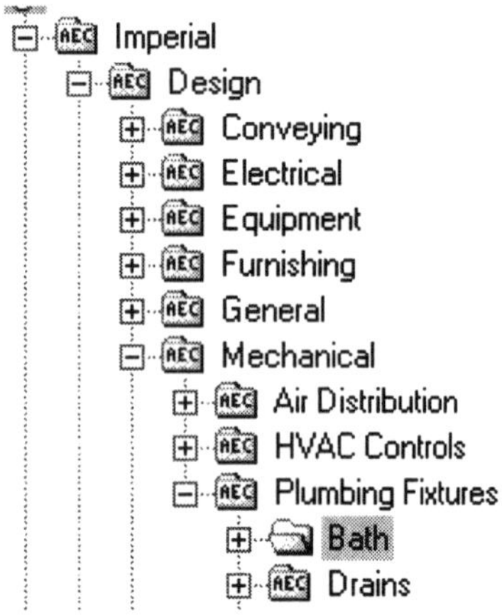

Locate the *Tub 30 x 66* file in the *Imperial/Design/Mechanical/Plumbing Fixtures/Bath* folder.

8. 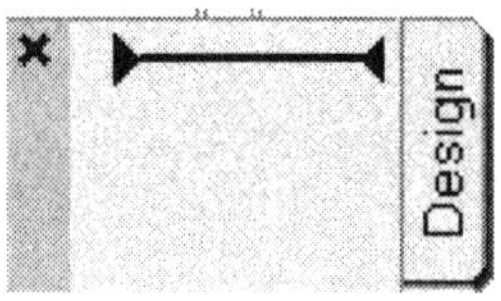

Drag and drop the *Tub 30 x 66* onto the Plumbing Palette. You can release when you see the bar as shown.

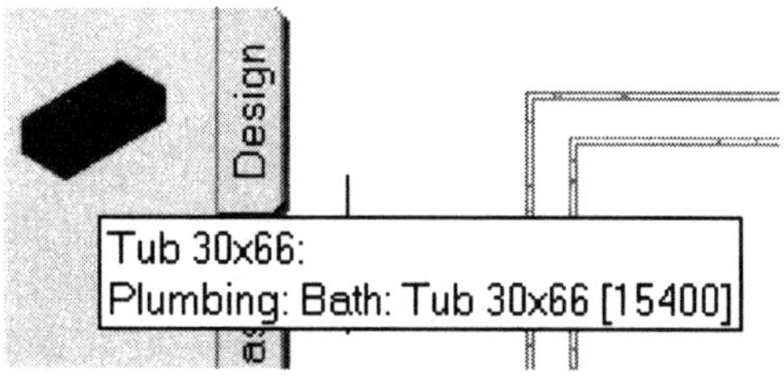

9. 

Locate *Tank 2* in the Toilet folder.
Drag and drop onto the Plumbing palette.

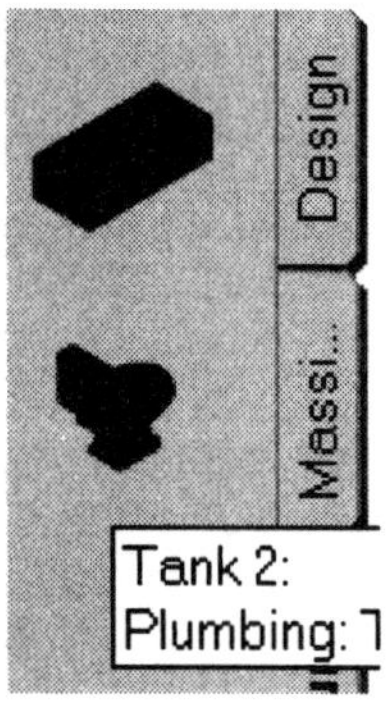

10.

Locate the *32 x 24* shower in the shower folder.
Drag and drop onto the Plumbing palette.

You change how icons appear on the tool palette by using the View options.

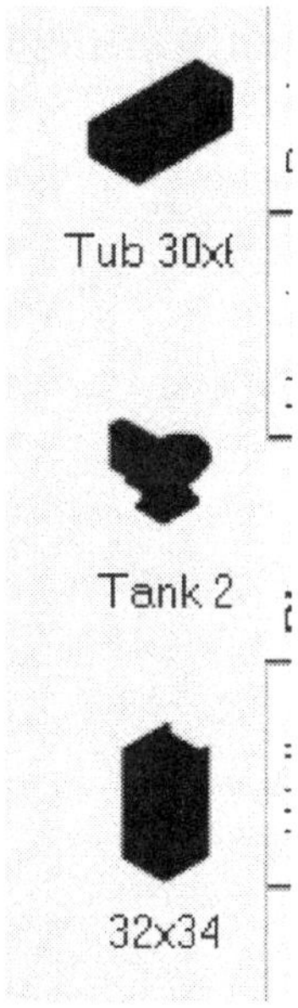

11.

Locate the *Vanity* in the *Lavatory* folder.
Drag and drop onto the Plumbing palette.

Close the Design Center.

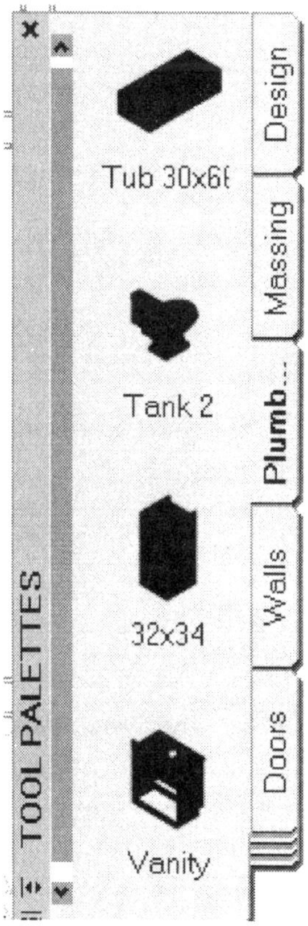

Adding Fixtures to Bathrooms

12. 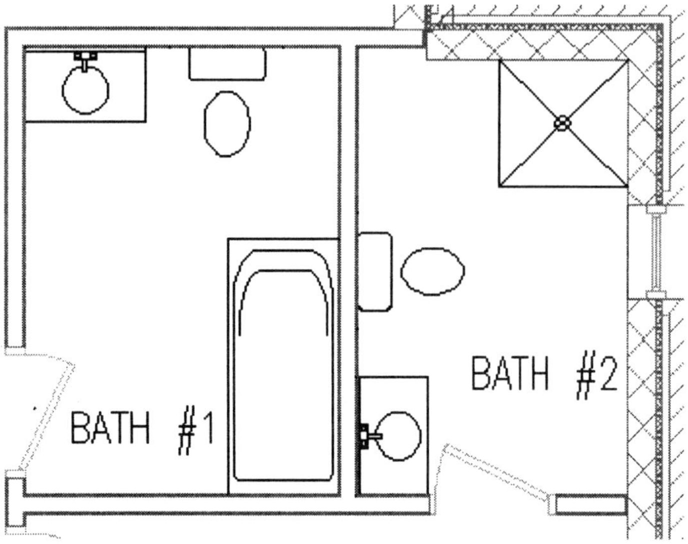

Using the tools on the new Plumbing Palette, equip the two bathrooms as shown.

13. Select the tub.

Note that the plumbing fixtures were automatically placed on the *P-Flor-Fixt* layer.

14. Save as *ex4-2.dwg*.

TIP: As an additional exercise, place towel bars, soap dishes and other items in the bathrooms.

TIP: The Space Planning process is not just to ensure that the rooms can hold the necessary equipment, but also requires the drafter to think about plumbing, wiring, and HVAC requirements based on where and how items are placed.

Exercise 4-3:

Furnishing the Common Areas

Drawing Name: Ex4-2.dwg
Estimated Time: 30 minutes

Common areas are the Living Room, Dining Room, and Family Room.

This lesson reinforces the following skills:

- Design Center
- Tool Palette
- Customization

You will need internet access in order to complete this exercise.

1.  Open *ex4-2.dwg.*
   Select the Model tab.
   Switch to a top view.

2.  Launch the Design Center.

3.  Launch the Tool Palette

Creating a Tool Palette

4. 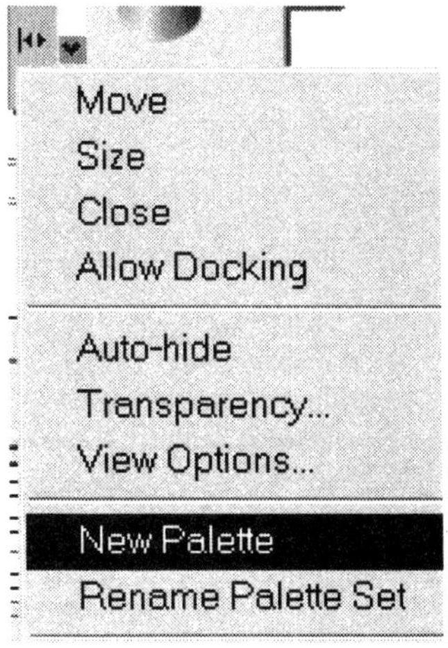

   Select the bottom of the Tool Palette below the expand/contract arrows.
   Right click and select **New Palette.**

5. 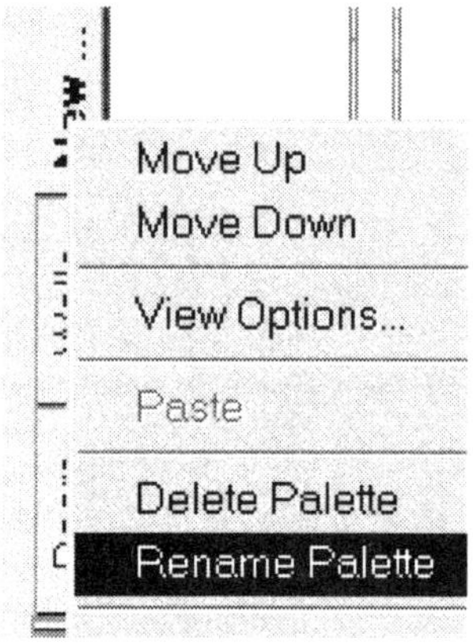

Pick the new palette tab.
Right click and select **Rename Palette.**

6. 

Rename the tool palette **Furniture**.

Adding Tools from DesignCenter Online

7. 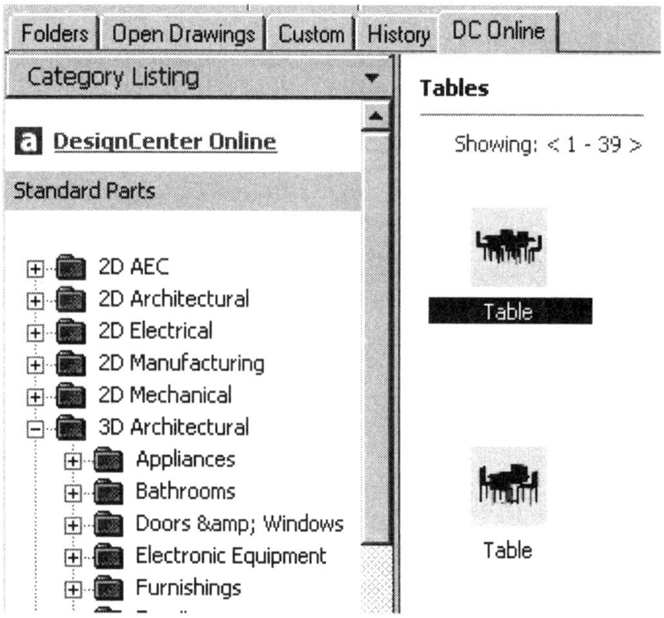

In the Design Center dialog, select the DC Online tab. Browse to *3D Architecture/ Furnishings/Tables.*
furniture

8. 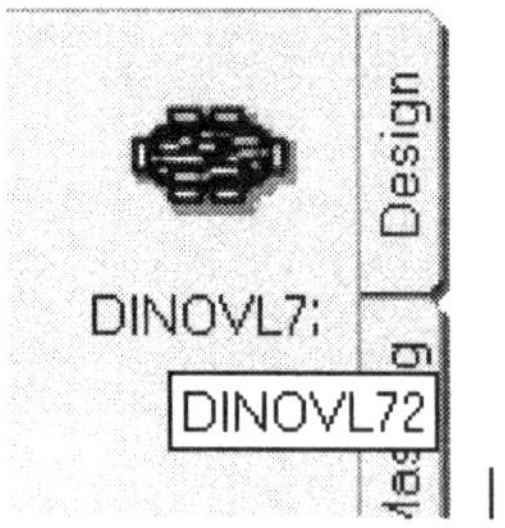

Drag and drop the file called **DINOVL72** onto the new palette. There may be slight pause while the file downloads from Autodesk's sever.

9. Select the DNOVL72 tool.
Right click and select **Properties.**

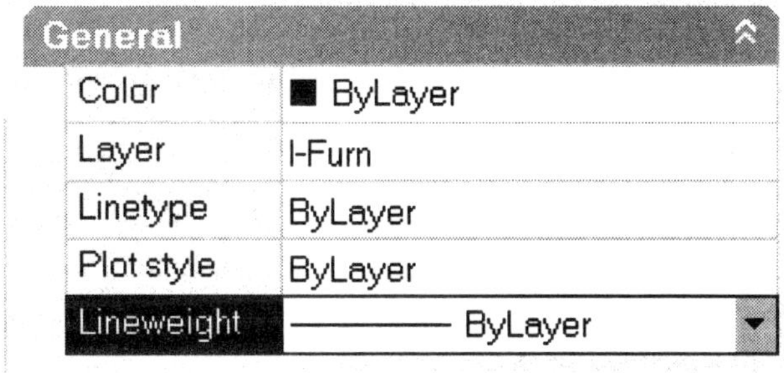

Scroll down and expand the General section.
Set the Layer to **I-Furn**.
Set Color to **ByLayer**.
Set Linetype to **ByLayer**.
Set Plot Style to **ByLayer.**
Set Lineweight to **ByLayer.**

10.

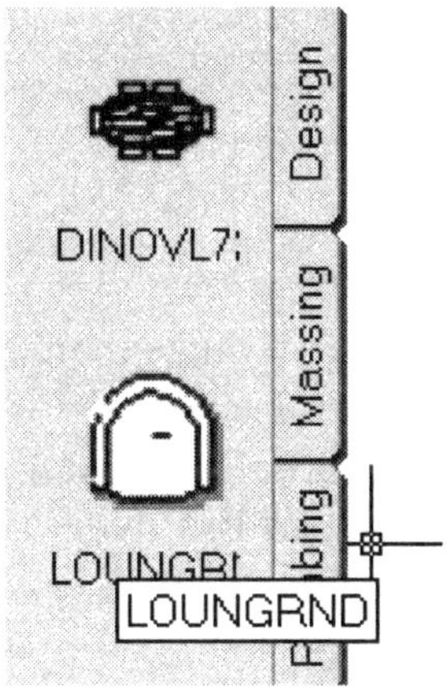

Browse to *3D Architecture/Furnishings/Chairs* folder.

Drag and drop the **loungrnd** chair onto the Furniture palette.

Select the LOUNGRND tool.
Right click and select **Properties.**

11.

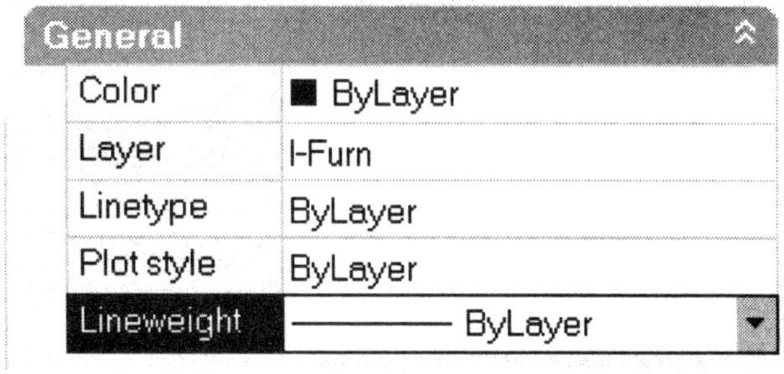

Scroll down and expand the General section.
Set the Layer to **I-Furn**.
Set Color to **ByLayer**.
Set Linetype to **ByLayer**.
Set Plot Style to **ByLayer.**
Set Lineweight to **ByLayer.**

12.

Browse to *3D Architecture/Furnishings/Sofas* folder.

Drag and drop the **loveset6** onto the Furniture palette.

Select the LOVESET tool.
Right click and select **Properties.**

13.

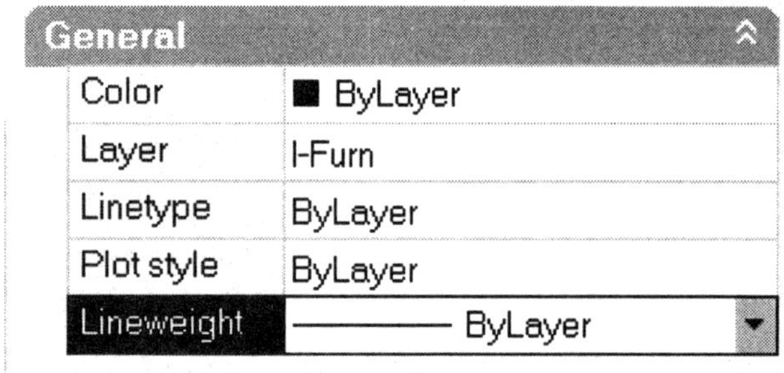

Scroll down and expand the General section.
Set the Layer to **I-Furn**.
Set Color to **ByLayer**.
Set Linetype to **ByLayer**.
Set Plot Style to **ByLayer.**
Set Lineweight to **ByLayer.**

14.

Browse to *3D Architecture/Furnishings/Tables* folder.

Drag and drop the **tblcoffe** onto the Furniture palette.

Select the TBLCOFFE tool.
Right click and select **Properties.**

15.

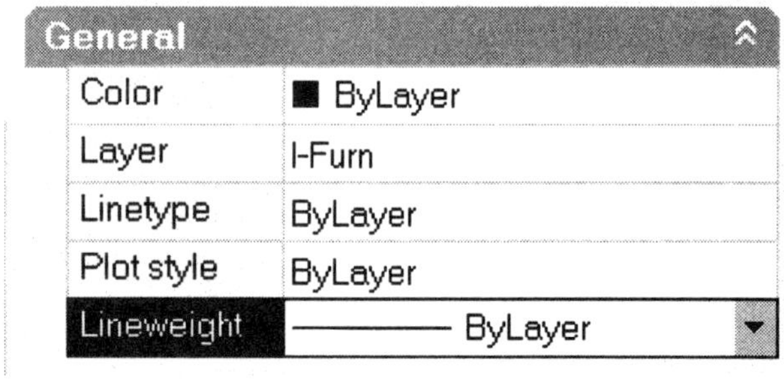

Scroll down and expand the General section.
Set the Layer to **I-Furn**.
Set Color to **ByLayer**.
Set Linetype to **ByLayer**.
Set Plot Style to **ByLayer.**
Set Lineweight to **ByLayer.**

16.

Browse to *3D Architecture/Furnishings/Entertainment enter* folder.

Drag and drop the **entcntr** onto the Furniture palette.

Select the ENTCNTR tool.
Right click and select **Properties.**

17.

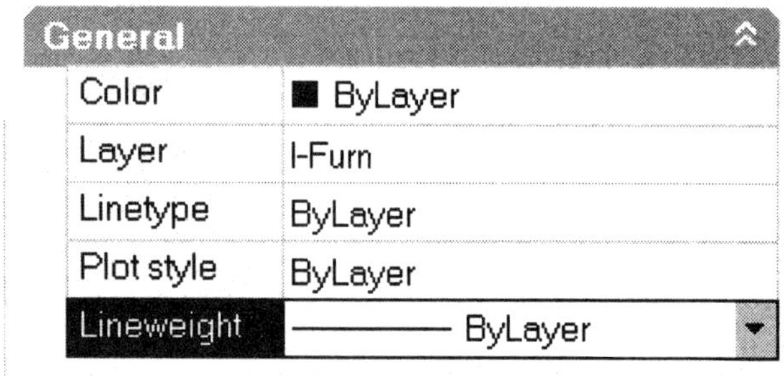

Scroll down and expand the General section.
Set the Layer to **I-Furn**.
Set Color to **ByLayer**.
Set Linetype to **ByLayer**.
Set Plot Style to **ByLayer.**
Set Lineweight to **ByLayer.**

18. Close the Design Center.

19.

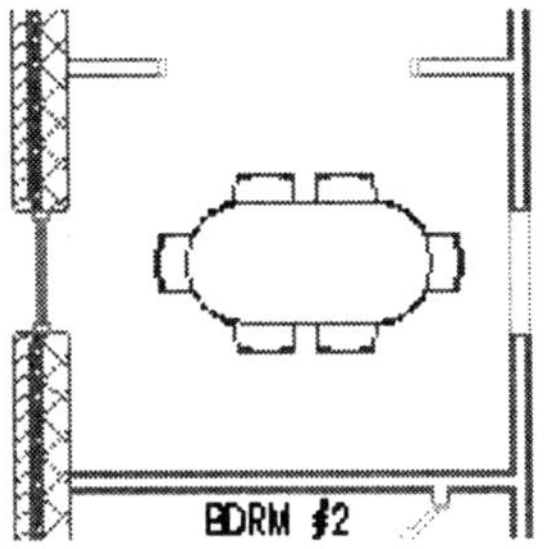

Add the **DINOVL72** to the dining room.

20.

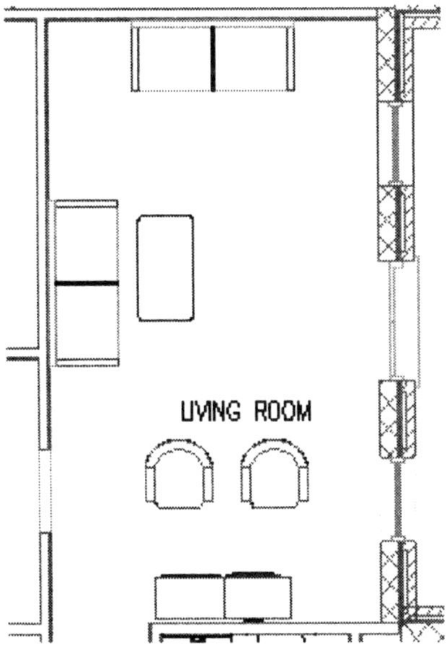

Furnish the living room with the lounge chair, sofa, coffee table, and entertainment center.

21.

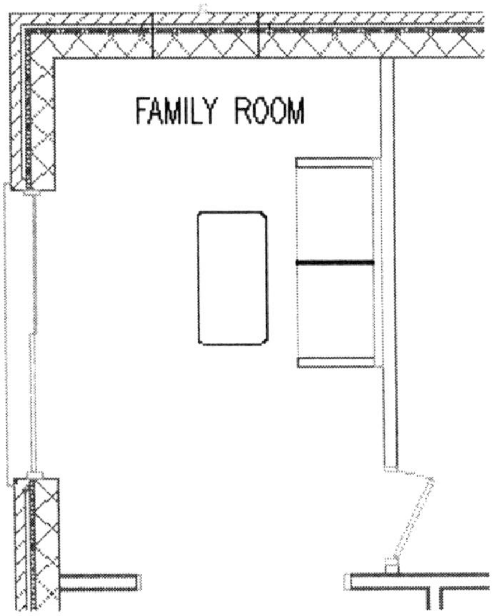

Add a sofa and coffee table to the family room.

22. Save the file as *ex4-3.dwg.*

Exercise 4-4

Adding to the Service Areas

Drawing Name: Ex4-3.dwg
Estimated Time: 30 minutes

1.  Open *ex4-3.dwg.*
   Select the Model tab.
   Switch to a top view.

2.  Launch the Design Center.

3. 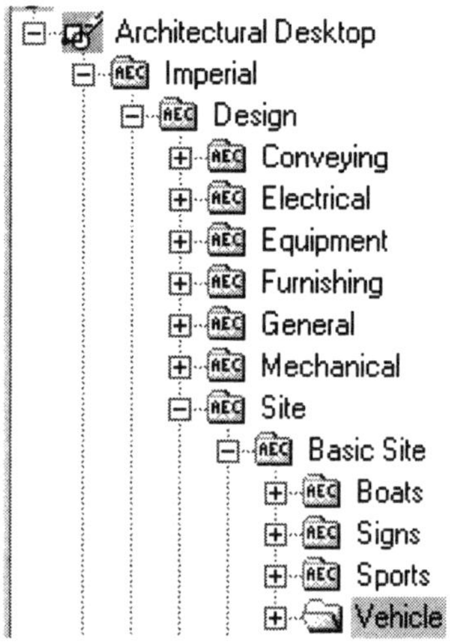

   Select the Custom tab.
   Browse to *Architectural Desktop/Imperial/Design/Site/Vehicles* folder.

4. 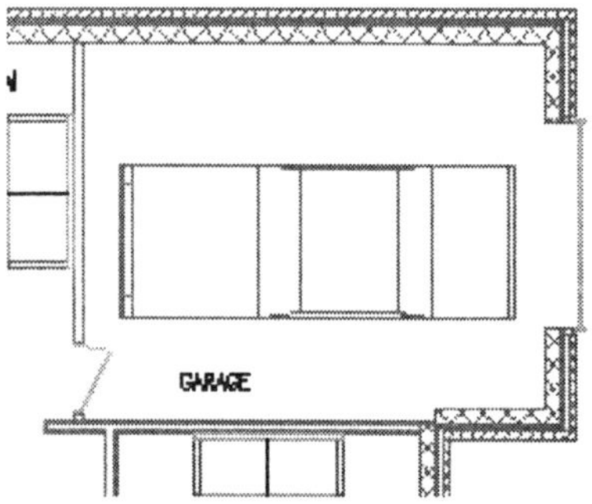

   Drag and drop the *Generic* car into the garage.

5. 

   If you pick the car, you see that it is placed on the *C-Site-Vhcl* layer automatically.

TIP: If the preview shown in the Design Center does not appear as a 3D object, then it is a 2D object. Don't select it for use in your model.

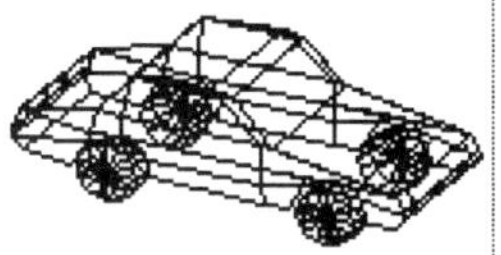

All that remains is the kitchen area.

6. 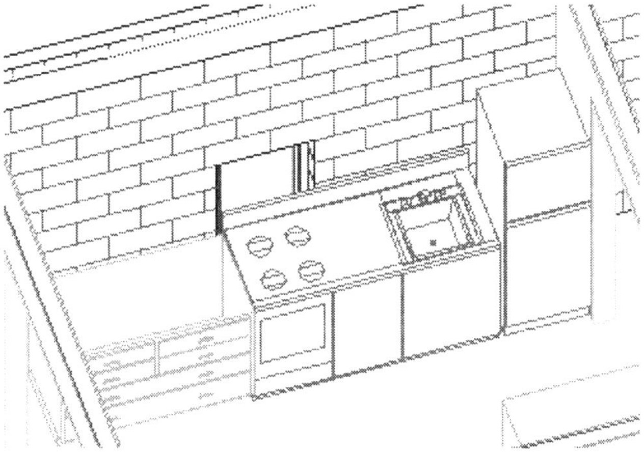

Use the Design Center to add casework, a kitchen sink, and an oven into the kitchen area.

We see now using our space planning that the window needs to be shifted up.

design equipment unit kitchen large

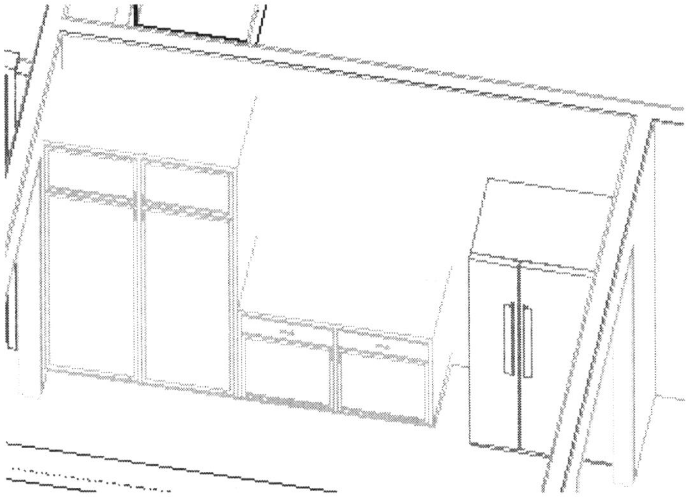

Add a refrigerator and additional cabinets to the other side of the kitchen.

7. 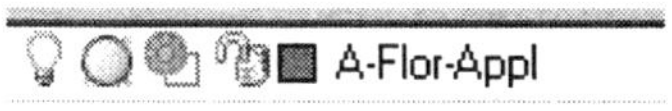

Select the refrigerator and the stove.
Note that these are placed on the *A-Flor-Appl* layer.

8. 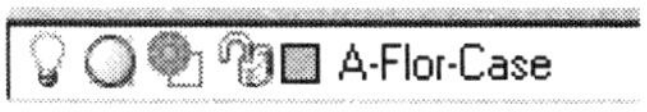

Select the cabinetry.
Note that these are placed on the *A-Flor-Case* layer.

9. 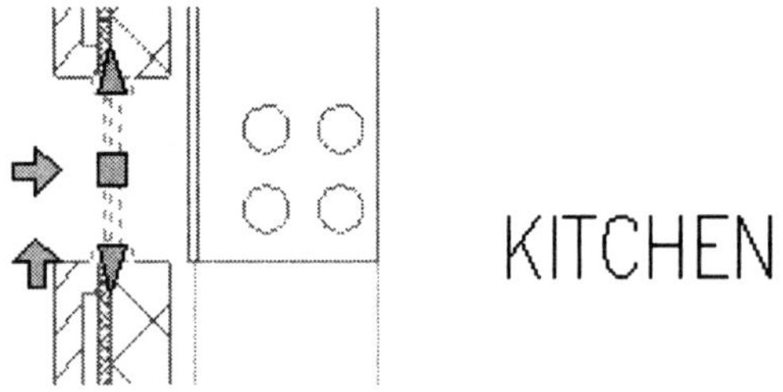

Select the kitchen window.
Right click and select **Properties.**

10. 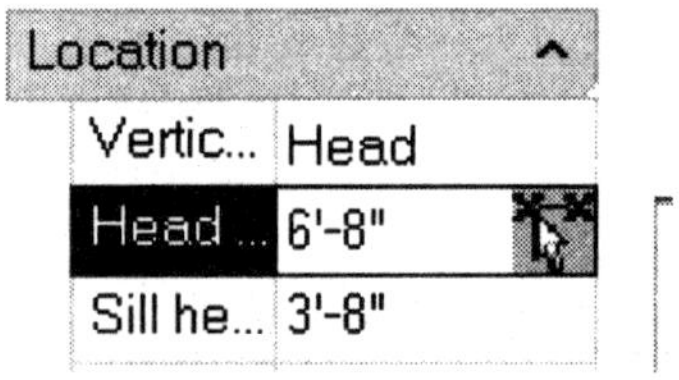

Change the Head Height to **6′-8″**.

11. 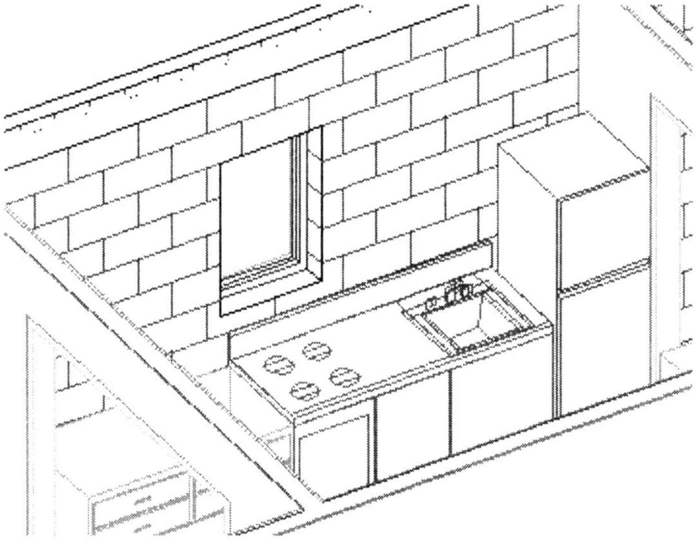

The window is now positioned properly.

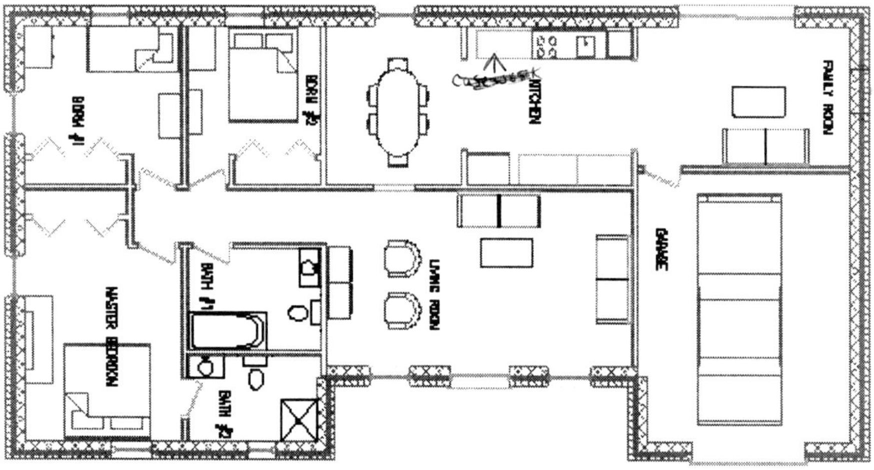

Our completed floor plan.

The image is rotated 90 degrees.

12. Save the file as *ex4-4.dwg.*

Exercise 4-5

Creating Layer Settings

Drawing Name: Ex4-4.dwg
Estimated Time: 30 minutes

This lesson reinforces the following skills:

- Layer Manager
- Layer Settings
- Layer Groups

1.  Open *ex4-4.dwg.*
   Select the Model tab.
   Switch to a top view.

2.  Select the **Layer Manager** tool.

3 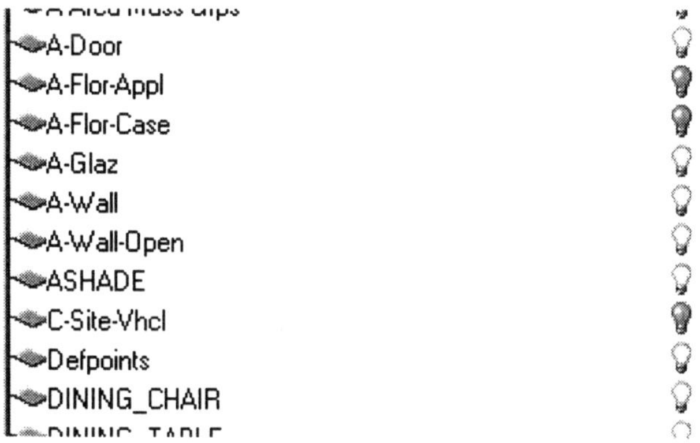

Freeze the layers used by the Space Planning items:

S-Flor-Appl
A-Flor-Case
I-Furn
C-Site-Vhcl
P-Flor-Fixt

4.  Select the **Snapshots** tool.

5. 

Select **New**.

6. 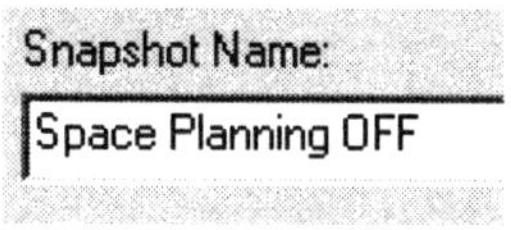

In the Snapshot Name field, type **Space Planning OFF**.

   Press **OK**.

7.

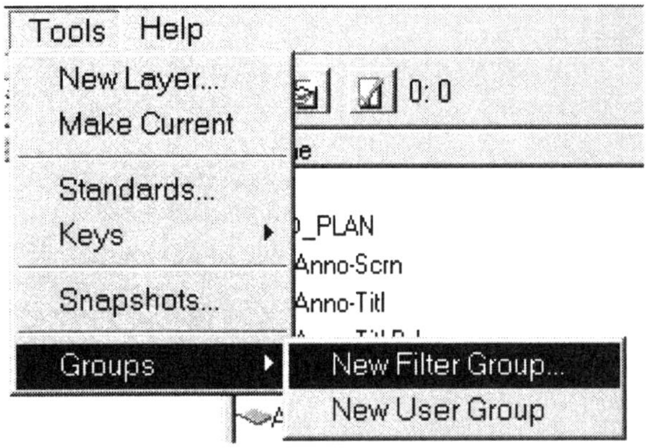

Go to **Tools→Groups→New Filter Group.**

8.

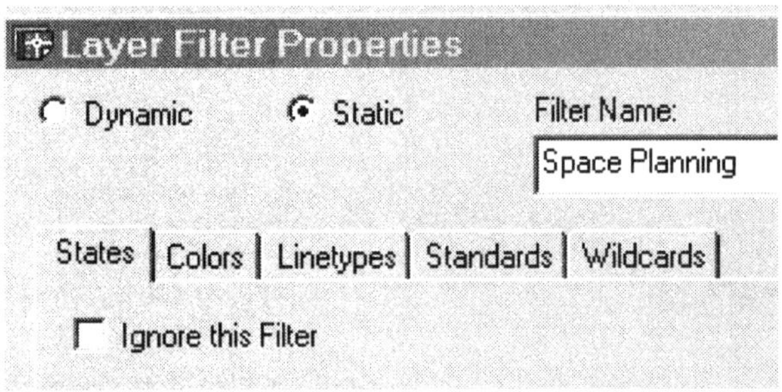

Enable **Static.**
In the Filter Name field, type **Space Planning.**
Disable **Ignore this Filter.**

Press **OK.**

9.

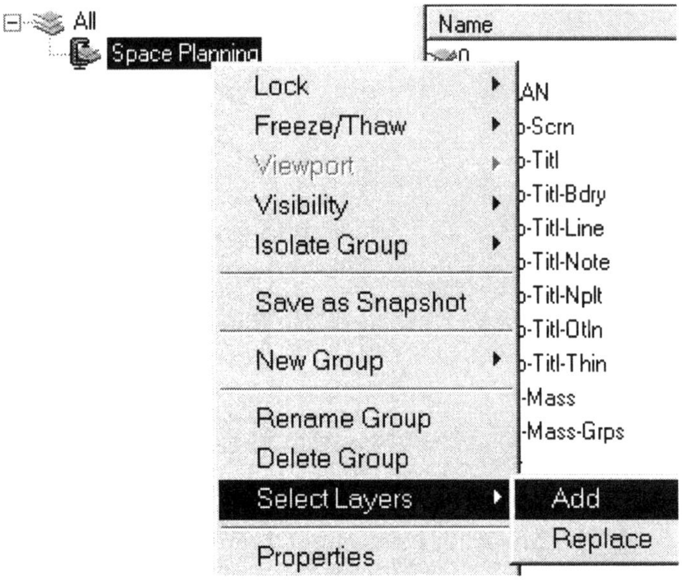

Select the Space Planning filter.
Right click and select **Select Layers→Add.**

10.

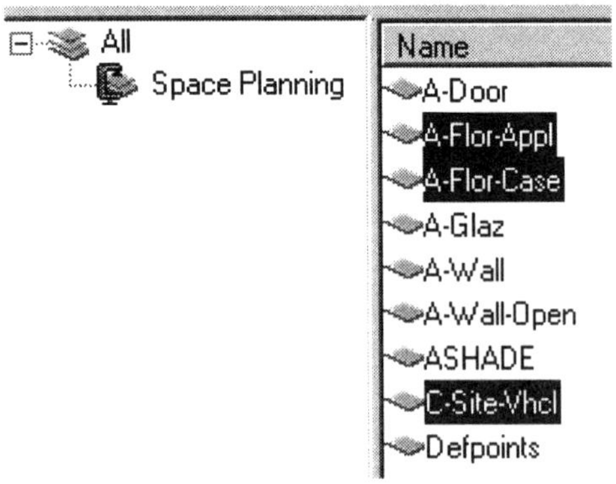

Select **All** so that all layer names are visible.

Control-Select all the layer names associated with the space planning items.
Drag and drop them over to the Space Planning folder.

11. 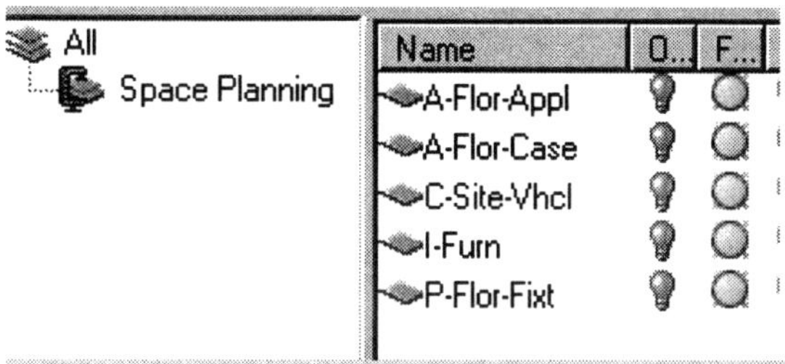

If you select Space Planning, you should see all the layers assigned to this group.

12. 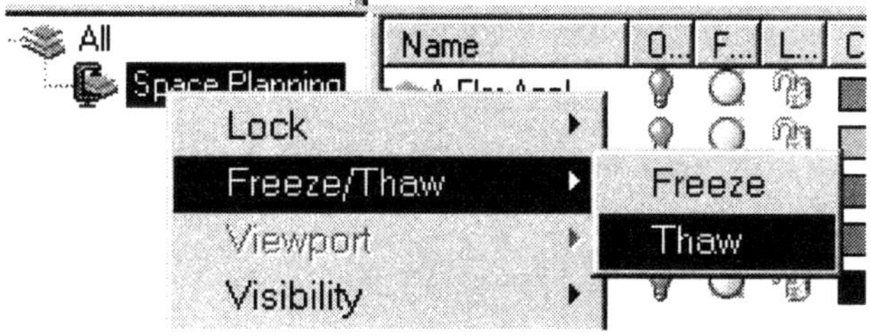

Select the **Space Planning** group.
Right click and select **Freeze/Thaw→Thaw.**

Close the dialog.

All the space planning items are now visible.

13. Save as *ex4-5.dwg*.

Notes:

Lesson 5
Roofs

Roofs can be created with single or double slopes, with or without gable ends, and with or without overhangs. Once you input all your roof settings, you simply pick the points around the perimeter of the building to define your roof outline. If you make an error, you can easily modify or redefine your roof.

You need to pick three points before the roof will begin to preview in your graphics window. There is no limit to the number of points to select to define the perimeter.

To create a gable roof, uncheck the gable box in the Roof dialog. Pick the two end points for the sloped portion of the roof. Turn on the Gable box. Pick the end point for the gable side. Turn off the Gable box. Pick the end point for the sloped side. Turn the Gable box on. Pick the viewport and then press ENTER. A Gable cannot be defined with more than three consecutive edges.

Roofs can be created using two methods: ROOFADD places a roof based on points selected or ROOFCONVERT which converts a closed polyline or closed walls to develop a roof.

TIP: If you opt to use ROOFCONVERT and use existing closed walls, be sure that the walls are intersecting properly. If your walls are not properly cleaned up with each other, the roof conversion is unpredictable.

TIP: The Plate Height of a roof should be set equal to the Wall Height.

Shape – Select the Shape option on the command line by typing 'S.'	Single Slope – Extends a roof plane at an angle from the Plate Height.	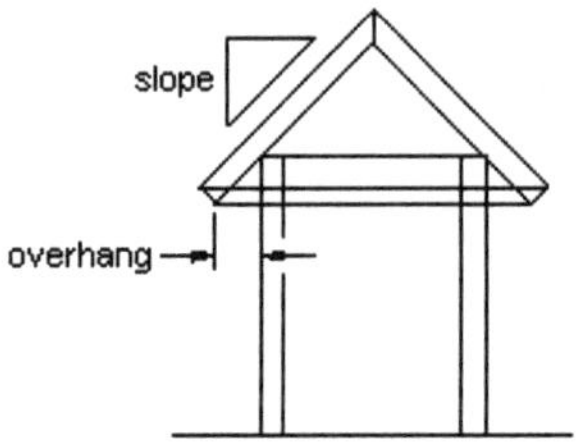 end elevation view
	Double Slope – Includes a single slope and adds another slope, which begins at the intersection of the first slope and the height specified for the first slope.	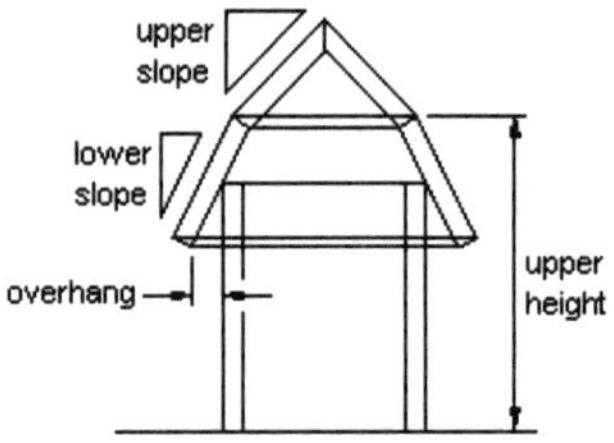 end elevation view
Gable – Select the Gable option on the command line by typing 'G.'	If this is enabled, turns off the slope of the roof place. To create a gable edge, select Gable prior to identifying the first corner of the gable end. Turn off gable to continue to create the roof.	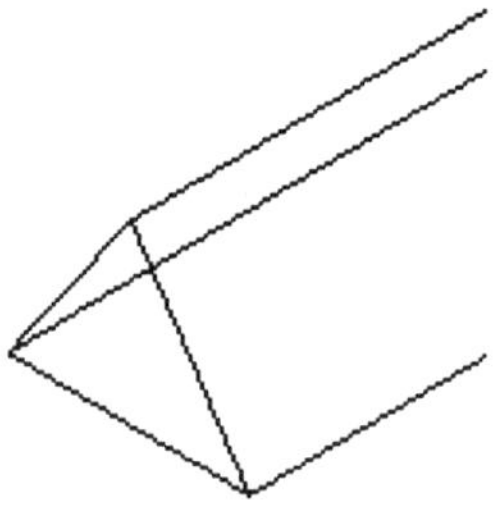 gable roof end
Plate Height – Set the Plate Height on the command line by typing 'PH.'	Specify the top plate from which the roof plane is projected. The height is relative to the XY plane with a Z coordinate of 0.	
Rise– Set the Rise on the command line by typing 'PR.'	Sets the angle of the roof based on a run value of 12	A rise value of 5 creates a 5/12 roof, which forms a slope angle of 22.62 degrees.
Slope – Set the Slope on the command line by typing 'PS.'	Angle of the roof rise from the horizontal.	If slope angles are entered, then the rise will automatically be calculated.
Upper Height - Set the Upper Height on the command line by typing 'UH.'	This is only available if a Double Slope roof is being created. This is the height where the second slope will start.	

Rise (upper) - Set the Upper Rise on the command line by typing 'UR.'	This is only available if a Double Slope roof is being created. This is the slope angle for the second slope.	A rise value of 5 creates a 5/12 roof, which forms a slope angle of 22.62 degrees.
Slope (upper) - Set the Upper Slope on the command line by typing 'US.'	This is only available if a Double Slope roof is being created. Defines the slope angle for the second slope.	If an upper rise value is set, this is automatically calculated.
Overhang- To enable on the command line, type 'O.' To set the value of the Overhang, type 'V.'	If enabled, extends the roofline down from the plate height by the value set.	
	The Floating Viewer opens a viewer window displaying a preview of the roof.	
	The match button allows you to select an existing roof to match its properties.	
	The properties button opens the Roof Properties dialog.	
	The Undo button allows you to undo the last roof operation. You can step back as many operations as you like up to the start.	
	Opens the Roof Help file.	

TIP: You can create a gable on a roof by gripping any ridgeline point and stretching it past the roof edge. You cannot make a gable into a hip using grips.

Exercise 5-1:

Creating a Roof using Existing Walls

Drawing Name: ex4-5.dwg
Estimated Time: 15 minutes

This exercise reinforces the following skills:

- Convert to Roof

1.  Open *ex4-4.dwg.*
   Select the Work tab.
   Activate the right viewport that shows the top view.

2. Freeze the equipment and furnishings layers to save screen regen time.

    Select the **Layer Manager** tool.

   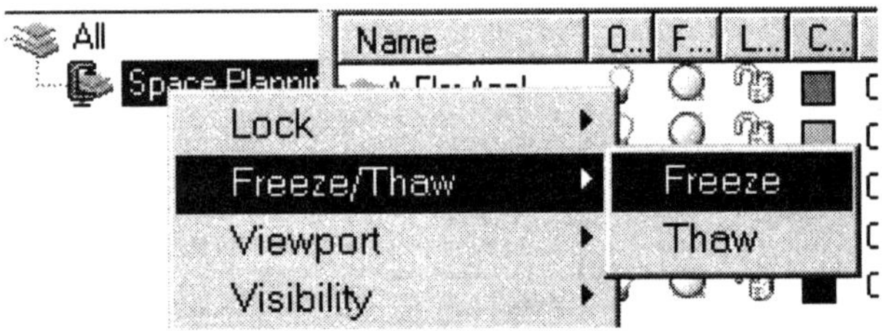

   Select the **Space Planning** group.

   Right click and select **Freeze/Thaw→Freeze.**

   Press **OK**.

3.  Launch the Tool Palette.

4. 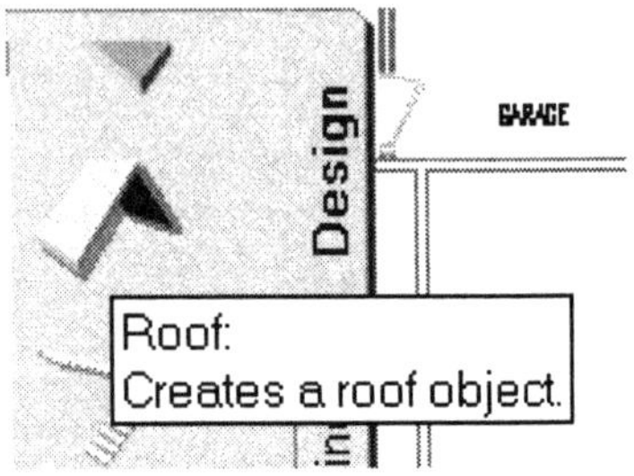

   Select the Design tab.
   Select the Roof tool.

5. Right click and select Apply Tool Properties to→Linework and Walls.

6. Select all the exterior walls in the drawing. You can select using a window for the entire building. (This selection method is applicable for this command – do not assume it will work for all commands.)

   Press Enter to continue.

Enter **NO** to retain the layout geometry.

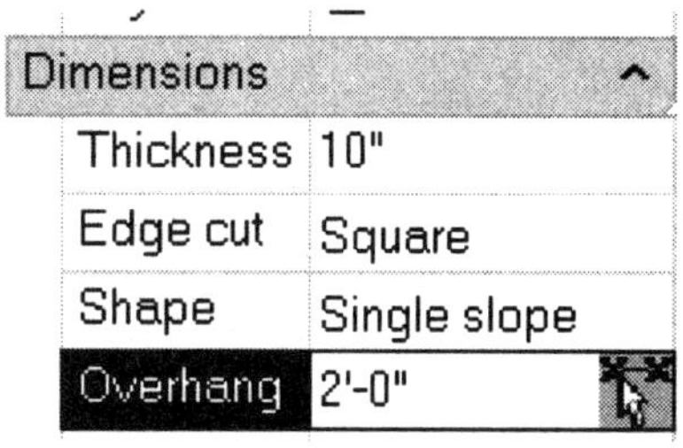

Expand the Dimensions section.
Set the Thickness to **10″**.
Set the Shape to **Single slope**.
Set the Overhang to **2′-0″**.

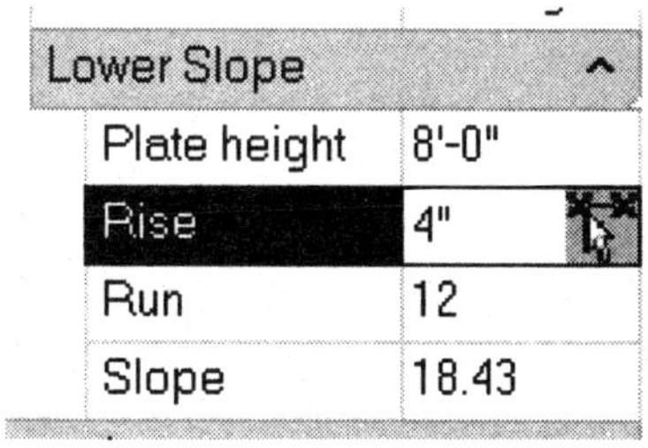

Expand the Lower Slope section.
Set the Plate height to **8′-0″**.
Set the Rise to **4″**.

7. Close the Properties dialog.
   Switch to paper space so you can see your roof in both viewports.

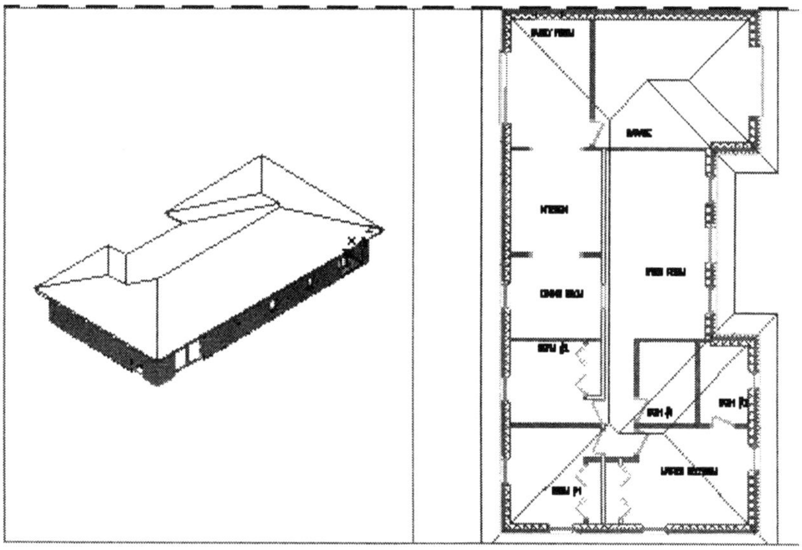

8. Save as *ex5-1.dwg*.

Exercise 5-2:
Roof Slabs

Drawing Name: ex5-1.dwg
Estimated Time: 15 minutes

This exercise reinforces the following skills:

- Convert to Roof
- Roof Slab Tools

Our roof works, but strictly speaking we can make it better with a couple of changes around the chimney. ADT allows us to cut holes through roofs (to allow for vents, chimneys and skylights), and to add other faces or subsidiary roofs such as dormers.

In order to edit a roof you have to convert it to Roof Slabs.

1.  Open *ex5-1.dwg.*
Select the Work tab.
Activate the left viewport that shows the isometric view.

2. 

Select the roof.

Right click and select **Convert to Roof Slabs.**
At the 'Erase layout geometry?' prompt type **Y,** then enter.
At the next prompt hit enter to accept the Standard roof slab type.
The Roof Slab Properties dialog appears.
Close it.

The roof will change appearance slightly. It now consists of individual slabs on the A-Roof-Slab layer.

3.

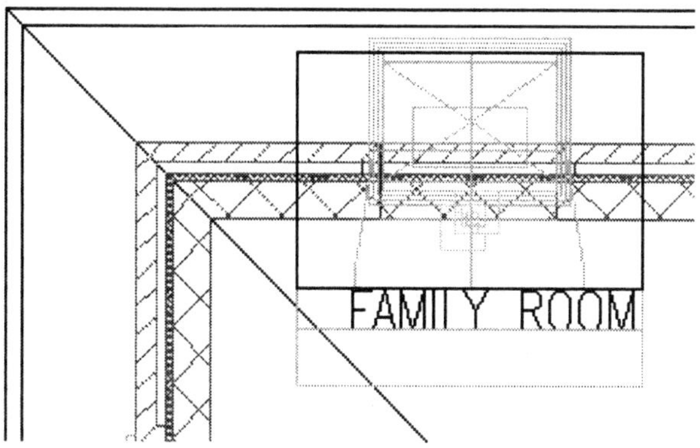

Activate the right viewport. Zoom into the area where the chimney is located.

Draw a rectangle over the outline of the chimney.

4.

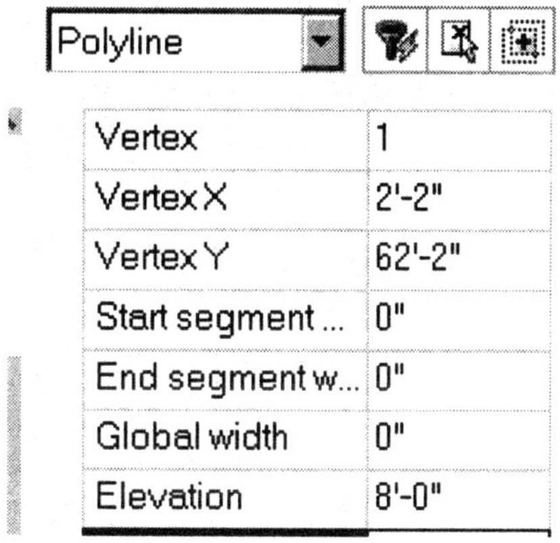

Select the rectangle.
Right click and select **Properties**.
Set the Elevation to **8′-0″.**

Close the Properties dialog.
Deselect the rectangle.

5.

Freeze the **A-Area-Mass-Grps** layer.
This is the layer the chimney is on.

6.

Select the roof slab located on top of the chimney.
Right click and select **Hole→Add**.

7. At the next prompt pick the rectangle. Be careful where you pick so you don't pick walls or furniture, which you can't see below the roof.
At the 'Erase Layout Geometry?' prompt hit, right click and select **Yes**.

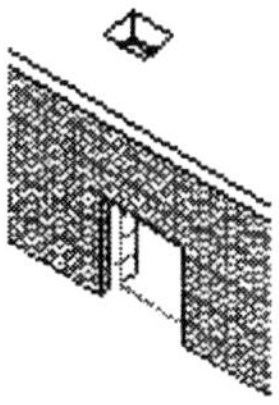

The hole will appear.

8. 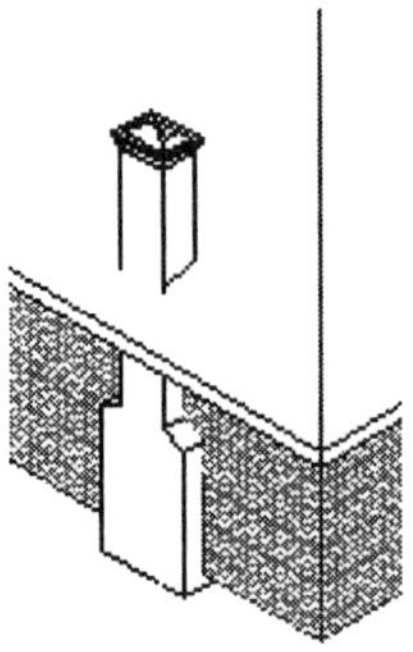

Thaw the **A-Area-Mass-Grps** layer.

Remember we see the mass elements as well as the mass groups.

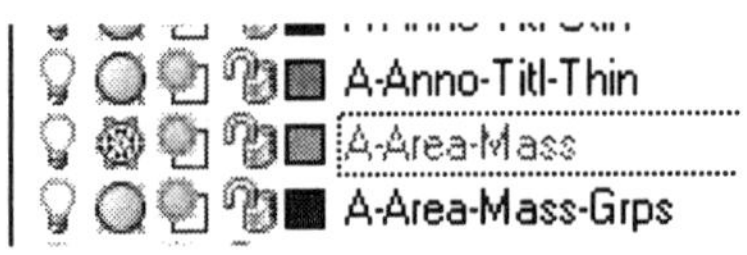

Freeze the **A-Area-Mass** layer.

The chimney now appears OK.

Our roof as it exists has one problem at the chimney. The 'uphill' side of the chimney will catch water and snow. It needs a tiny little roof gable, called a cricket, to divert water away from the chimney.

9. Save as *ex5-2.dwg.*

Exercise 5-3:

Creating a Roof Cricket

Drawing Name: ex5-2.dwg
Estimated Time: 30 minutes

This exercise reinforces the following skills:

- Layer User Groups
- Make Layer Current
- Isolate Layer Group

1.  Open *ex5-2.dwg.*

Creating a Layer User Group

2.  Select the **Layer Manager** tool.

3. 

Select **All**.
Right click and select **New Group→User.**

4. 

Rename the group **Roof**.

5. 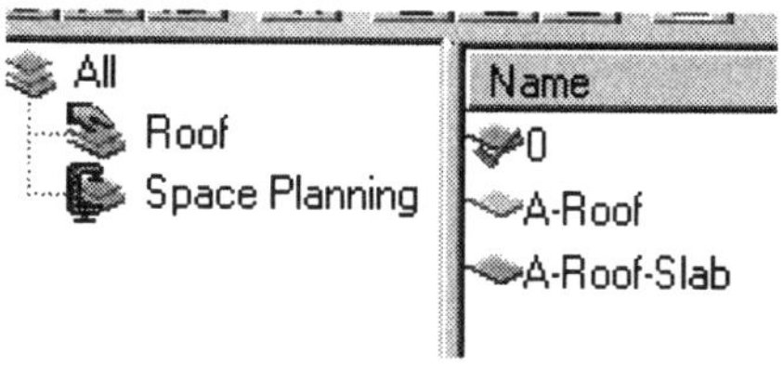

Place the layers 0, A-Roof, and A-Roof-Slab in that group.

Make Layer Current

6. Select layer **0**.

Right click and select **Make Current.**

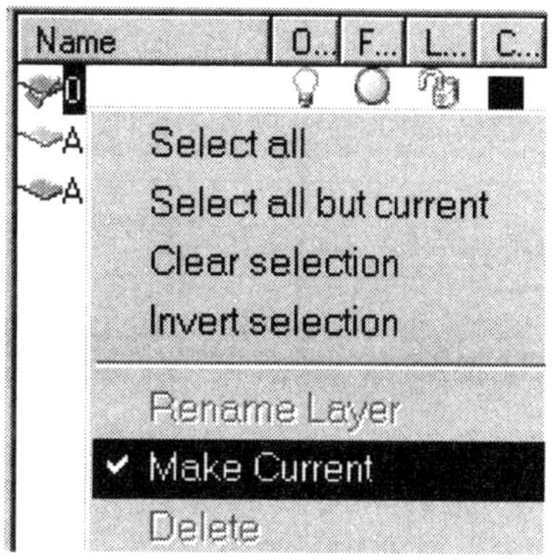

Isolate Group

Isolate the layer group so you only see those layers.

7. 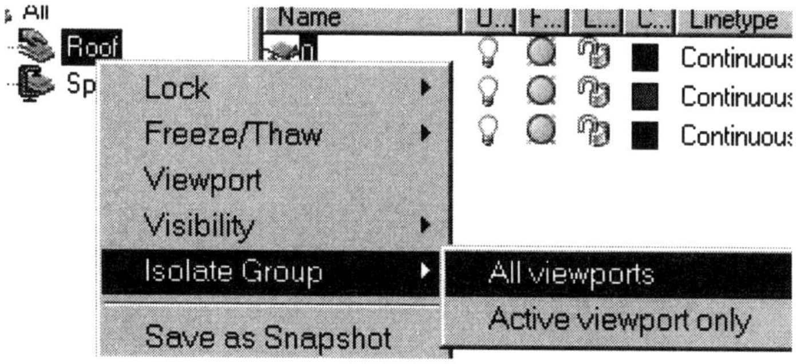

Select the Roof group. Right click and select **Isolate Group→All Viewports.**

Press **OK** to close the Layer Manager.

8. 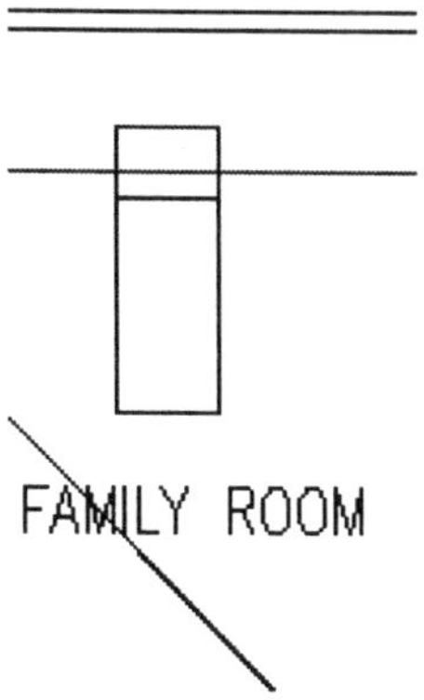

Draw a rectangle 1′6″ wide by 36″ long, using the SE corner of the roof hole as the start point and going away from the hole.

9.  Launch the Tool Palette.

10. 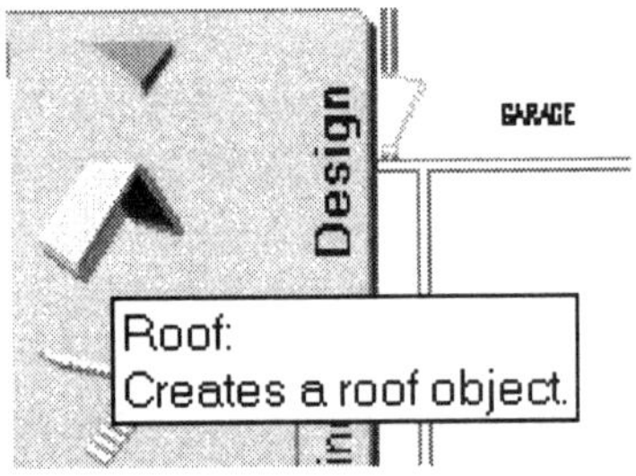

Select the Design tab.
Select the Roof tool.

11. Right click and select Apply Tool Properties to→Linework and Walls.

12. 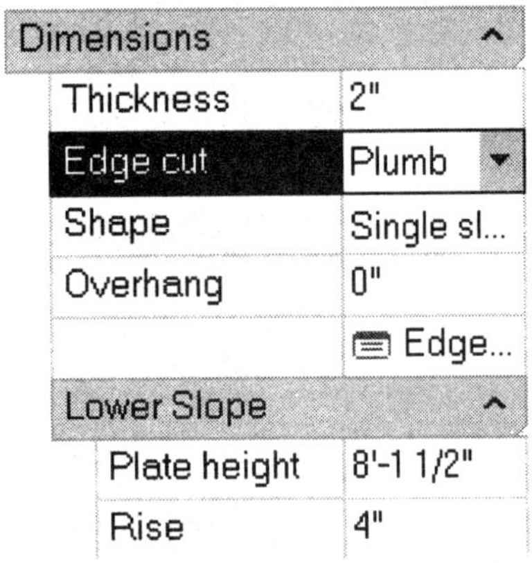

Pick the polyline (you can type 'l' for 'last' at the Select Objects prompt) and hit enter. Right click and select **No** for the 'Erase layout geometry?' prompt.

Sett the Thickness to **2″**.
Set the Edge cut to **Plumb**.
Set the Overhang to **0″**.
Accept the plate height.
Make the rise **4″**.
Close the Properties dialog.

13. 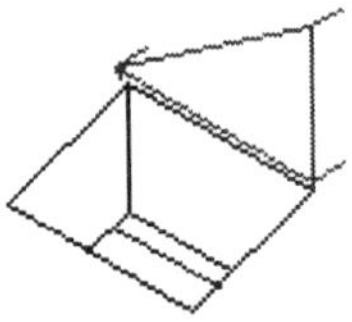

Move the cricket into position so it is aligned with the opening on the top of the roof.

14. The new roof is hipped. Grip edit its ridge to make the exposed face a gable. Pick the vertex of the triangle and stretch so it is aligned with the top horizontal line to create the gable.

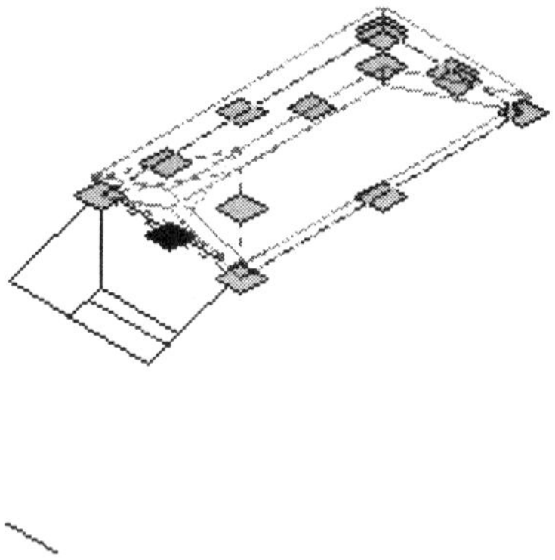

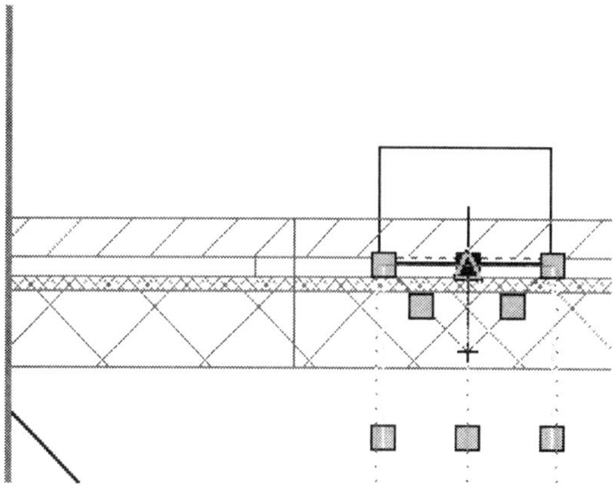

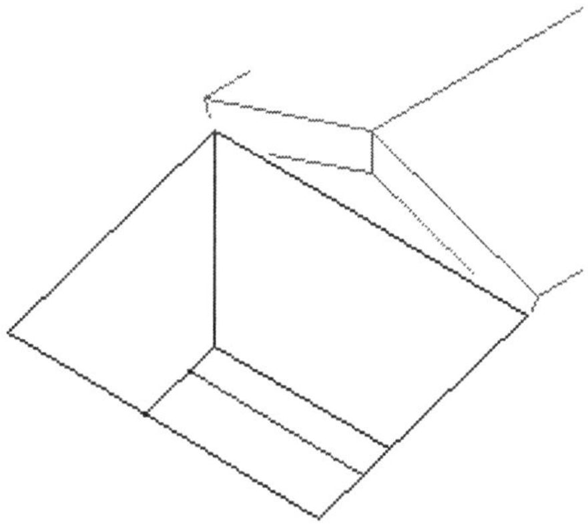

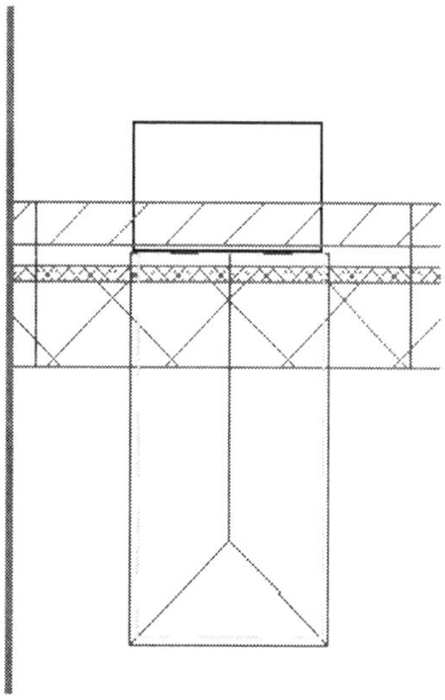

15. Turn on any layers you may have turned off for visibility, including the chimney.

Here's a shaded view from the other direction

Save as ex5-3.dwg.

Notes:

QUIZ 3

True or False

1. Custom content can be located in any subdirectory and still function properly.
2. The sole purpose of the Space Planning process is to arrange furniture in a floor plan.
3. The Design Center only has 3D objects stored in the Content area because ADT is a strictly 3D software.
4. Appliances are automatically placed on the APPLIANCE layer.
5. When you place a wall cabinet, it is automatically placed at the specified height.
6. You can create tools on a tool palette by dragging and dropping the objects from the Design Center onto the palette.

Multiple Choice

7. A residential structure is divided into:

   A. Four basic areas
   B. Three basic areas
   C. Two basic areas
   D. One basic area

8. Kitchen cabinets are located in the _______________ subfolder.

   A. Casework
   B. Cabinets
   C. Bookcases
   D. Furniture

9. Select the area type that is NOT part of a private residence:

   A. Bedrooms
   B. Common Areas
   C. Service Areas
   D. Public Areas

10. To set the layer properties of a tool on a tool palette:

    A. Use the Layer Manager
    B. Select the tool, right click and select Properties.
    C. Launch the Properties dialog
    D. All of the above

11. Vehicles placed from the Design Center are automatically placed on this layer:

    A. A-Site-Vhcl
    B. A-Vhcl
    C. C-Site Vhcl
    D. None of the above

12. Layer Filter User groups are used to:

    A. Set the visibility of a set of layers.
    B. Set the display of the layer list
    C. Set the properties of layers
    D. All of the above

13. The **Roof** tool is located on this tool palette:

    A. DESIGN
    B. GENERAL DRAFTING
    C. MASSING
    D. TOOLS

ANSWERS:

1) T; 2) F; 3) F; 4) F; 5) T; 6) T; 7) B; 8) A; 9) D; 10) B; 11) C; 12) D; 13) A

Lesson 6
Structural Members

Architectural documentation for residential construction will always include plans (top views) of each floor of a building, showing features and structural information of the floor platform itself. Walls are located on the plan but not shown in structural detail.

Wall sections and details are used to show:
- the elements within walls (exterior siding, sheathing, block, brick or wood studs, insulation, air cavities, interior sheathing, trim)
- how walls relate to floors, ceilings, roofs, eaves,
- openings within the walls (doors/windows with their associated sills and headers)
- how walls relate to openings in floors (stairs).

Stick-framed (stud) walls usually have their framing patterns determined by the carpenters on site. Once window and door openings are located on the plan, and stud spacing is specified by the designer (or the local building code), the specific arrangement of vertical members is usually left to the fabricators and not drafted, except where specific structural details require explanation.

The structural members in framed floors that have to hold themselves and/or other walls and floors up are usually drafted as framing plans. Designers must specify the size and spacing of joists or trusses, beams and columns. Plans show the orientation and relation of members, locate openings through the floor and show support information for openings and other specific conditions.

In the next exercises, we shall create a floor framing plan. Since the ground floor of our one-story lesson house has already been defined as a concrete slab, we'll assume that the ground level slopes down at the rear of the house and create a wood deck at the sliding door to the family room. The deck will need a railing for safety.

Autodesk Architectural Desktop includes a Structural Member Catalog that allows you to easily access industry-standard structural shapes. To create most standard column, brace, and beam styles, you can access the Structural Member Catalog, select a structural member shape, and create a style that contains the shape that you selected. The shape, similar to an AEC profile, is a 2D cross-section of a structural member. When you create a structural member with a style that you created from the Structural Member Catalog, you define the path to extrude the shape along.

You can create your own structural shapes that you can add to existing structural members, or use to create new structural members. The design rules in a structural member style allow you to add these custom shapes to a structural member, as well as create custom structural members from more than one shape.

All the columns, braces, and beams that you create are sub-types of a single Structural Member object type. The styles that you create for columns, braces, and beams have the same Structural Member Styles style type as well. When you change the display or style of a structural member, use the Structural Member object in the Display Manager and the Structural Member Styles style type in the Style Manager.

If you are operating with the AIA layering system as your current layer standard, when you create members or convert AutoCAD entities to structural members using the menu picks or toolbars, Architectural Desktop assigns the new members to layers: A-Cols, A-Cols-Brce or A-Beam, respectively. If Generic Architectural Desktop is your standard, the layers used are A_Columns, A_Beams and A_Braces. If your layer standard is Current Layer, new entities come in on the current layer, as in plain vanilla AutoCAD.

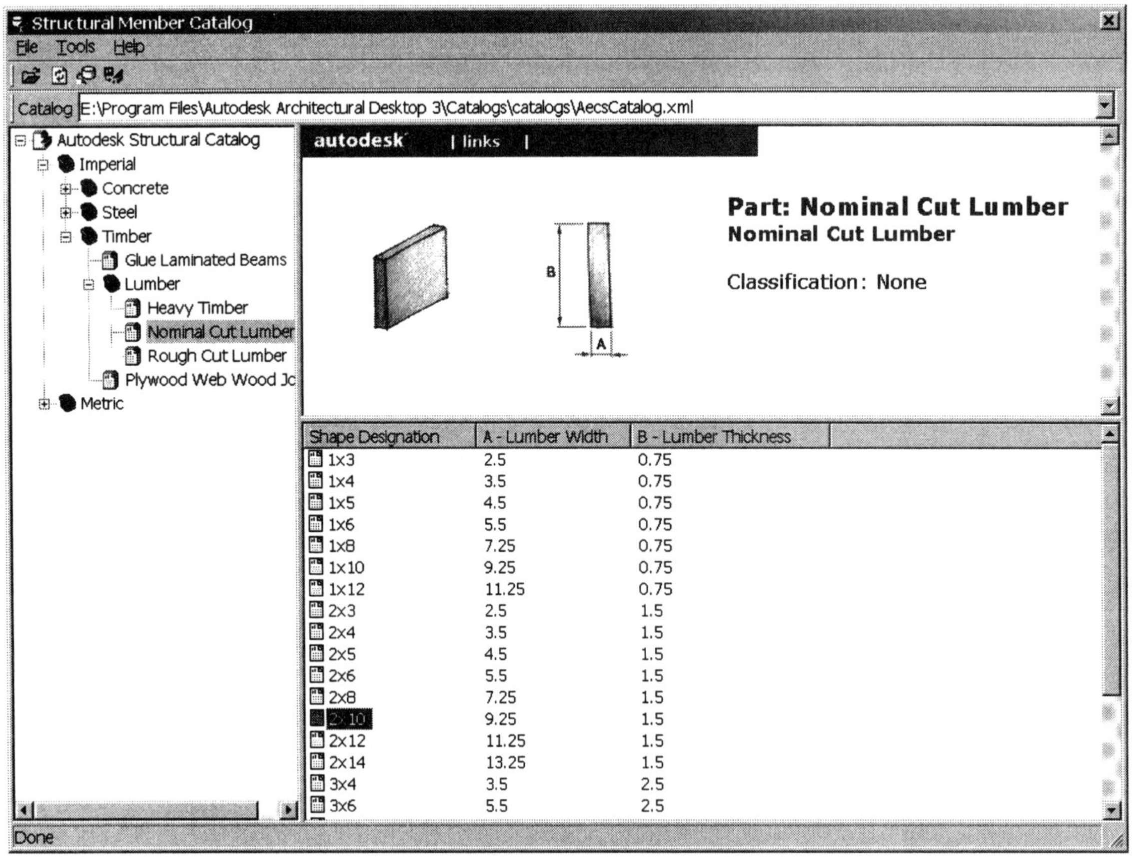

The Structural Member Catalog includes specifications for standard structural shapes. You can choose shapes from the Structural Member Catalog, and generate styles for structural members that you create in your drawings.

The left pane of the Structural Member Catalog contains a hierarchical tree view. Several industry standard catalogs are organized in the tree, first by imperial or metric units, and then by material.

	Open a catalog file - The default is the catalog that comes with ADT, but you can create your own custom catalog. The default catalog is located in the following directory path: \\Program Files\Autodesk Architectural Desktop R3\Catalogs\catalogs.
	Refresh Data
	Locate Catalog item based on an existing member – allows you to select a member in a drawing and then locates it in your catalog.
	Generate Member Style – allows you to create a style to be used.

Exercise 6-1:

Creating Member Styles

Drawing Name: ex5-3.dwg
Estimated Time: 15 minutes

This exercise reinforces the following skills:

- Creating Member Styles
- Use of Structural Members tools

1.  Open *ex5-3.dwg.*
Select the Work tab.
Activate the right viewport.

Create a User Filter Group

2.  Select the **Layer Manager** tool.

3. 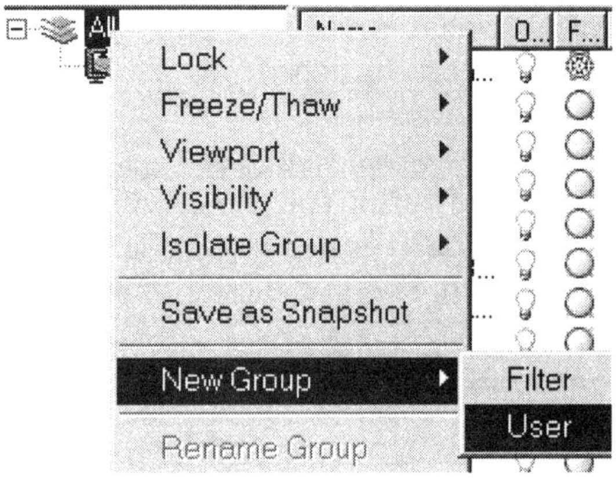

Select **All**.
Right click and select
New Group→User.

4. Set Layer 0 as current.

A green checkmark next to the layer name indicates it is current.

5. 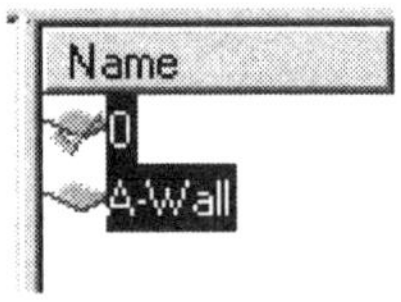

Add layers **0** and **A-Wall** to the **Deck Framing** user group.

6. 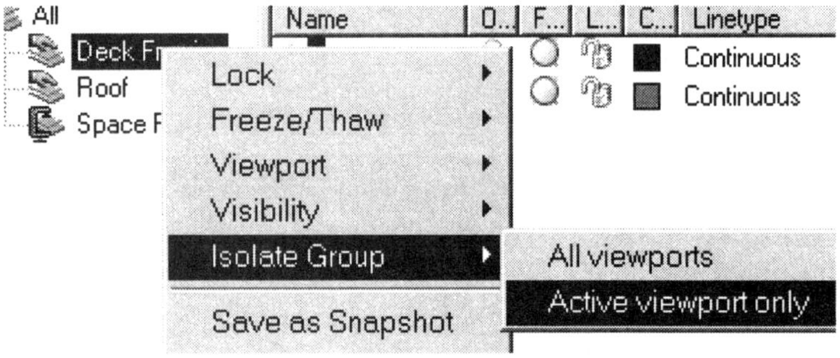

Pick the Deck Framing group name, right click and pick **Isolate Group→ Active Viewport only.**
Click **OK**.

We will be adding a wood framed deck, 14′ x 9′, to the back of the house. For purposes of this exercise we will assume that the ground level is 12″ below the slab at the back of the house and falls away so that grade level below the edge of the deck away from the house is 6′ below floor level: -6′-0″ a.f.f. (above finish floor) in architectural notation. We will place the top of the deck floorboards even with the top of the floor slab.

We will use support and rim joists as in standard wood floor framing, and they will all be at the same level, rather than joists crossing a support beam below. In practice this means the use of metal hangers, which will not be drawn. Once the floor system is drawn we will add support columns at the outside rim joist and braces at the columns.

Creating Structural Member Styles

7. 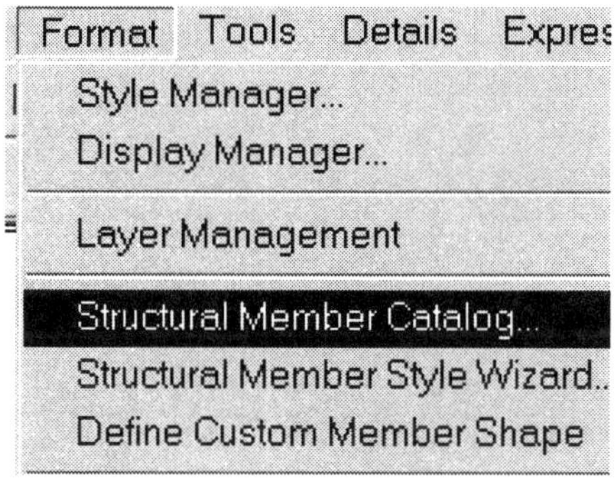

Go to Format→Structural Member Catalog.

8. 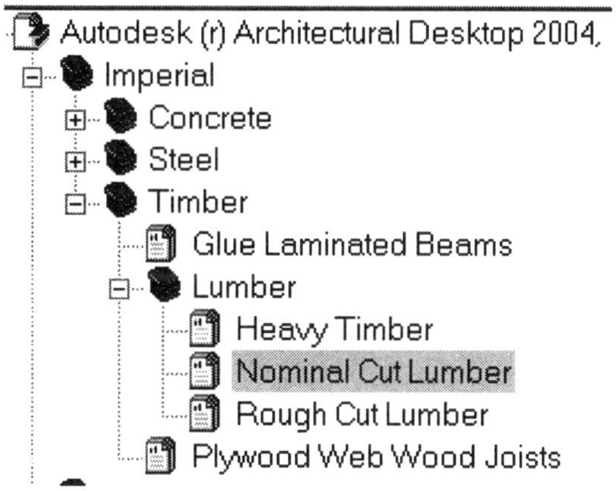

Browse to the *Imperial\Timer\Lumber\ Nominal Cut Lumber* folder.

9. 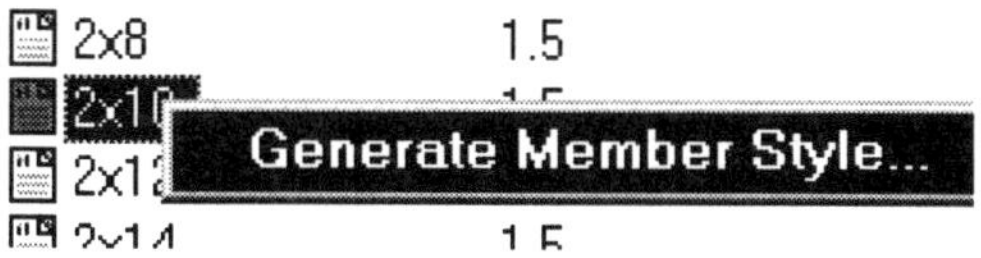

Locate the **2x10** shape designation. Right click and select **Generate Member Style.**

10. 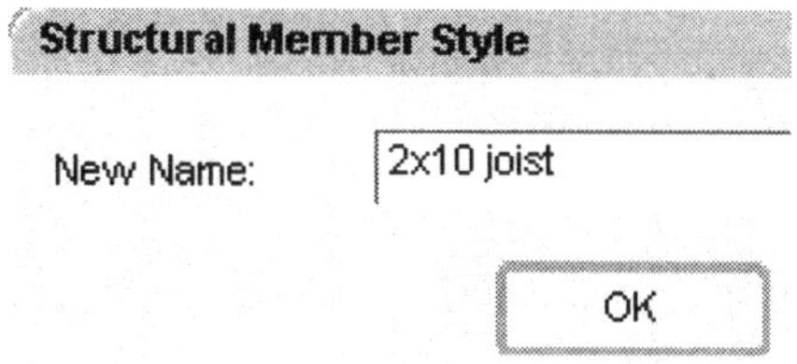

In the Structural Member Style dialog box, type **2x10 joist** - the name for your style, Click **OK**.

A style that contains the catalog shape that you selected is created. You can view the style in the Style Manager, create a new structural member from the style, or apply the style to an existing member.

When you add a structural member to your drawing, the shape inside the style that you created defines the shape of the member. You define the length, justification, roll or rise, and start and end offsets of the structural member when you draw it.

You cannot use the following special characters in your style names:

- less-than and greater-than symbols (< >)
- forward slashes and backslashes (/ \)

- quotation marks (")
- colons (:)
- semicolons (;)
- question marks (?)
- commas (,)
- asterisks (*)
- vertical bars (|)
- equal signs (=)
- backquotes (`)
-

11. 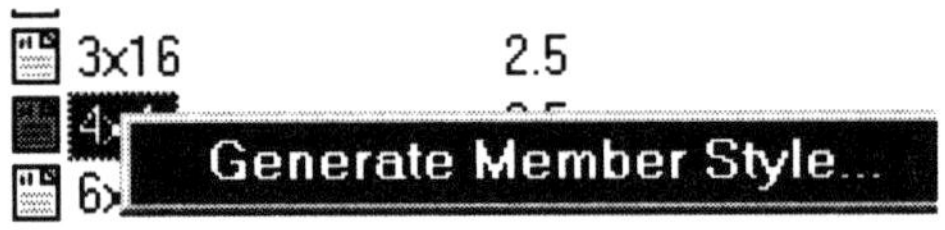

Locate the **4x4** Shape Designation. Right click and select **Generate Member Style.**

12. 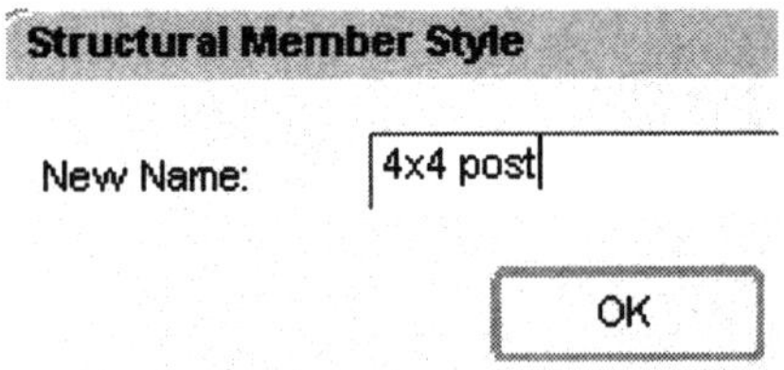

Type **4x4 post** in the New Name field. Press **OK.**

13. 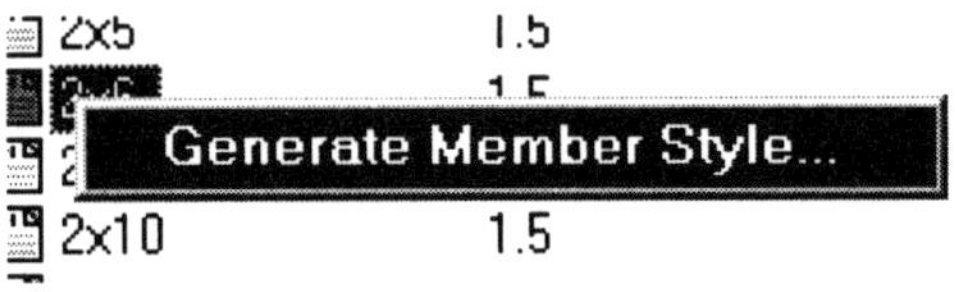

Select the **2x6** Shape Designation. Right click and select **Generate Member Style.**

14. 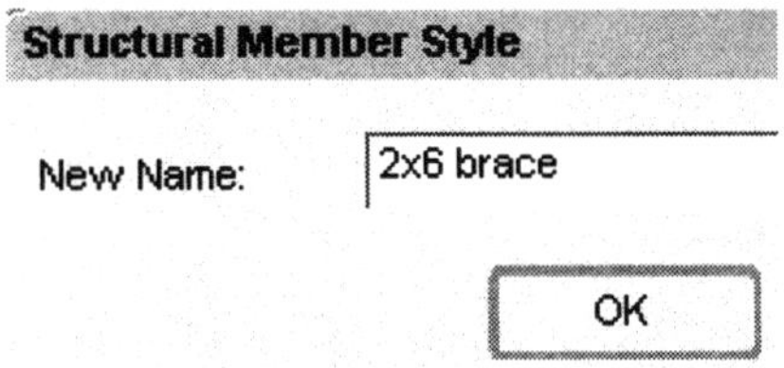

Type **2x6 brace** in the New Name field. Close the catalog.

15.  Launch the Tool Palette.

16. 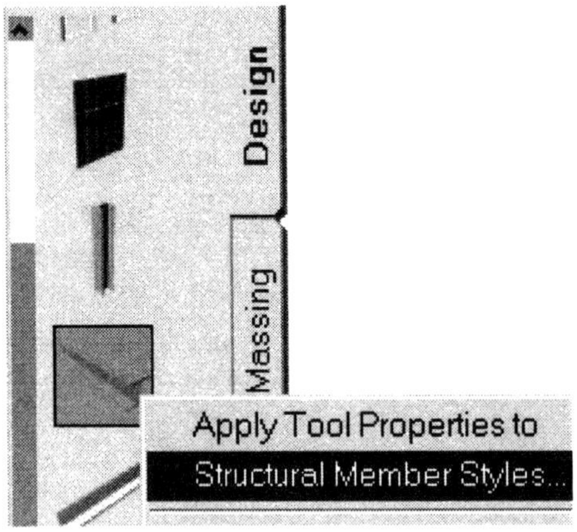

Select the Design tab.

Select the Structural Beam tool. Right click and select **Structural Member Styles.**

17. 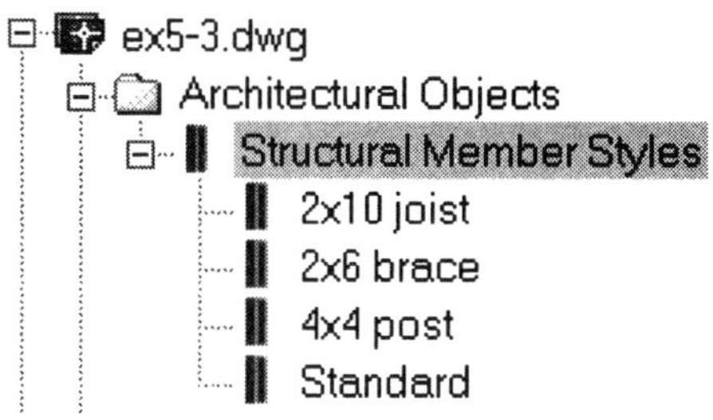

Under Architectural Objects, expand the Structural Member Styles.

We see the styles we just created.

Close the Style Manager dialog.

18. Save as *ex6-1.dwg.*

Exercise 6-2:
Adding Structural Members

Drawing Name: ex6-2.dwg
Estimated Time: 15 minutes

This exercise reinforces the following skills:

- Creating Member Styles
- Use of Structural Members tools

1.  Open *ex6-1.dwg.*
Select the Work tab.
Activate the right viewport.

2. 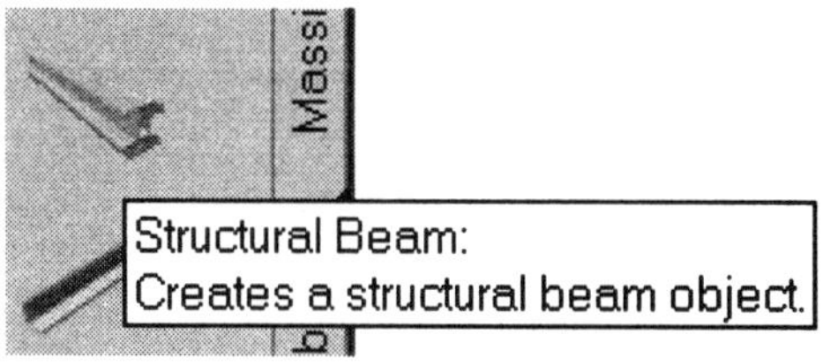

Select the Structural Beam tool on the Design Palette.

3. 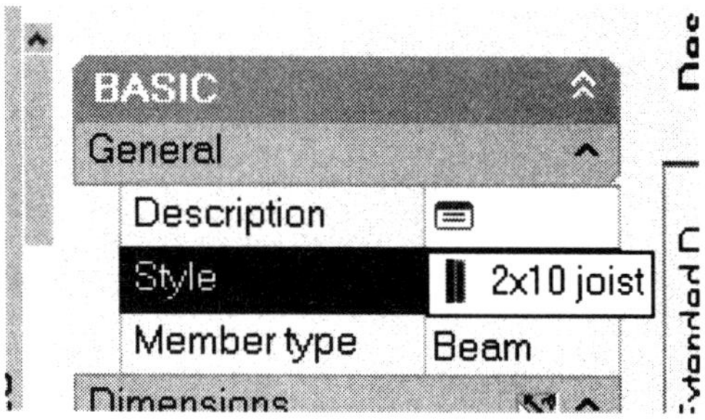

Select the 2x10 joist from the Style drop-down.

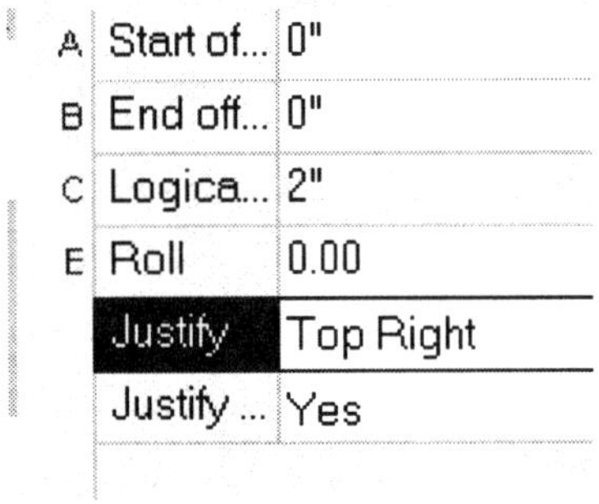

Set Justify to Top Right.
Set the Roll to 0.
Set the Start Offset to 0″.

Zoom into the family room area (the top left of the floor plan).

4. Use the From Osnap, pick the upper left corner of the house wall, and type '@1.5<-90' for the Offset; Press ENTER.
This shifts the first beam slightly below the wall.

Pull the cursor down at a 270° angle, and type in 13′-9″ for the length.
DO NOT EXIT THE COMMAND.

```
Command: _AecsBeamAdd
Start point or [STyle/STArt offset/ENd offset/Justify/Roll/Match]: _from Base
point: <Offset>: @1.5<-90

End point or [STyle/STArt offset/ENd offset/Justify/Roll/Match]: 13'-9"

End point or [STyle/STArt offset/ENd offset/Justify/Roll/Match/Undo]:
```

5. Change the Justification to Top Left.
Pull the cursor to the left (180°) and enter 9′ for the length.

Hit enter to terminate the command:

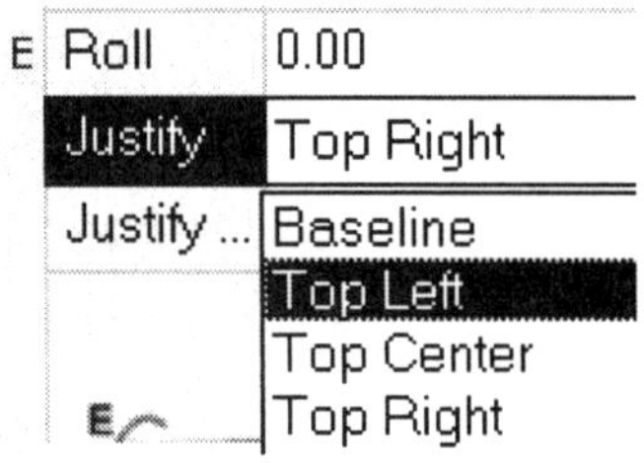

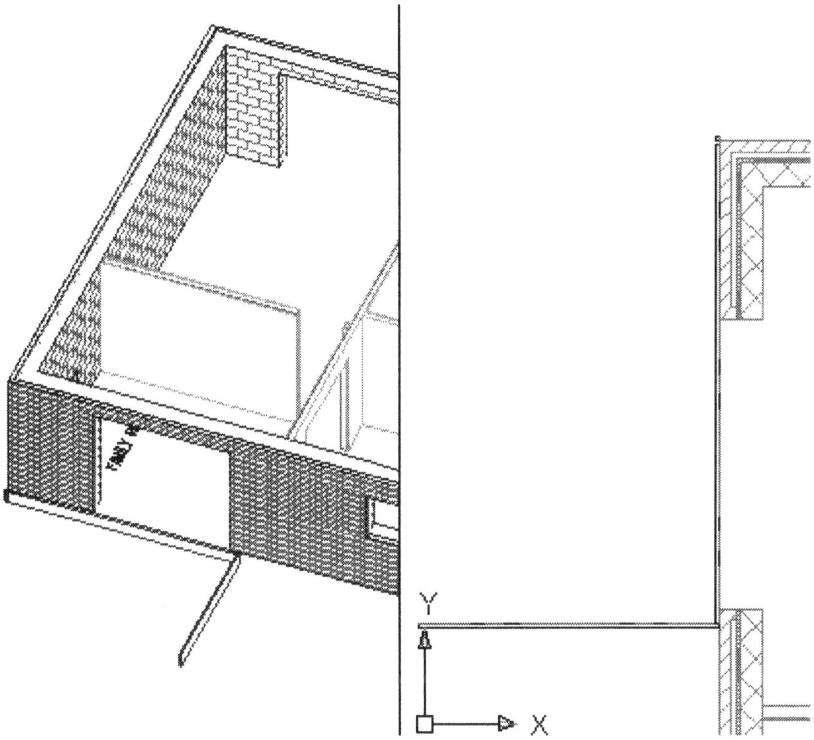

6. 

Mirror the first joist. (Use the Midpoint Osnap with Polar or Ortho.)

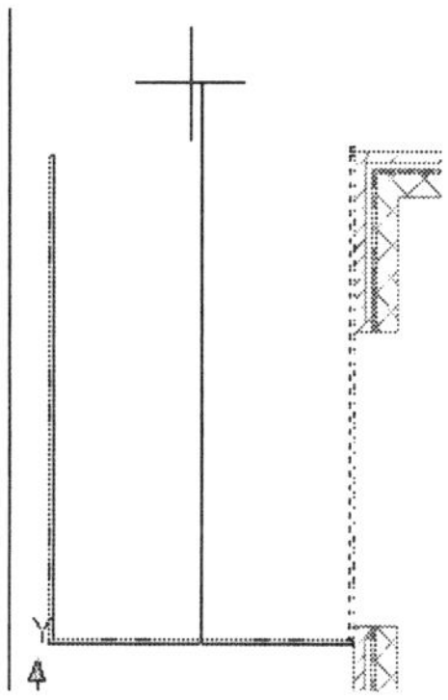

7. 

Mirror the second from bottom to top (use the Midpoint Osnap with Polar or Ortho) to finish the outside of the frame:

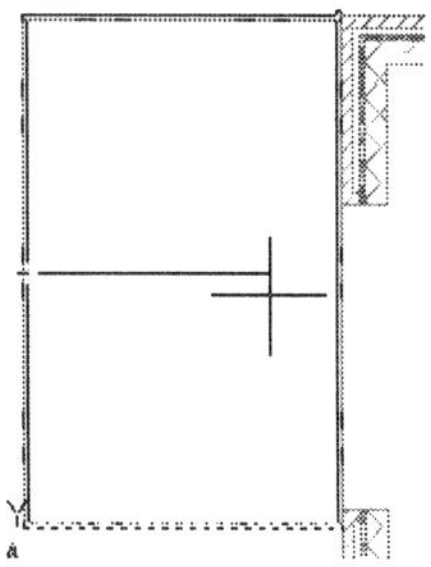

8. 

Copy the left (outside) joist 1.5″ to the right to form a beam to support the rest of the joists we are about to create.

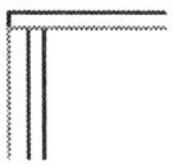

9. 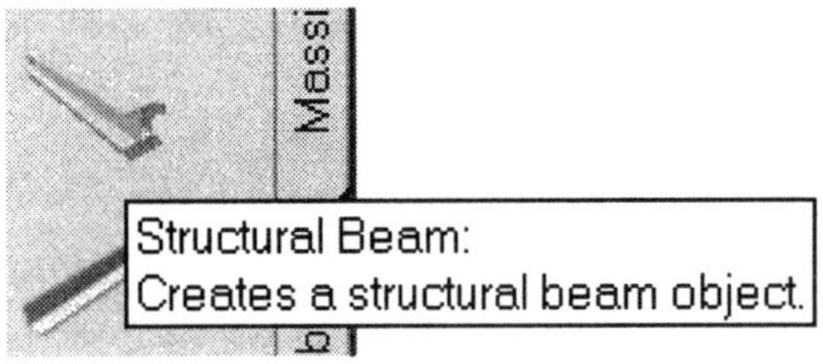

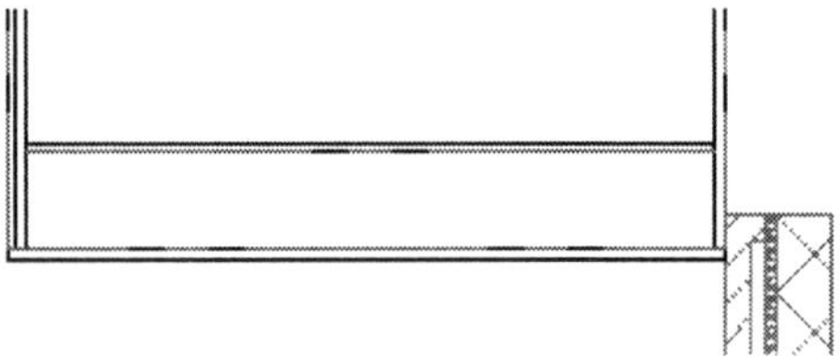

Select the Structural Beam tool from the Design Palette.
Sketch the beam horizontally between the two vertical beams.

10. Move the new joist 13.75″ up, so that the center of it is 1′-4″ from the bottom edge of the bottom horizontal joist.

TIP: Starting a 16″ spacing from one edge to centers minimizes waste when using flooring (boards or sheets of sub floor) in nominal 4′ increments. The same patterning usually holds for wall studs and drywall.

11. Use a rectangular array to copy the last joist 10 times at a 16″ distance to finish the floor joist framing:

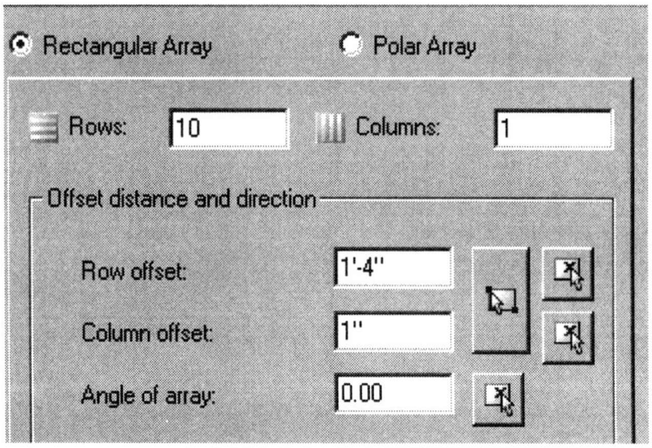

12.

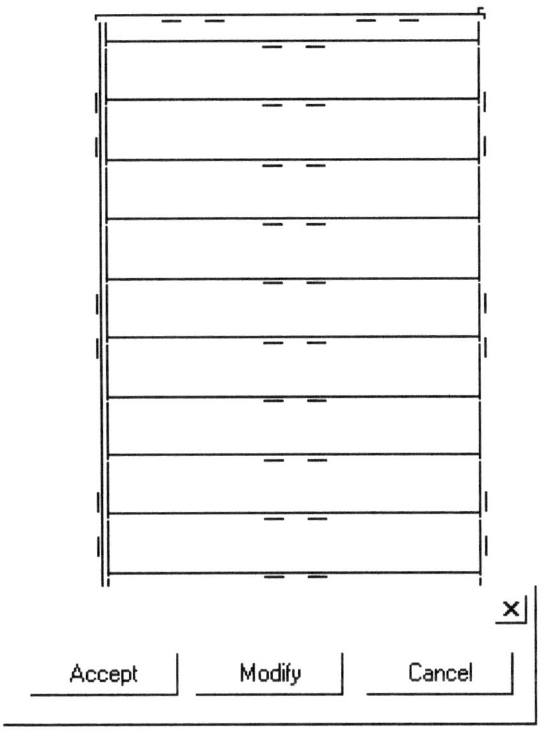

Use the  button to check your array.

Press **Accept**.

Adding Columns

13.

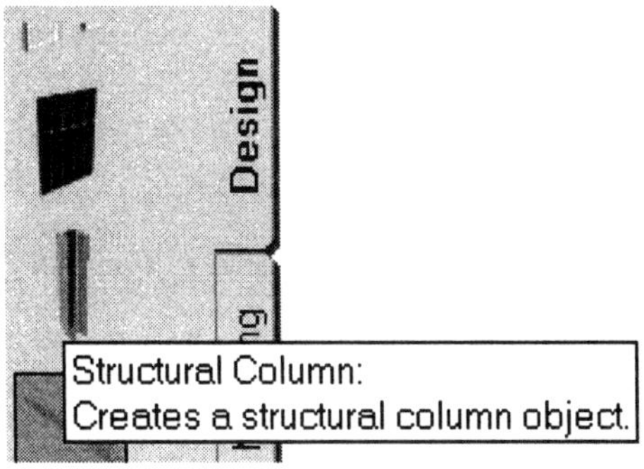

Select the **Structural Column** tool from the Design Palette.

14. Set the Style to **4x4 post**.
Set the Length to **6′-0″**.
Set Justify to **Bottom Left**.
Set the Roll to **0**.

At the 'Select grid or RETURN:' prompt, hit Enter.

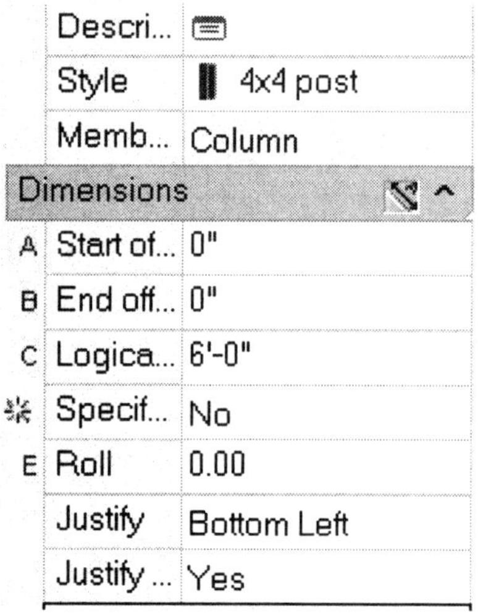

15. 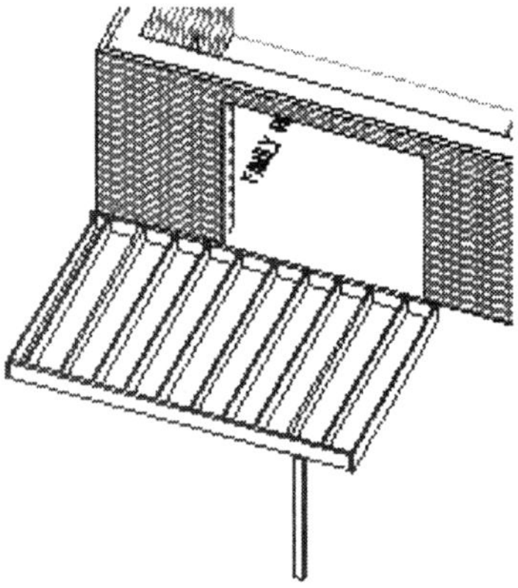

In the right viewport, use the From Osnap, pick the lower left corner of the joist frame, and enter '@0,24,-6′-10″' to place the post so the left face aligns with the outside of the doubled joist, the bottom face is 2′ from the bottom edge, and the top is even with the bottom of the joists.

16. Mirror the post to place another column 2′ in from the top (left side) of the frame.

17. Zoom in close to the base of one of the columns in the left viewport.

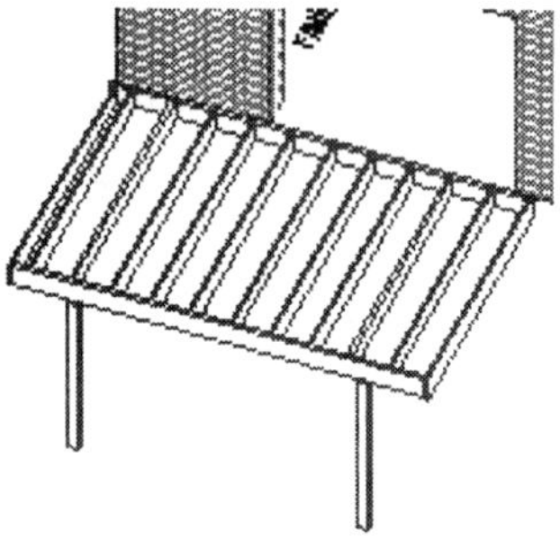

Adding Braces

18. 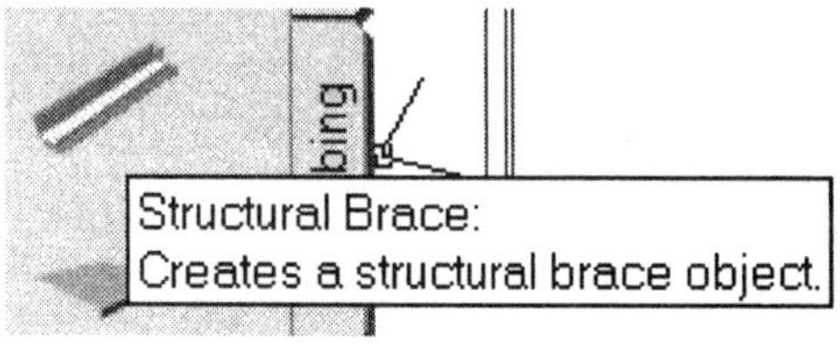

Select the **Structural Brace** tool from the Design Palette.

19.

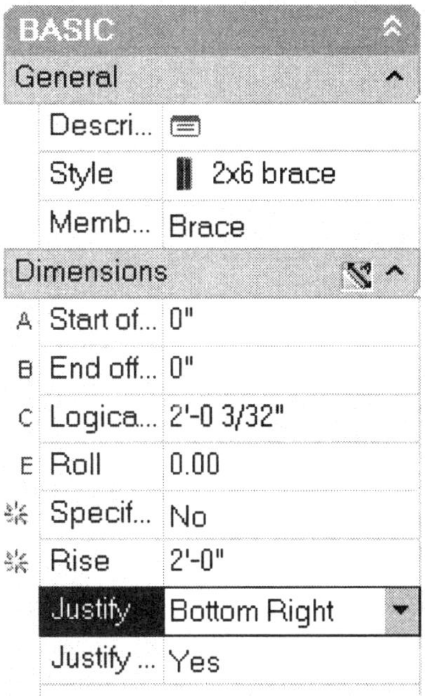

Set the Style to **2x6 brace.**
Set the Roll to **0**.
Set Specify on Screen to **No**.
Set the Rise to **2′-0″**.
Set Justify to **Bottom Right.**

20.

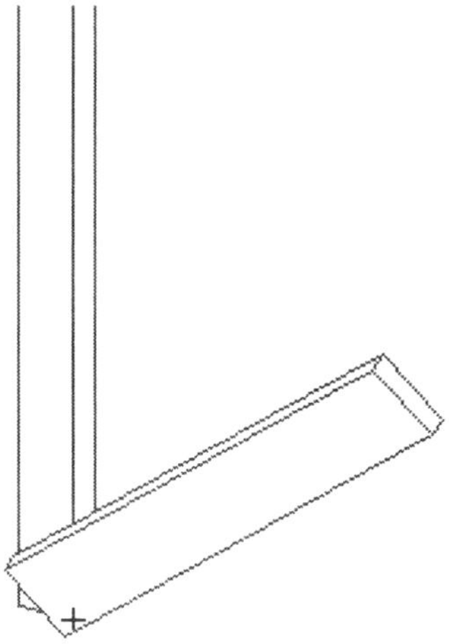

Pick the outside bottom endpoint of the column, pull the cursor to the right so the Polar angle reads 270°, type in 24 for the distance and return, then return again to end the command. If you can't get the polar angle, type in @24<270 at the prompt and press ENTER.

In order to show the brace as it will be cut and placed, we need to add trim planes.

21. Select the brace.

Right click and select **Properties**.
Scroll down to the Advanced Section.
Select the info button.

22. Select the Add tool.

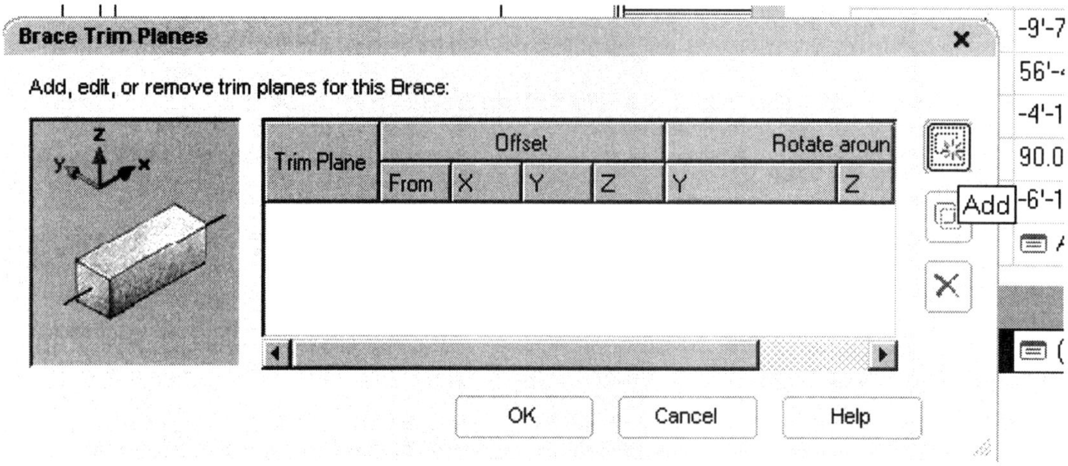

23.

Trim Plane	Offset			Rotate around	
	X	Y	Z	Y	Z
1	3"	0"	0"	45.00	0.00
2	-3"	0"	0"	315.00	0.00

Add two trim planes with the settings shown. Note that you need to set the first trim plane From Start and the second trim plane From End.

24.

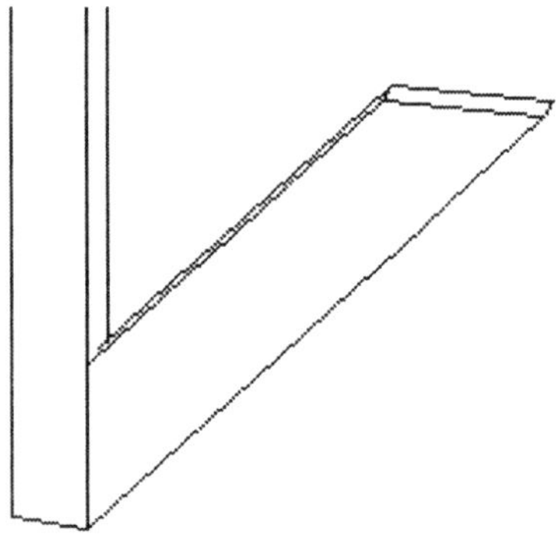

Use Rotate3D to position the brace against the column.

25. 

Mirror the brace to the other side of the column.

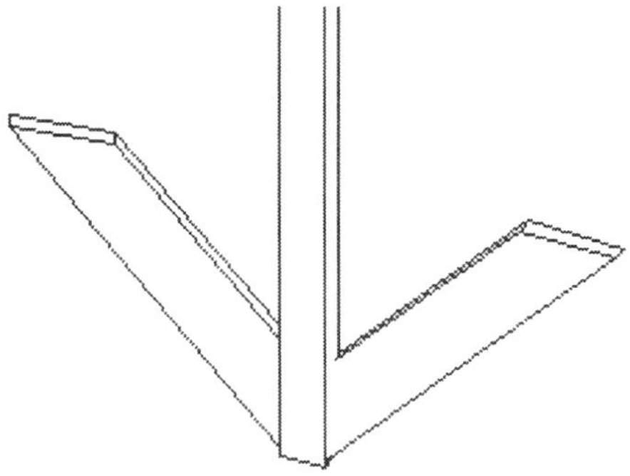

26. 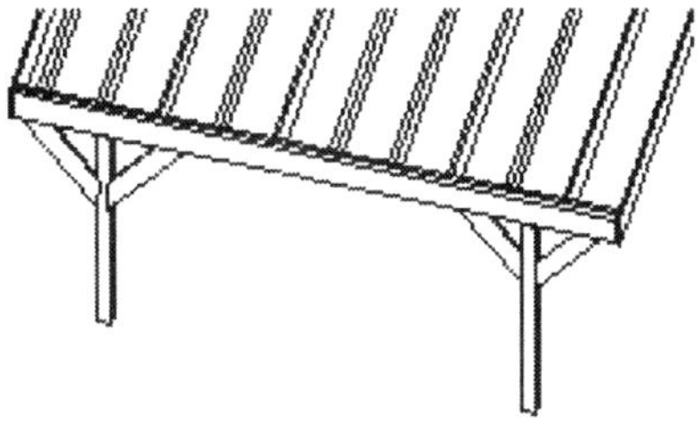

Move the two braces up so their tops touch the underside of the joists. Use the Endpoint and Perpendicular Osnaps. Copy the two braces from one post to the other.

27. Save as *ex6-2.dwg.*

Exercise 6-3:

Add Floorboards

Drawing Name: ex6-2.dwg
Estimated Time: 15 minutes

This exercise reinforces the following skills:

- Structural Members
- Use of Structural Members tools

The top of the joist frame we created in the last exercise is sitting even with the top of the floor slab. It needs to be lowered to allow for nominal 2x6 deck boards.

1.  Open *ex6-2.dwg.*
Select the Work tab.
Activate the right viewport.

Using Quick Select

2. 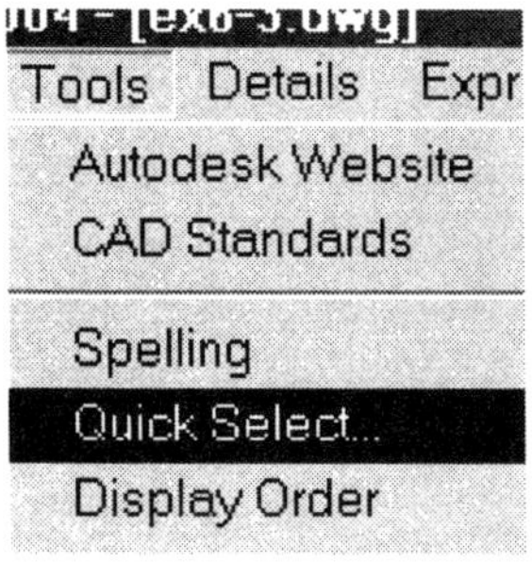

Go to **Tools→Quick Select.**

3.

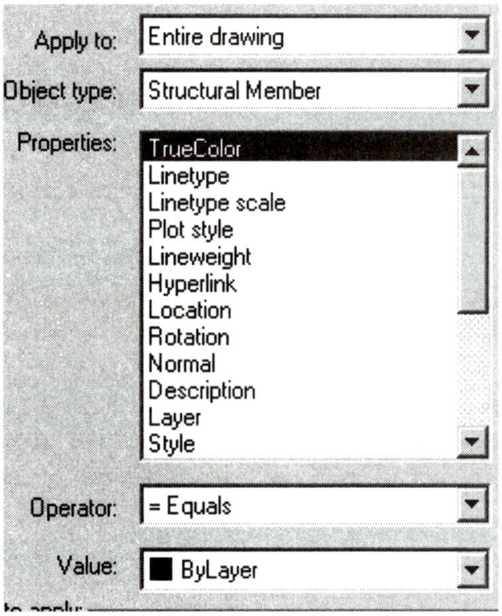

– Greater than

Set the Object Type to **Structural Member**.

Set the Properties to TrueColor =Equals ByLayer.

Press **OK**.

All structural members are selected.

4.

Select the MOVE tool.
When prompted for the base point, select the left end point of one of the joists.
When prompted for the destination point, type **@0, 0, -1.5**.

5.

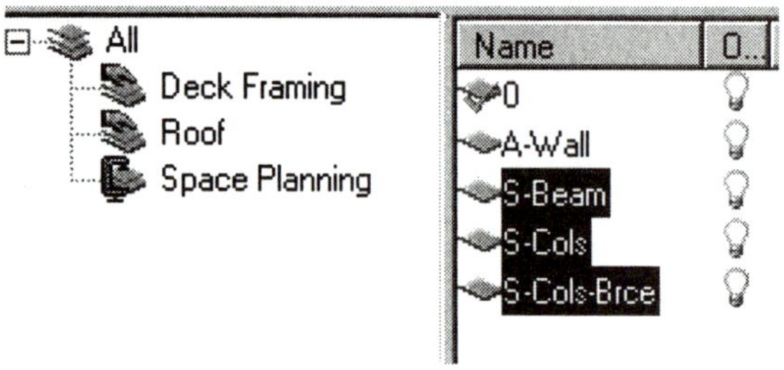

Activate the Layer Manager.
Drag the S-Beam, S-Cols, and S-Cols-Brce layers into the Desk Framing User Group.

These layers were automatically created when you placed your structural members.

Press **OK** to close the Layer Manager.

6. Select the Structural Beam tool.

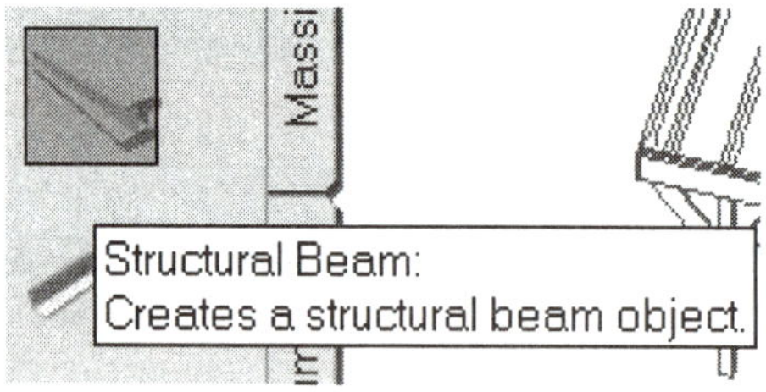

7. 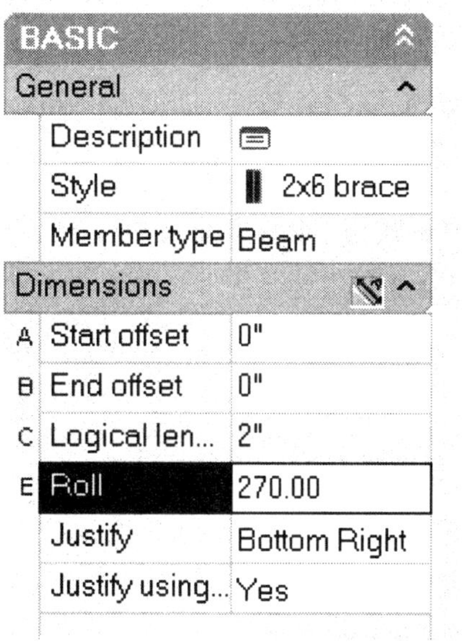

Set the Style to **2x6 brace**.
Set the Roll to **270°**, so that it lies flat rather than vertical.
Set the Justification to **Bottom Right**, so the board sits on top of the joists.

8. 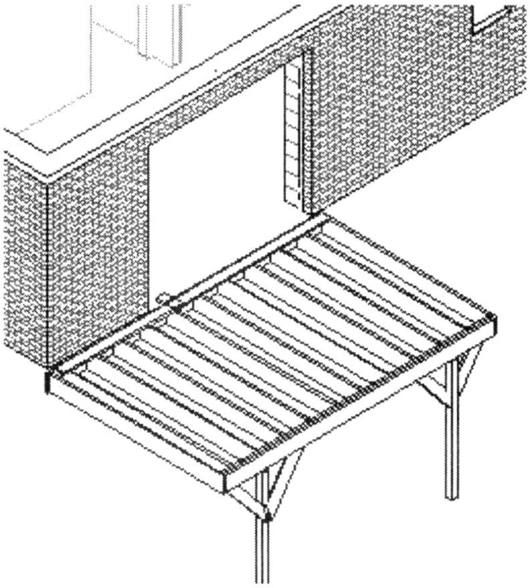

Pick the lower right corner of the joist at the house wall, drag the cursor up (90°), and give the board a length of 8′. Drag the cursor up at 90° and add a second board of length 6′.

9. 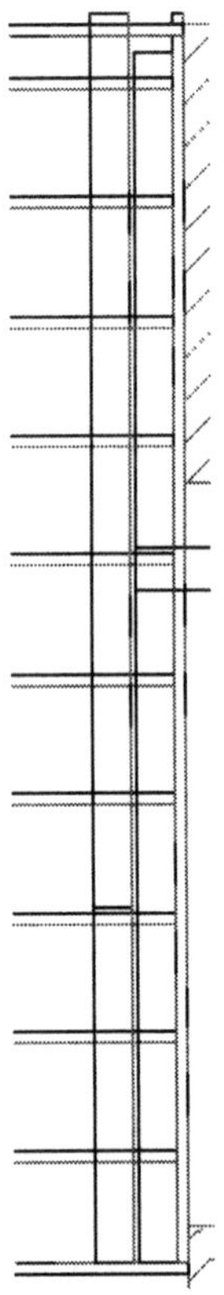

Enter twice to terminate and restart the command so you can pick a new starting point.

Pick the lower left corner of the first deck board you created, pull the cursor up at 90°, enter a distance of 4′, then pull the cursor up at 90° and enter a distance of 10′. (Although not strictly necessary, we are providing suggested lengths of deck boards to minimize wastage.) Deck boards are laid with a nominal ½″ space between them to allow for drainage and board warping, so move the last two deck boards ½″ to the left.

10. Array the 4 deck boards to fill the deck: 1 row, 9 columns with a column offset of –1′0″.

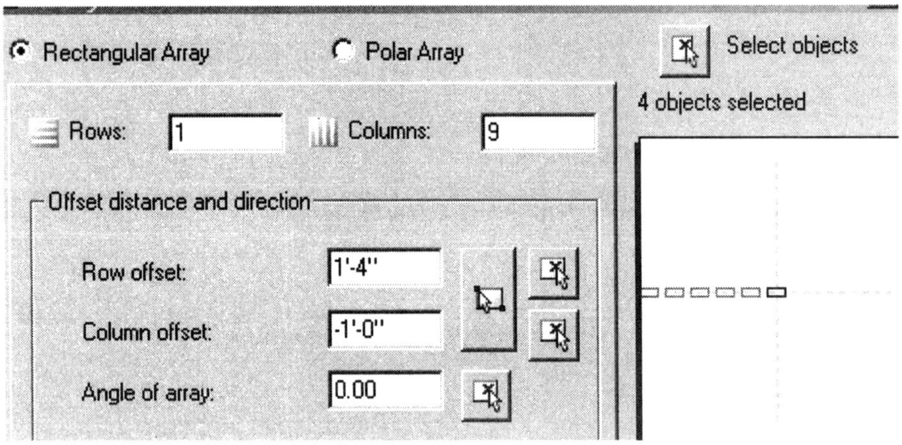

11. 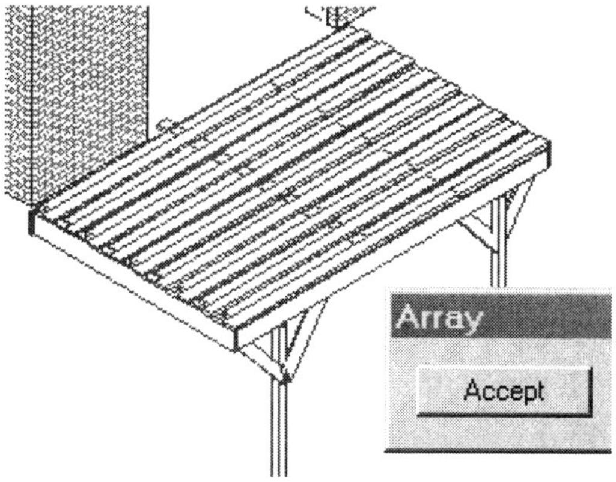

Use the Preview option of the Array to check your array.

Press **Accept**.

12. Save as *ex6-3.dwg.*

Exercise 6-4:

Add Railing

Drawing Name: Ex6-3.dwg
Estimated Time: 15 minutes

This exercise reinforces the following skills:

- ❑ Railings
- ❑ Railing Styles

Next, we create a railing for the deck.

1.  Open *ex6-3.dwg.*
Select the Work tab.
Activate the right viewport.

2. 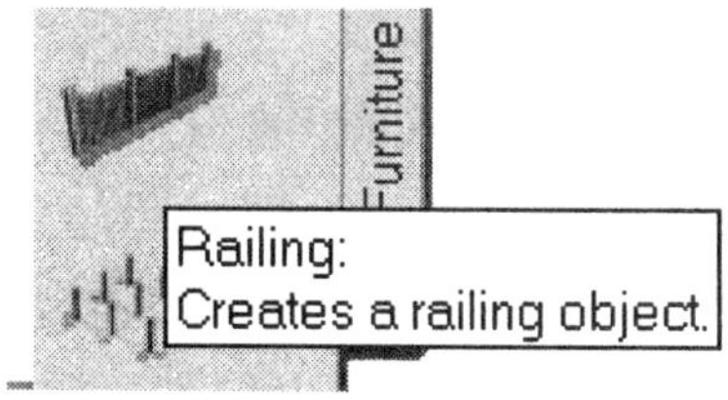

Select the Railing tool from the Design palette.

3.

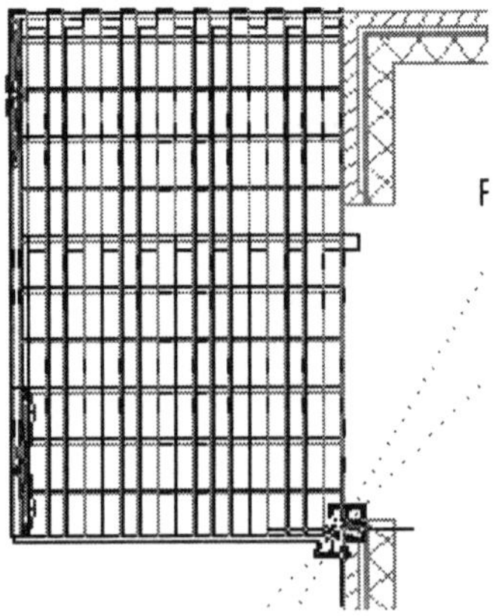

Pick the lower right corner of the deck for the start point.

Create endpoints at 9′ to the left (180°), then 14′ up (90°), and 6′ to the right (0°). This leaves a 3′ opening at the corner of the house.

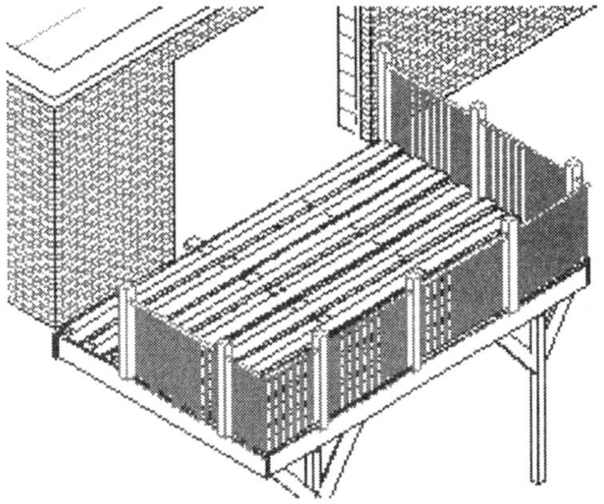

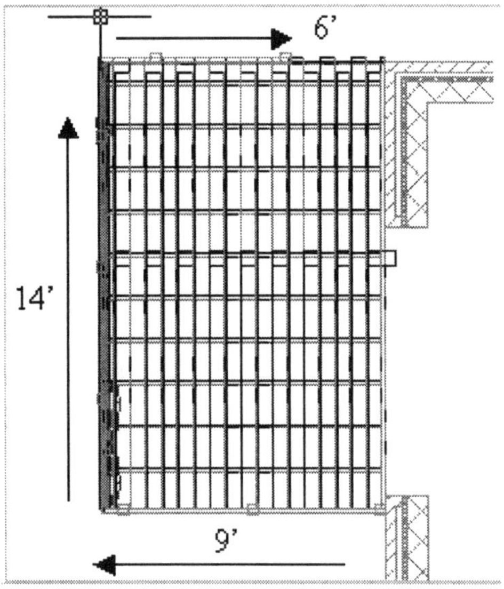

Railing Styles

4.

Select the **Railing** tool from the Design Palette.
Right click and select **Railing Styles**.

5.

Select **Standard** under Railing Styles.
Right click and select **New**.

6. 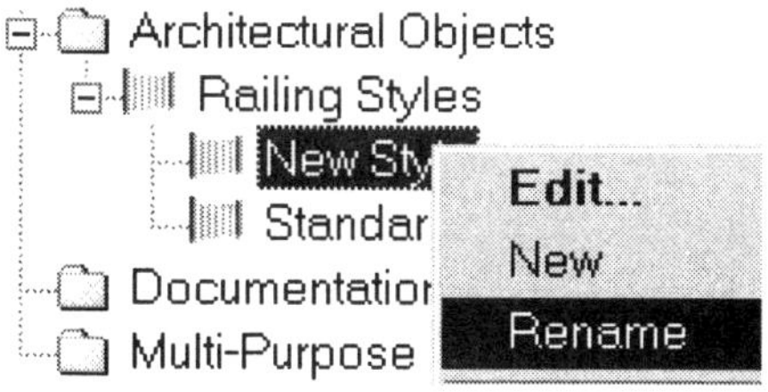

Select the **New Style**.
Right click and select **Rename**.

7. 

Name the new railing style **Deck**.

8. 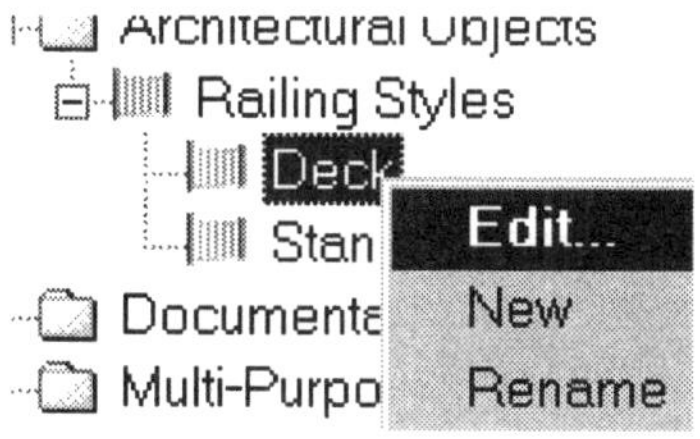

Pick the new style, right click and pick **Edit**.

9. 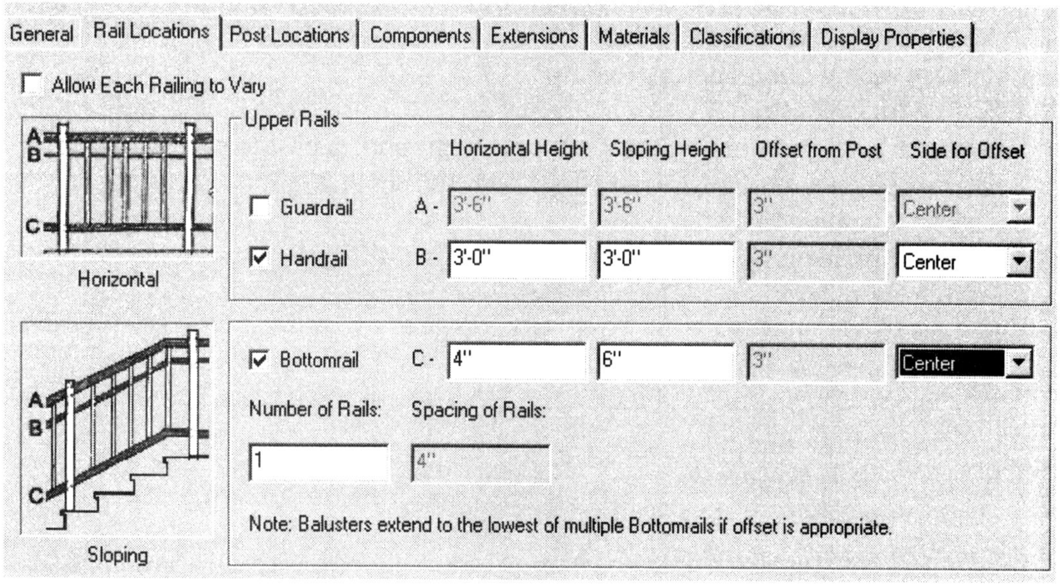

Select the **Rail Locations** tab.
Enable **Handrail** for the Upper Rails.
Set the Horizontal Height to **3′.**
Set the Sloping Height to **3′**.
Set the Side for Offset to **Center**.
Enable the **Bottom Rail**. (This adds a bottom rail)
Set the Horizontal Height to **4″**.
Set the Sloping Height to **6″**.
Set the Number of Rails to **1**.

10. 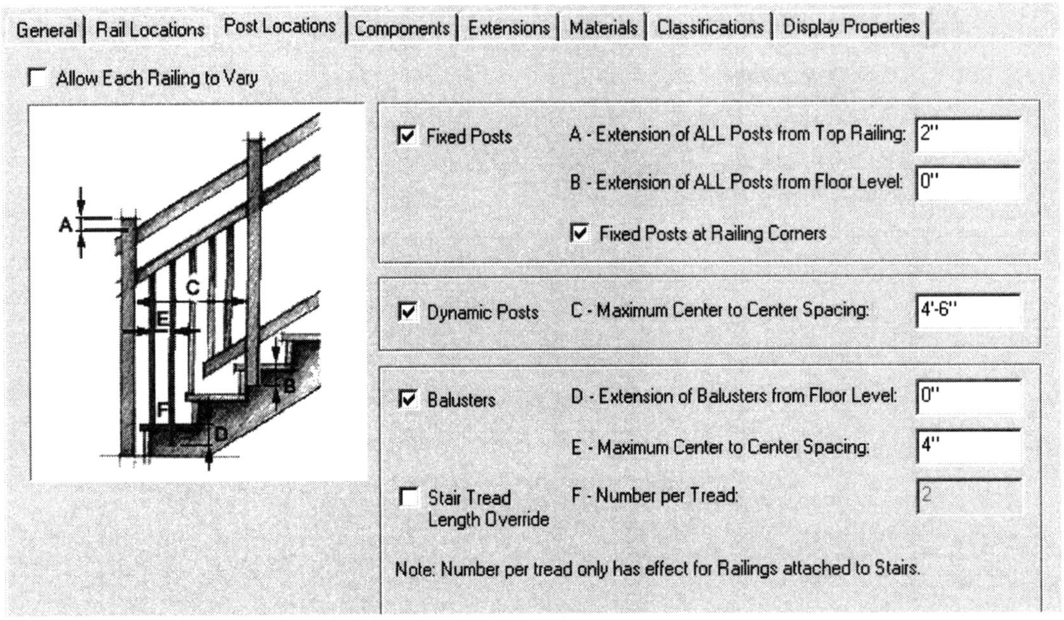

Select the **Post Locations** tab.
Disable **Allow Each Railing to Vary**.
Enable **Fixed Posts.**
Enable **Fixed Posts at Railing Corners**. (This adds a post to each corner)
Set the Extensions of ALL Posts from Top Railing to **2″**.
Enable **Dynamic Posts**.
Set the Maximum Center to Center Spacing to **4′-6″**.
Enable **Balusters**.
Set the Maximum Center to Center Spacing to **4″**.
Disable the **Stair Tread Length Override**.

11. Select the **Components** tab.
Change the Width of the Guardrail to **3″**.
All the other settings are unchanged.

General | Rail Locations | Post Locations | Components | Extensions | Materials | Classifications | Display Properties

Component	Profile Name	Scale	Width	De...	Rotation	Justification
A - Guardrail	*circular*	Scale To...	3"	2"	-	Middle Center
B - Handrail	*circular*	Scale To...	1 1/2"	1 1/2"	-	Middle Center
C - Bottomrail	*circular*	Scale To...	1"	1"	-	Middle Center
D - Fixed Post	*rectangular*	Scale To...	4"	4"	0.00	Middle Center
E - Dynamic Post	*rectangular*	Scale To...	4"	4"	0.00	Middle Center
F - Baluster	*rectangular*	Scale To...	1"	1"	0.00	Middle Center

Press **OK** to close the dialog box.

Press **Apply** and **OK**.

Changing a Railing Style

12. 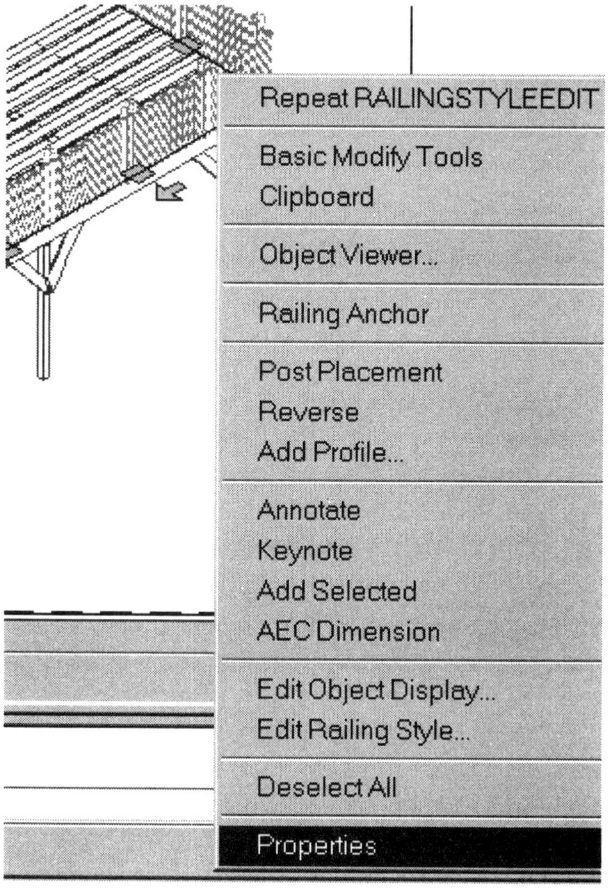

Select the Railing.
Right click and select **Properties**.

13. 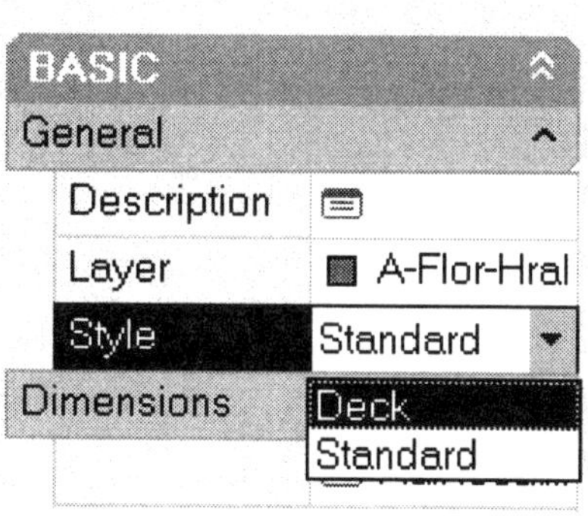

Change the Style to **Deck.**
Close the dialog.

14. Save as *ex6-4.dwg*.

Stairs

A house may have main stairs (from the first floor to the second floor) and/or a set of service stairs. Main stairs are usually constructed using pre-fabricated parts and are generally of better quality than service stairs. Service stairs are built on location. They are generally constructed of construction lumber.

There are six general types of stairs commonly used in residential construction. They are straight-run, L stairs, double-L stairs, U stairs, winder stairs and spiral stairs.

Straight run stairs are the most common. They are the least expensive to build, but they require a long open space.

Common terms associated with stairs include:

Balusters:	vertical members that support the handrail on open stairs
Enclosed stairs:	stairs that have a wall on both sides (also known as closed, housed, or box stairs). These can be stairs leading down to a basement or cellar.
Headroom:	The shortest clear vertical distance measured from the nosing of the tread and the ceiling.
Housed stringer:	A stringer that has been routed or grooved to accommodate the treads and risers.
Landing:	The floor area at either end of the stairs; also the area between a set of stairs, such as in an L stairs.
Newel:	The main posts of the handrail at the top and bottom or at points where the stairs change direction.
Nosing:	The rounded projection of the tread which extends past the face of the riser.

We will be adding service stairs to our deck.

Exercise 6-5:

Add Stairs

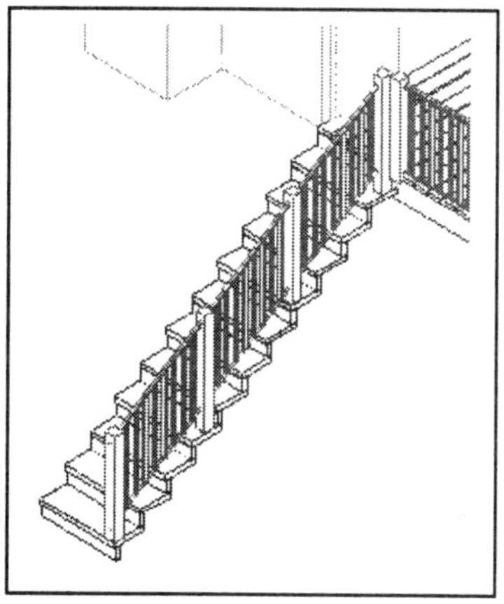

Drawing Name: Ex6-4.dwg
Estimated Time: 15 minutes

This exercise reinforces the following skills:

- Add Stairs
- Add Railing

1.  Open *ex6-4.dwg.*
   Select the Work tab.
   Activate the right viewport.

2. Stairs run from the foot of the stair to the top of the stair, so before we can place our stairs, we need to reset our UCS so the Z depth is at the foot of the stairs.

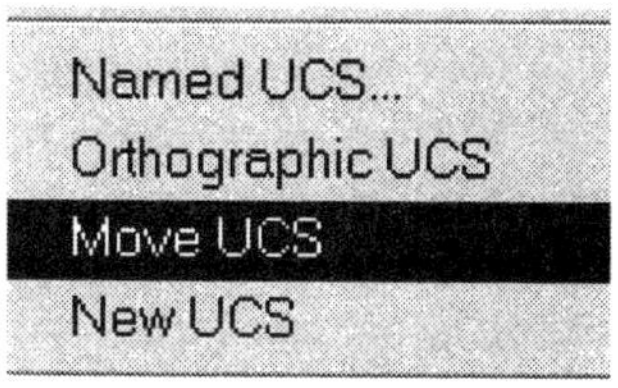

Go to **Tools→ Move UCS**.

3. 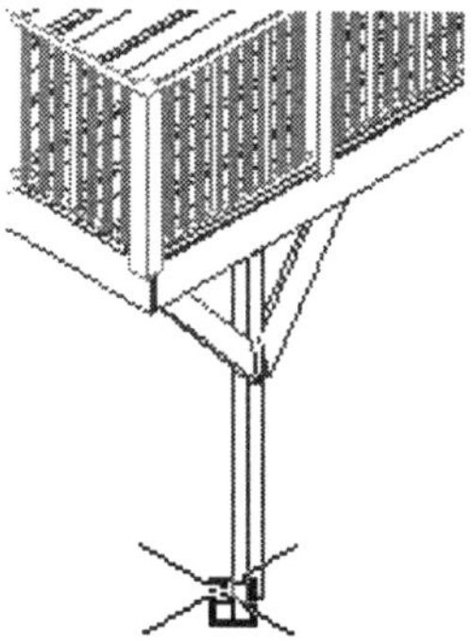

Select one of the endpoint corners of the columns placed to support the decking.

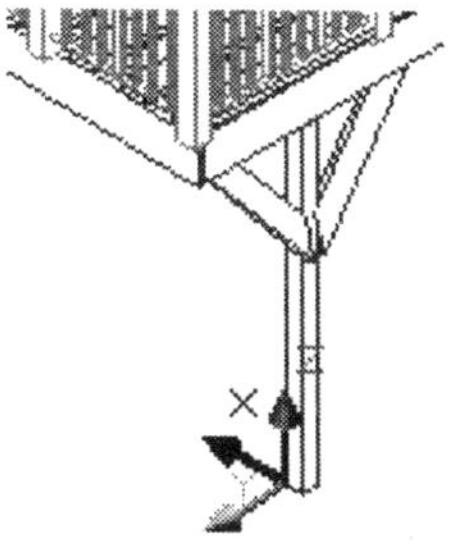

You see the UCS icon moved to the new location.

4.

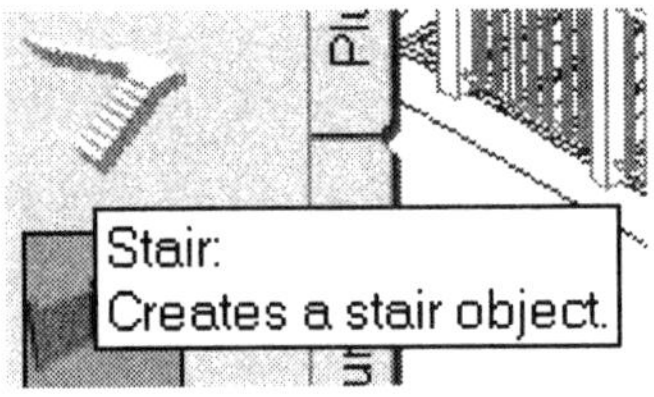

Select the **Stair** tool from the Design Palette.

5.

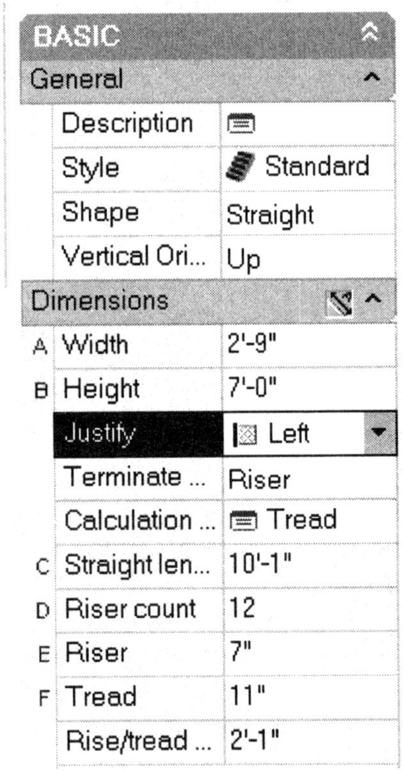

Set the Style to **Standard**
Set the Shape to **Straight.**
Set the Width to **2′-9″**.
Set the Height to **7′**.
Set the Tread to **11″**.
Set Justify to **Left**.

Note that the Straight length is automatically calculated at 10′-1″.

6.

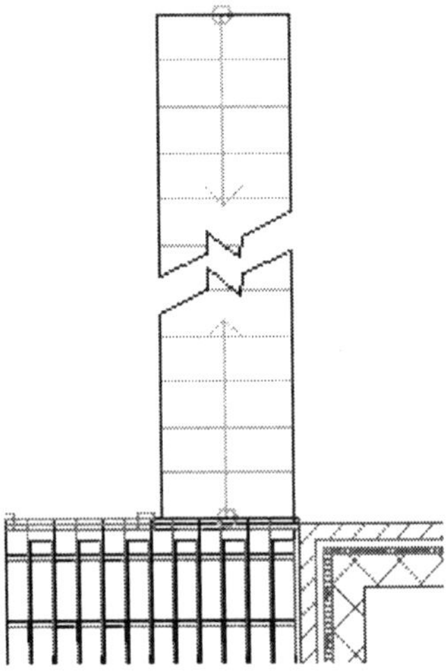

Pick a point 10′-1″ above the deck for the start point of the stairs.

Pick a point near the top of the deck for the end point of the stairs.
Close the dialog box.

Stair Representation

7. We see the stair as a broken view because of the Options setting in our AEC Stair Defaults.

   Bring up the **Options** Dialog box.

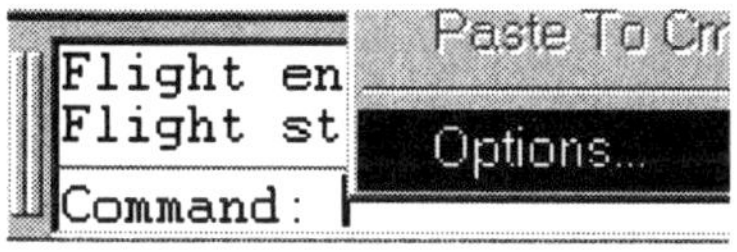

   Place your cursor in the command line.
   Right click and select **Options.**

   Select the **AEC Object Settings** tab.
   Enable the Presentation Format.

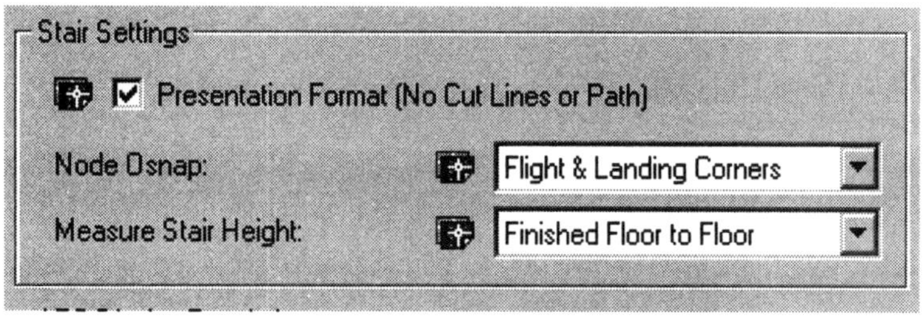

   Press **Apply** and **OK**.
   Notice that the stairs appearance does not change.

8. Type **Regen.**
   The stairs now appear without a break mark.

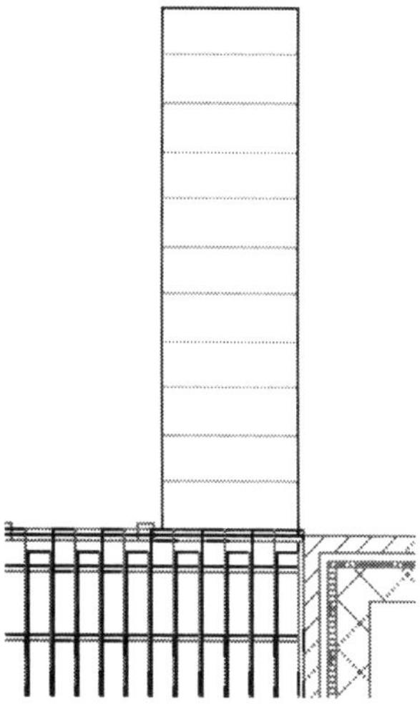

9. 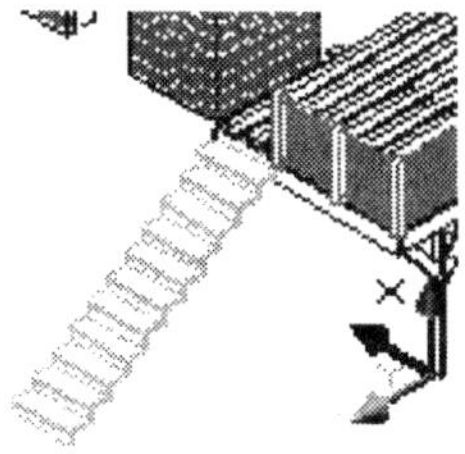

   The stairs are placed, but they need to be shifted slightly to fit with the deck.
   Use the MOVE tool to position the stairs properly.
   Safety regulations require a handrail down the stairs.

Add Railing

10.

Select the **Railing** tool from the Design Palette.

11.

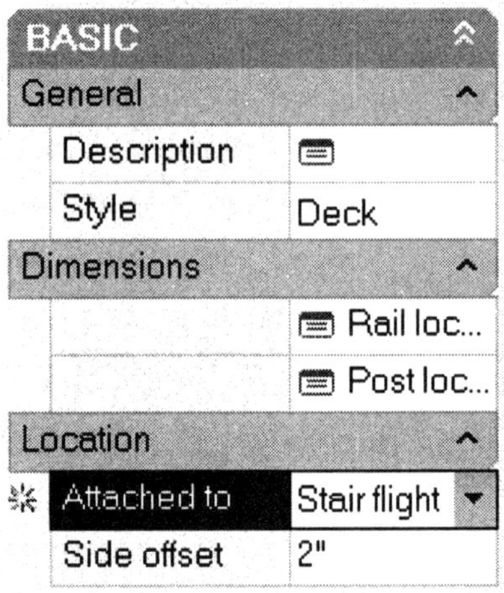

Set the Style to **Deck**.
Set Attached to: **Stair Flight**.
Set Offset to **2″**.

12.

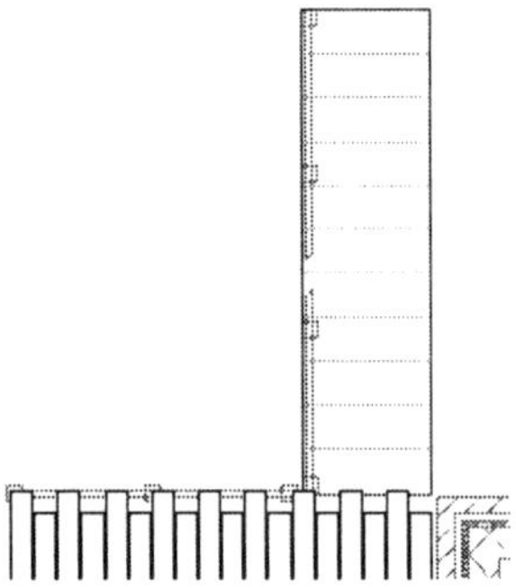

You will be prompted to select the stairs.
Pick the left side of the stair to place railing on the left side.

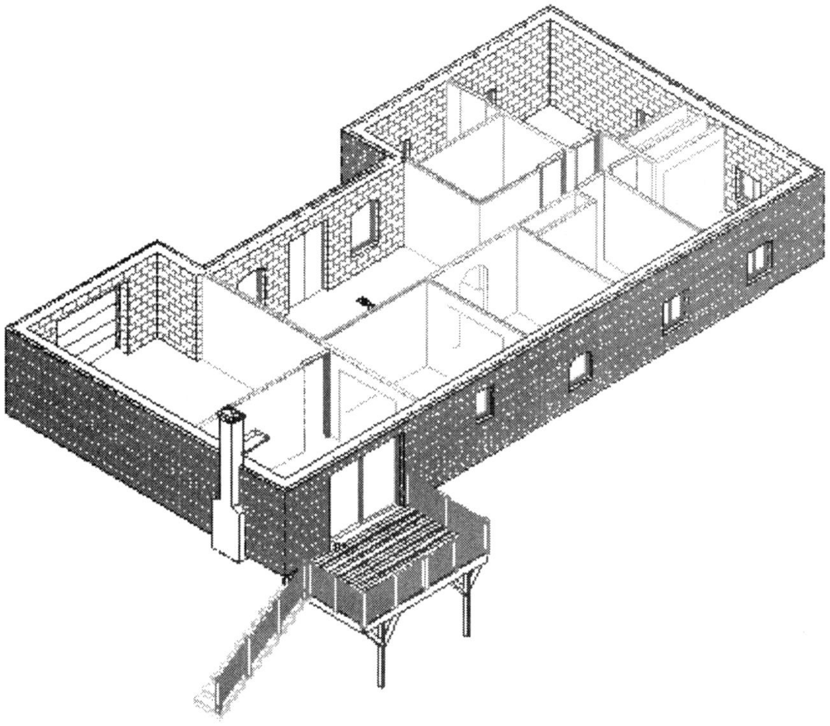

13. Save as *ex6-5.dwg.*

Notes:

Lesson 7
Layouts

Before we can create our construction drawings, we need to create layouts or views to present the design. Architectural Desktop is similar to AutoCAD in that the user can work in Model and Paper Space. Model Space is where we create the 3D model of our house. Paper Space is where we create or setup various views that can be used in our construction drawings. In each view, we can control what we see by turning off layers, zooming, panning, etc.

To understand paper space and model space, imagine a cardboard box. Inside the cardboard box is Model Space. This is where your 3D model is located. On each side of the cardboard box, tear out a small rectangular window. The windows are your viewports. You can look through the viewports to see your model. To reach inside the window so you can move your model around or modify it, you double-click inside the viewport. If your hand is not reaching through any of the windows and you are just looking from the outside, then you are in Paper Space.

You can create an elevation in your current drawing by first drawing an elevation line and mark, and then creating a 2D or 3D elevation based on that line. You can control the size and shape of the elevation that is generated. Unless you explode the elevation that you create, the elevation remains linked to the building model that you used to create it. Because of this link between the elevation and the building model, any changes to the building model can be made in the elevation as well.

When you create a 2D elevation, the elevation is created with hidden and overlapping lines removed. You can edit the 2D elevation that you created by changing its display properties. The 2D Section/Elevation style allows you to add your own display components to the display representation of the elevation, and create rules that assign different parts of the elevation to different display components. You can control the visibility, layer, color, linetype, lineweight, and linetype scale of each component. You can also use the line work editing commands to assign individual lines in your 2D elevation to display components, and merge geometry into your 2D elevation.

After you create a 2D elevation, you can use the AutoCAD BHATCH and AutoCAD DIMLINEAR commands to hatch and dimension the 2D elevation.

Exercise 7-1:
Creating a Custom Titleblock

Drawing Name: Architectural Title Block.dwg
Estimated Time: 15 minutes

This exercise reinforces the following skills:

- Title blocks
- Attributes
- Layouts

1. 

   Browse to
   Documents and Settings\All Users\Application Data\Autodesk\Autodesk Architectural esktop 2004\R16.0\enu\Templates\AutoCAD Templates.

   Open the *Architectural Title Block.dwg*

2. Perform a **File→Save as.**

   Save the file to your work folder.
   Rename **Architectural Title Block-Asize.dwg.**

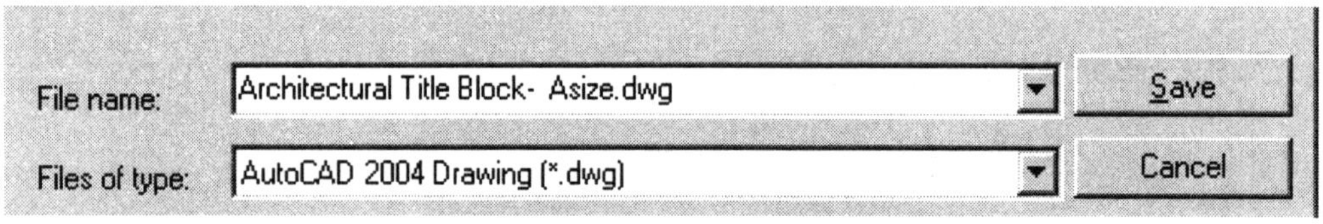

3. 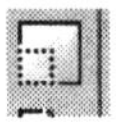 Select the **Scale** tool.

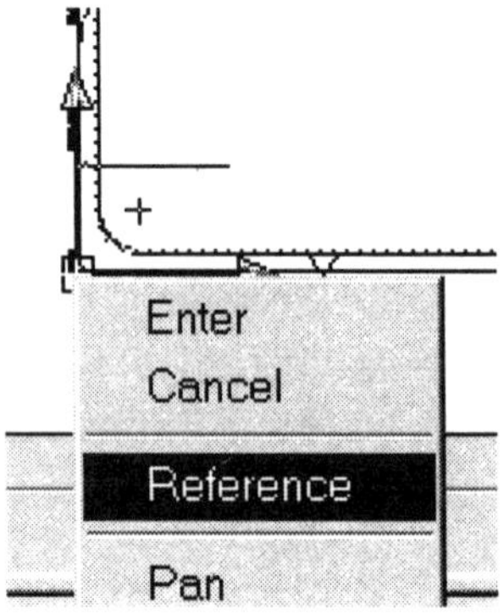

Type **ALL** to select the title block.
Select the lower left point as the base insertion point.
Right click and select **Reference.**
When prompted for the reference length,
select the left point of the bottom horizontal line, then select the right point of the bottom horizontal line to specify the existing titleblock's length.
When prompted for the new length,
Enter **11″**.

The titleblock is now re-scaled to be placed on an 8-1/2″ x 11″ sheet.

4.

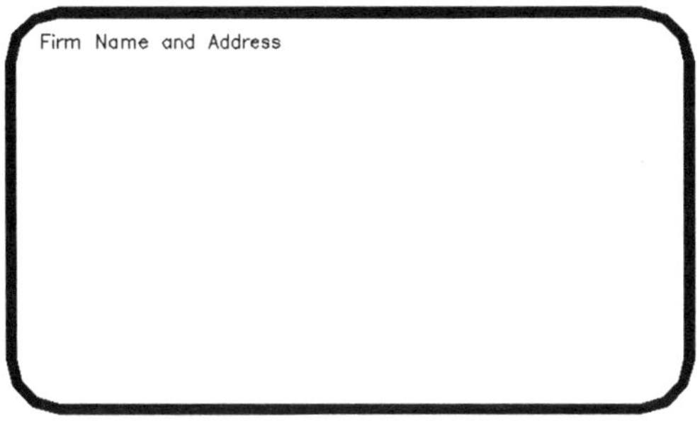

Zoom into the Firm Name and Address rectangle.

5.

Select the **MTEXT** tool.

Set the Font to **Verdana**.
Enter the name and address of your college.

6.

Use **SCALE** and **MOVE** to locate the text properly.

Inserting a Logo

7.

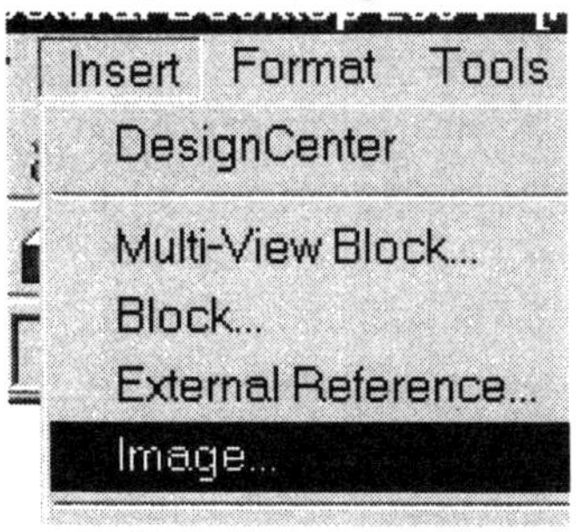

Go to **Insert→Image**.

8.

Locate and select the image of your choice.
(You can download *evc-logo.jpg* from www.schroff1.com.

Place the image in the rectangle.

Add a Hyperlink

9. Select the image.
Right click and select **Properties**.

10.

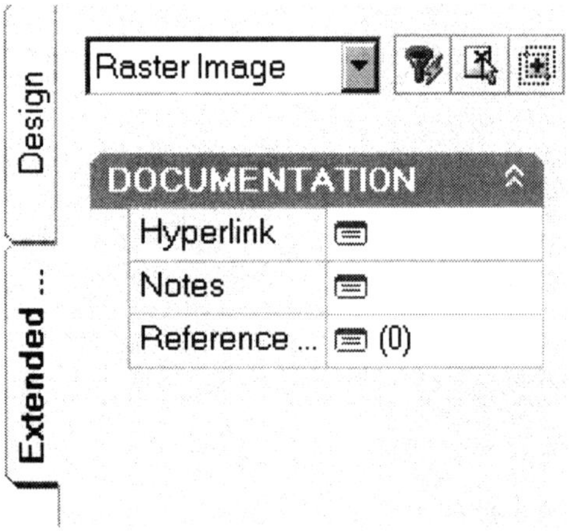

Select the **Extended** Tab.
Pick the Hyperlink field.

11.

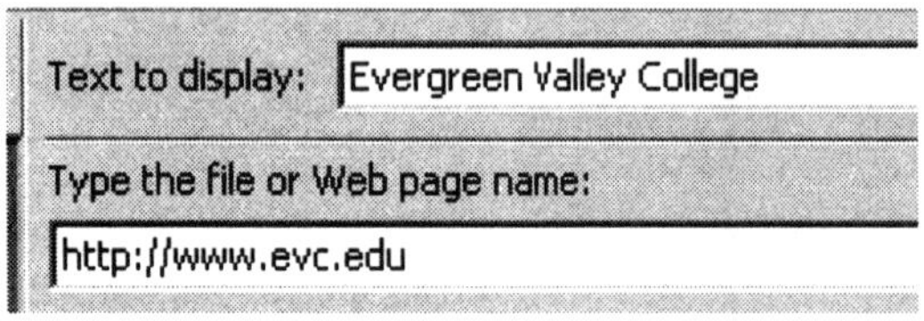

Type in the name of the school in the Text to display field.
Type in the website address in the Type the file or Web page name field.

Press **OK**.

12.

To turn off the image frame/boundary:

Type **IMAGEFRAME** at the command line.
Right click and select **OFF**.

13.

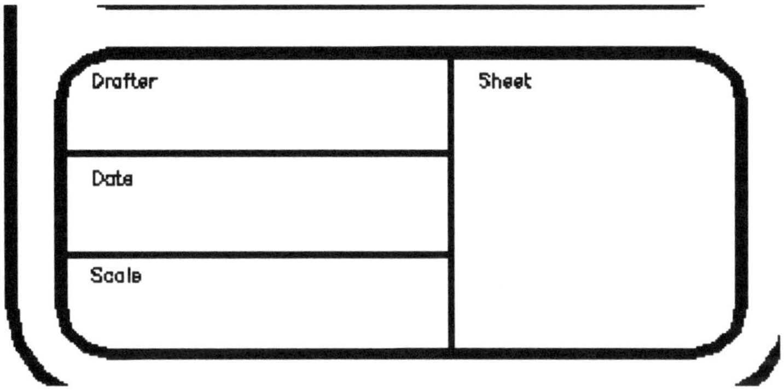

Change the text for Project to **Drafter.** To change, simply double click on the text and an edit box will appear.

Accessing the Attribute Creation tools

14.

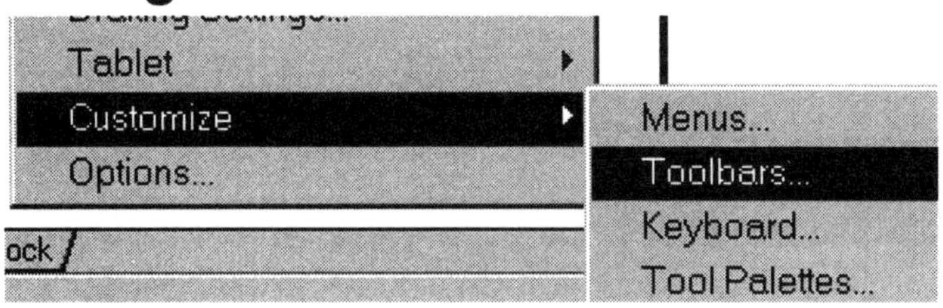

Go to **Tools→ Customize→Toolbars**.

15.

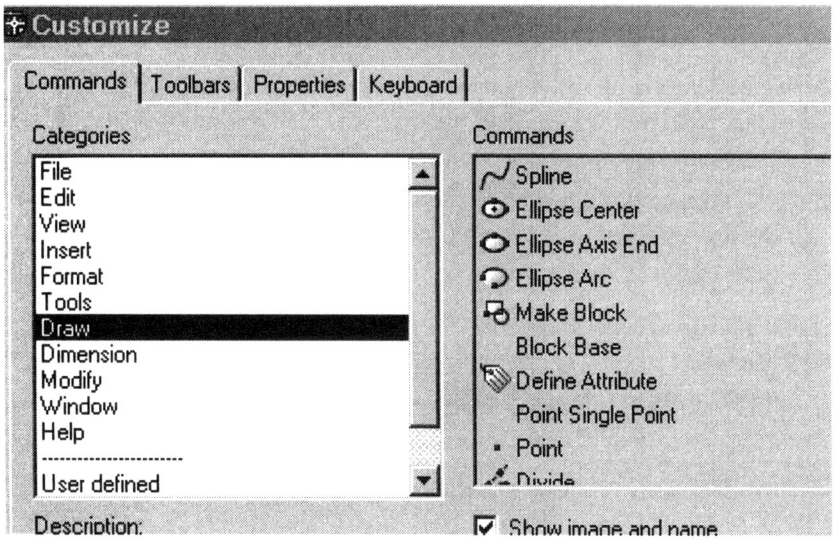

Select the **Commands** tab.

Select the **Draw** Category.

Locate the **Define Attribute** tool.

16.

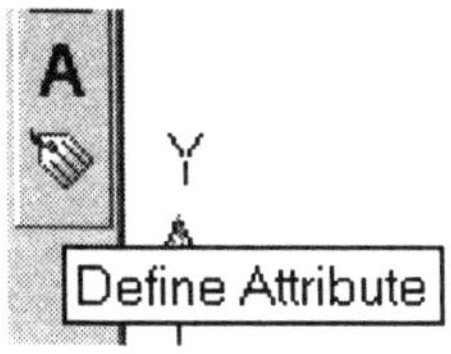

Drag and drop the tool onto the Draw toolbar.

17.

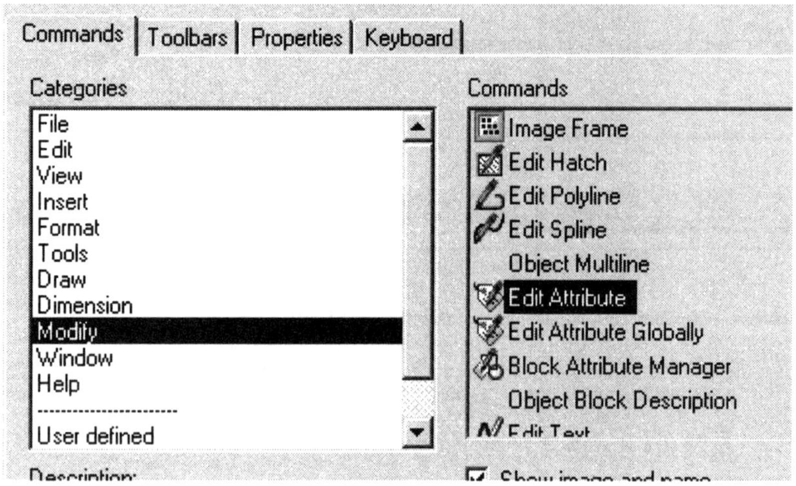

Select the **Modify** Category.

Locate the **Edit Attribute** tool.

18.

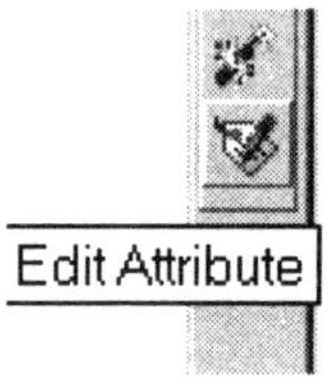

Drag and drop the tool onto the Modify toolbar.

Close the Customize dialog.

19. 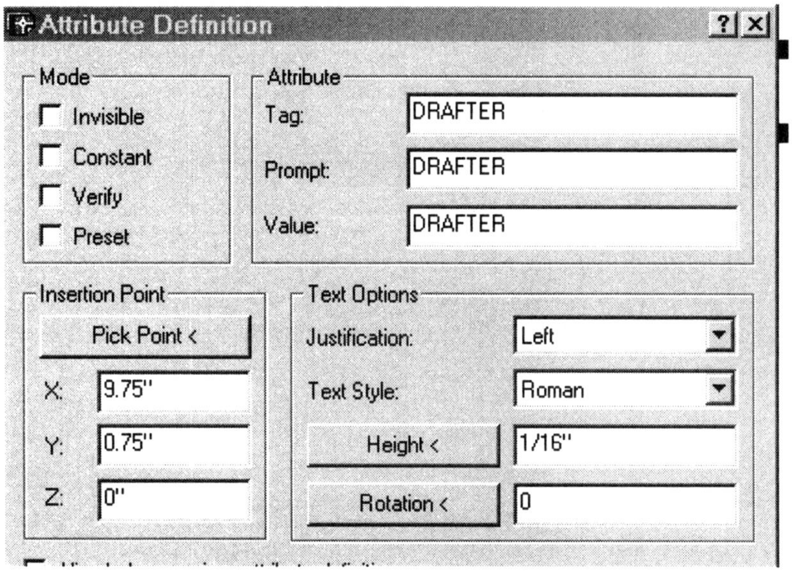

 Select the **Define Attribute** tool.

In the Tag field, enter **DRAFTER**.
In the Prompt field, enter **DRAFTER**.
In the Value field, enter your initials.
In the Insertion Point area:
  In the X field, enter: **9.75″**.
  In the Y field, enter: **0.75″**.
  In the Z field, enter: **0″**.
In the Text Options area:
  Set the Justification to **Left**.
  Set the Text Style to **Roman.**
  Set the Height to **1/16″.**

Press **OK.**

20. 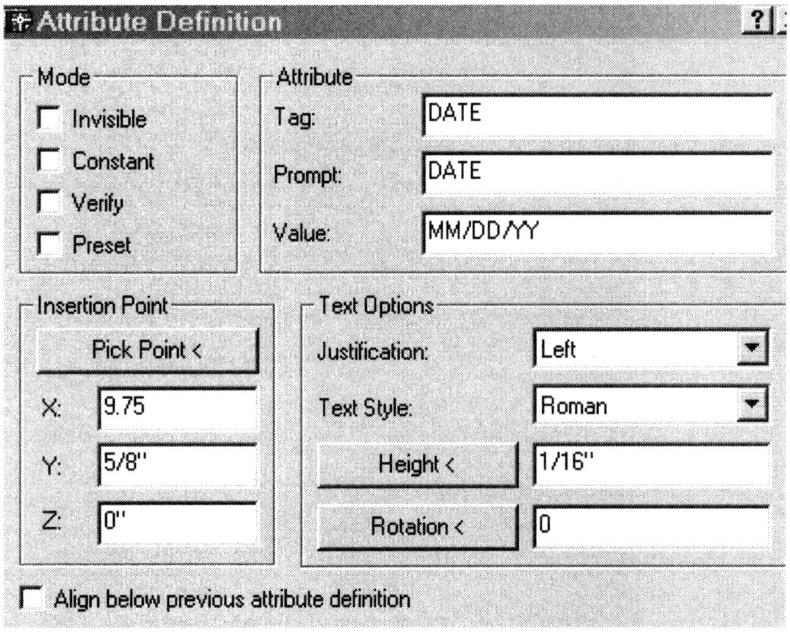

 Select the **Define Attribute** tool.

In the Tag field, enter **DATE**.
In the Prompt field, enter **DATE**.
In the Value field, enter **MM/DD/YY**.
In the Insertion Point area:
   In the X field, enter: **9.75″**.
   In the Y field, enter: **5/8″**.
   In the Z field, enter: **0″**.
In the Text Options area:
   Set the Justification to **Left**.
   Set the Text Style to **Roman.**
   Set the Height to **1/16″.**

Press **OK.**

21.

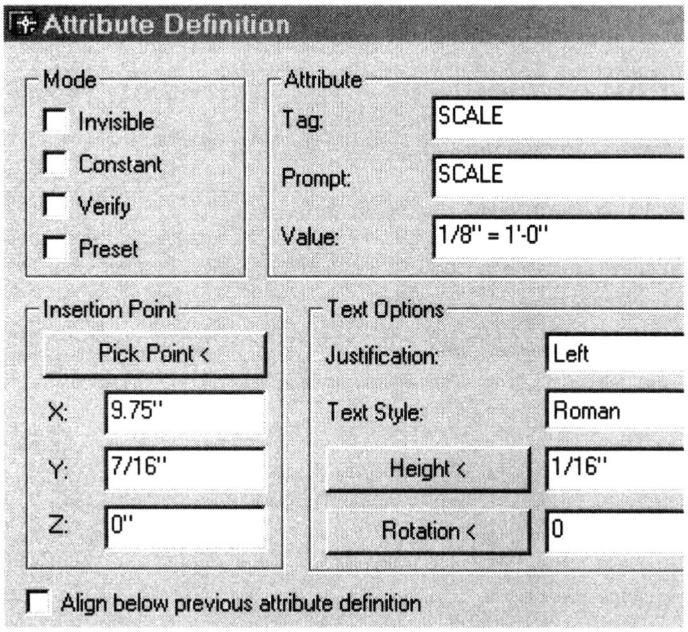

 Select the **Define Attribute** tool.

In the Tag field, enter **SCALE**.
In the Prompt field, enter **SCALE**.
In the Value field, enter **1/8″= 1′-0″**.
In the Insertion Point area:
- In the X field, enter: **9.75″**.
- In the Y field, enter: **7/16″**.
- In the Z field, enter: **0″**.

In the Text Options area:
- Set the Justification to **Left**.
- Set the Text Style to **Roman.**
- Set the Height to **1/16″.**

Press **OK.**

22.

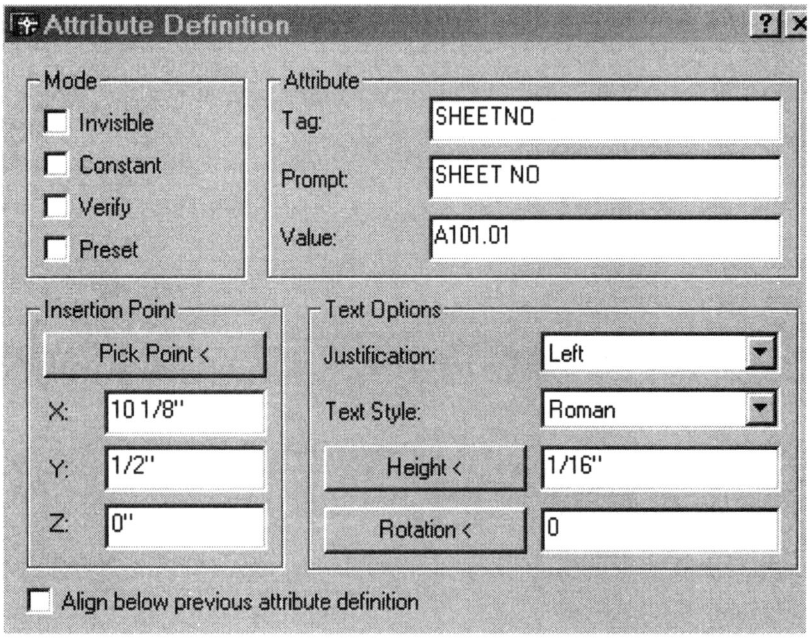

 Select the **Define Attribute** tool.

In the Tag field, enter **SHEETNO**.
In the Prompt field, enter **SHEET NO**.
In the Value field, enter **A101.01**.
In the Insertion Point area:
    In the X field, enter: **10 1/8″**.
    In the Y field, enter: **1/2″**.
    In the Z field, enter: **0″**.
In the Text Options area:
    Set the Justification to **Left**.
    Set the Text Style to **Roman.**
    Set the Height to **1/16″.**

Press **OK.**

TIP: A common error for students is to forget to enter the insertion point. The default insertion point is set to 0,0,0. If you don't see your attributes, look for them at the lower left corner of your titleblock and use the MOVE tool to position them appropriately.

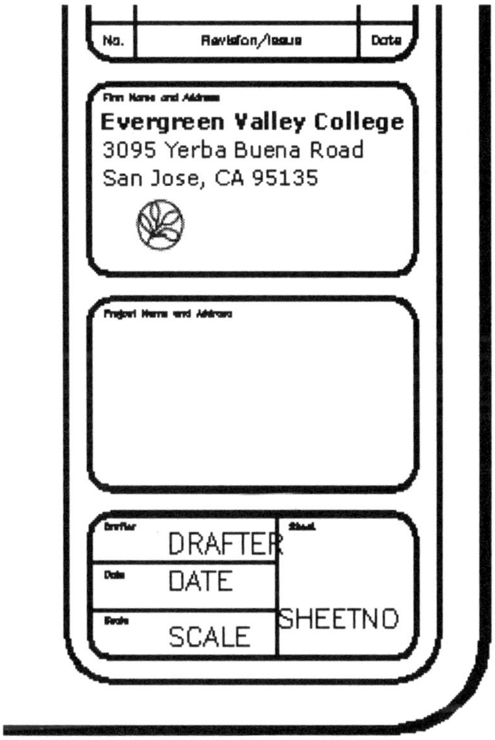

Your titleblock should look similar to the image shown.

Do not worry about the fact that the DRAFTER attribute is too long as you only have three initials in the value field.

23. Save the file and go to **File→Close.**

Exercise 7-2:

Creating an Elevation Label

Drawing Name: NEW
Estimated Time: 15 minutes

This exercise reinforces the following skills:

- Blocks
- Elevation Labels
- Create AEC Custom Content
- Attributes

1.  Select the **QNEW** tool.

2.  Launch the Design Center.

3. 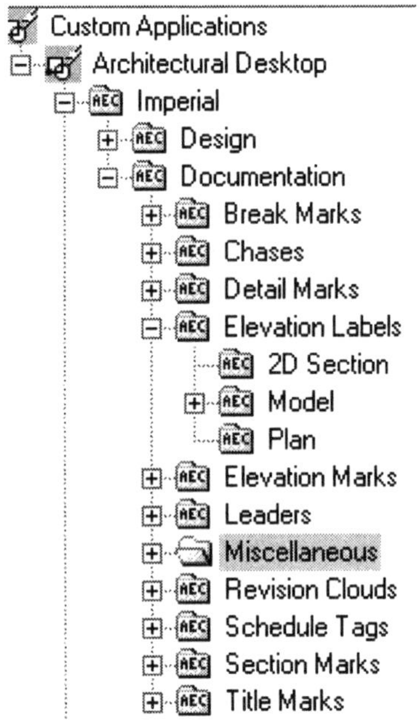

Select the **Custom** tab.
Browse to *Architectural Desktop\Imperial\Documentation\Miscellaneous*.
Locate the **Datum Point** file.

4. 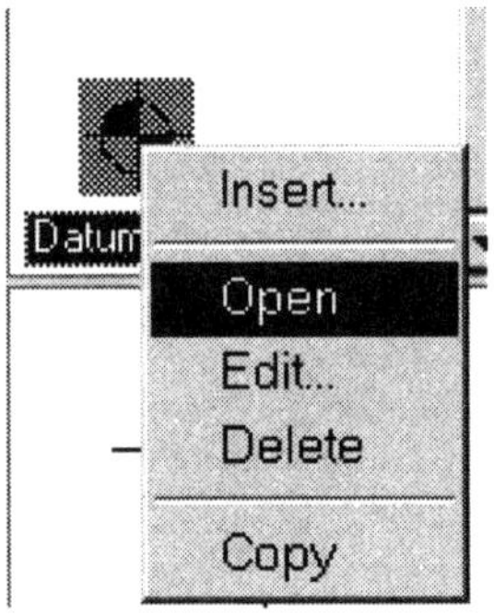

Select the Datum Point file.
Right click and select **Open**.

5. Select **File→Save as.**
Browse up to the Documentation folder.
Select the **Create New Folder** tool.

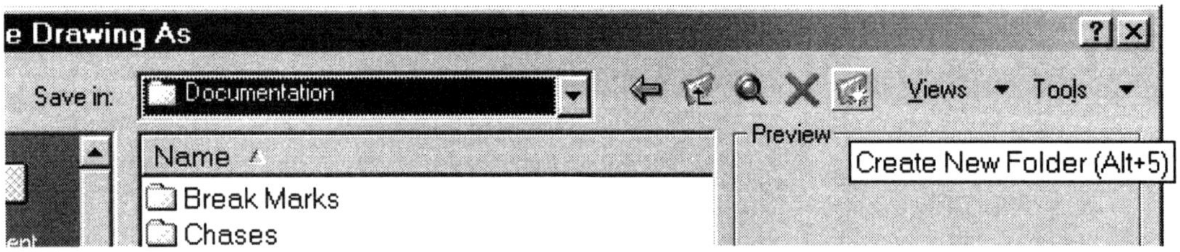

6.

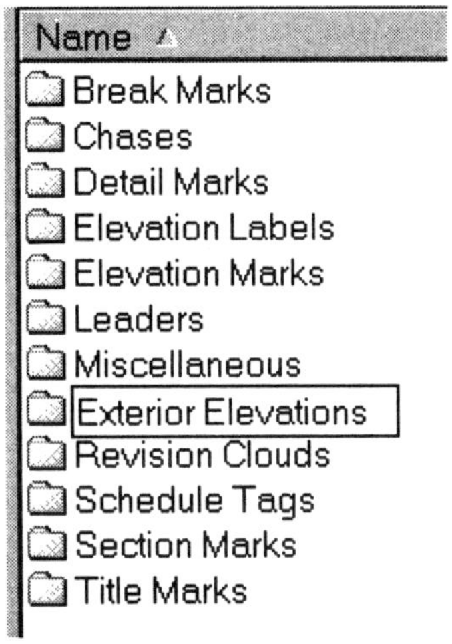

Rename the folder **Exterior Elevations**.

7.

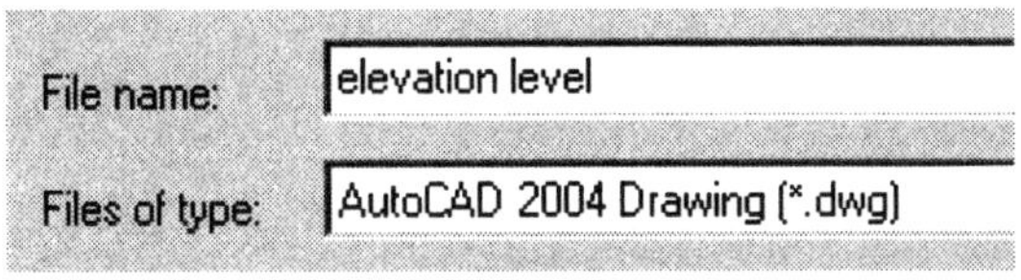

Name your file **elevation level.**
Press **Save.**

8. Draw a 6″ long horizontal line.
Add two attributes: One for level and one for elevation.

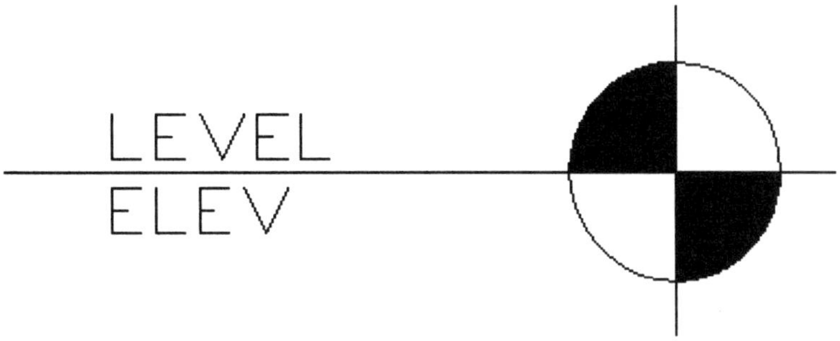

9.

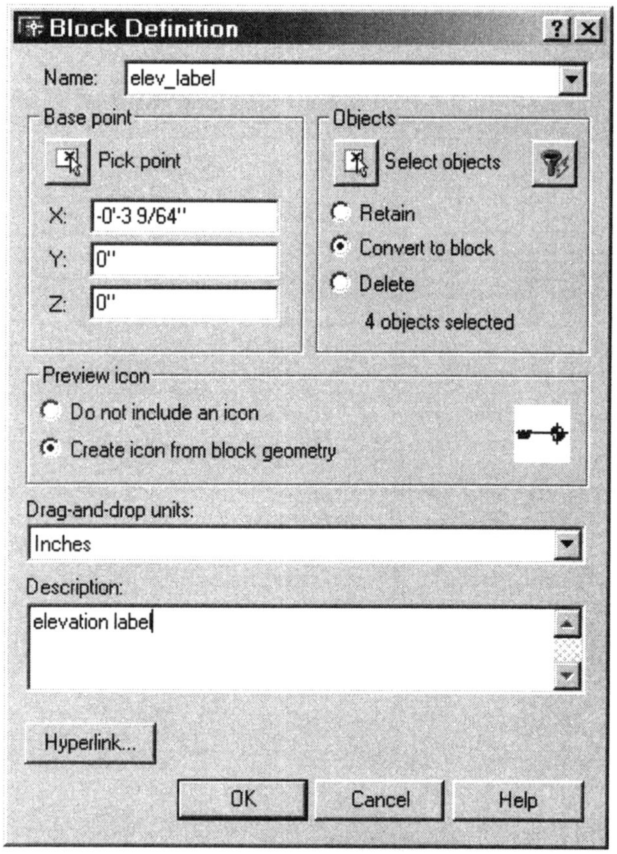

Select the **Make Block** tool.

In the Name field, enter **Elev_label.**
Select the objects in the drawings.
Select the end point of the horizontal line as the insertion point.
Select **Convert to Block.**
Enable **Create icon from block geometry.**
Press **OK**.

10.

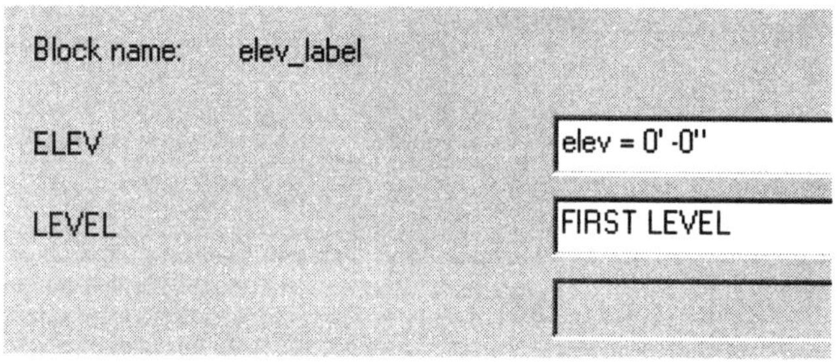

The Edit Attributes dialog will appear.

Press **OK.**

11.

Go to **Format→AEC Content Wizard.**

12. Enable **Custom Command**.
Select the **elev_label** block using the Add tool and remove any other blocks listed in the Content File window.
In the Command String field enter **AecAnnoSymbolAdd SYMBOL elev_label.**
Press **Next.**

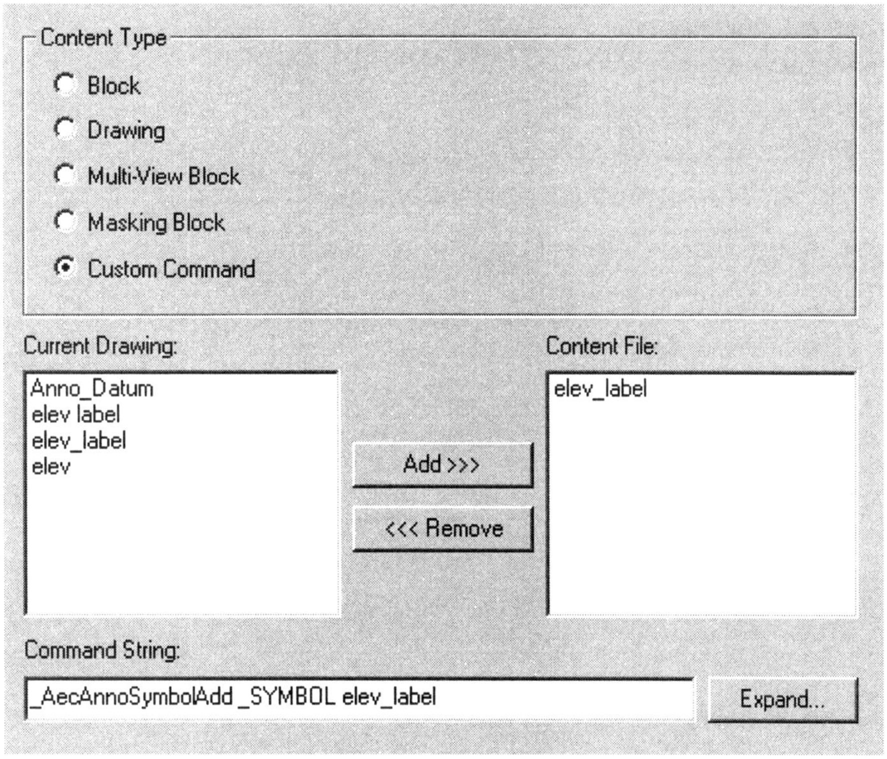

13. Enable **Enable AEC Unit Scaling**.
This automatically scales your block to the current viewport.
The Layer Key assigns the layer to place your block.
Press **Next.**

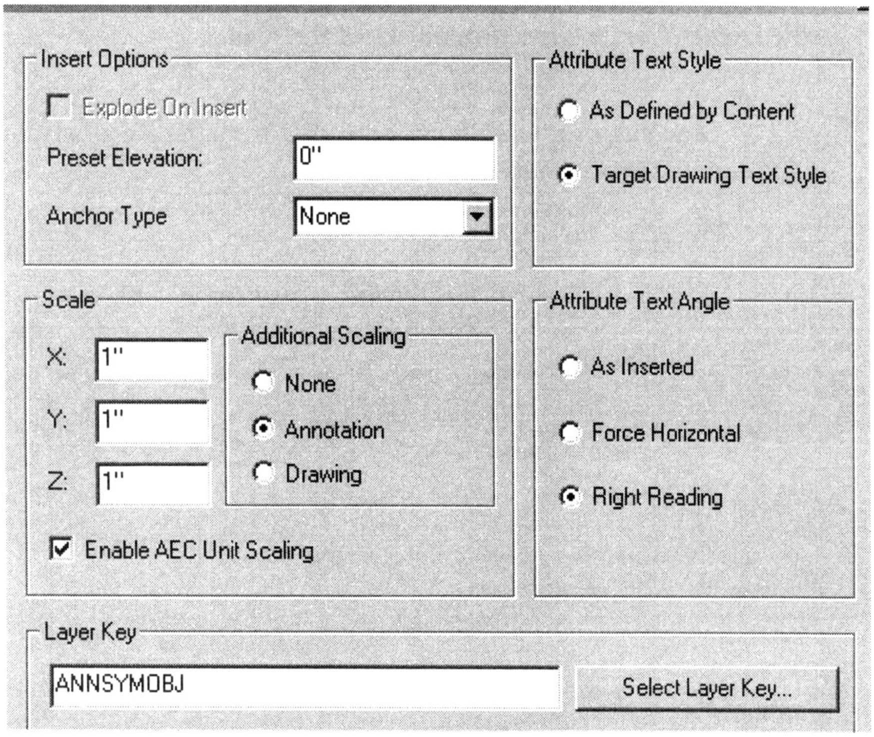

14. Enable Current Drawing.
Press Default Icon to select the drawing's preview icon.

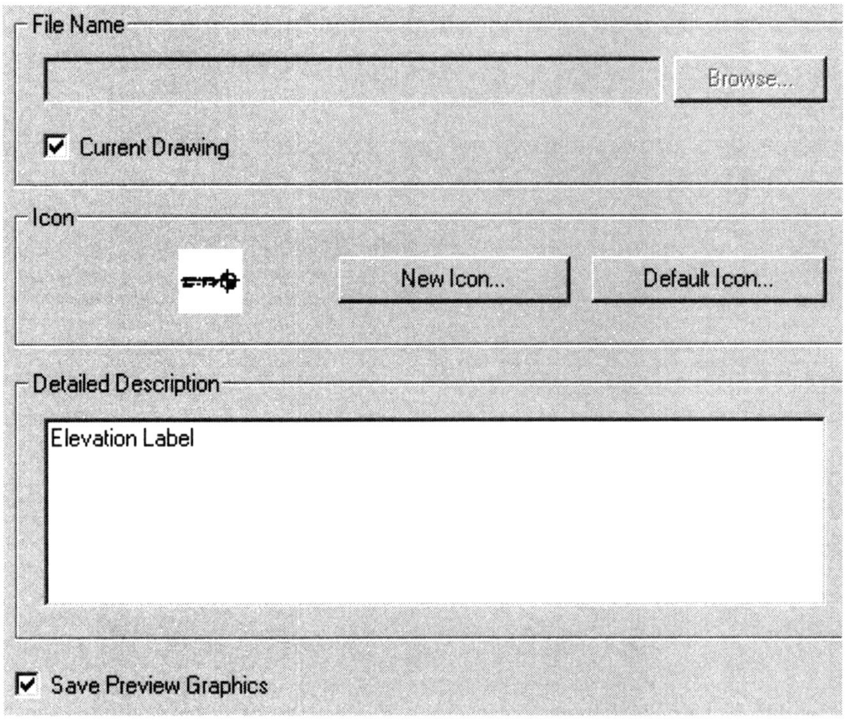

Press **Finish.**

15. Press **Save** and **Close.**

16. Right click in the Design Center Window and select **Refresh.**

17. 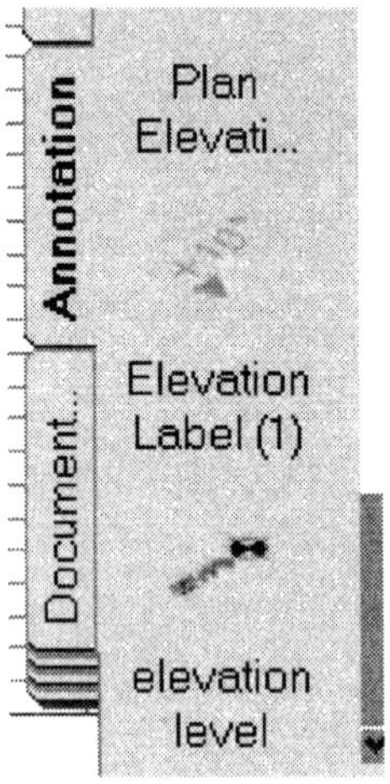

Drag and drop the **Elevation Label** from the Design Center onto the Annotation Palette.

Close the Design Center.

Exercise 7-3:

Creating an Elevation Window Tag

Drawing Name: NEW
Estimated Time: 15 minutes

This exercise reinforces the following skills:

- ❑ Blocks
- ❑ Elevation Labels
- ❑ Create AEC Custom Content
- ❑ Attributes

1. 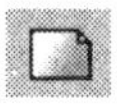 Select the **QNEW** tool.

2.  Select the **Polygon** tool.

   Set the number of sides to **6**.
   For the center point, enter **0,0,0**.
   Set the polygon to **Inscribed.**
   Set the Radius to **1/8″**.

3.  Select the Define Attribute tool.

   The tag should be set to **WINDOWOBJECTS:NUMBER.**
   The prompt should be set to **WINDOW NO**.
   The default value should be set to **000**.
   The Insertion Point should be set to **0,0,0**.
   Set the Justification to **Center**.
   Press **OK**.

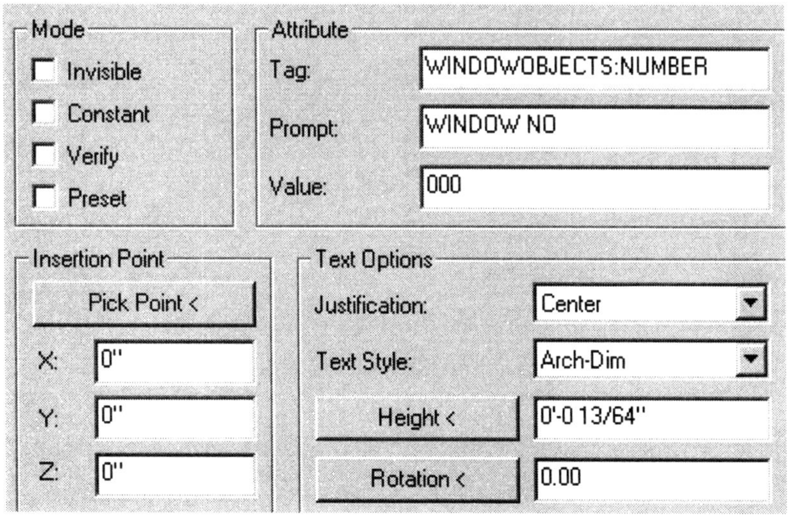

4. Select the Define Attribute tool.

The tag should be set to **WINDOWSTYLES:TYPE.**
The prompt should be set to **TYPE**.
The default value should be set to **STD**.
Ste the Mode to **Invisible**.
Enable **Align below previous attribute definition.**

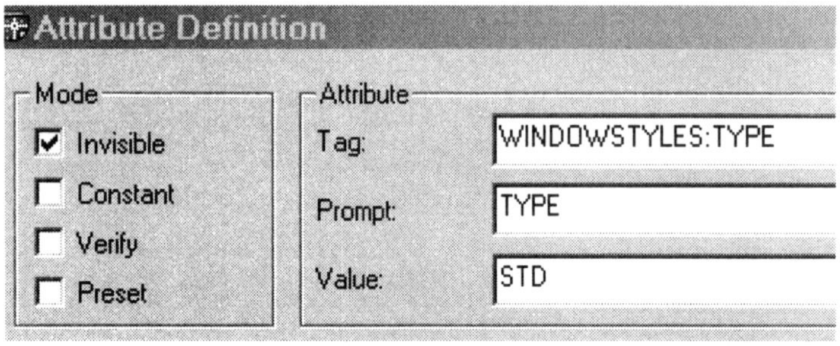

5. 

Select **Save.**
Enter **elev_window_tag** for the file name.

> **TIP:** ADT only allows the user to specify a single path for Content. You can create a custom subdirectory under the Content path in order to protect your custom files.

6. Go to **Format→Style Manager.**

7. Select the **Open** tool.
Browse to *Document and Settings\All Users\Architectural Desktop 2004\R16.0\enu\AEC Content\Imperial\Documentation\Schedule Tags\Property Set Defs.dwg.*

8.

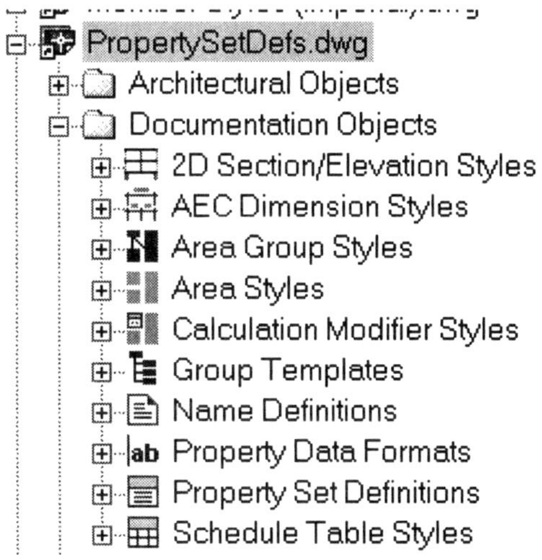

Browse to Property Set Definitions. Copy **Window Objects and Window Styles.**

9.

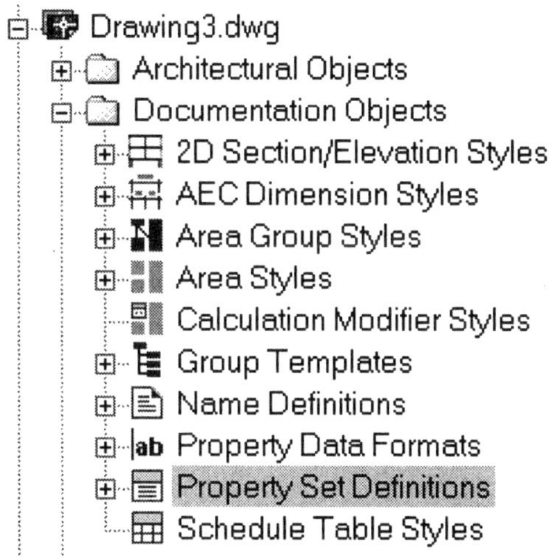

Locate the Property Set Defintions in your current drawing.

10. Paste **Window Objects** and **WindowStyles.**

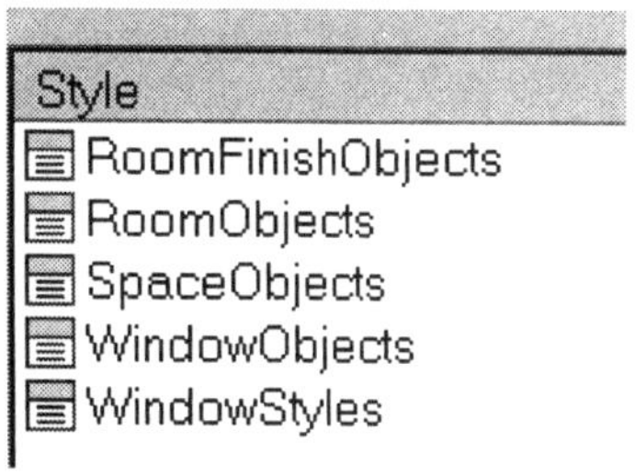

11. Go to **Format→AEC Content Wizard.**

12.

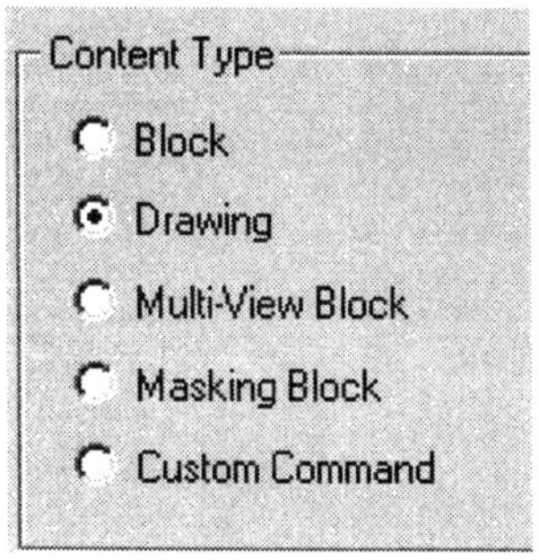

Enable **Drawing.**
Press **Next.**

13. 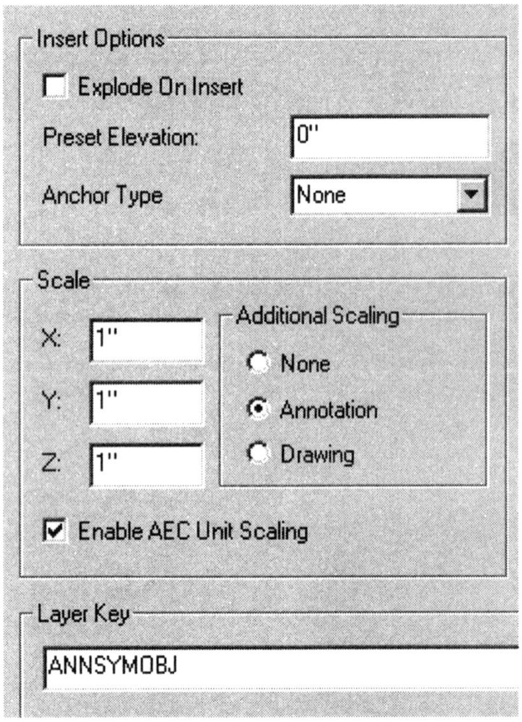

Enable **Enable AEC Unit Scaling.**
Set the Layer Key to **ANNSYMOBJ.**
Press **Next.**

14. 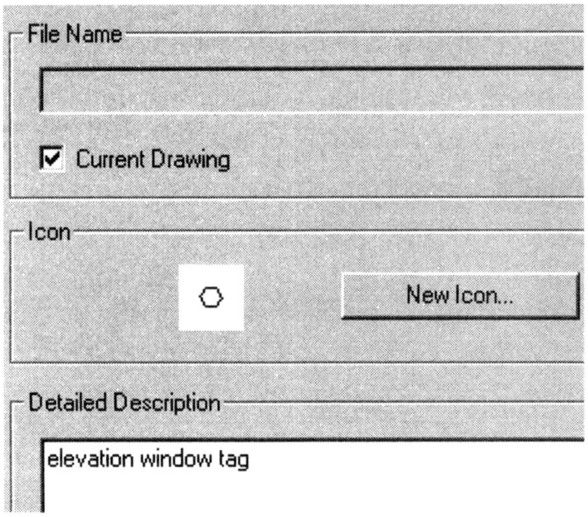

Enable **Current Drawing.**
In the Detailed Description field, enter **elevation window tag.**

Press **Finish**.

15. Save as *elev_window_tag.*
Close the file.

Exercise 7-4:
Creating Elevation Views

Drawing Name: ex6-5.dwg
Estimated Time: 15 minutes

This exercise reinforces the following skills:

- VPORTs
- Locking and Unlocking Display
- Layouts

1.  Open *ex6-5.dwg.*

Creating a Layout

2. 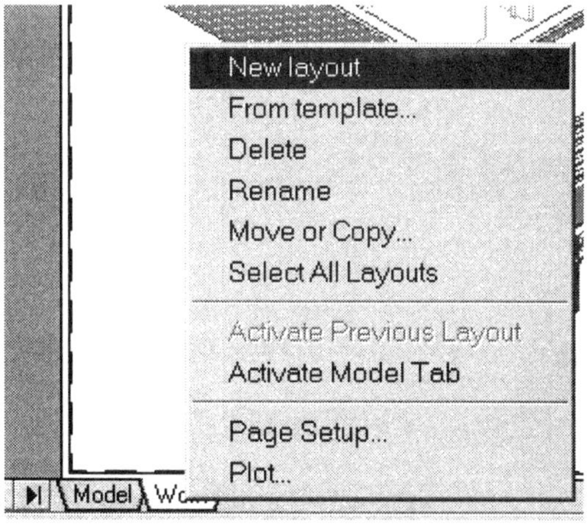

Place your mouse over the Work tab. Right click and select **New Layout**.

3. 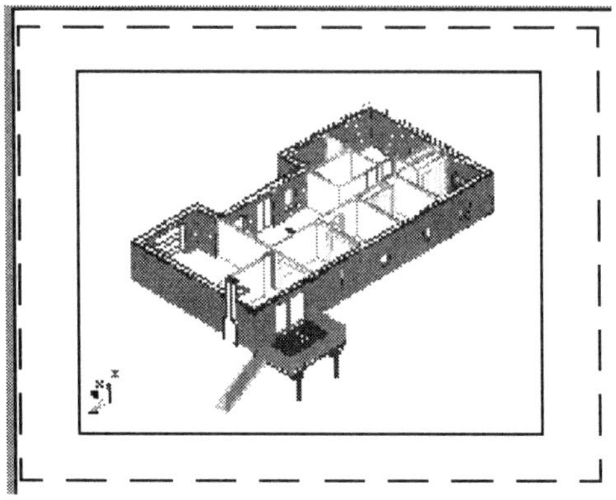

The layout appears with one viewport.

4. 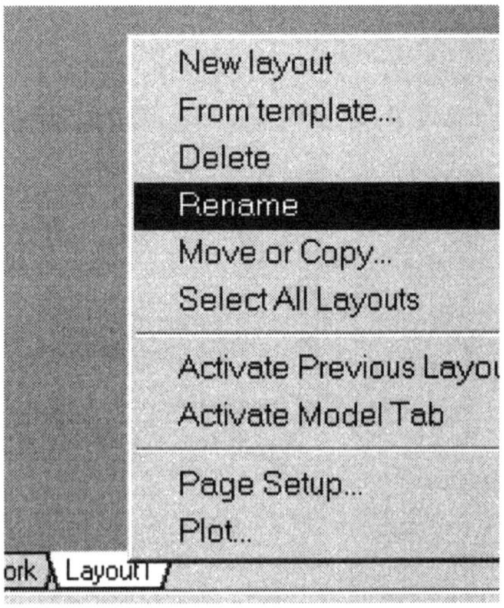

Select the new layout tab.
Right click and select **Rename**.

Change the name to
Elev-North & South.

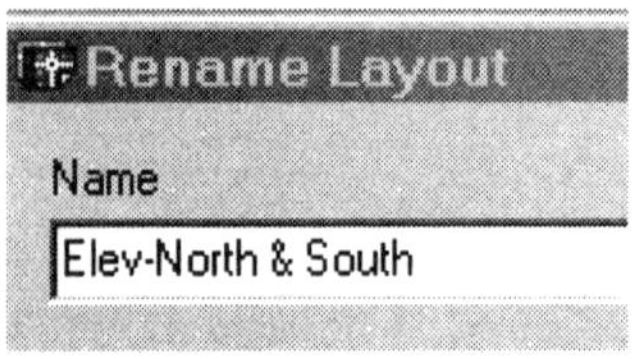

Press **OK**.

5. 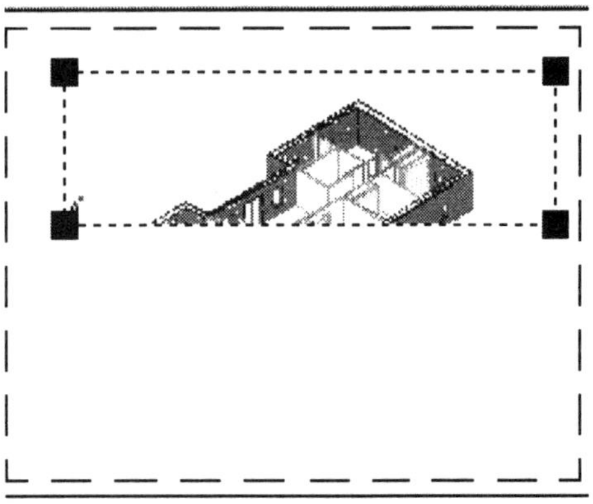

Using grips, move and resize the viewport so it takes up top of the sheet.

6. 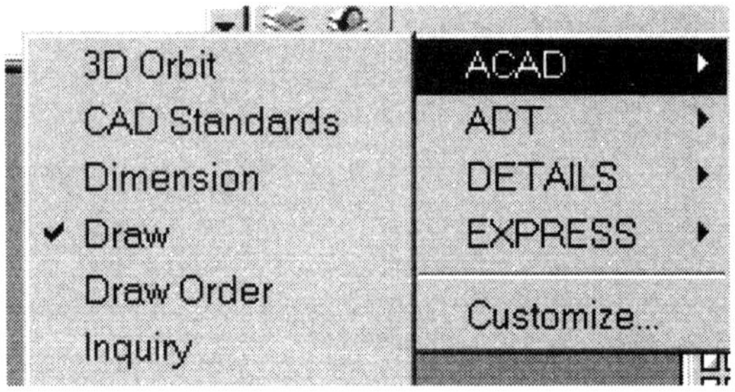

Right click in the grey area of any toolbar.
Select **ACAD→Viewports**.

This activates the **Viewports** toolbar.

7. 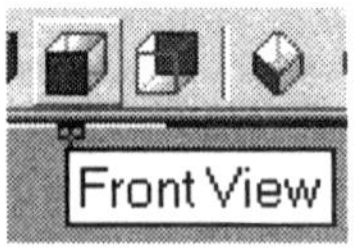

Select inside the viewport to activate it.
Select the **Front View** tool.

This tool is on the View toolbar. You can activate this toolbar if it is not visible.

8. 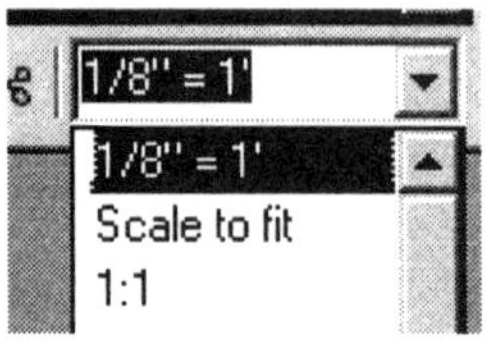

Set the viewport scale to **1/8″ = 1′**.

9. 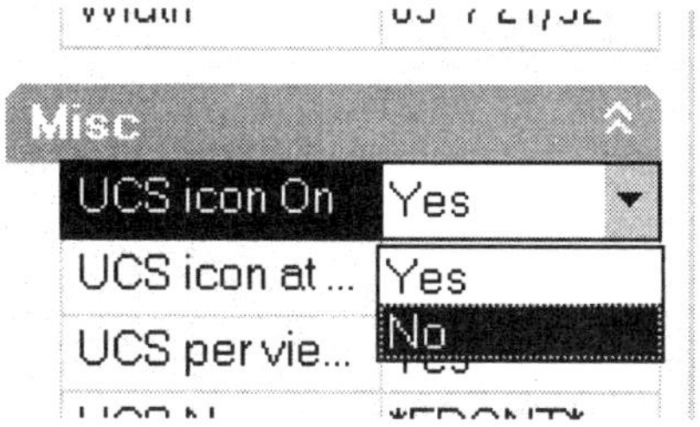

Select the viewport.
Right click and select **Properties**.
Under **Misc:** Set the UCS icon On to **No**.
This turns off the display of the UCS icon in the viewport.

10. 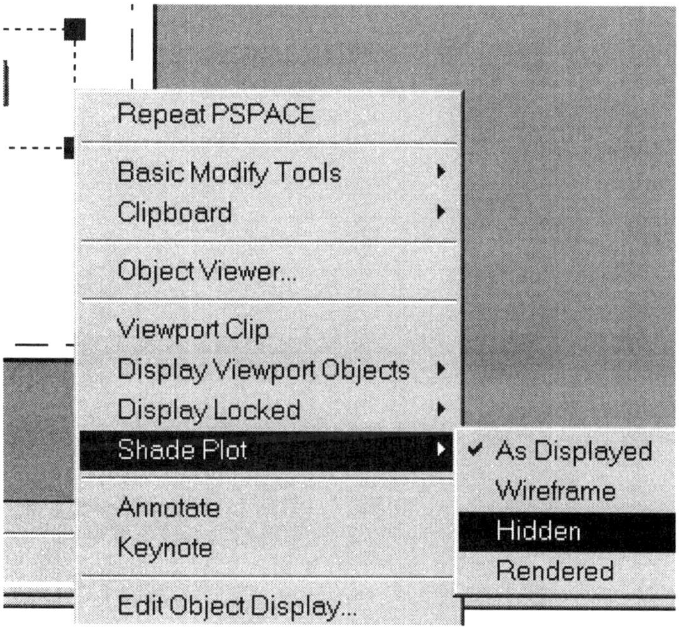

Select the viewport.
Right click and select
Shade Plot→Hidden.

Create a New Layer User Group

11.  Select the **Layer Manager** tool.

12.  Select **All**.
Select the **New User Group** tool.

13. 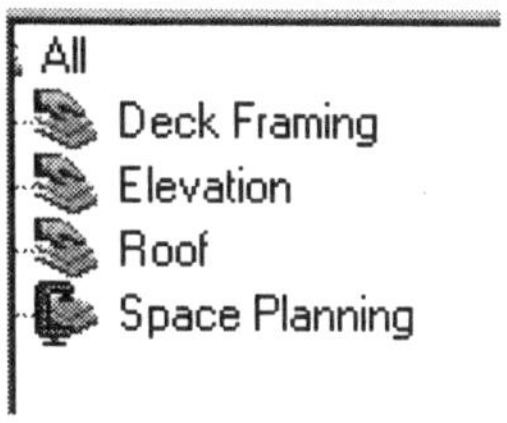

Rename the user group **Elevation.**

14. 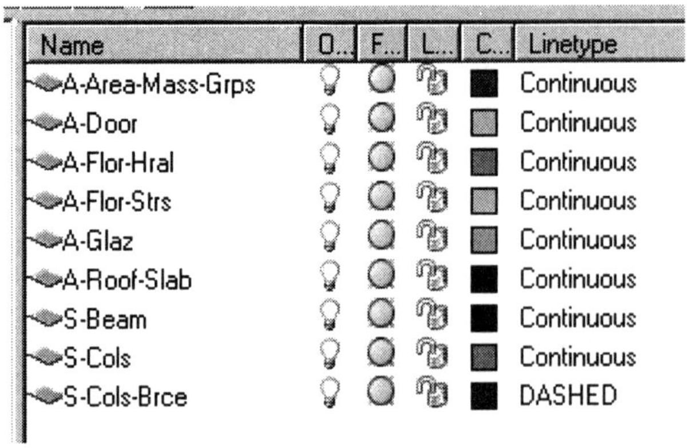

Place the layers listed in the Elevation user group.

Set them so they are all visible – ON and THAWED.

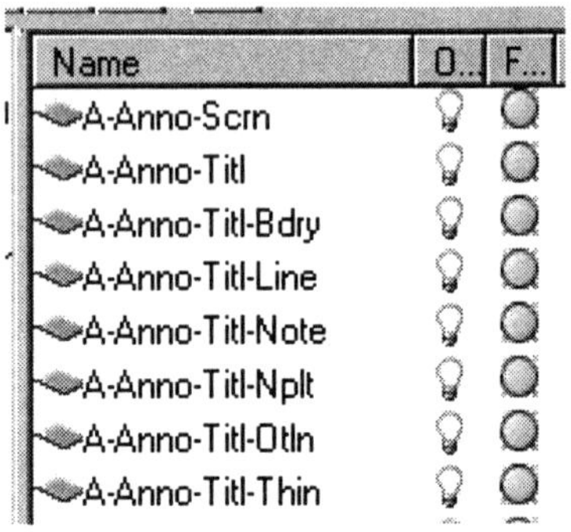

Close the dialog.

15.  Select the Elevation user group.
Select the **New Layer** tool.

16. 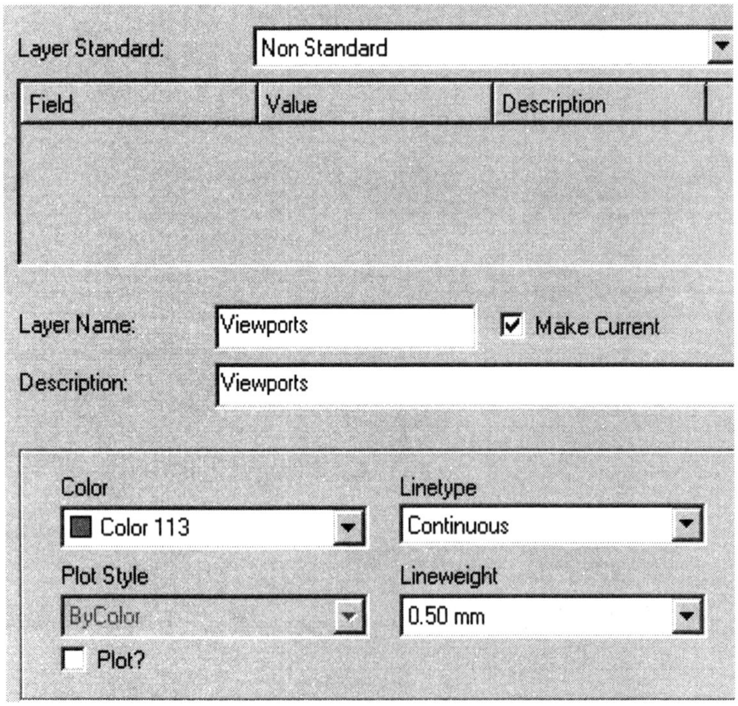

Set the Layer Standard to **Non Standard**.
Set the Layer name to **Viewports.**
Enable **Make Current**.
Set the Description to **Viewports**.
Set the Color to **113**.
Disable the **Plot** option.

Press **OK** twice to exit the dialog.

17. The viewport should appear as shown.

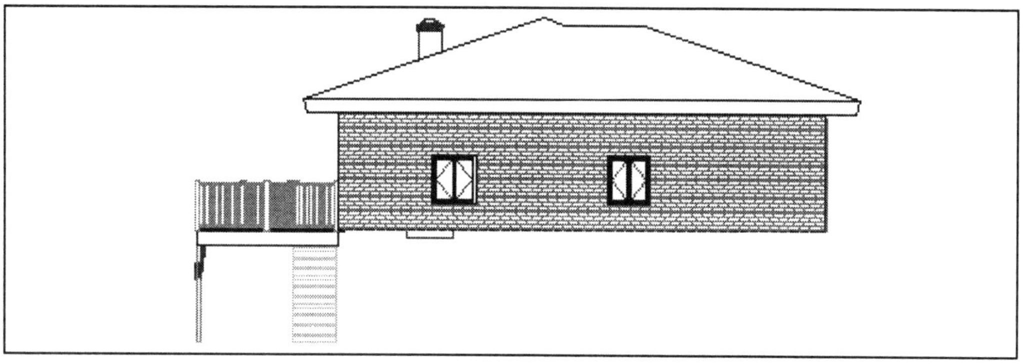

Select the viewport and move it to the **Viewports** layer.

18.  Select the **Single Viewport** tool.

19. 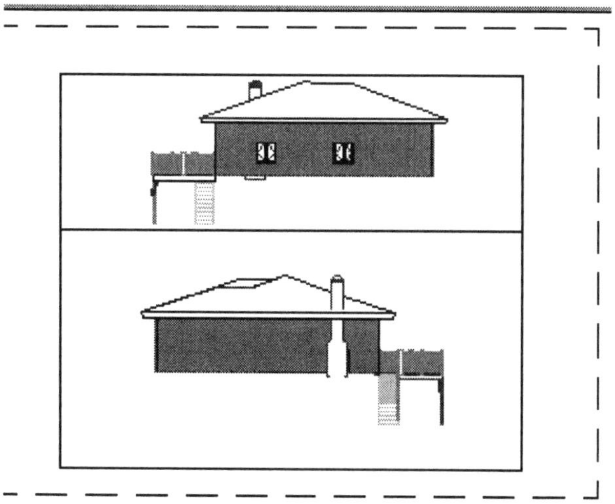

Place a second viewport below the first viewport.

Set the view to **Back**.

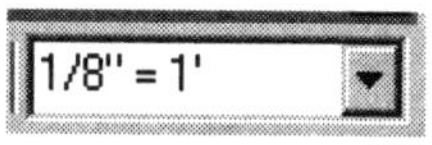

Set the scale to **1/8″=1′**.
Set the Shade Plot to **Hidden.**

20. 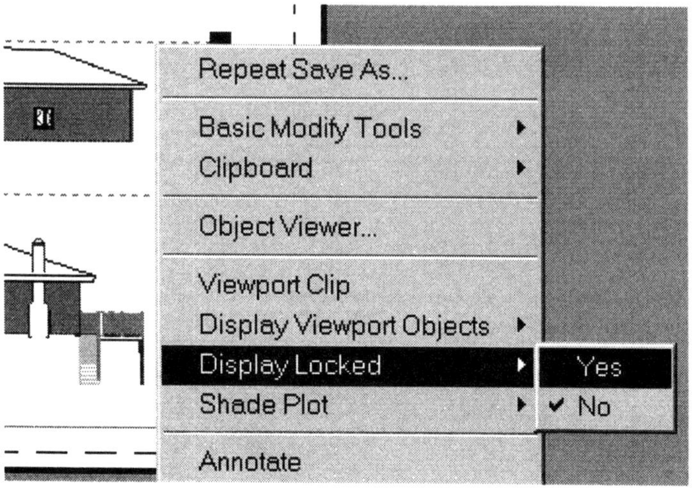

Select each viewport. Right click and set the Display Locked to **Yes**.

21. Save as *ex7-4.dwg*.

Exercise 7-5:
Annotating Elevation Views

Drawing Name: ex7-4.dwg
Estimated Time: 15 minutes

This exercise reinforces the following skills:

- Inserting a Titleblock
- Adding Material Callouts
- Adding a Scale bar

1.  Open *ex7-4.dwg.*

2. 

Set the Layer **A-Anno-Titl** as Current.

Inserting a Titleblock

3. 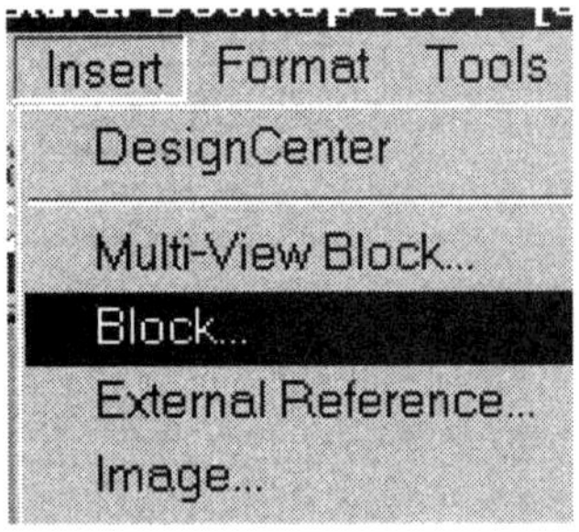

Go to **Insert→Block**.

TIP: To turn off the UCSICON, activate the viewport. Type UCSICON and OFF at the command line. You can only turn the UCSICON OFF/ON in model space.

4. Locate the titleblock you created in Exercise 7-1.dwg.
Set the Insertion point to **0,0,0**.
Set the Scale to **1** and enable **Uniform Scale.**
Press **OK.**

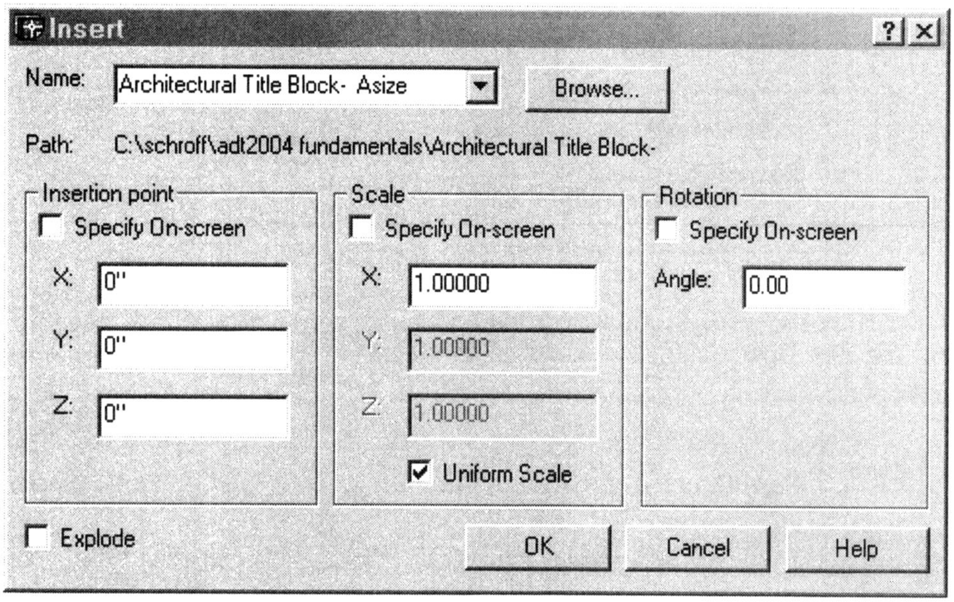

5.

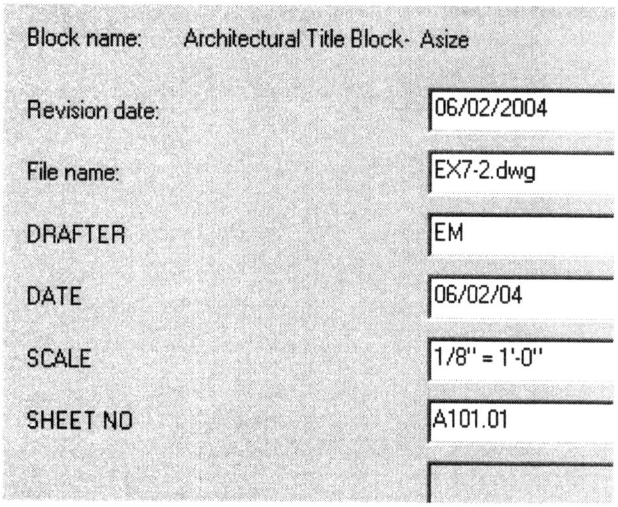

Fill in the attribute values. Use today's date for the date fields.

Use your initials in the DRAFTER field.

Press **OK.**

6. Shift the viewports so they fit inside the titleblock.

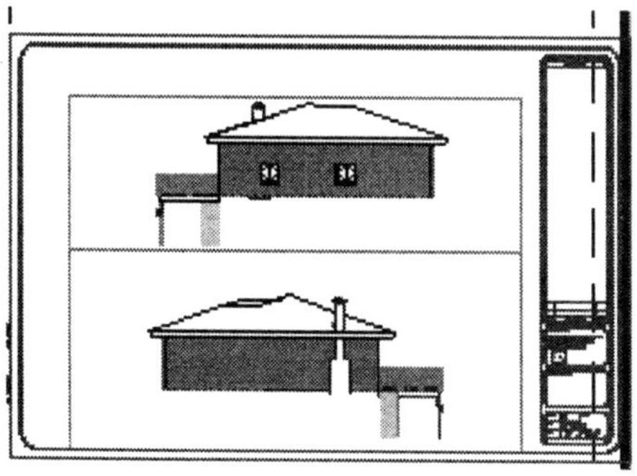

Accessing Page Setup

7. 

The dotted lines on the sheet indicate the margin.
You may notice that the margin cuts off part of the titleblock.
Place your mouse over the layout tab.
Right click and select **Page Setup**.

8. Select the Plot Device tab.
Select your plotter.

Select the **Properties** button.

9. 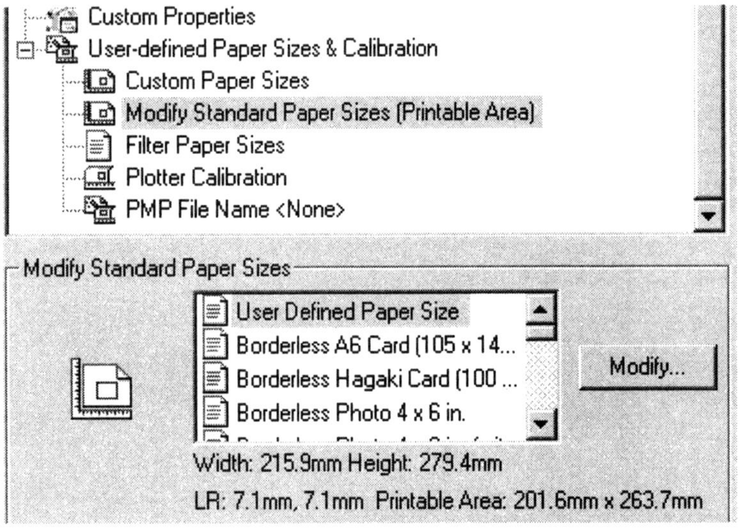

Select Modify Standard Paper Sizes (Printable Area).
Select User Defined Paper Size.
Select **Modify**.

10. 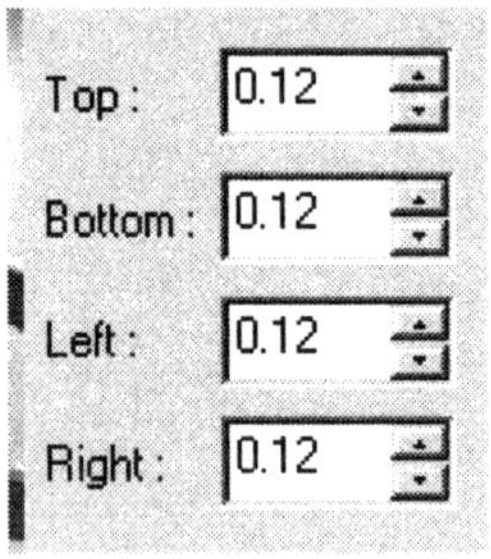

Set the Margins to **0.12**.

Press **OK** as prompted to close the dialog.

11. The title block now fits properly in the sheet.

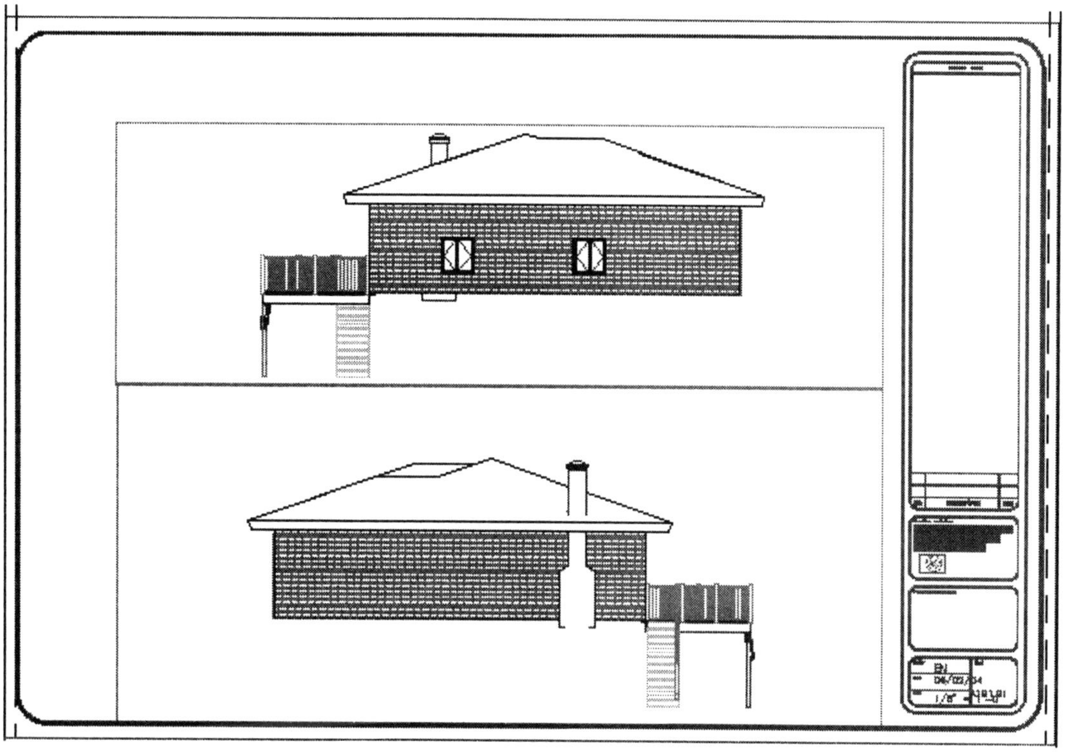

Adding Material Annotations

12. 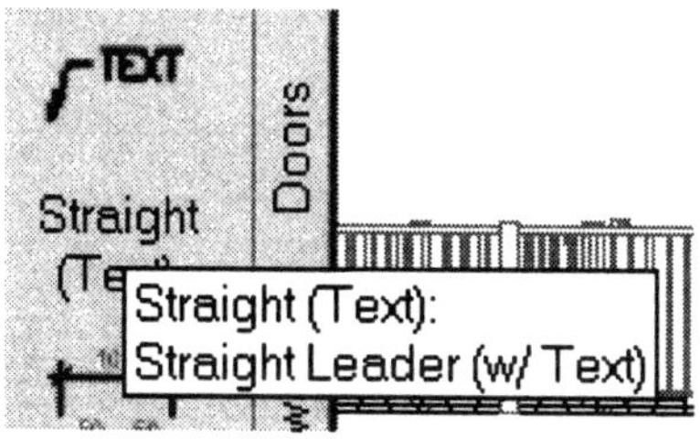

Launch the Tool Palette.
Select the **Straight Leader** tool from the Annotation Palette.

13. Add the text by entering **SHINGLE W/2" INSUL.**

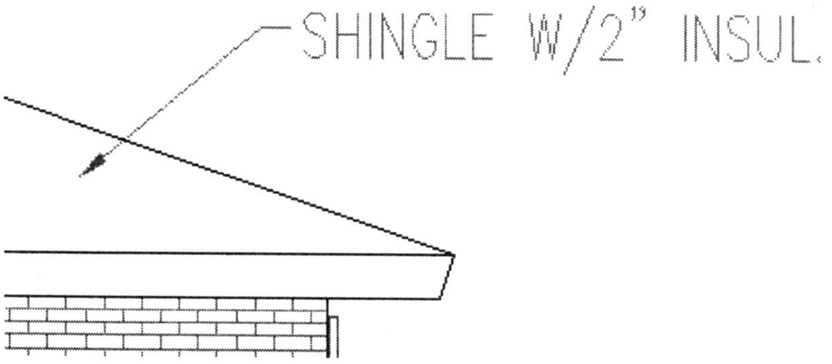

14.

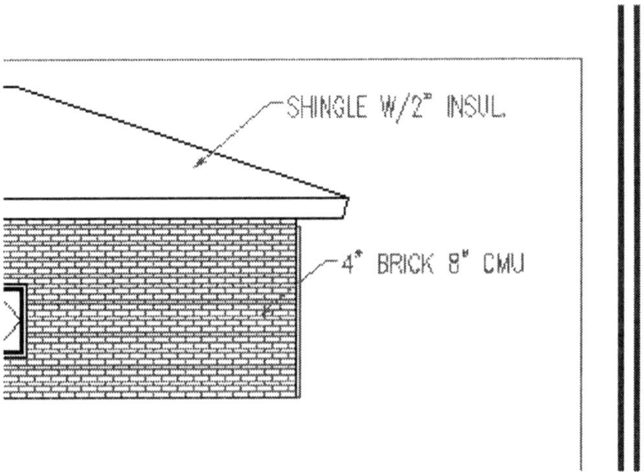

Add the text by entering **4″ BRICK 8″ CMU.**

Adding Elevation Labels

15. Launch the Tool Palette.
Select the Annotation Palette.
Locate the elevation label you created.
Pick the right bottom of the building.
When prompted for the rotation, enter 0.
The attribute edit dialog will appear.
Press **OK.**

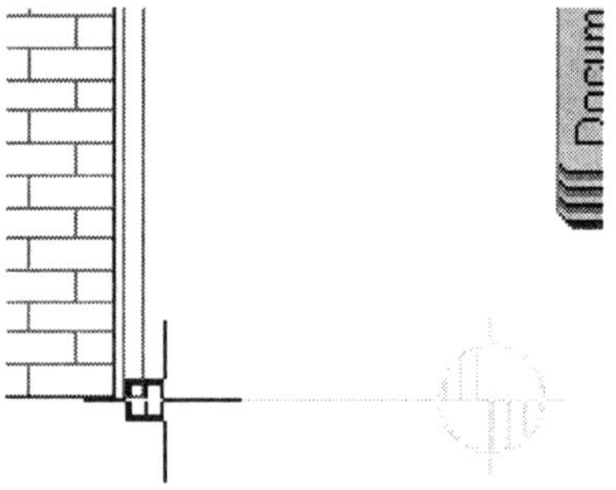

16.

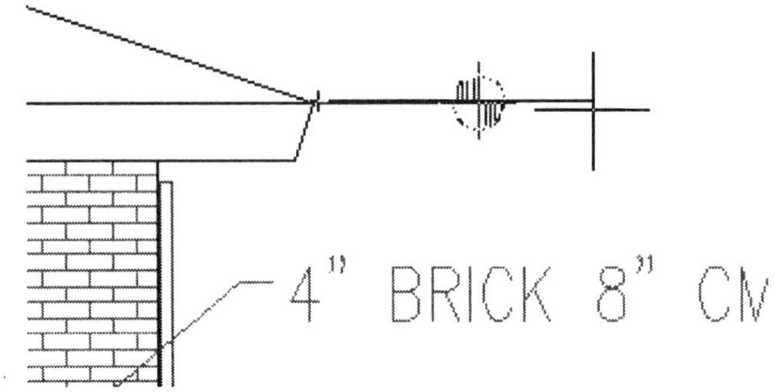

Select the elevation label.
Pick the roof edge.
When prompted for the rotation, enter 0.
The attribute edit dialog will appear.

17.

Edit the attributes.
Change LEVEL to **TOP OF PARAPET.**
Change ELEV to **Elev = 8′-0″.**
Press **OK.**

18.

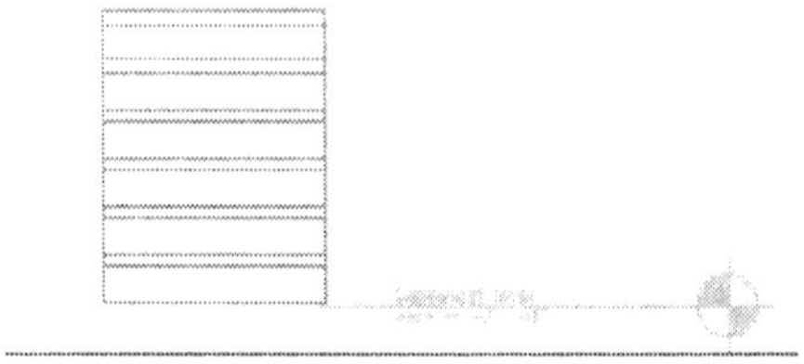

Add an elevation label for the bottom of the stairs.

Name the level **Basement level.**
Set the elev to **elev = -7′-0″.**

Adding Window Tags

19. Launch the Design Center.
    Locate the *elev_window_tag* drawing you created earlier.
    Select, right click and select **Insert as Block**.

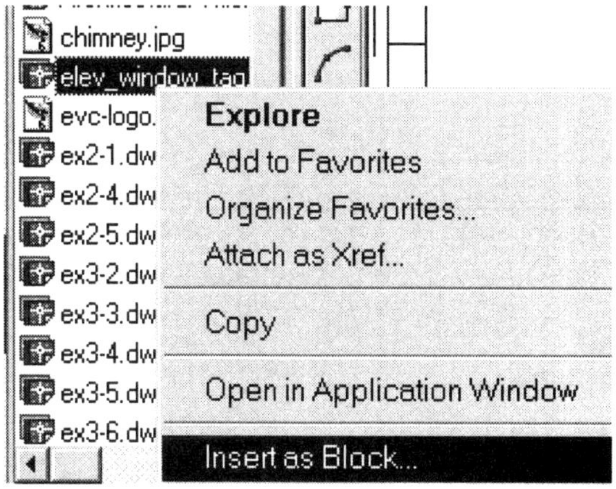

20. Add the elev_window_tag block to the two windows in the top viewport.

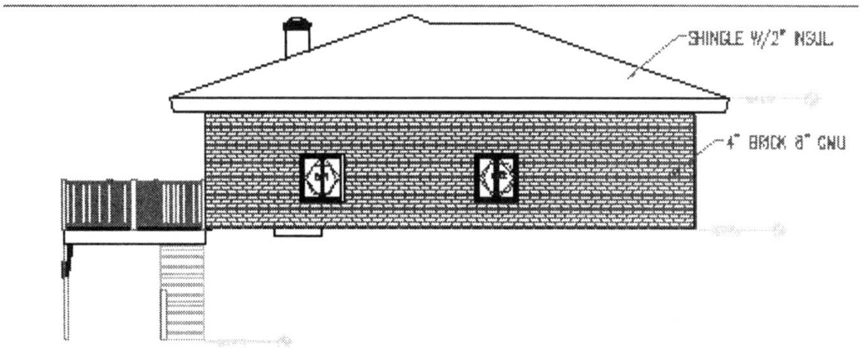

21. Save the file as *ex7-5.dwg.*

Sections

You can draw a section line in your drawing by specifying a start point, an endpoint, a length, and a height for the section. You can specify additional points between the start and endpoint to create jogs in your section. The section line acts as a cutting plane when you create the section, slicing a section from the building model.

Section marks are placed to create a cutting plane line and a section identifier. The section identifier includes the section number and the sheet number where the section is located. ADT comes with four standard section marks: two allow you to define a section identifier and two allow you to define a section identifier and a sheet number. You can also create custom section marks and define them using Create AEC Content.

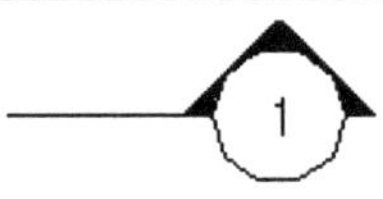	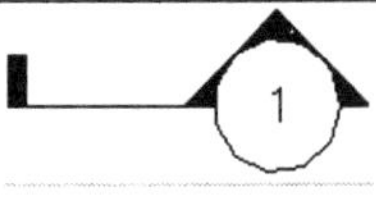	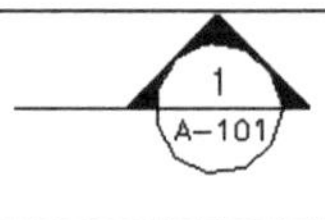	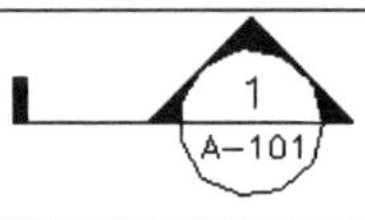
Section Mark A1	Section Mark A1T	Section Mark A2	Section Mark A2T

When you place a section mark, you are prompted 'Add AEC Object?' A yes response to this prompt will use the section line as a section object for the development of a section. This allows you to generate a section drawing.

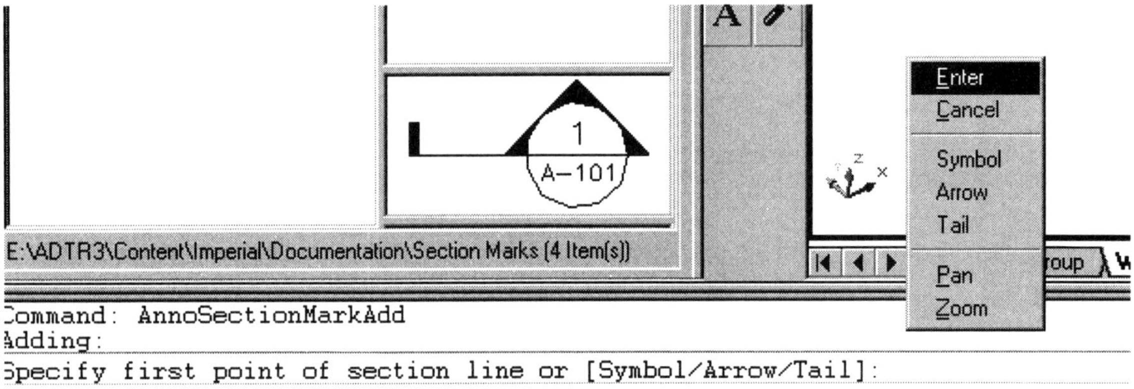

The command AnnoSectionMarkAdd has several options that allow the user to specify the symbol, the arrow, and whether or not the section mark has a tail. You can specify a custom symbol or a custom arrow as long as these drawing files reside in the Content path.

The section line and mark should be placed on the A-Sect-Iden layer and is greenish-blue in color.

It will not automatically be placed onto the correct layer unless you drag and drop from the Design Center and have your layer standards set up properly.

Exercise 7-6:

Creating Section Views

Drawing Name: ex7-5.dwg
Estimated Time: 15 minutes

This exercise reinforces the following skills:

- Creating a Layout
- Creating Section Lines
- Creating Section Marks
- Using AEC Content

1.  Open *ex7-5.dwg.*

2. 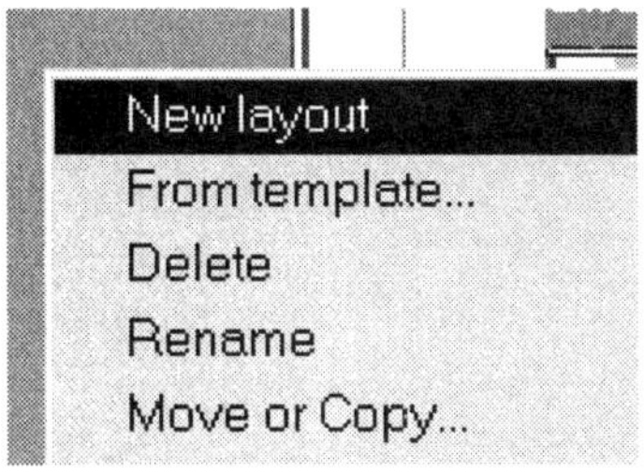

Right click on any of the existing layout names. Select 'New Layout' from the popup menu.

3. 

A new tab will appear at the end of all the existing tabs. The new tab is called *Layout1*.

4. Left clicking (selecting) the Layout1 tab will bring up the Page Setup dialog box. This allows you to set the page size, scale, printer, etc. for the new layout.

TIP: This dialog box comes up automatically the first time you select a newly created layout. To modify any of the settings after the initial setup, you can select the tab, right click, and select **Page Setup.**

5. Select the Plot Device tab.
In the Layout name edit box, change the name from Layout1 to **Sections.**
Select the **DWF55 ePlot** as the device.

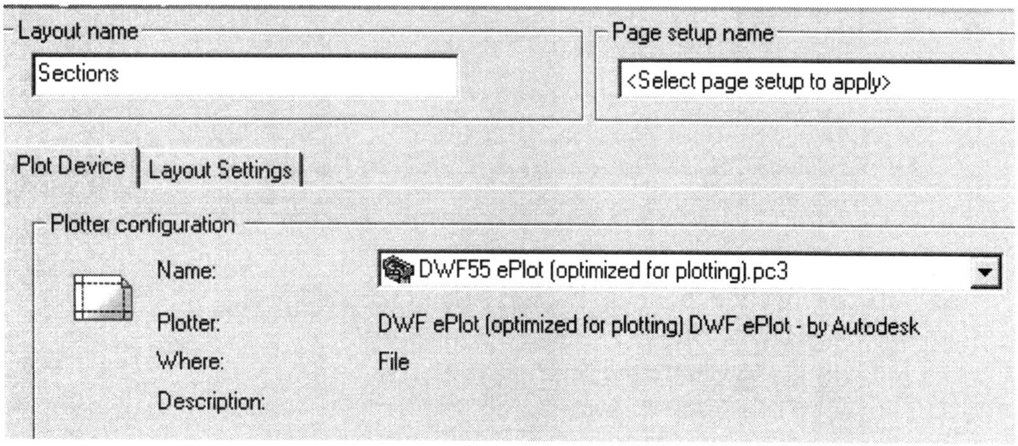

6. Select the Layout Settings tab.
Set the Paper size to ARCH D (36 x 24 Inches).
Press **OK**.

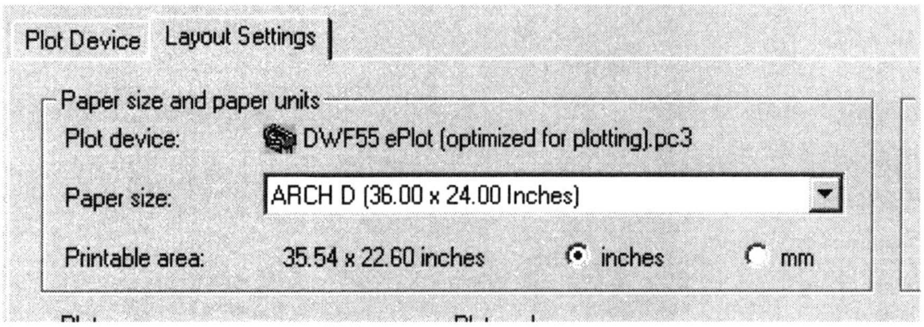

7. Select the Sections tab. You should have a single viewport.

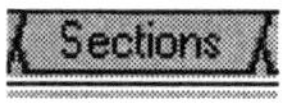

8.  Select the Top View icon.

When prompted to select a viewport, pick the viewport in your graphics area. It will automatically switch to a top view.

If you set the Model tab to top view then all new viewports will default to that view.

9. Pick the viewport. Right click and select 'Properties.'
Locate the Standard Scale field.
1/16″ = 1′-0 will fit well on a nominal D sheet.

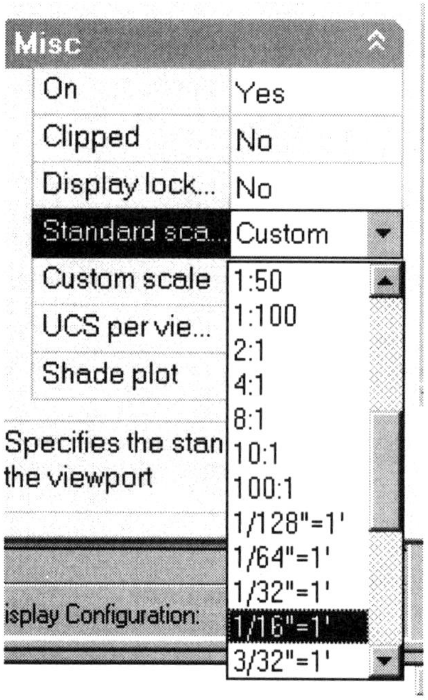

10. **Activate MODEL Space.**
Use PAN to move the model to the left side of the viewport.
Turn the **UCSICON** off.
Lock the Display to ensure the scale stays at 1/16″ = 1′.

11.  Launch the tool palette.

12. 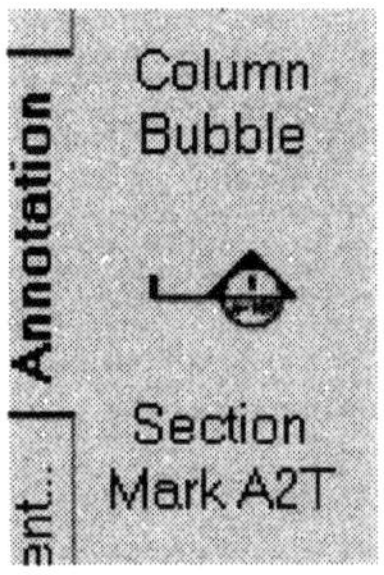

Select **Section Mark A2T** on the Annotation Palette.

13. 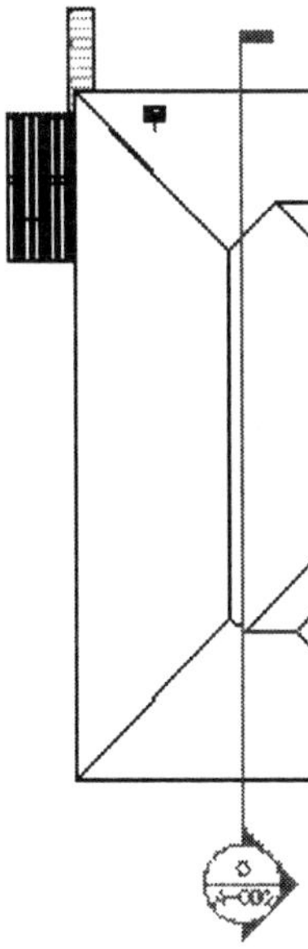

Verify that you are still in Model Space.
Place the section line as shown, going from top to bottom. Setting ORTHO ON will help create a straight line.
When prompted to *Add Building Section Line object? [Yes/No] <No>:*
Type **Y**.

14. 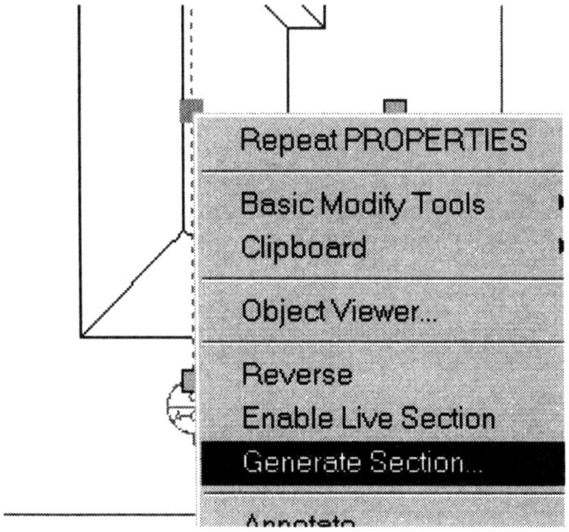

Select the Section line.
Right click and select **Generate Section**.

15.

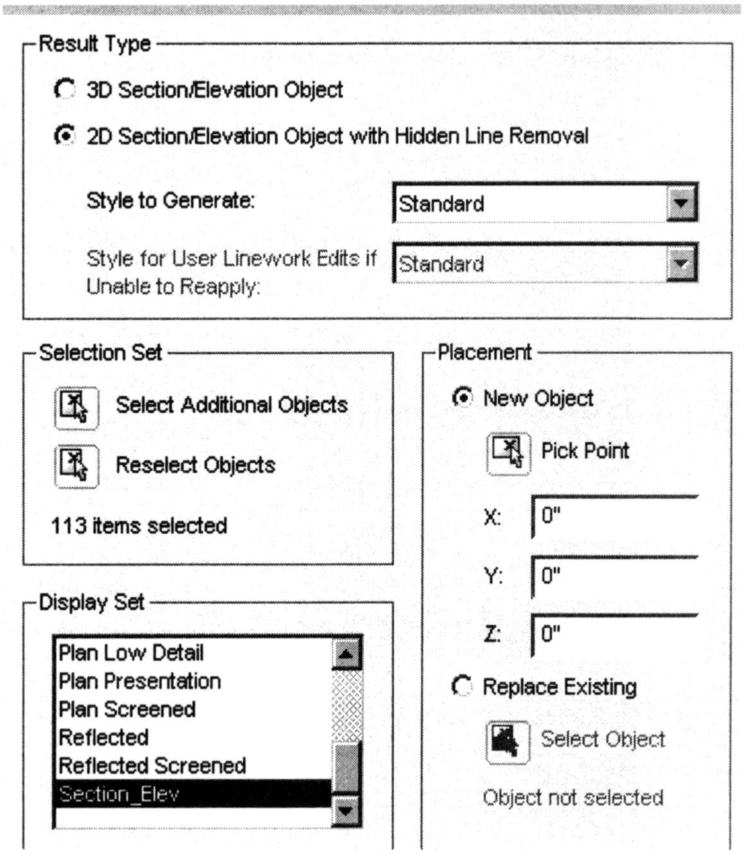

Set the Result Type to **2D Section/ Elevation Object**.

For the Selection Set, window around the entire building. Do not include the section line and viewport.

Set the Display Set to **Section_Elev**.

Select the **Pick Point tool** in the Placement section.

16. Pick a point to the right of your plan view to place your elevation. You may need to enlarge your viewport or shift your views.

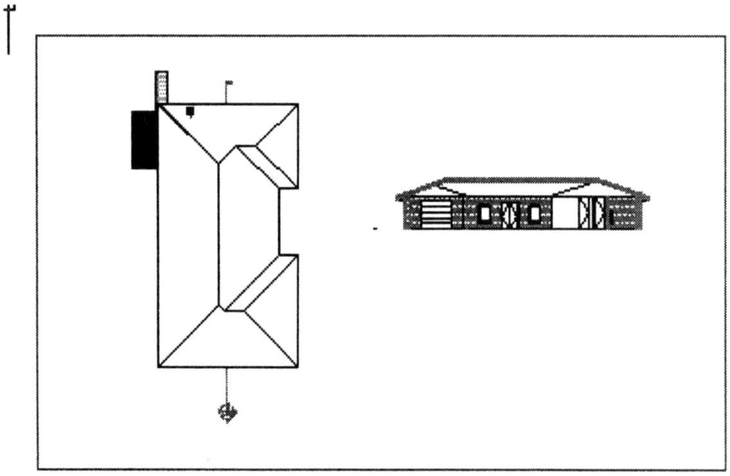

Changing the Section Line Display

17.

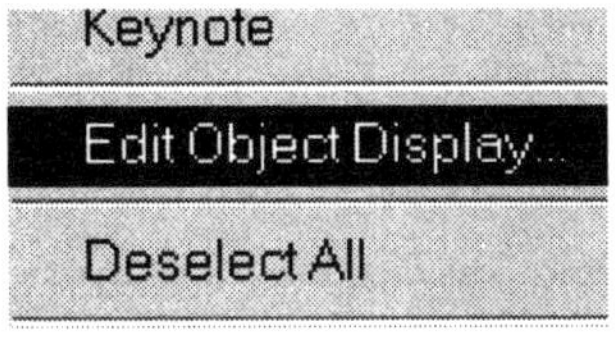

Select the Section Line.
Right click and select **Edit Object Display**.

18.

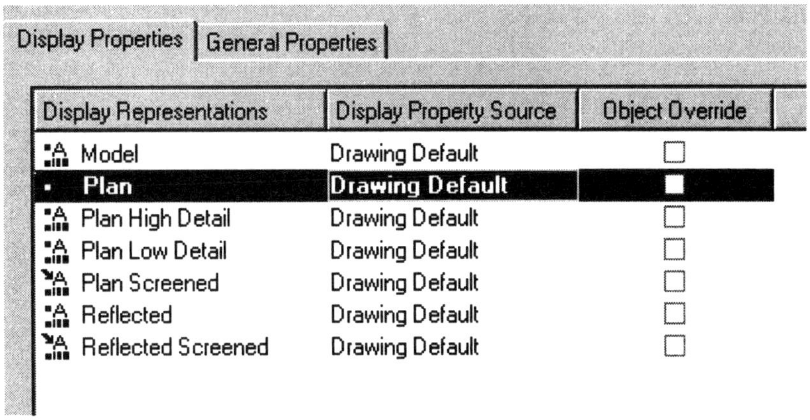

Select **Object Override.**

19.

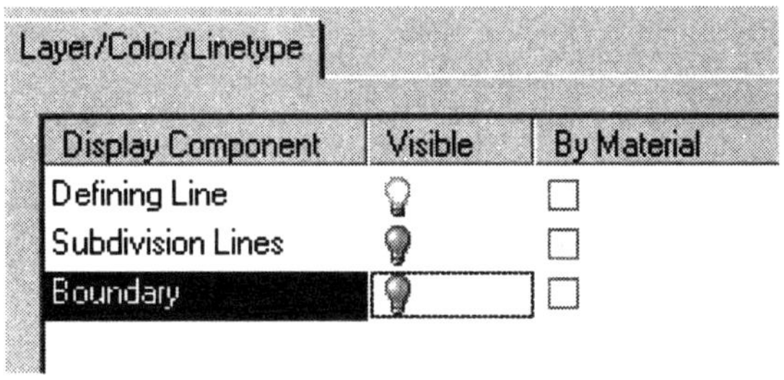

Set the Subdivision Line and Boundary so Visibility is turned **OFF**.

Press **OK** twice to exit the dialog box.

20.

Select the **Edit Attibute** tool.
Select the section header.

21.

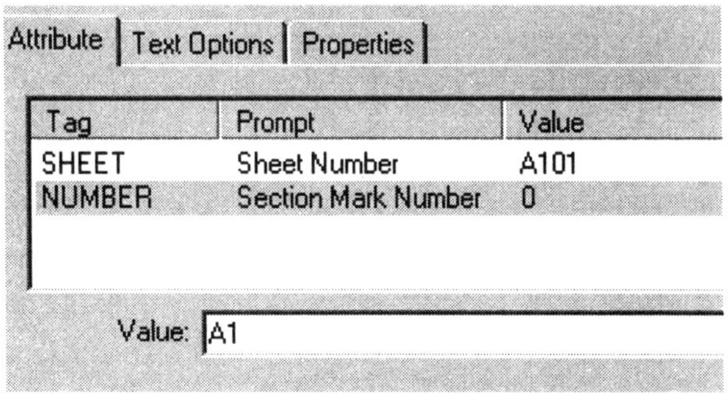

Change the values of the attributes.
Change the Sheet Value to **A101**.
Change the Number Value to **A1**.

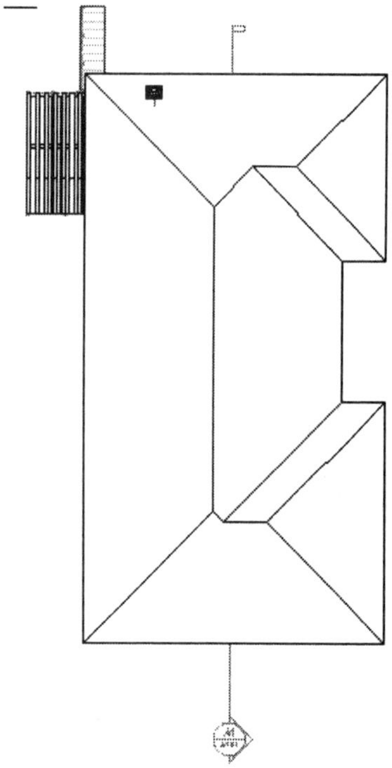

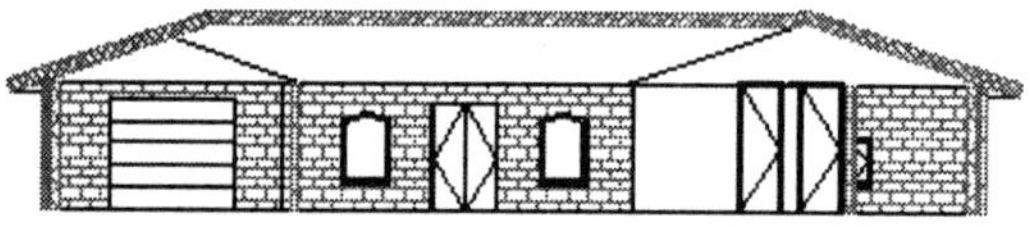

Reverse the Section Display

22.

Select the Section Line.
Right click and select **Reverse**.

Change the Section Depth

23.

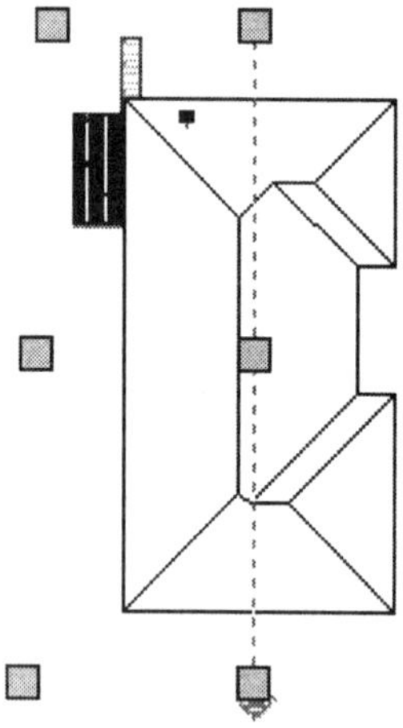

Pick the Section Line.
Use the blue grips of the boundary line to move the section depth into the model.

24.

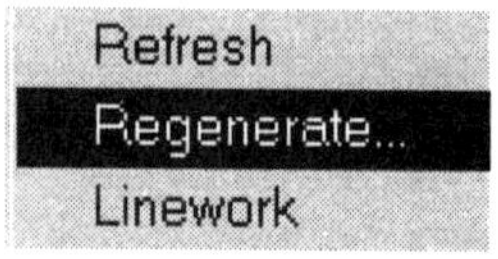

Select the Section View.
Right click and select **Regenerate.**

25. 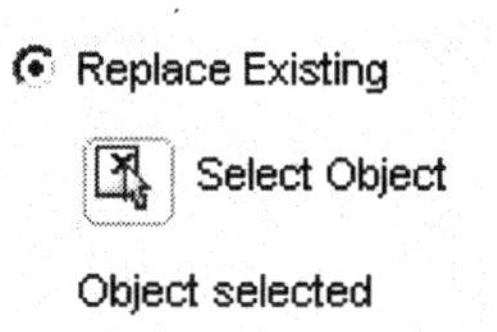

Enable **Replace Existing**.
Pick **Select Object a**nd select the existing section view.

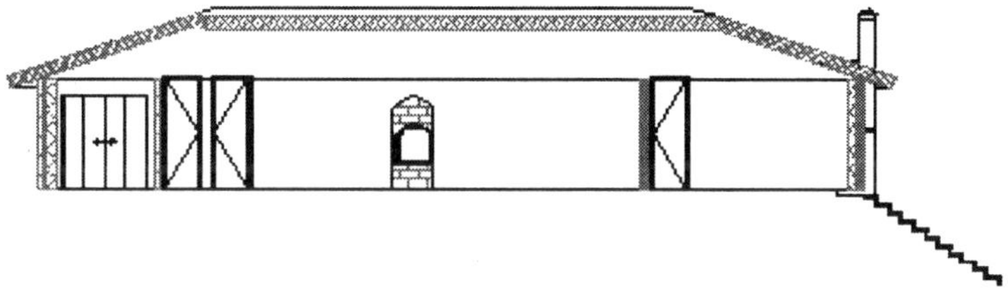

26. Save the file as *ex7-6.dwg.*

Exercise 7-7:

Creating 3D Section Views

Drawing Name: Ex7-6.dwg
Estimated Time: 15 minutes

This exercise reinforces the following skills:

- Creating a Layout
- Creating Section Lines
- Creating Section Marks
- Using AEC Content

1.  Open *ex7-6.dwg.*

2. Create a new layout and name it **3D Section**.

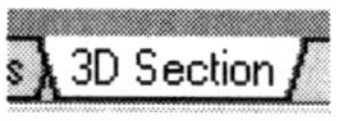

3. Use STRETCH to set the single viewport so it only occupies half the paper.
Set the viewport to TOP view.
Set the Scale to ¼″ = 1′.
Lock the Display.

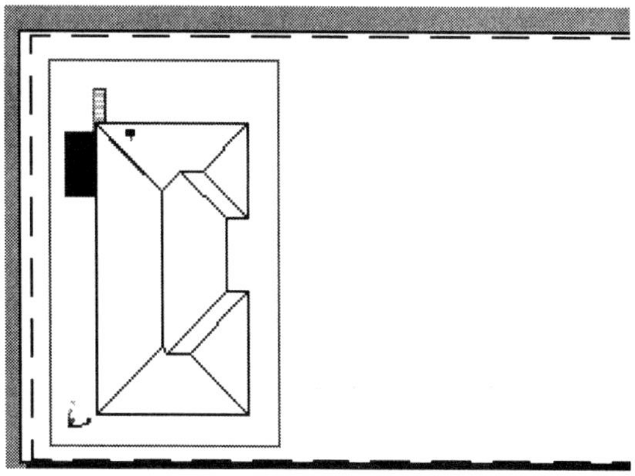

4. 

Select the viewport.
Right click and select
Basic Modify Tools→Copy.

5. Place the second viewport next to the first as shown.

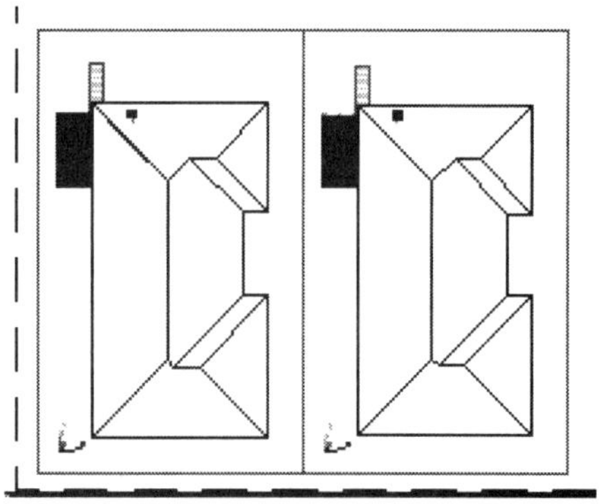

6. Create a New Layer called **3D Section.** Set the Color as **White** and the Linetype as **Continuous**. Enable **Make Current.** Enable **Plot.**

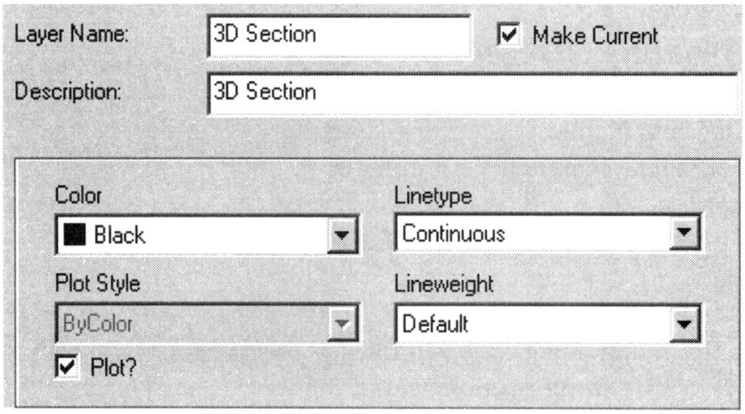

7. Unlock the Display of the right viewport.
Pan the model space so that you have an empty area displayed in the right viewport.

8. Launch the Design Center.

9. Activate the model space for the plan view viewport on the left.

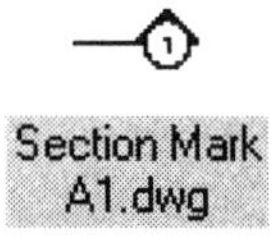

Select **Section Mark A1** to drag and drop into the left viewport.

10.

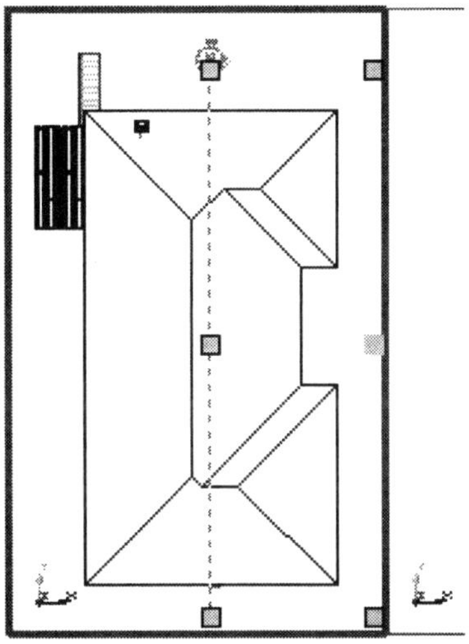

Type **A2** for the Section Mark Number.

Specify the right side of the model for the arrow side.
At the ADD AEC section object? prompt, type **Y** for YES.
(This creates the 2D/3D section object).

11.

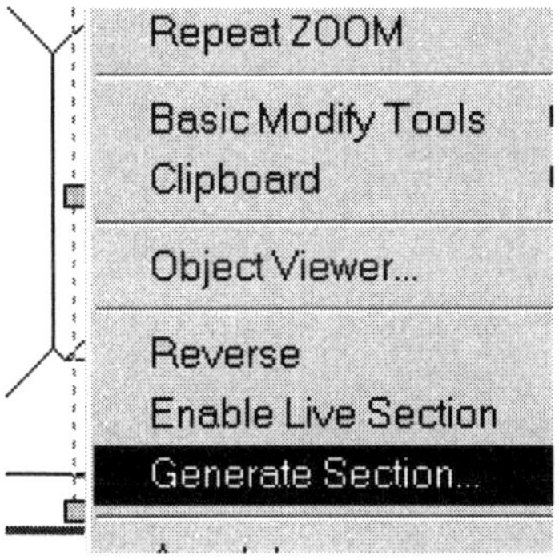

Select the section line you just created.
Right click and select **Generate Section.**

12.

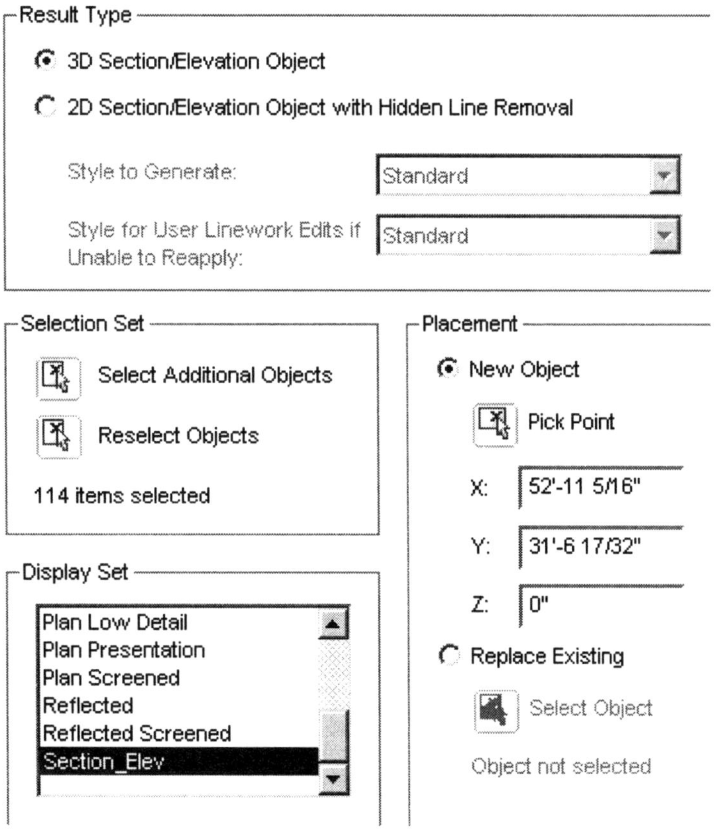

Enable **3D Section/ Elevation Object.**
Select the house model.
Set the Display Set to **Section_Elev.**
For placement, select the viewport on the right.
Press **OK**.

13. With the right viewport activated, switch to an isometric view. 

14. You can move the section view so it has a greater separation from the house view using the MOVE tool.

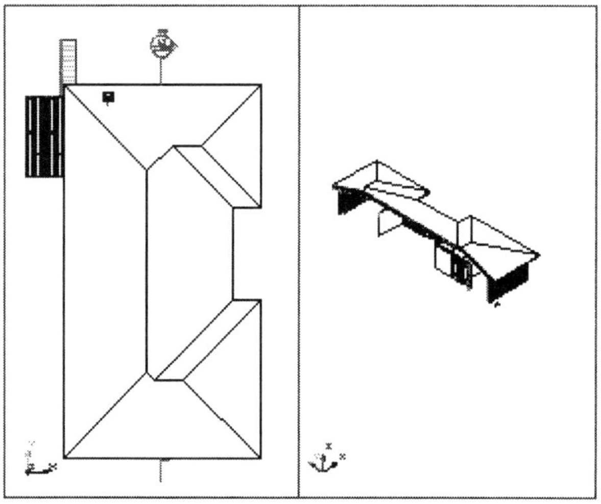

You can also use the PAN and ZOOM tools to position your 3D Section view. Make sure that you set a standard scale for both your viewports and lock the display.

If you don't like the section view generated, you can move the section line and regenerate the section view.

15. Save as *ex7-7.dwg*

TIP: Placing your viewports on the layer 'Defpoints' will ensure that they will never plot.

Quiz 4

True or False

1. Columns, braces, and beams are created using Structural Members.
2. When you isolate a Layer User Group, you are freezing all the layers in that group.
3. You can isolate a Layer User Group in ALL Viewports, a Single Viewport, or a Selection Set of Viewports.
4. When placing beams, you can switch the justification in the middle of the command.
5. Standard AutoCAD commands, like COPY, MOVE, and ARRAY cannot be used in ADT.

Multiple Choice

6. Before you can place a beam or column, you must:

   A. Generate a Member Style
   B. Activate the Structural Member Catalog
   C. Select a structural member shape
   D. All of the above

7. Select the character that is OK to use when creating a Structural Member Style Name.

   A. -
   B. ?
   C. =
   D. /

8. Identify the tool shown.

   A. Add Brace
   B. Add Beam
   C. Add Column
   D. Structural Member Catalog

9. Setting a Layer Key

    A. Controls which layer AEC objects will be placed on.
    B. Determines the layer names created.
    C. Sets layer properties.
    D. All of the above.

10. There are two types of stairs used in residential buildings:

    A. INSIDE and OUTSIDE
    B. METAL and WOOD
    C. MAIN and SERVICE
    D. FLOATING and STATIONARY

11. Select the stair type that does not exist from the list below:

    A. Straight-run
    B. M Stairs
    C. L Stairs
    D. U Stairs

12. The first point selected when placing a set of stairs is:

    A. The foot/bottom of the stairs.
    B. The head/top of the stairs
    C. The center point of the stairs
    D. Depends on the property settings

ANSWERS:

1) T; 2) F; 3) T; 4) T; 5) F; 6) D; 7) A; 8) A; 9) A; 10) C; 11) B; 12) D

Lesson 8
Documentation

We can create the best 3D model in the world, but if we cannot produce working 2D drawings that can be read by a contractor or builder, then we have not done our job.

The AIA has established a set of rules for drawings, including how sheets are to be numbered, colors, and dimensioning standards.

Drawing Annotation includes

- Dimensions
- Notes
- Schedules
- Symbols

Prior to annotation being placed, you need to set the Drawing Scale. The drawing scale determines that size of symbols and text. The command is DWGSCALESETUP.

To access the drawing scale can be accessed using **Format→Drawing Setup** and selecting the Scale tab.

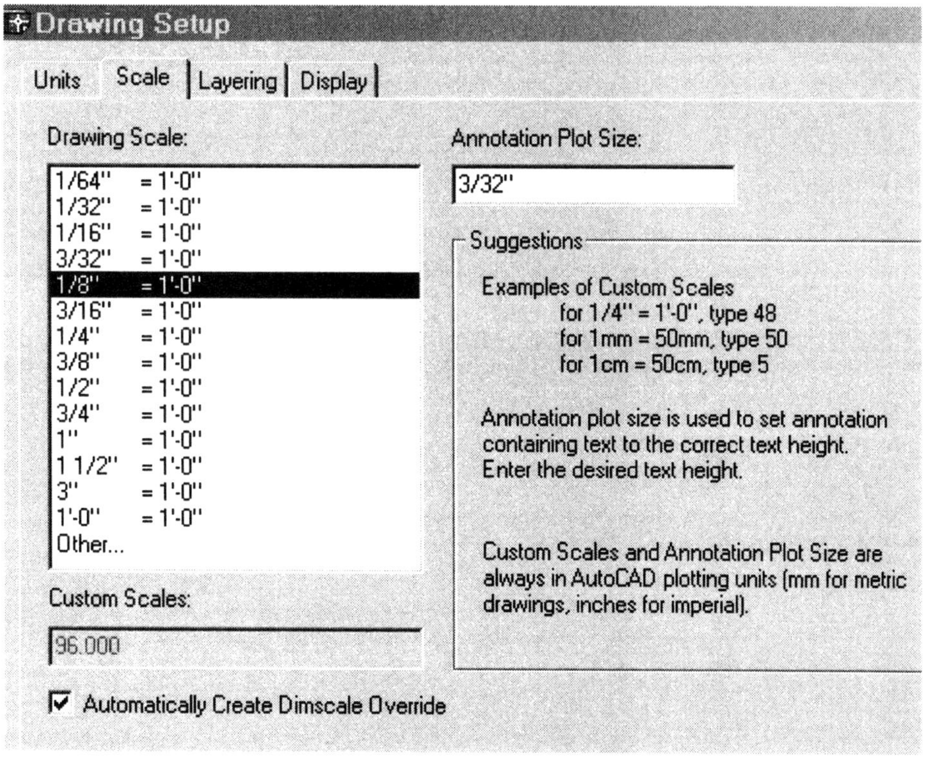

Scale-dependent objects in an Autodesk Architectural Desktop drawing are scaled automatically to reflect the units set in a drawing. Any styles that you create in metric or imperial units are scaled appropriately. You can also set the scale for the plot size of annotation in your drawing. If you are using a drawing template, then you can customize the drawing scale in your template and save the changes.

TIP: The Annotation Plot Size value can be restricted by the Linear Precision setting on the Units tab. If the Annotation Plot Size value is more precise than the Linear Precision value, then the Annotation Plot Size value is not accepted.

Most of the documentation tools can be accessed using the Design Center.
You simply drag and drop the desired symbol into the drawing.

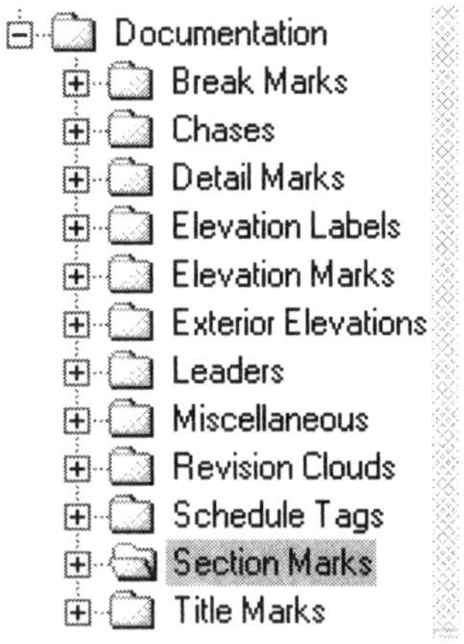

Break Marks	AnnoBreakMarkAdd SETIMPBREAKMARKS	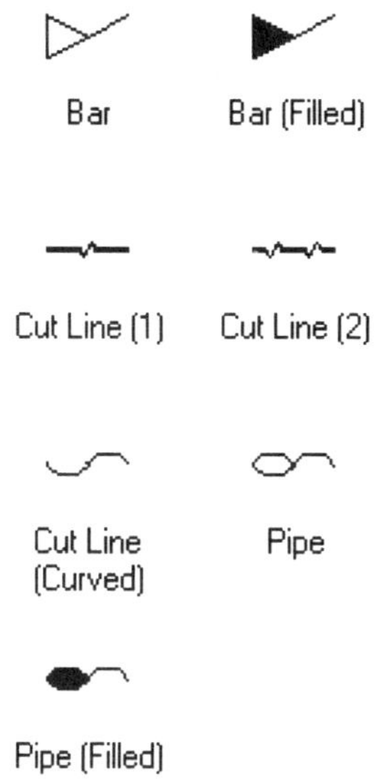
Chases	AECCannomVblockInterferenceAdd SETIMPCHASES	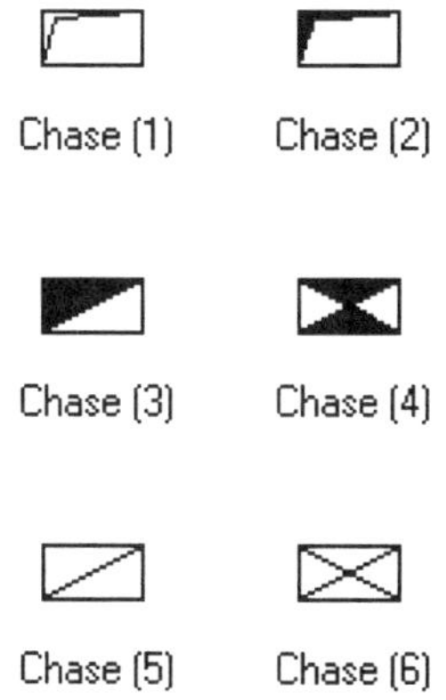
Detail Marks	AnnoDetailMarkAdd SETIMPDETAILMARKS	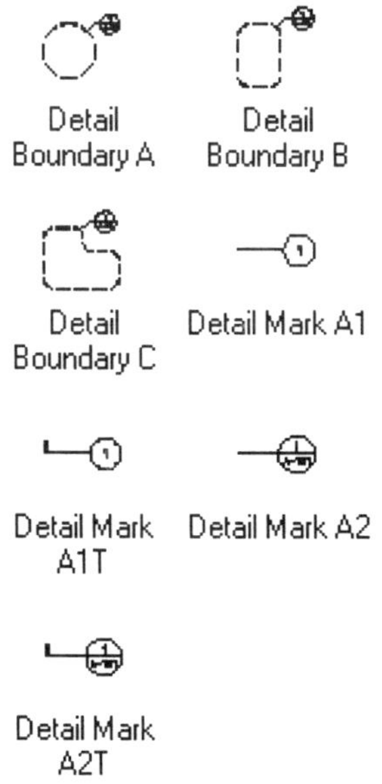

Elevation Labels	AnnoElevationLabelAdd SETIMPELEVATIONLABELS	2D Section 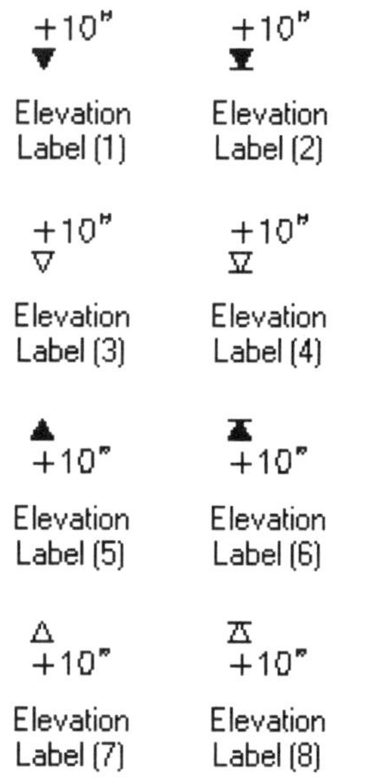 Model 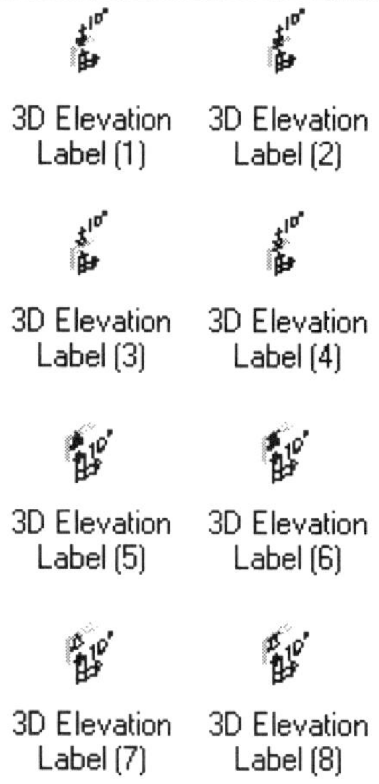
Elevation Labels	AnnoElevationLabelAdd	Plan 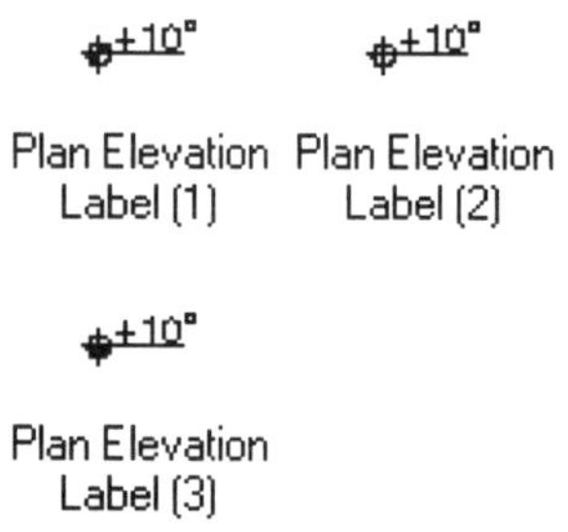

Elevation Marks	AnnoElevationMarkAdd SETIMPELEVATIONMARKS	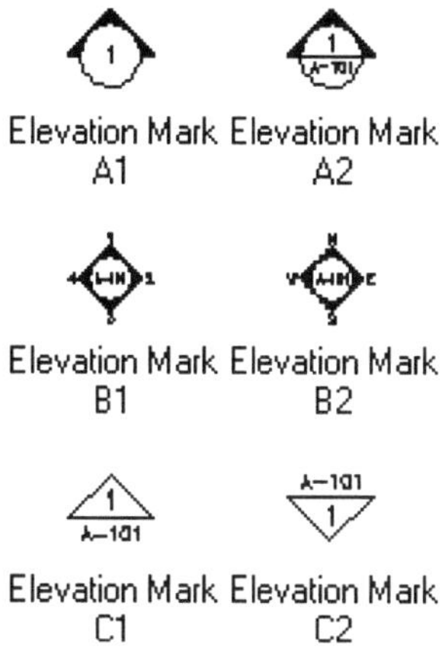
Leaders	AnnoLeaderAdd SETIMPLEADERS	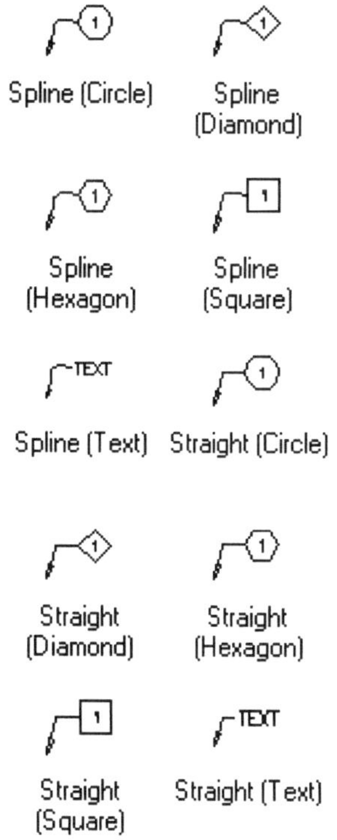

<table>
<tr>
<td>Miscellaneous</td>
<td>SetImpMiscellaneous</td>
<td>
Dimensions
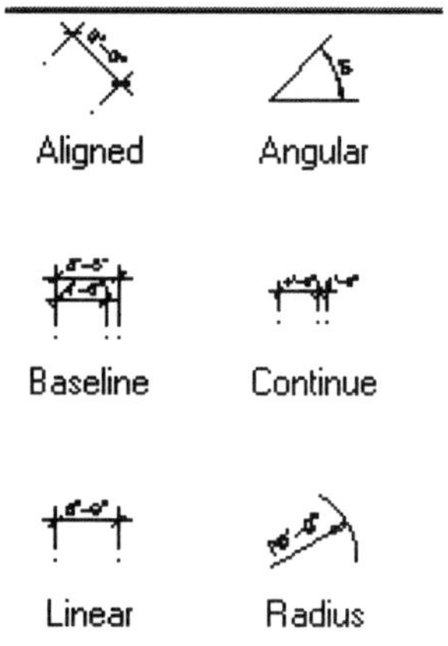

Fire Rating Lines
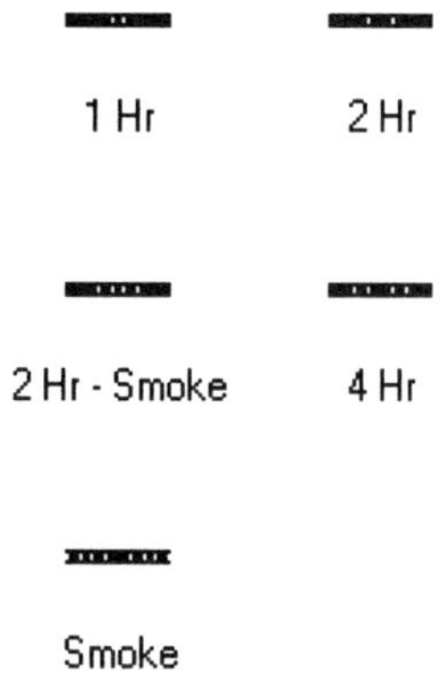

Match Lines
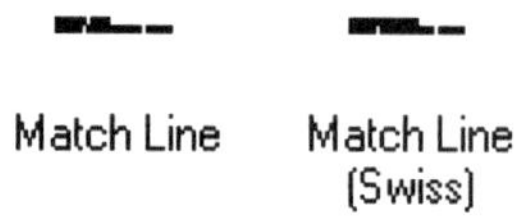

</td>
</tr>
</table>

Miscellaneous	SetImpMiscellaneous	North Arrows 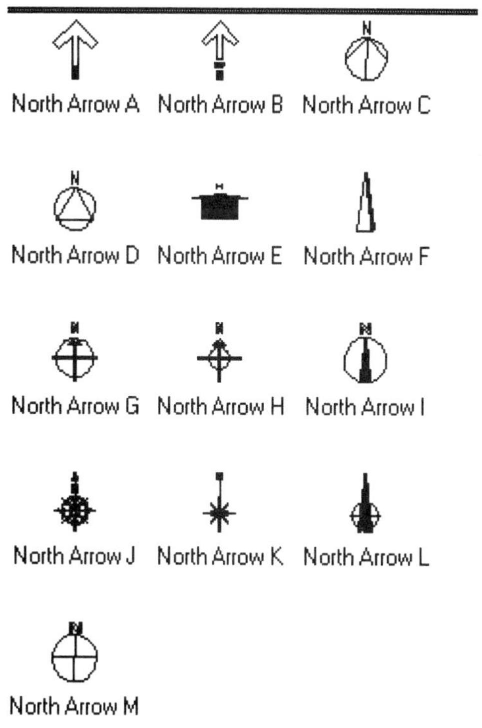
Revision Clouds	AnnoRevisionCloudAdd SETIMPREVISONCLOUDS	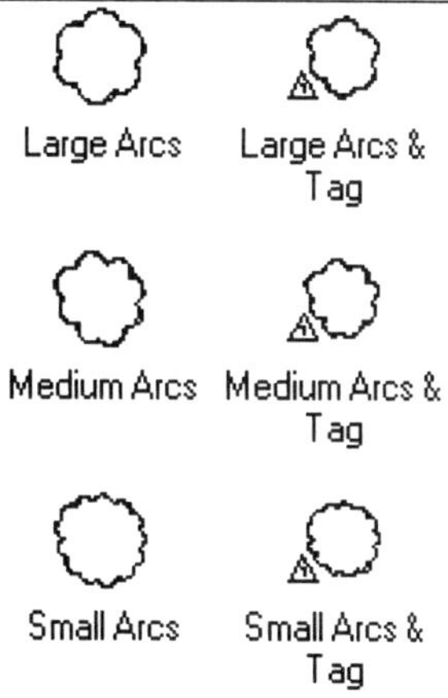

<table>
<tr>
<td>Schedule Tags</td>
<td>AecAnnoScheduleTagAdd</td>
<td>
Area Tags

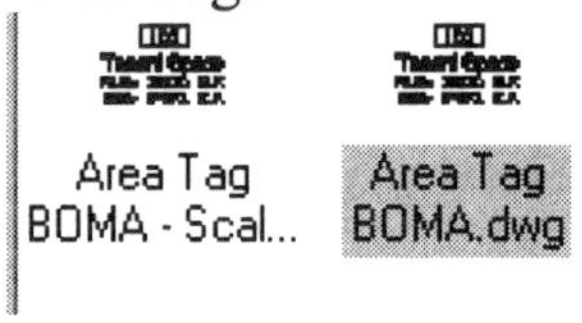

Door and Window Tags

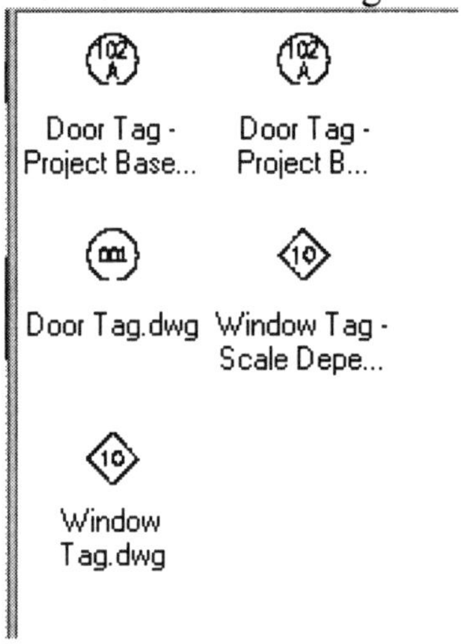

Object Tags

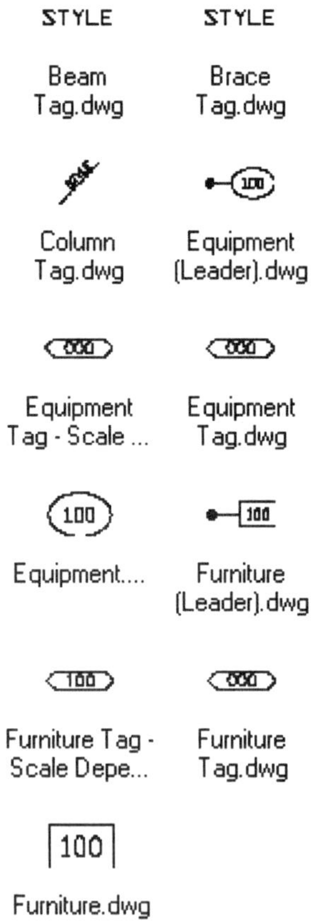

</td>
</tr>
</table>

Schedule Tags		Room & Finish Tags 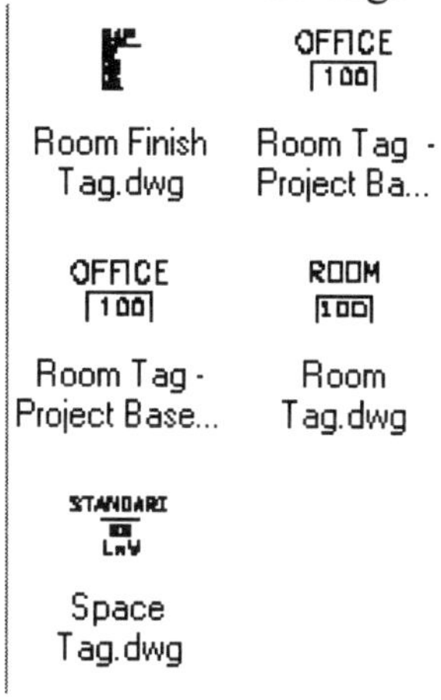 Wall Tags 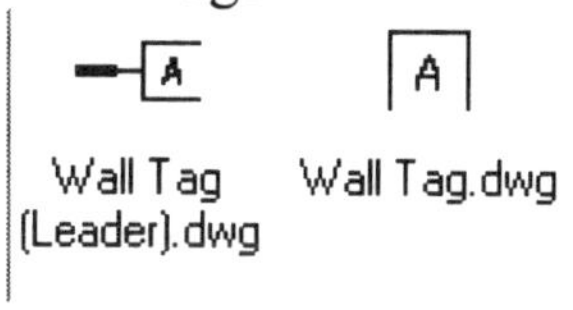
Section Marks	AnnoSectionMarkAdd SETIMPSECTIONMARKS	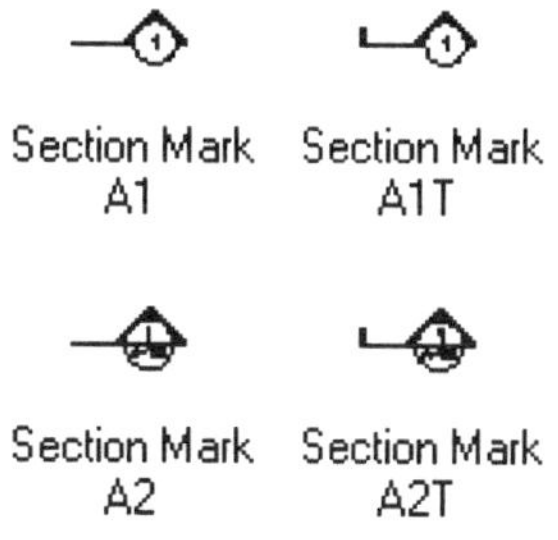
Title Marks	AnnoTitleMarkAdd SETIMPTITLEMARKS	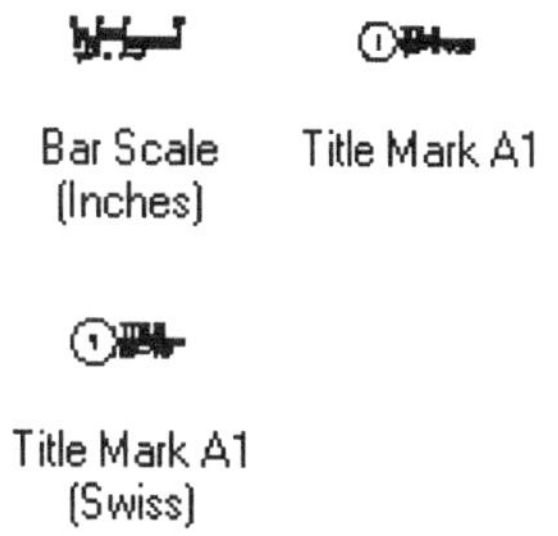

Many users make the mistake of using the standard AutoCAD dimension tools to dimension their ADT plans. ADT comes with a set of tools specifically for dimensioning ADT objects. By using these tools, dimensions are automatically placed on the correct layers.

Exercise 8-1:
Dimensioning a Floor Plan

Drawing Name: ex7-7.dwg
Estimated Time: 30 minutes

This exercise reinforces the following skills:

- Drawing Setup
- Dimension Styles
- AEC Dimensions

1. Open the Lesson 7-7.dwg.

2. 

Create a layout sheet called **Plot-Flr.**
Set the layout sheet **to A-size.**

3.  Select the **Layer Manager** tool.

4. Create a Layer User group called **Floor Plan.**
Place all the layers in this group that you want included in your floor plan.

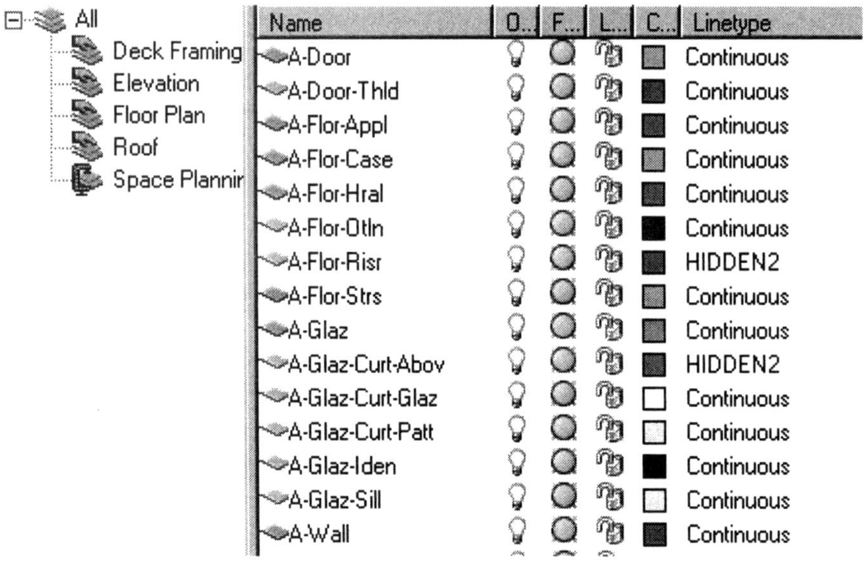

5. Activate the viewport on the Plot-Flr layout.
   Select Floor Plan.
   Right click and select **Isolate Group→Active Viewport only.**

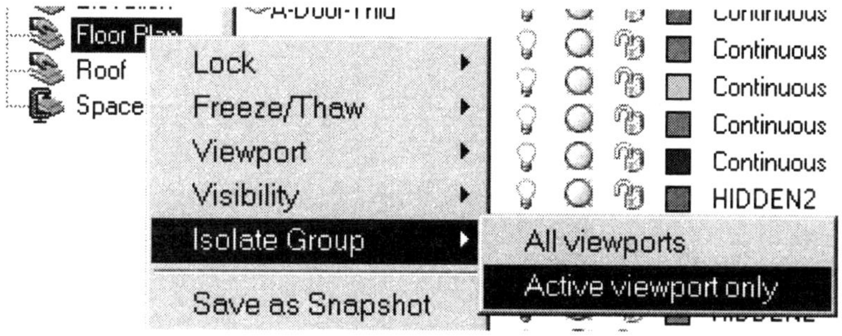

6. 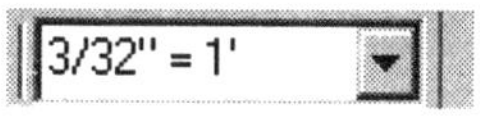

Set the viewport scale to **3/32″ = 1′.**

7. 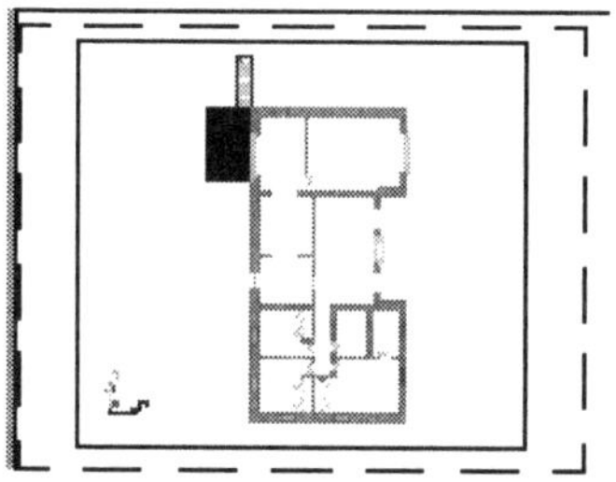
Adjust the viewport so the entire floor plan is visible.
Position the floor plan centered in the viewport.

8. Type **UCSICON.**
   Enter **OFF.**

9. Place the viewport on the *viewports* layer.

Add Title Mark

10. Lauch the Tool Palette.

11. 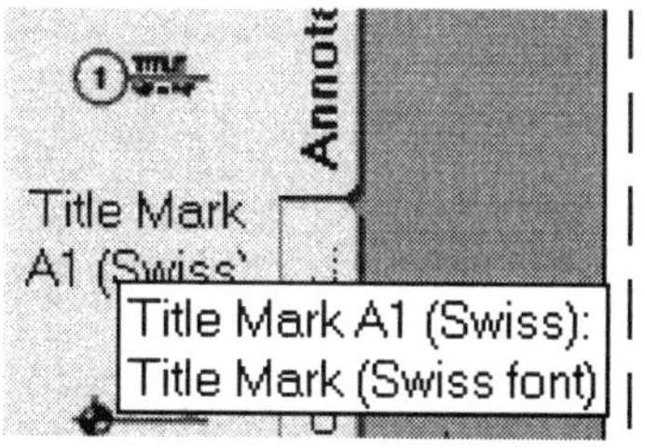

Select the **Title Mark** tool from the Annotation Palette.
Pick below the view to place the title mark.

12. 

In the Scale field, enter **3/32″ = 1′-0″.**
In the Title field, enter **FLOOR PLAN.**
Press **OK.**

13. 

Pick to place the end point of the title mark line.
The title mark is placed on the sheet.

You can apply AEC Dimensions to Walls with door and window openings and Grids.

Before you can apply AEC Dimensions, you need to check several user system options.

✓ Verify Dimension Settings

14. 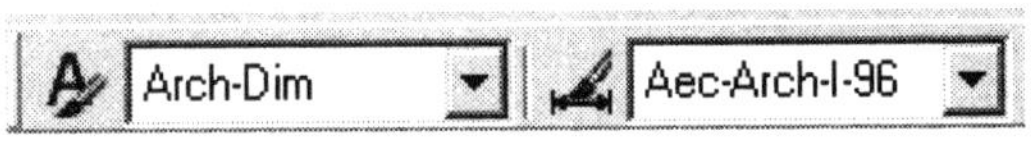

Verify the dimension style is set to *Aec-Arch-I-96.*

15. 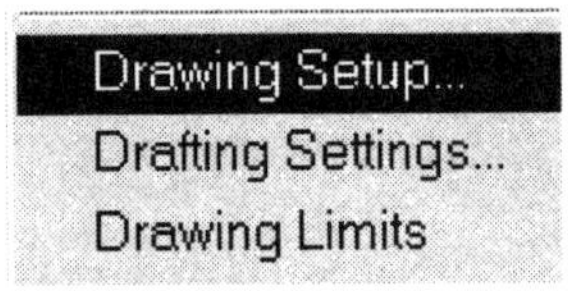

Go to **Format→Drawing Setup.**

16. 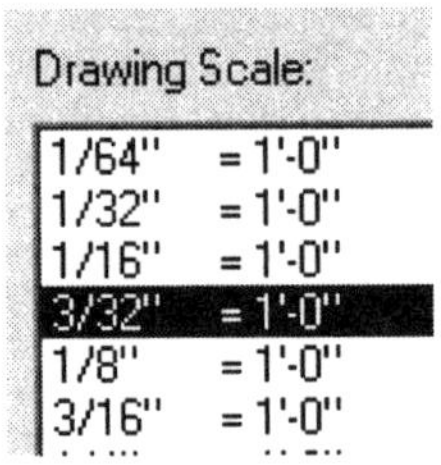

Set the Drawing Scale to **3/32″ to 1′-0″**.

Press **OK**.

Activate the floor plan viewport.

Add Wall Dimensions

17. 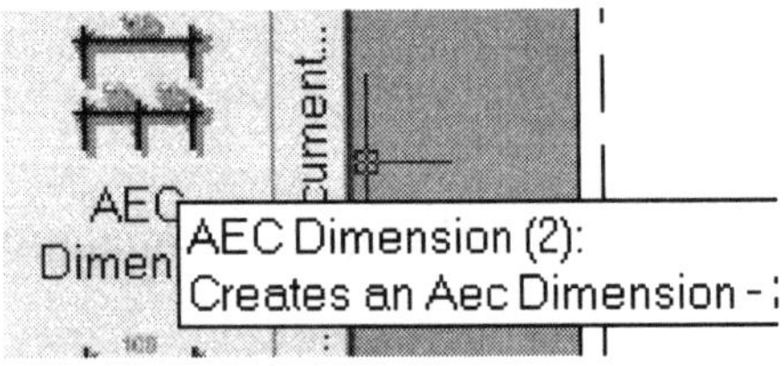

Select the **AEC Dimension (2)** tool on the Annotation Palette.

18. Add Wall Dimensions is only available in Model Space. Dimensions are automatically placed on A-Anno-Dims layer when the Layering Standard is set to AIA.

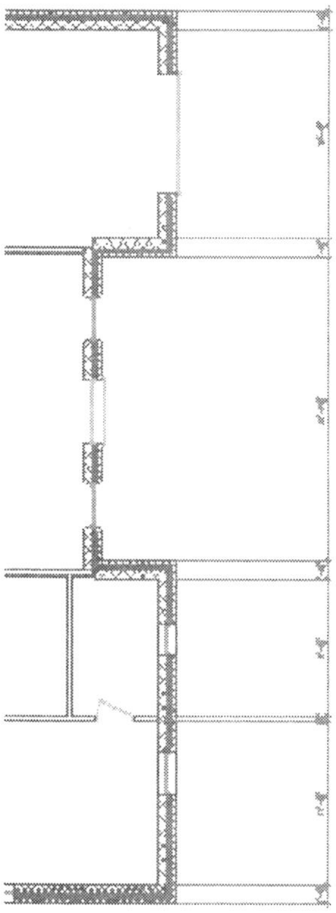

Select the wall(s) you wish to dimension.
Select the side of the wall where you wish the dimension to be placed.
All dimensions relevant to the wall will be placed.

19.

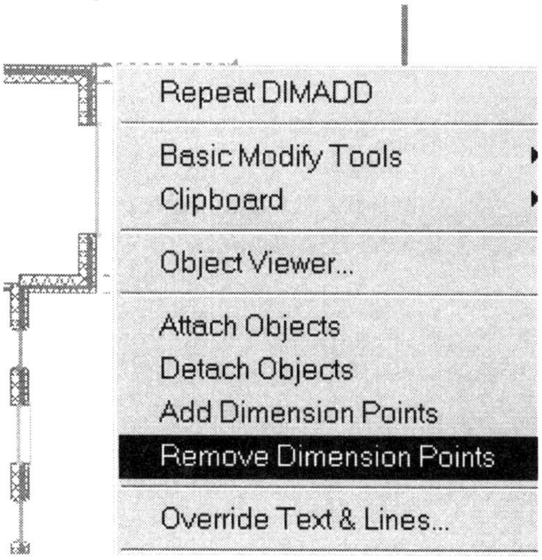

Select the Dimension you just placed.
Right click and select
Remove Dimension Points.

20. 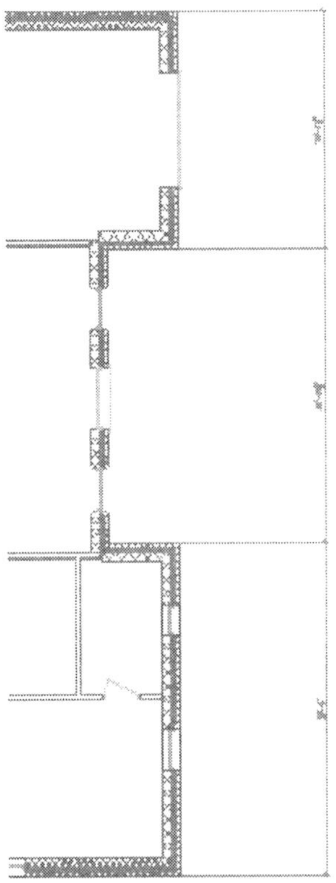

Select the extension lines for the walls that are not necessary.

21. 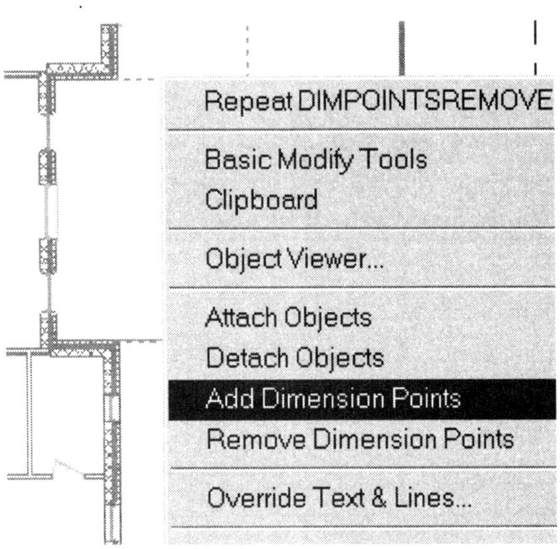

Select the Dimension you just placed.
Right click and select **Add Dimension Points.**

22.

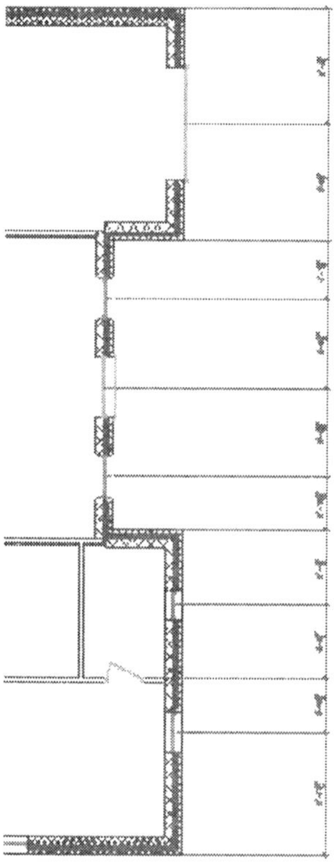

Select the midpoints of the doors and windows.
Then, select the dimension you just placed.

23. Save as *ex8-1.dwg.*

TIP: You can insert blocks into model or paper space. Note that you did not need to activate the viewport in order to place the Scale block.

Notes:

Lesson 9
Schedules

Schedules can be created to list doors, windows, walls, or any other object in your drawing. The schedule provides detail information regarding the size, construction, and vendor for each object type. Each object in a schedule is usually assigned a mark, which is placed as a tag, next to the object. Schedules form the basis of a Bill of Materials or shopping list for the contractor/builder.

The information included in the schedule is extracted from the property data attached to the drawing object (window/door/wall/etc.). Some properties are automatically generated when the object is inserted and placed in the drawing. However, other properties may be edited manually. You can also export schedule data to a .TXT file, a .XLS file or a .CSV file for use in a database. This would allow you to perform a cost analysis on required building materials.

Schedule Table Styles

The format of schedule tables can be controlled using three methods:

- Use the default schedule table
- Import a style from another drawing
- Create a Custom Style

Using the Style Manager

Menu	Format →Style Manager
Command Line	TableStyle

The TableStyle tool brings up the Style Manager dialog box. This dialog has its own toolbar and menu.

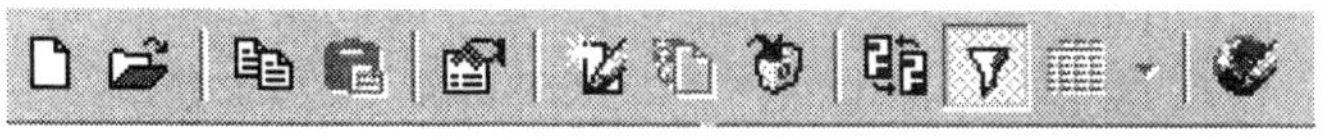

The first four icons in the dialog are standard WINDOW icons: NEW, OPEN, COPY, and PASTE. These allow users to create new styles, open an existing style, copy a style from another source, or paste from another source.

Edit Style

The Edit Style button allows you to modify an existing schedule style. There are six tabs, plus a Notes button.

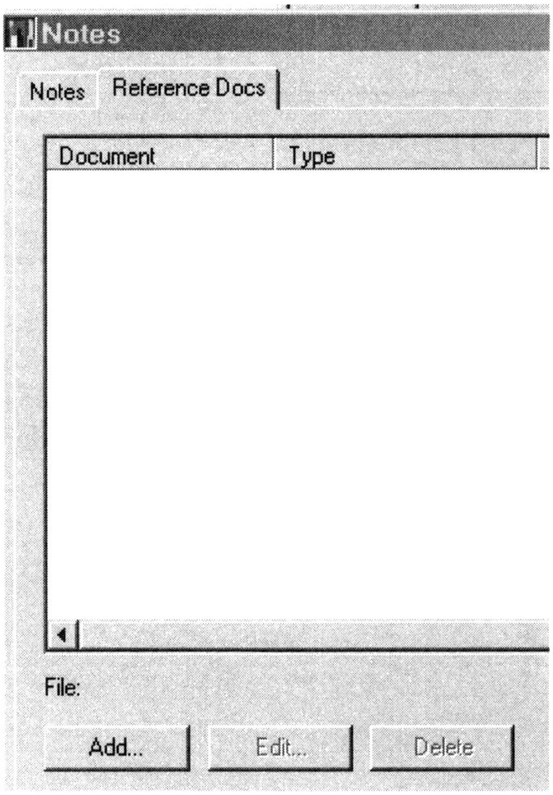

Pressing the Notes button brings up a Notes dialog box.

The user can reference specifications to support the schedule definition style or create a note to explain the schedule style.

To use an existing document, select the **Reference Docs** tab and select **Add**.

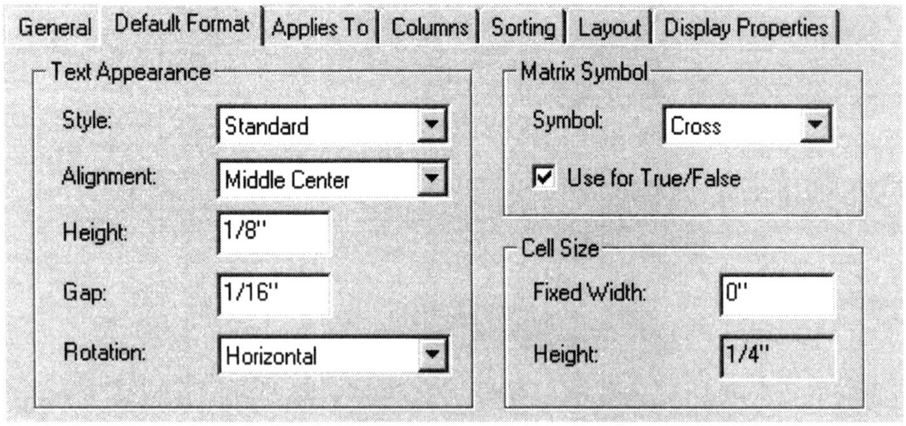

Style	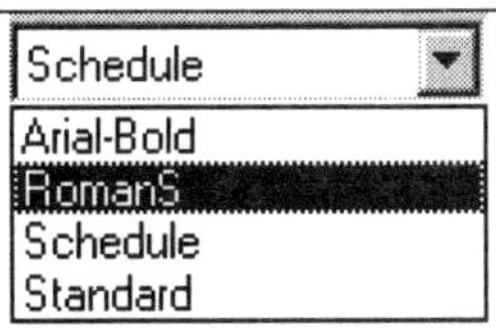	Sets the Text Style to be used. You can assign any text style as long as it is defined and loaded.
Alignment	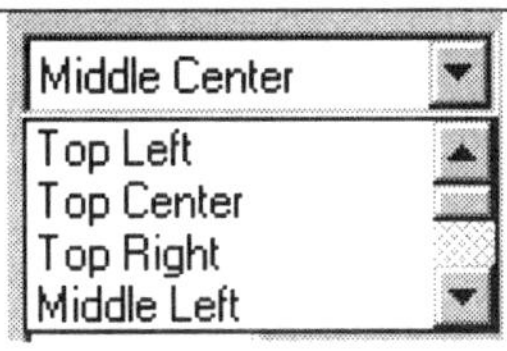	Sets the Alignment of the text
Height	Sets Text Height	
Gap	Set the prescaled gap between the text and the schedule table lines.	
Rotation	Set the Rotation, which changes the text orientation within the cell. For the table title and for group titles, this option also controls the location of the cell relative to the rest of the table.	
Matrix Symbol	Select a Matrix Symbol, which is used by matrix displays and optionally for true/false values.	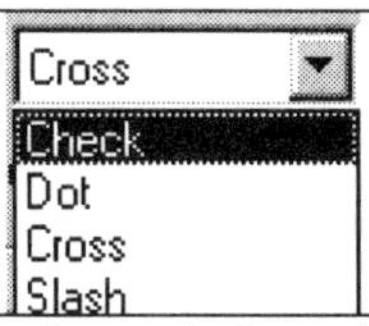
Use for True/False	Select or clear Use for True/False to control whether matrix symbols or the data format text are used for true/false values.	
Cell Size		
Fixed Width	Set the Fixed Width for a given column.	Specify 0.0 for widths that adjust to fit the data within them.
Height	Cell Size Height is a read-only field. The height is calculated from the Text Height and Gap.	

TIP: The text style must be defined as an AutoCAD text style before you can apply it to the schedule table. If you want to use a different font for part of your schedule, you must first define an AutoCAD text style that uses the desired font. The text style must be loaded before it can be accessed by the Schedule Styles Manager.

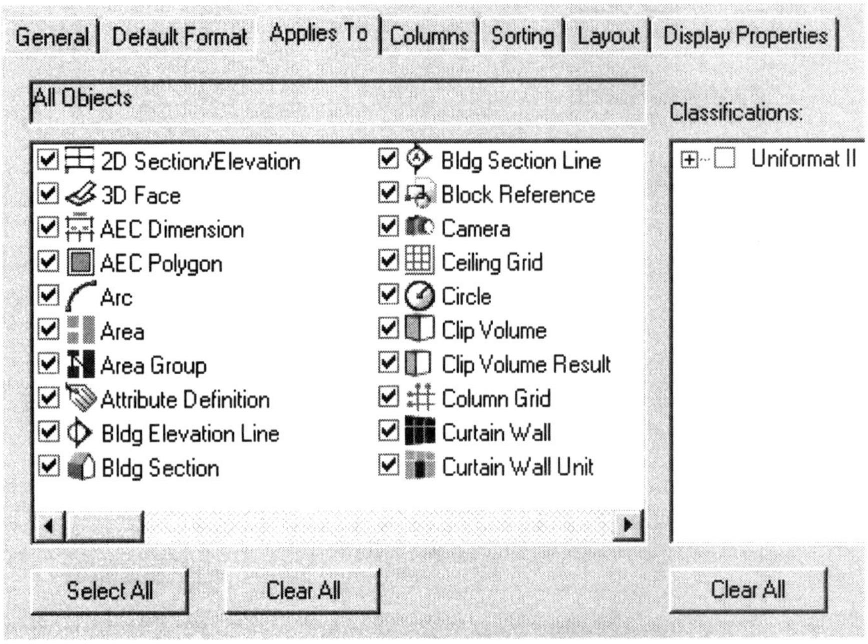

The **Applies To** tab is used to select the Objects the schedule applies to.

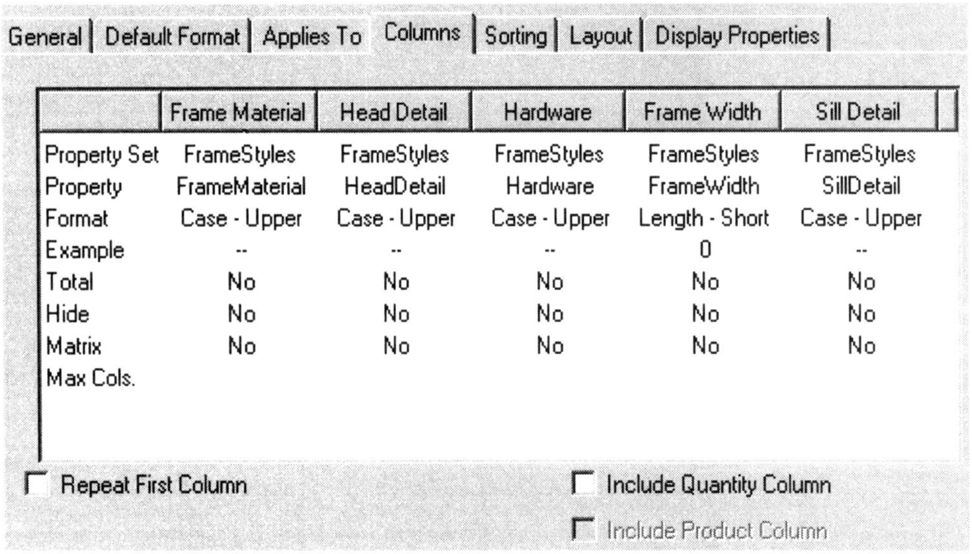

To add a Column, select the Add Column button.
To Add a Header, select the Add Header button.
To Modify a Column, select the Modify button.
To Delete a Column, select the Delete button.

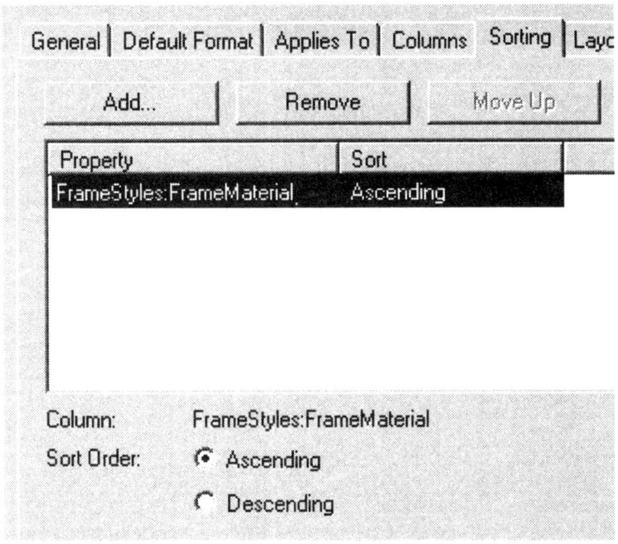

If assigned, the current property for sorting the schedule displays.

Click Add to add additional properties to sort by. The "Select Property' dialog will appear.

Select a property to sort by, and click OK. The selections presented are the columns defined on the Columns tab that are not already selected for sorting.

Select the property from the list, and then select either Ascending or Descending as the sorting method for that property.

To remove a property from the sorting list, select the property and then click Remove.

To move a property higher or lower in the sorting order, select the property and then either Move Up or Move Down.

When you finish making changes, click OK to return to the Style Manager.

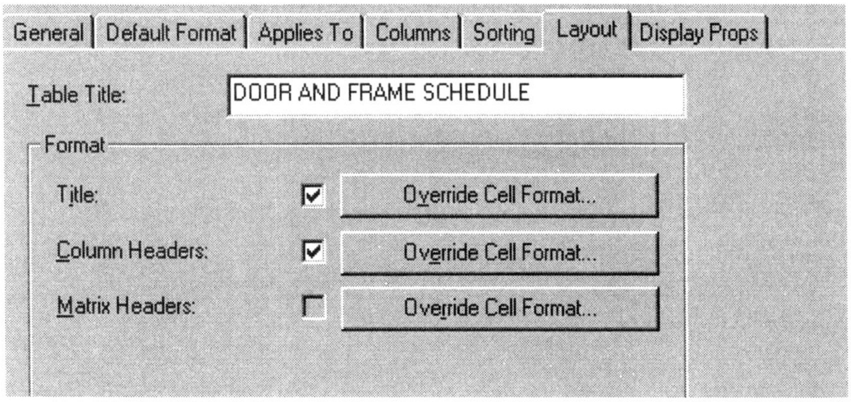

To modify the title for your schedule, click the Layout tab and edit the text in the Table Title edit box.

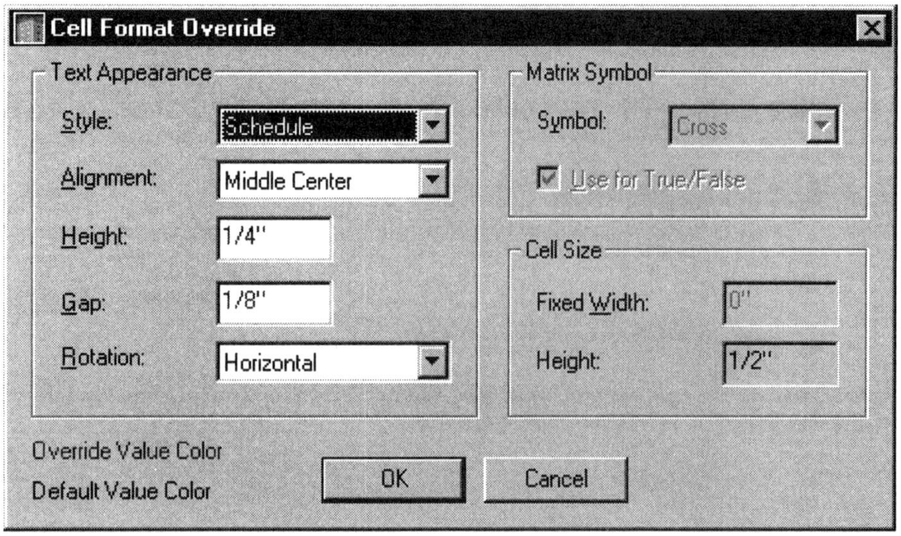

Pressing the Override Cell Format will allow you to modify the properties for each cell.

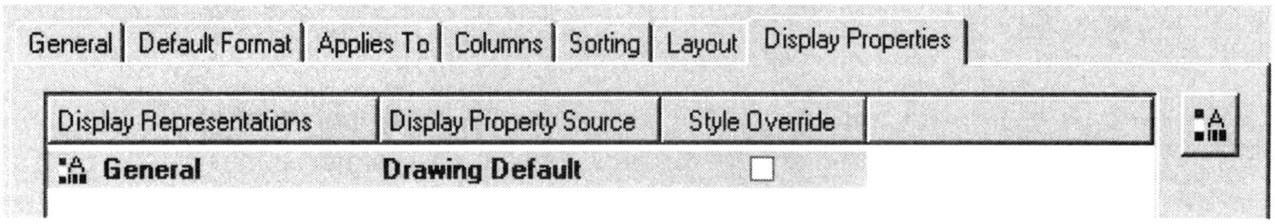

The display properties of an object affect the way the object appears in the drawing. You can override the default display for the current display configuration by setting a different visibility, layer, color, linetype, hatching, and cut plane height for the selected object.

New Style

This icon allows the user to create a new Schedule Style. Styles are listed in alphabetical order in the style tree.

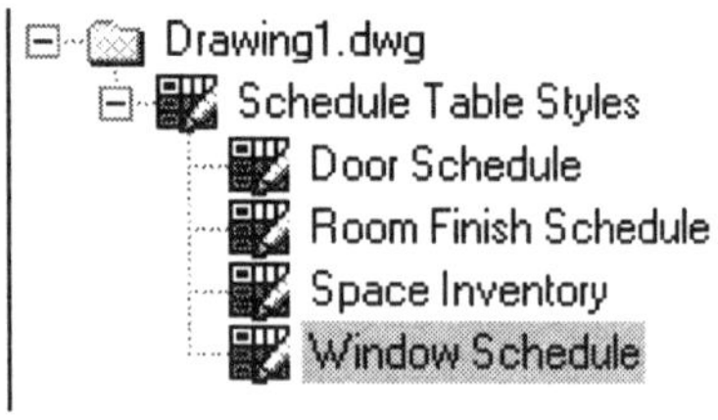

Purge

Purges unused schedule tables from the drawing.

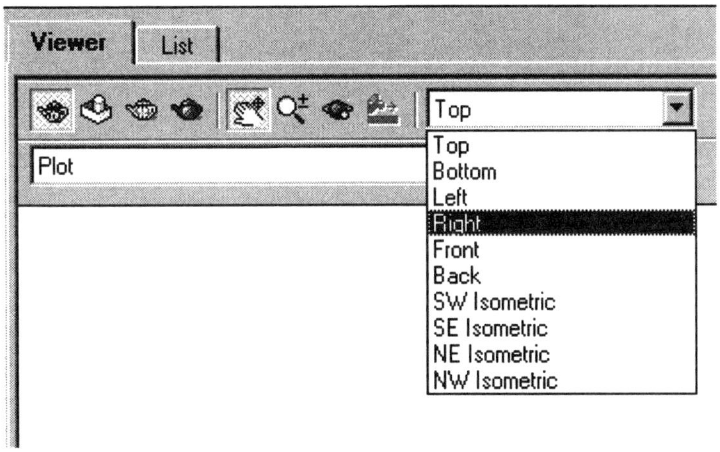

The Style Manager includes a Viewer that allows the user to change the view of the schedule that will be inserted into the drawing. You can zoom in, window, change shading, orbit, etc.

Exercise 9-1:

Creating a Schedule Table

Drawing Name: Ex8-1.dwg
Estimated Time: 15 minutes

This exercise reinforces the following skills:

- ❑ Schedule Table Styles
- ❑ Style Manager

1. Open *ex8-1.dwg.*

2. 

Activate the Plot-FLR tab.

3. 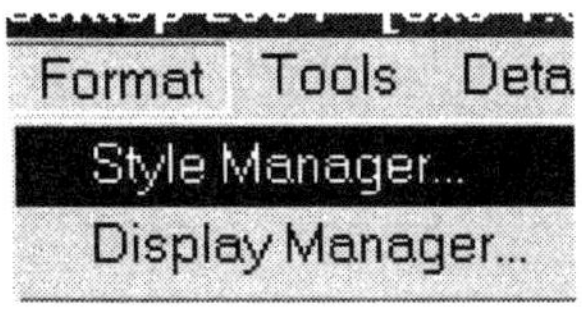

Select **Format→Style Manager**.

4. Open the *PropertySetDefs.dwg.*
The file can be located in the path indicated.

PropertySetDefs.dwg
In Folder: C:\Documents and Settings\All Users\Application Data\Autodesk\Autodesk Architectural Desktop 2004\R16.0\enu\AEC Content\Metric\Documentation\Schedule Tags

Locate the **Window Schedule** under Schedule Table Styles.

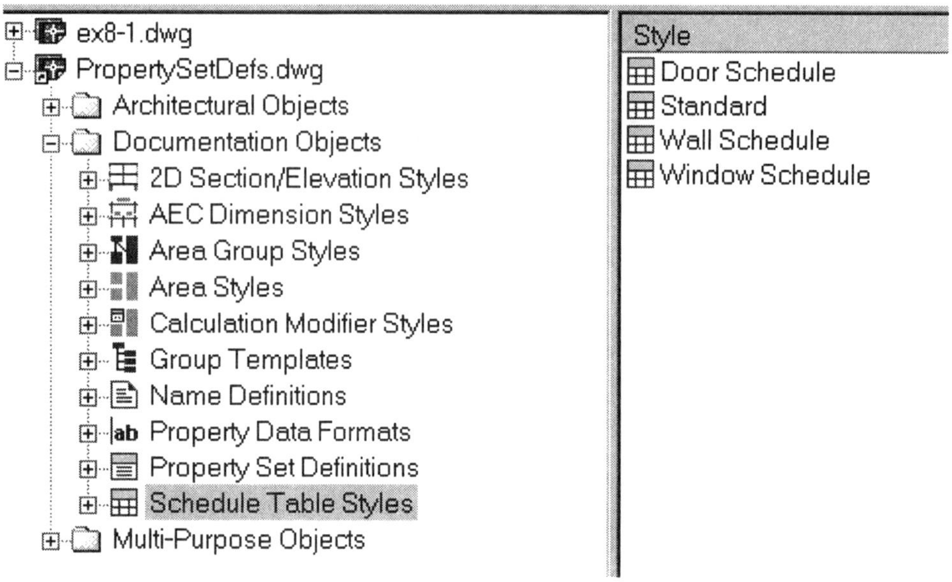

5. 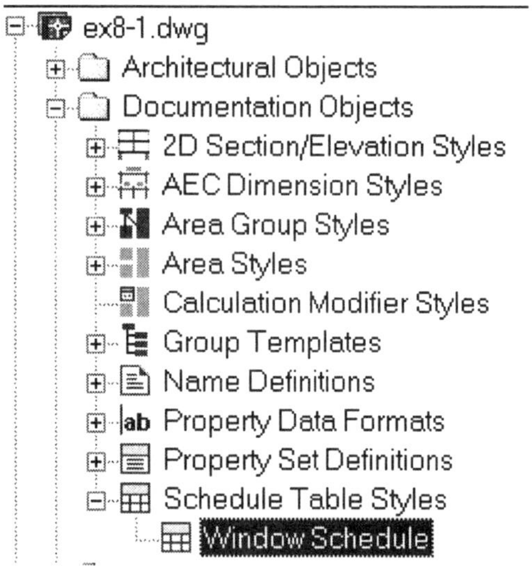

Copy and Paste into the *ex8-1.dwg*.

6. 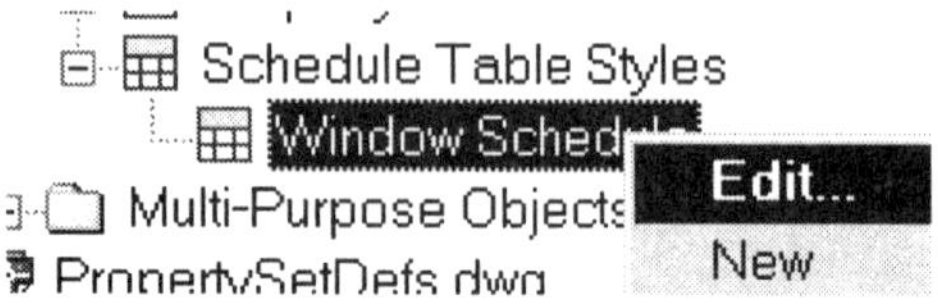

Select the Window Schedule.
Right click and select **Edit**.

7. 

Select the Columns tab.
Select **Add Column.**

8.

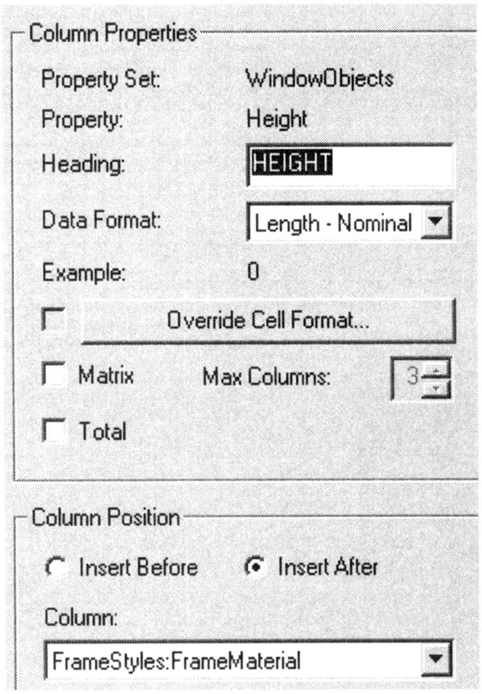

Select **Height** under the WindowObjects.
Edit the Heading to **HEIGHT.**

Press **OK.**

9.

Select the Columns tab.
Select **Add Column.**

10.

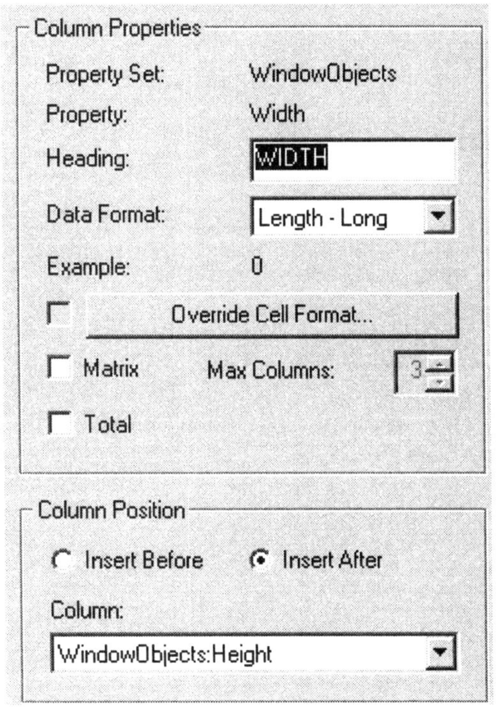

Select **Width** under the WindowObjects.
Edit the Heading to **WIDTH.**

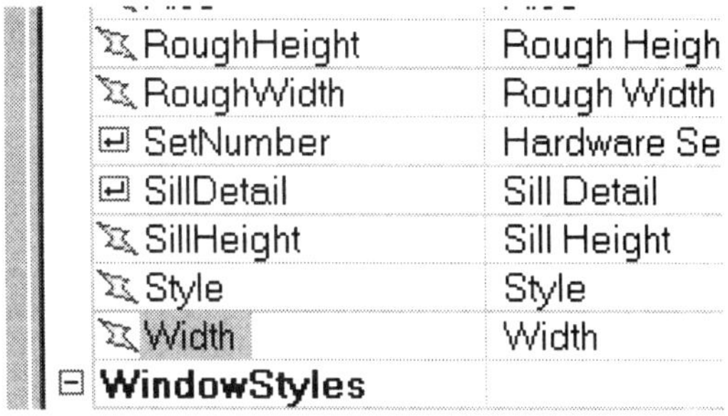

Press **OK.**

Add Header

11. Hold down the Control key and select the HEIGHT and WIDTH columns. Select **Add Header.**

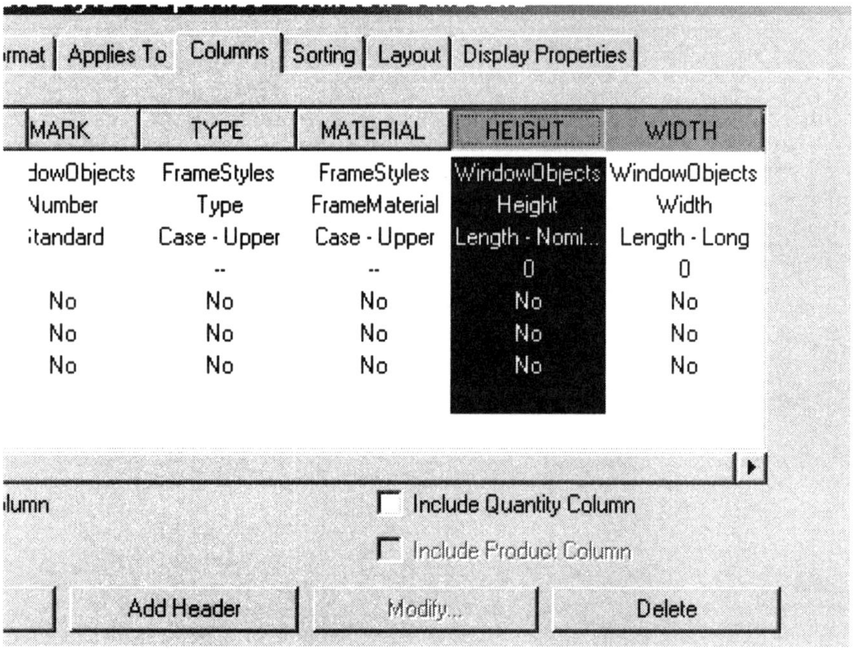

12.

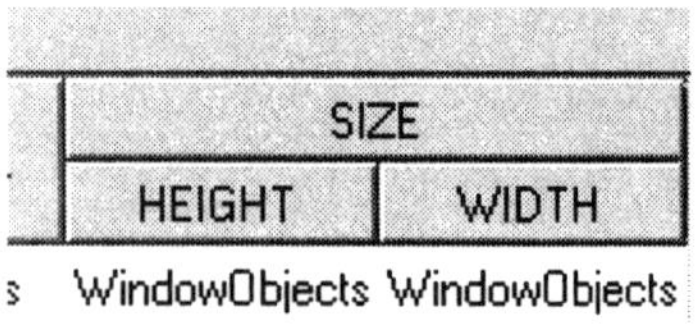

Enter **SIZE** as the header title.

Press **OK.**

13.

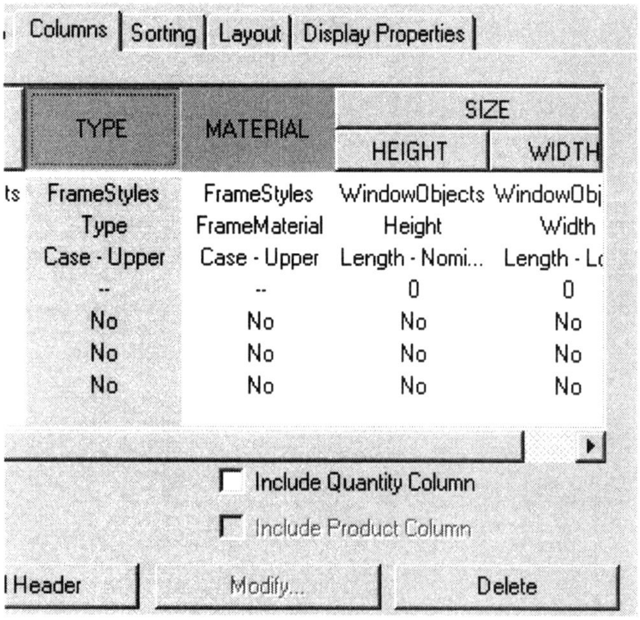

Select the TYPE and MATERIAL columns.

Select the **Delete** button.

14.

WINDOW SCHEDULE		
	SIZE	
MARK	HEIGHT	WIDTH

The preview window shows what the schedule will look like.

15. Save as *ex9-1.dwg.*

Exercise 9-2:

Adding Door & Window Tags

Drawing Name: Ex9-1.dwg
Estimated Time: 15 minutes

This exercise reinforces the following skills:

- Add Schedule Table
- Schedule Tags

1. Open *ex9-1.dwg.*

2. 

Select the **Window Tag** tool from the Annotations Palette.

3. 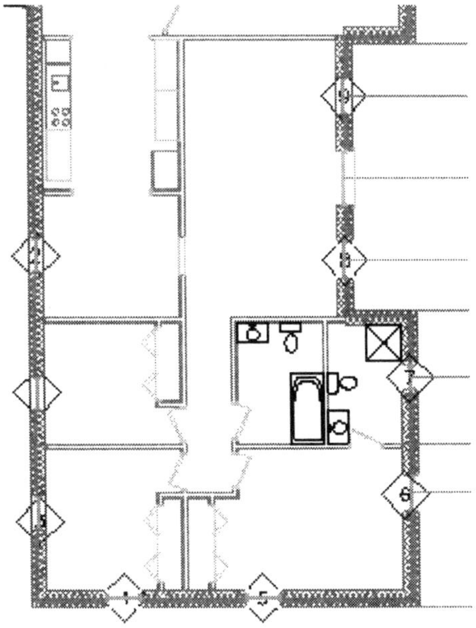

Select each window.
Press **ENTER** to center the tag on each window.
Press **OK** to accept the default properties.

4. 

Select the **Door Tag** tool from the Annotations Palette.

5. 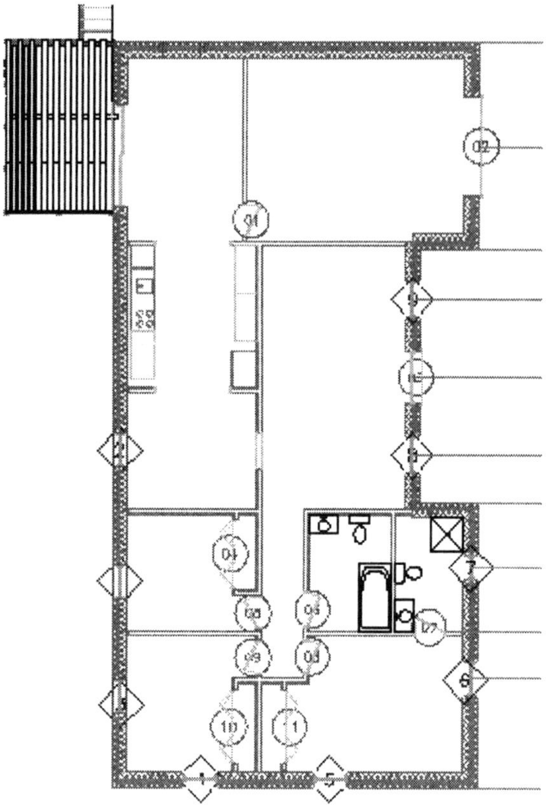
Select each door.
Press **ENTER** to center the tag on each window.
Press **OK** to accept the default properties.

TIP: The Window Tags should automatically be placed on the **A-Glaz-Iden** Layer.

6. Save as *ex9-2.dwg.*

Exercise 9-3:

Adding a Schedule Table

Drawing Name: Ex9-2.dwg
Estimated Time: 15 minutes

This exercise reinforces the following skills:

- ❑ Add Schedule Table
- ❑ Schedule Tags

1. Open *ex9-2.dwg.*

2. 

Create an 81/2 x 11 sheet called Schedules.

3. 

Place the viewport on the viewports layer.

Pan the view so you are in a blank area.

Select the **Plot-Flr** layout tab.

4. 

Select the **Window Schedule** tool from the Documentation Palette.

5. 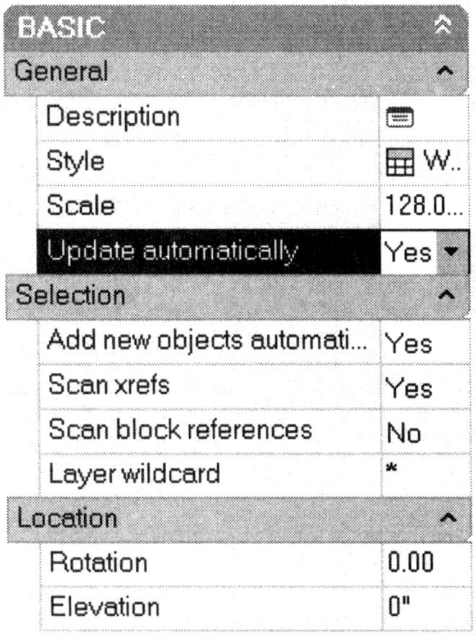

Window around the floor plan.
The windows will automatically be selected and all other objects will be filtered out.
In the Properties dialog, set
Update Automatically to **Yes.**
Set Add new objects automatically to **Yes**.
Press **Enter.**

6. 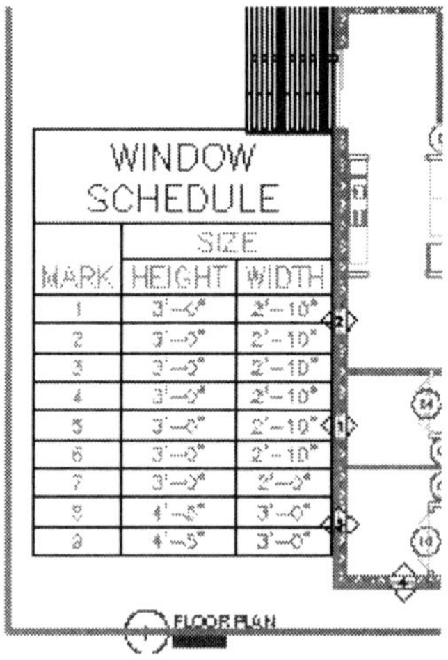

When prompted for the upper left corner of the table, pick inside the viewport.

When prompted for the lower right corner of the table, press RETURN.

Place the schedule in the viewport.

7. 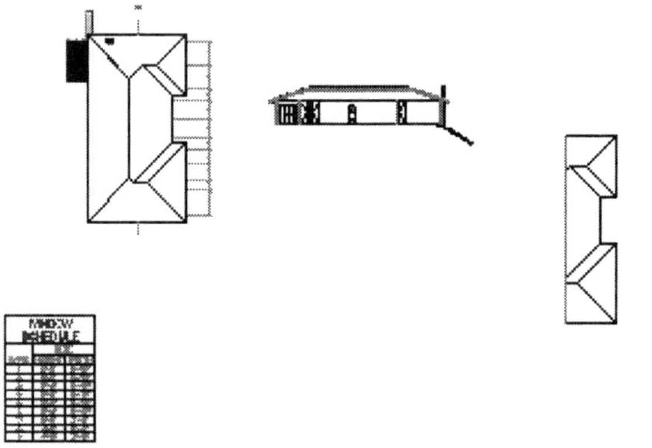

Switch to the Model tab.
Move the schedule away from the other views.

8. Switch to the Schedules layout tab.
Adjust the viewport so it displays the window schedule.
Lock the Display.

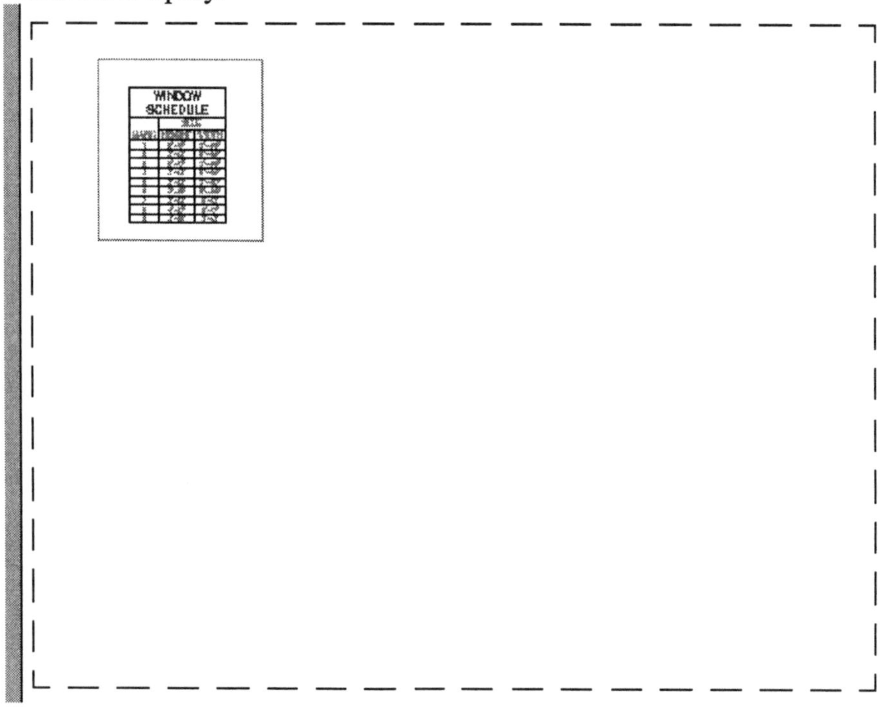

Import Schedule Style

9. Select the Door Schedule tool on the Documentation Palette.
Right click and select Import Door Schedule Schedule Table Style.

This copies the door schedule table style from the PropertyDefs.dwg without opening the Style Manager.

10. 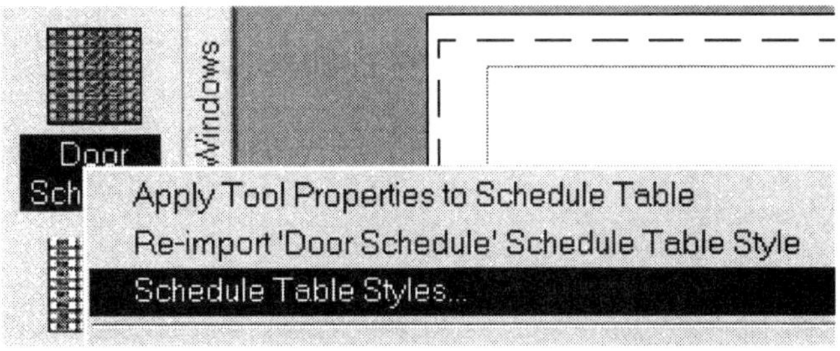

Select the Door Schedule tool.
Right click and select **Schedule Table Styles.**

11. 

The Door Schedule is now listed in your Style Manager.

Press **OK** to close the dialog.

12. 

Activate model space on the Plot-Flr tab.
Select the Door Schedule tool.
Window around the floor plan.
Place the door schedule.

13. 

Switch to the Model tab.
Move the door schedule away from the model.

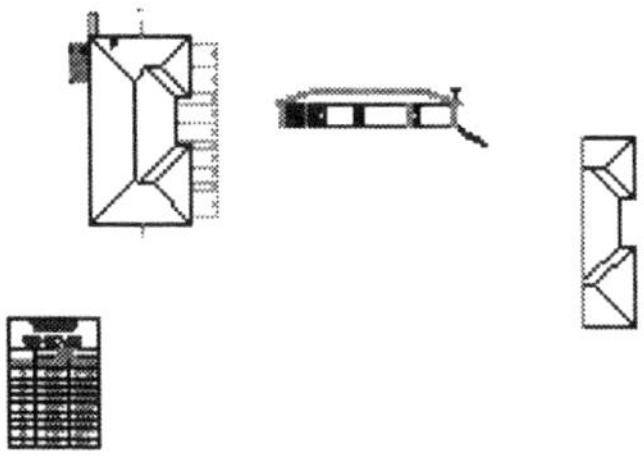

14. — — — — — — — — — — — — — —

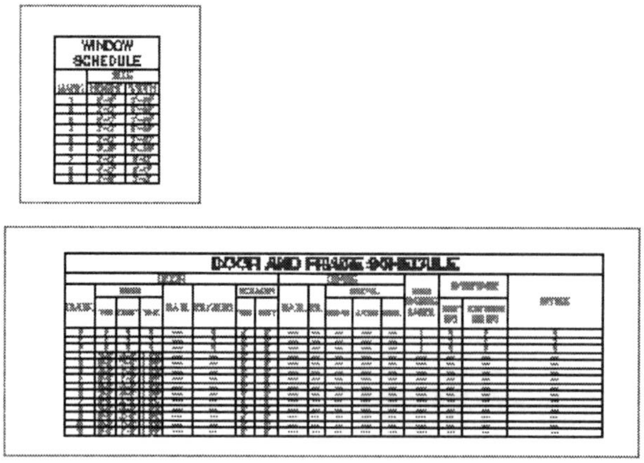

Select the Schedules layout tab.
Create a second viewport.
Place on the viewports layer.
Set the viewport to display the door schedule.

15. Save as *ex9-3.dwg.*

Exercise 9-4:

Exporting a Schedule

Drawing Name: Ex9-3.dwg
Estimated Time: 15 minutes

This exercise reinforces the following skills:

- Table Styles
- Creating a New Table Style
- Exporting an Exiting Schedule Table

1. Open *ex9-3.dwg.*

2.

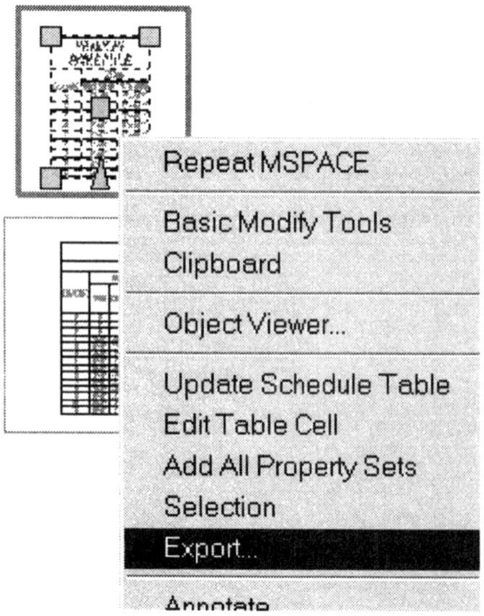

Select the Schedules layout tab.
Activate Model space.
Select the window schedule.
Right click and select **Export.**

3. You have three options of file type you can export: Excel, text, or csv.

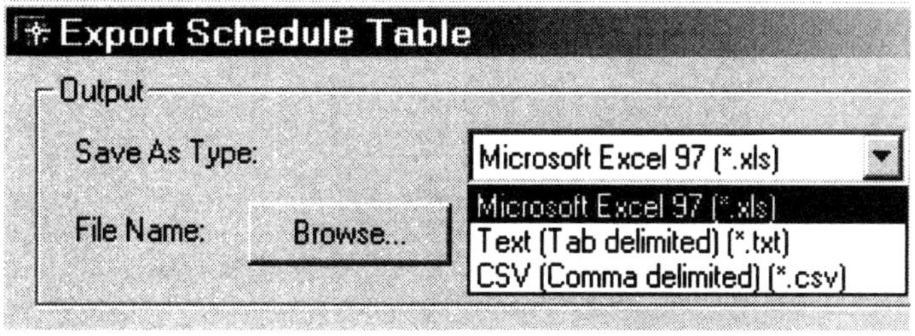

Select .txt.

4. Pressing the Browse button will allow you to set the path where the export file will be saved.

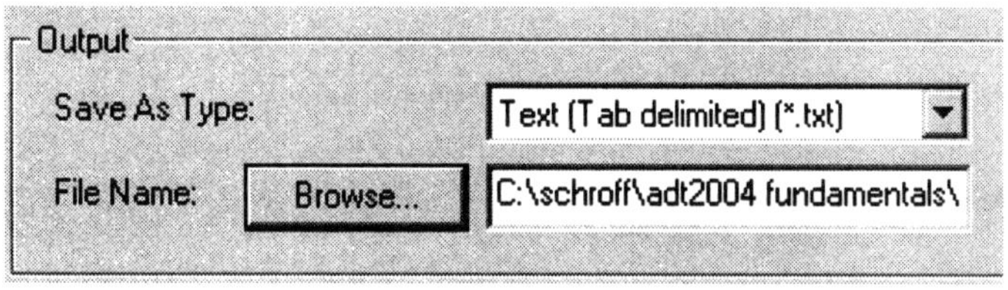

Change the file name to **Window Schedule.**
Press **Save.**

Press **OK.**

5. 

Locate the file you just created and open using Notepad.

6. 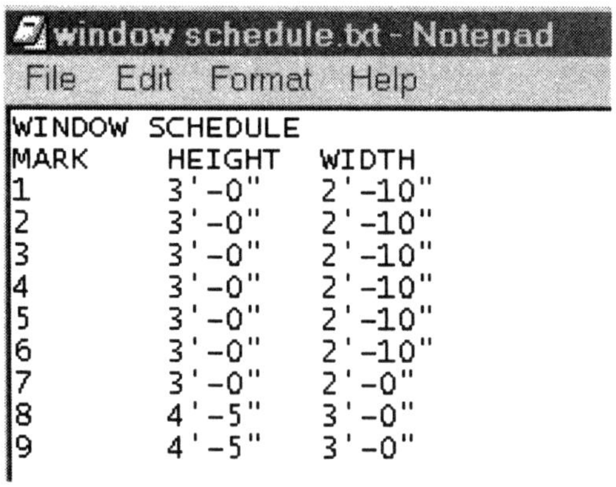

WINDOW SCHEDULE

MARK	HEIGHT	WIDTH
1	3'-0"	2'-10"
2	3'-0"	2'-10"
3	3'-0"	2'-10"
4	3'-0"	2'-10"
5	3'-0"	2'-10"
6	3'-0"	2'-10"
7	3'-0"	2'-0"
8	4'-5"	3'-0"
9	4'-5"	3'-0"

The file shows the data.

Close the text file.

7. Close the ADT file.

Notes:

Lesson 10

Creating a Video

One of the more fun (and the more frustrating) tools within Architectural Desktop is the ability to create a video.

A video requires two basic things:

A path – this is the path, which the camera will travel along. The path must be an open or closed polyline, circle, or rectangle.

A camera – the camera can be set to point to different angles and elevations along the path.

Exercise 10-1:

Adding a Path

Drawing Name: Ex9-3.dwg
Estimated Time: 10 minutes

This exercise reinforces the following skills:

- Creating a path

1.  Open *ex9-3.dwg.*

2. 

Activate the Model tab.

3.  Select the Layer Manager.

4.  Select the New User Group tool.

5. 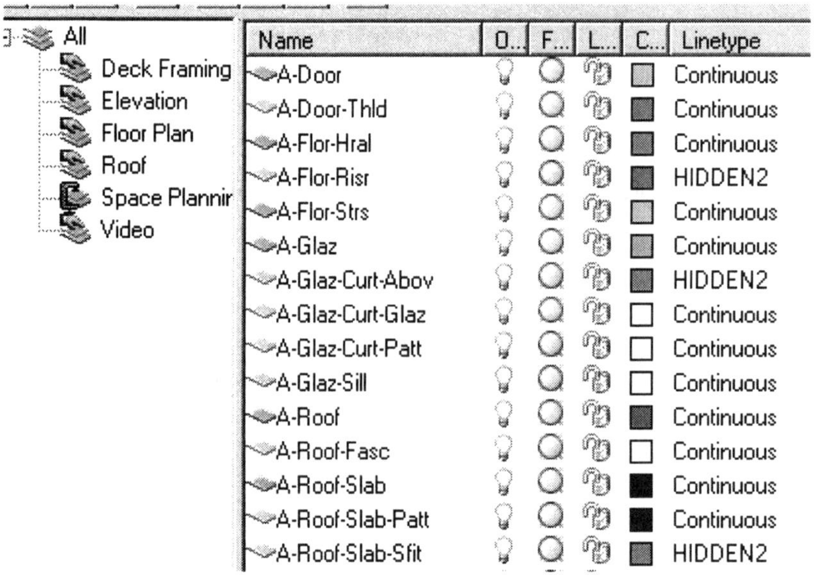

Name the user group **Video** and place all the layers for the house in the group.

6. 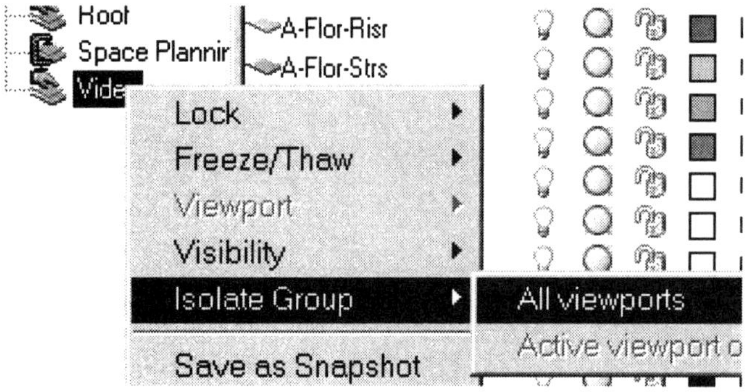

Select Video.
Right click and select **Isolate Group→All viewports.**

Press **OK** to close the Layer Manager.

3. Draw a circle around the house.

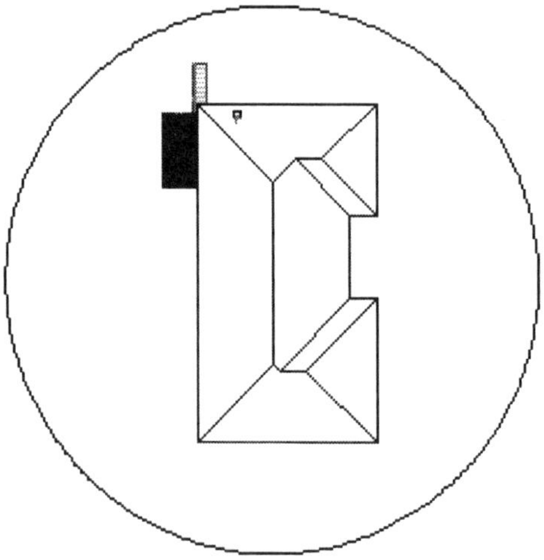

4. Select the circle.
Right click and select **Properties.**

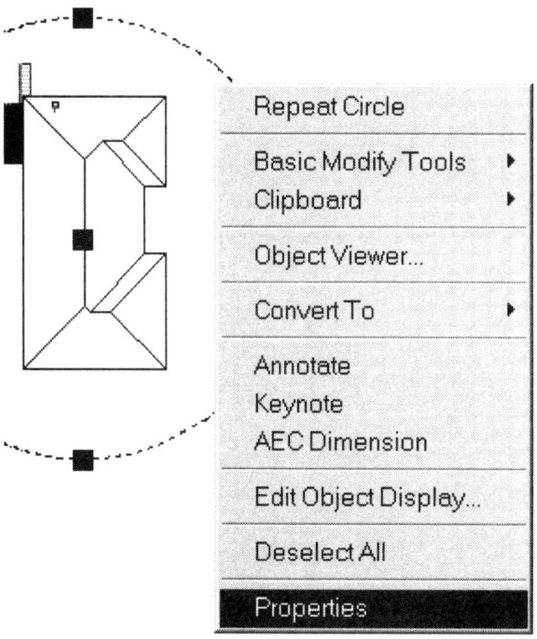

5. Set the Center Z to 5′-6″. This changes the elevation of the circle.
This will move the camera path so it is approximately eye level.

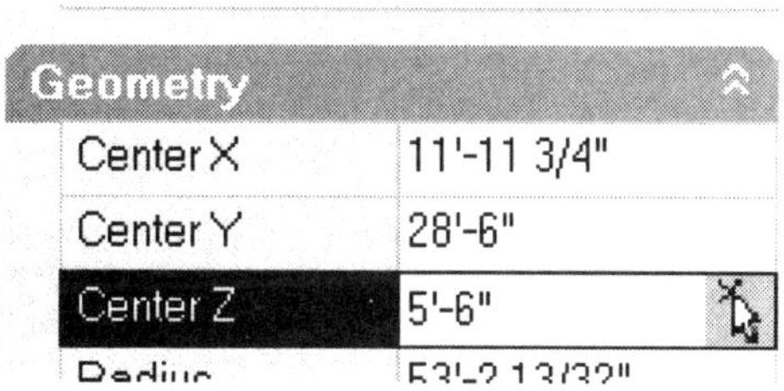

6. Save the file as *ex10-1.dwg.*

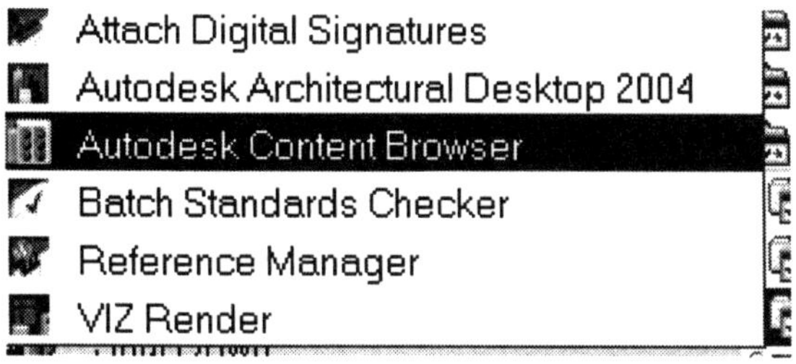

The Camera tool is loaded from the Content Browser and added to an existing palette. The Content Browser lets you store, share, and exchange ADT files, tools, and tool palettes. The Content Browser runs independently outside of ADT.

To launch the Content Browser, go to your Start Menu under Windows.

Exercise 10-2:

Adding a Camera Tool to a Palette

Drawing Name: Ex10-1.dwg
Estimated Time: 10 minutes

This exercise reinforces the following skills:

- Accessing the Content Browser
- Adding a Camera Tool to a Tool Palette
- Adding a Camera View
- Adjust Camera View

1.  Open *ex10-1.dwg.*

Accessing the Content Browser

3.

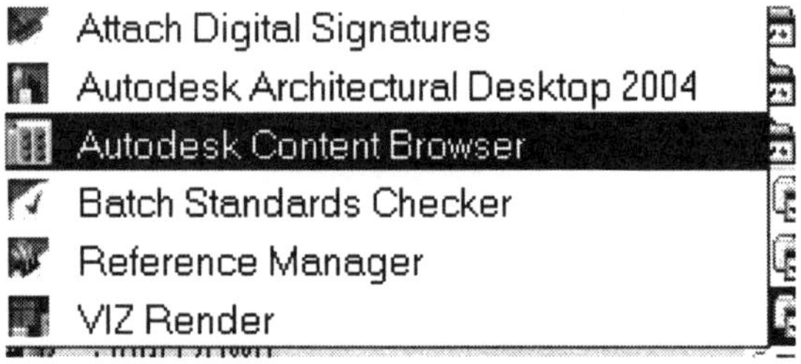

Launch the Autodesk Content Browser.

4.

Autodesk® Architectural Desktop Stock Tool Catalog

Select the Autodesk Architectural Desktop Stock Tool Catalog.

TIP: The Content Browser is a great resource for all sorts of content and tools. Take some time to explore what's available.

5. 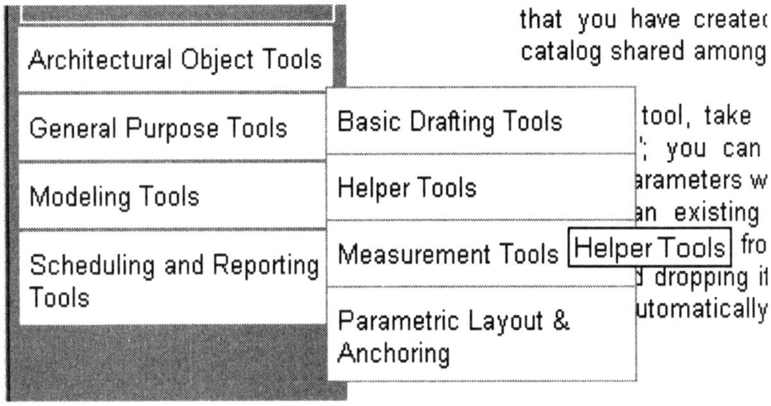

Select **Helper Tools** under **General Purpose Tools.**

6. 

Locate the Camera tool.
Notice the idrop symbol next to the camera image. This indicates that the Camera tool is idrop-enabled.

7. 

Select the Camera.
Right click and select **Copy**.

8. 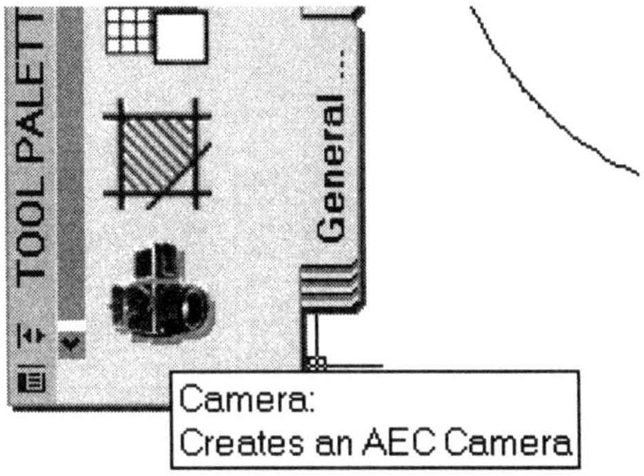

Select the **General Drafting** Palette on the Tool Palettes.
Right click and select **Paste**.
This adds the Camera tool to the palette.

9. 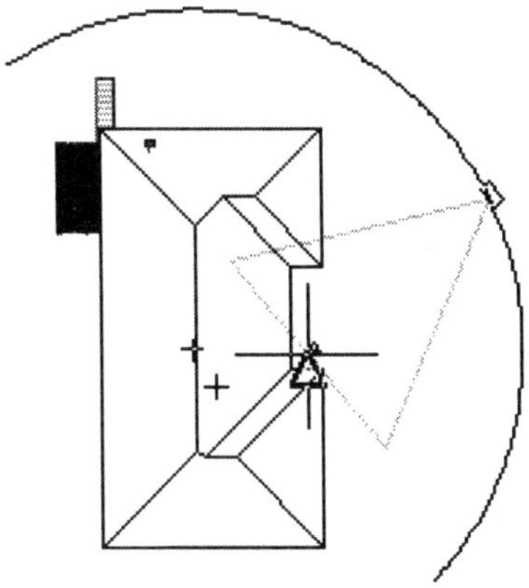

Place the camera on the circle.
With ORTHO OFF, you can direct the camera's viewpoint.
Select the front door as the target point.

10.

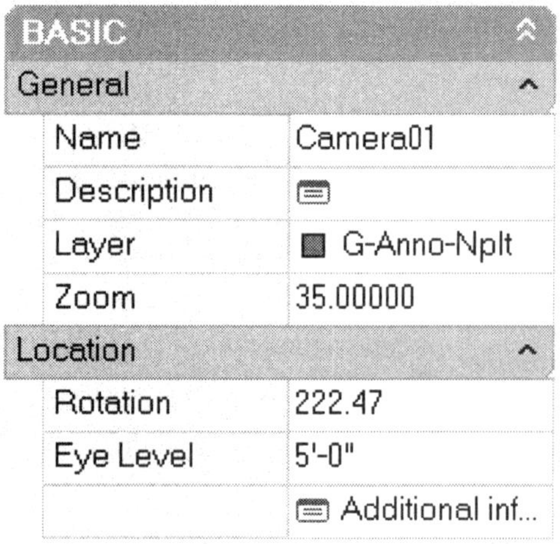

It is important to give the camera a name so you can keep track when you want to switch from one camera to another when creating your video.

The Zoom indicates lens size. A value of 50 represents a 50 mm lens. This is similar to what the average human eye sees. Above 50 is considered a telephoto lens. Below 50 is considered a wide-angle (panoramic) lens, allowing you to see more of the scene.

The Eye level sets the initial height of the camera.

The Generate View After Add box allows you to apply the camera view to a selected viewport after the camera is placed.

The Viewport Association box associates the camera with a particular viewport.

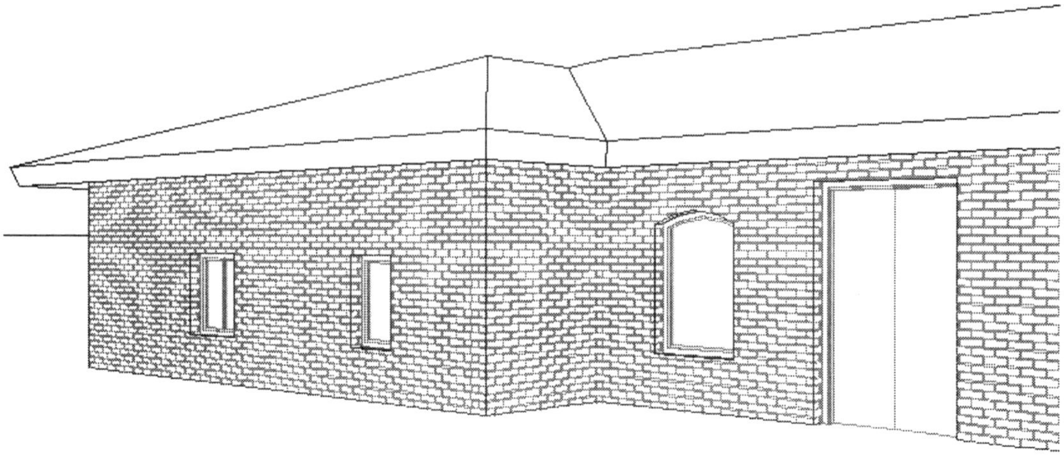

The camera automatically creates a view from the camera.

11. Set up two viewports. You can use the viewport on the right to check your camera view.

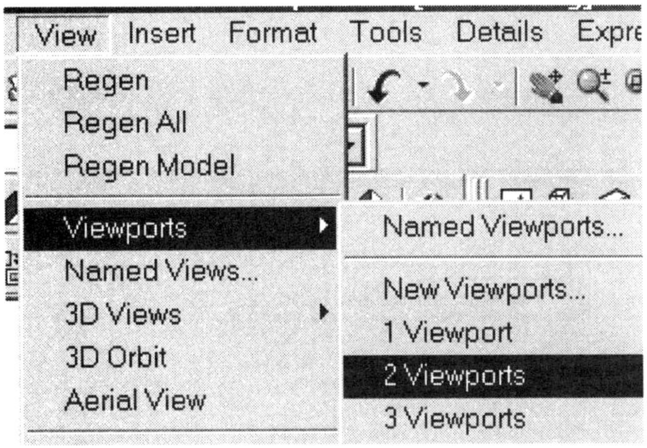

Go to
**View→Viewports→
2 Viewports.**

Select **ENTER** to accept the **Vertical** default.

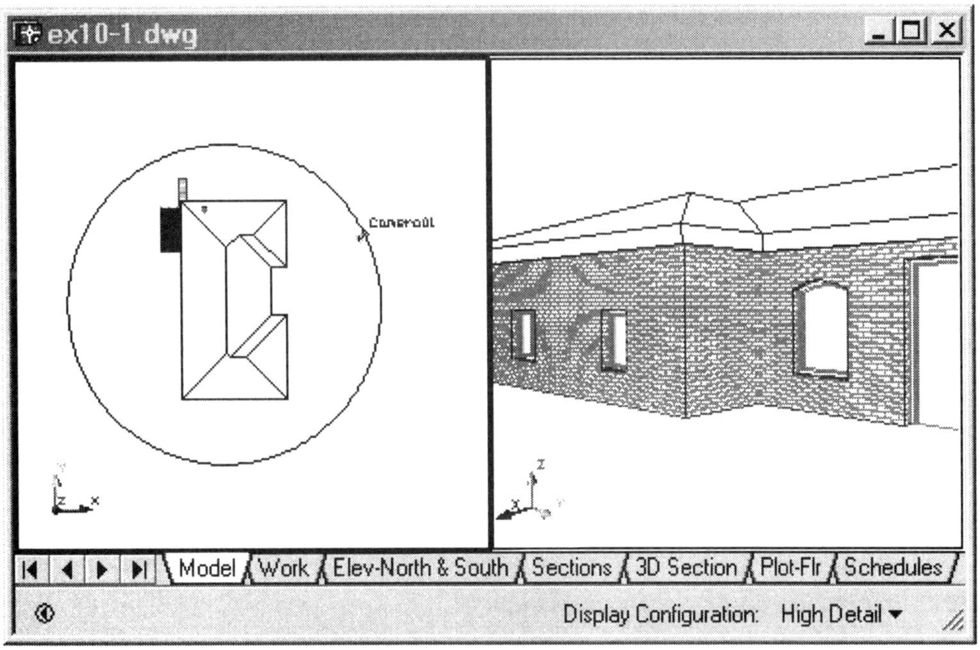

12.

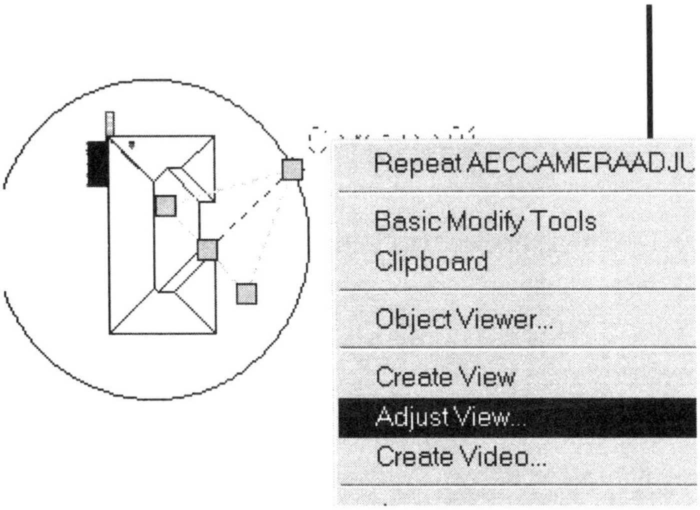

Select the Camera. Right click and select **Adjust View.**

13. Select **Zoom In.**
    Select **Turn Right.**
    Press **OK.**

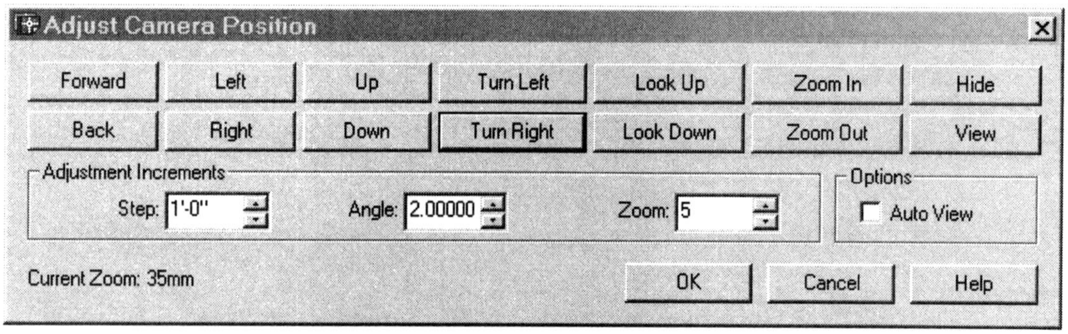

The left viewport changes to show the adjusted view.

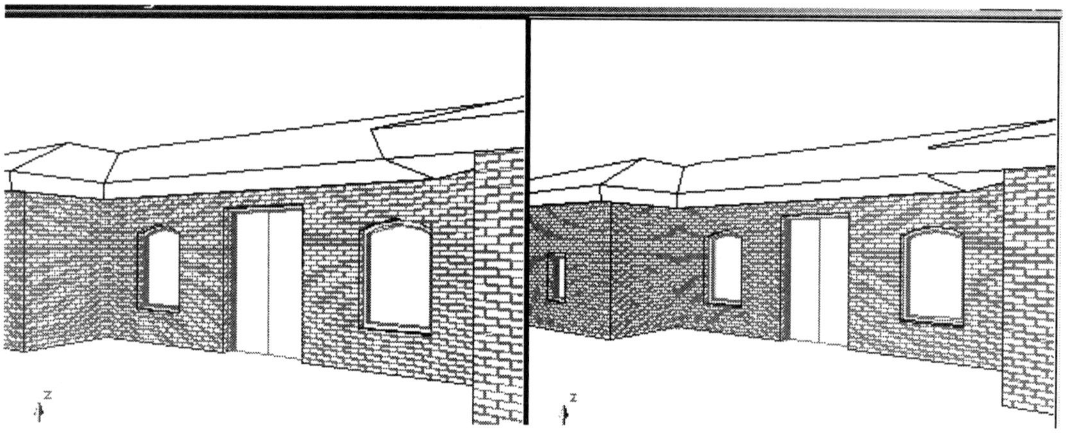

14. Set the left viewport back to a top view.

> **TIP:** You can use the camera grips to change the rotation, lens length, and camera position.

15. Experiment with different camera perspectives until you get the camera view you like.

16. Save as *ex10-2.dwg.*

Exercise 10-3:

Creating a Video

Drawing Name: Ex10-2.dwg
Estimated Time: 30 minutes

This exercise reinforces the following skills:

- Creating a Video

1.  Open *ex10-2.dwg.*

2. 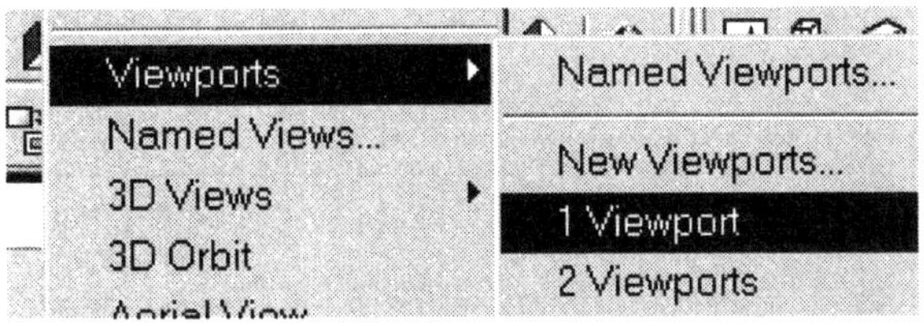

Go to **View→Viewports→ 1 Viewport.**

This sets your screen to a single viewport.

3. 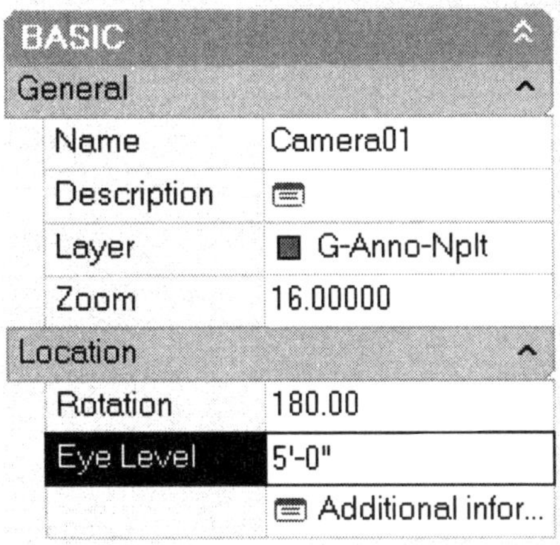

Select the Camera.
Right click and select **Properties.**

Set the Zoom Length to **16.**

Set the Eye Level to **5′-0″.**

Set the angle to **180.00**.

4. 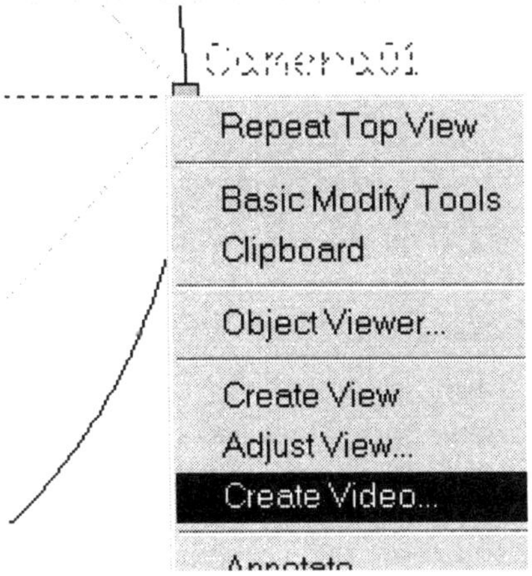

Select the Camera.
Right click and select **Create Video.**

5. 

Select the **Pick Path** button under Camera Path.
Select the circle.

6. 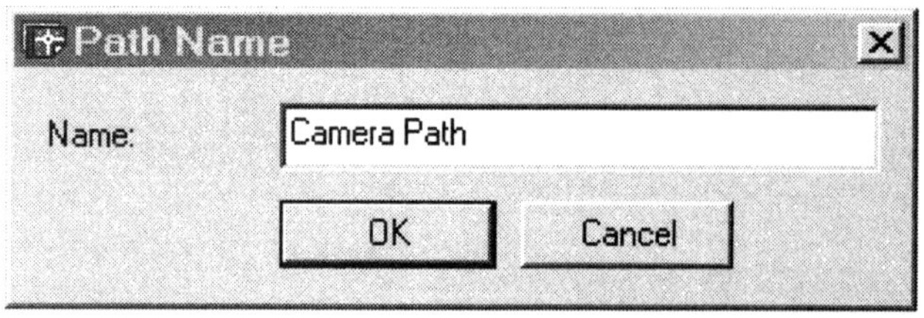

Enter **Camera Path** in the Name field.
Press **OK**.

7. 

Select **Pick Point** under Target Path. Select a point approximately in the center of the house.

8. 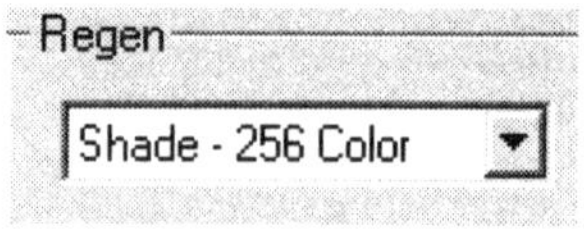

Set the Regen to **Shade – 256 Color.**

TIP: Selecting a regen option other than As Displayed performs a full regeneration of each frame and specifies the shading options for the AVI file generated.

9. 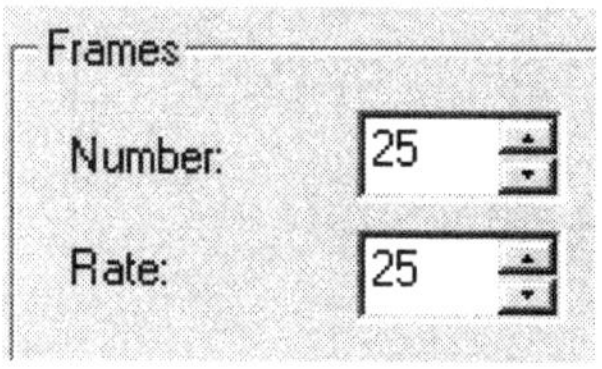

Set the Frames to 25 and Rate to 25.

Press **OK.**

TIP: Enable **Corner Deceleration** for the camera to move slower as it turns corners on the path.

10. 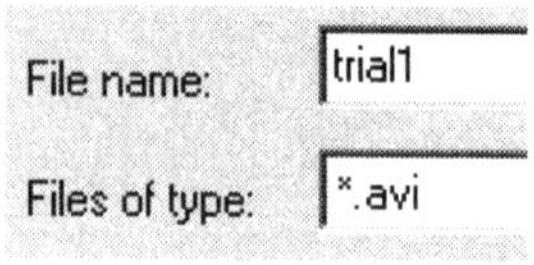

Browse to your work folder.
Name your video *trial1.avi* and select **Save.**

11.

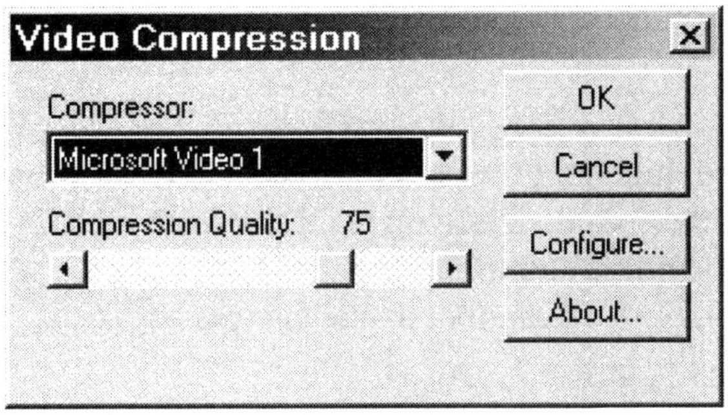

Select **Microsoft Video 1** as the Compressor.
Set the Compression Quality to **75**.
Press **OK**.

TIP: The avi format can be played using Microsoft Video Player or Real Player. If you use an incompatible Compressor, you will not be able to play your avi file.

It will take a few minutes for the avi to be created.

12.

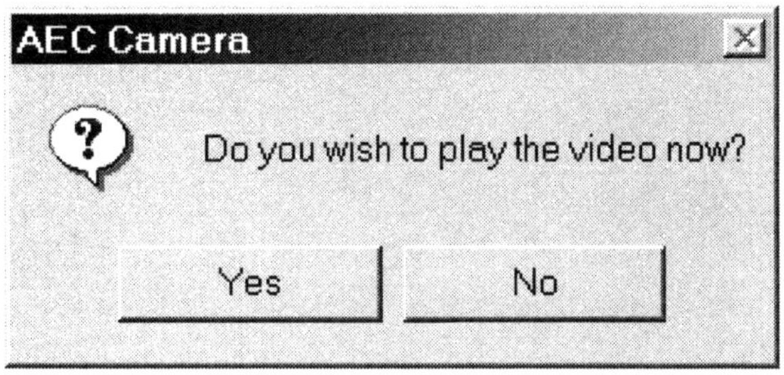

A dialog will appear asking if you would like to view the video.

Press **Yes.**

13. Save as *ex10-3.dwg.*

Playing your video shows an animated movie of your home. It looks a bit cartoonish, but that's OK.

ADT only allows you to animate shaded, hidden, or wire frame. It will not allow you to create a rendered animation of your model. To do that, you need software like 3D Studio Viz. Likewise, you can only select one camera at a time. You can modify the path to change elevations (using a 3D polyline), but you cannot change camera angles or perspectives.

TIP: The Content Browser can be launched by typing Ctl+4 or by using the Content Browser tool from ADT's Navigation toolbar.

COMPREHENSIVE EXAM

True or False

1. Doors, windows, and stairs are inserted into a drawing as objects.
2. The Object Viewer is a dialog box that allows you to view an object prior to placement.
3. The handle for placing a wall is located at the bottom of the Wall Justification line.
4. The Offset option of the Add Wall command shifts the justification handle off the justification line the Offset Value distance.
5. Wall Grips are located at the beginning, middle, and end on the bottom of the justification line of a wall.
6. AutoCAD commands such as OFFSET, TRIM, and EXTEND can be used to create and modify walls.
7. You can use wall grips to copy, stretch, or move walls.
8. Polylines can be converted to walls.
9. Door styles can not be copied.
10. Flip Hinge can be used to change the location and swing of a door or window.
11. You can change the location of a door or window using GRIPS.
12. If you remove a door or window from a wall, it will leave a gap. You will then need to "heal" the wall to close the opening.
13. Openings can be created with a specified width and height.
14. You can import door and window styles from external sources.
15. Roof properties define the thickness of the roof plane and the angle of the fascia.
16. The angle of a roof can be defined by the ratio of the rise to run or by a slope angle.
17. The CONVERT TO ROOF command is used to create a roof from a roof slab.
18. The ADDRAILING command can place a railing attached to stairs ONLY.
19. The scale for symbols and annotation is set with the OPTIONS dialog.
20. The Create AEC Content Wizard can be used to create a tool for a Tool Palette.
21. The Model Explorer allows you to view mass groups and elements.
22. The Model Explorer allows you to name mass groups and elements.
23. Grouping Mass Elements is the same as Joining them together.
24. A camera can be used to obtain views of a building.
25. In order to create a video, you must create a path.

Multiple Choice

1. The Menu Group that includes Architectural Desktop toolbars is:

    A. ACAD
    B. ACCOV
    C. ADT
    D. EXPRESS

2. To launch the Tool Palette, press:

    A. Ctl+2
    B. Ctl+3
    C. Shift+2
    D. Shift+3

3. To launch the Design Center, press:

    A. Ctl+2
    B. Ctl+3
    C. Shift+2
    D. Shift+3

4. To freeze all layers except those layers in a Layer User Group, use:

    A. Isolate User Group
    B. Filter User Group
    C. Quick Select
    D. Freeze Invert User Group

5. The default layer standard for the Imperial template is:

    A. None
    B. AIA (256 Colors)
    C. Generic Architectural Desktop
    D. Standard

6. The limits of the AEC_Arch Imperial templates is set to this by default:

A. 1′, 9′
B. 288′-0″,192′-0″
C. 144′-0″, 96′-0″
D. None of the above

7. The default scale factor for symbols and dimensions of the AEC_Arch Imperial template is:

A. ¼″ = 1′
B. ½″ = 1′
C. 1″ = 1′
D. 1/8″ = 1′

8. Walls have all of the following properties EXCEPT:

A. Width
B. Height
C. Justification
D. Thickness

9. The command to Convert a Polyline to a Wall is:

A. WALLCONVERT
B. POLYLINECONVERT
C. CONVERT
D. WALLPROPS

10. Select the entity type that CAN NOT be converted to a wall:

A. LINE
B. POLYLINE
C. SPLINE
D. ARC

11. The command to insert a Door into a drawing is:

A. DOORADD
B. ADDDOOR
C. INSERT
D. DOORINSERT

12. The Style of a door is defined using this command:

    A. DOORSTYLE
    B. STYLEDOOR
    C. DOORTYPE
    D. STYLETYPE

13. A single hinged door will display at an angle of 90 degrees if the opening percent is set to:

    A. 90
    B. 50
    C. 25
    D. 0

14. The _____ of an Arch Window defines its radius.

    A. RADIUS
    B. RISE
    C. HEIGHT
    D. DIAMETER

15. Roofs are created with the command:

    A. ADDROOF
    B. ROOFADD
    C. INSERT
    D. INSERTROOF

16. The following entity type CAN NOT be used by the CONVERT TO ROOF command:

    A. Roof slab
    B. Line
    C. Polyline
    D. Walls

17. The command to insert stairs into a drawing is:

A. STAIRADD
B. ADDSTAIR
C. INSERT
D. INSERTSTAIRS

18. Straight stairs are created using this Shape setting:

A. Multi-Landing
B. Spiral
C. Straight
D. U-Shaped

19. The Shape options for stairs include all those listed below EXCEPT:

A. U-SHAPED
B. Multi-Landing
C. Floating
D. Straight

20. To launch the Autodesk Content Browser, use:

A. Ctl+2
B. Ctl+3
C. Ctl+4
D. Ctl+5

21. Setting the Drawing Scale establishes the ______ of dimensions.

A. units
B. text height
C. text style
D. placement

22. Mass Elements can be created using the ______ Command:

A. MassElementAdd
B. ElementAdd
C. MassAdd
D. None of the above

23. Mass Elements are placed on this layer (using the AIA standard):

    A. A-AREA-MASS
    B. A-SOLIDS
    C. A-ELEMENTS
    D. A-MASS-ELEMENT

24. Which components make up the display system in Architectural Desktop?

    A. Scale, objects, and linetype settings.
    B. The viewports, layer settings, and scale.
    C. The plotscale, objects, and linetype settings.
    D. A viewport, objects, and a viewing direction for the objects.

25. What does the priority for components represent when creating or modifying wall styles?

    A. Importance values for use in wall cleanup at intersections.
    B. Relative structural strength values for the components of the wall style.
    C. Priority controls the display order of the individual wall components for the style.
    D. The assembly order of the individual wall components for construction purposes.

ANSWERS:

True-False
1) T; 2) T; 3) T; 4) T; 5) T; 6) T; 7) T; 8) T; 9) F; 10) T; 11) T; 12) F; 13) T; 14) T; 15) T; 16) T; 17) F; 18) F; 19) F; 20) T; 21) T; 22) T; 23) F; 24) T; 25) T

Multiple Choice
1) C; 2) B; 3) A; 4) A; 5) B; 6) B; 7) D; 8) D; 9) A; 10) C; 11) A; 12) A; 13) B; 14) B; 15) B; 16) A; 17) A; 18) C; 19) C; 20) C; 21) B; 22) A; 23) A; 24) B; 25) A

INDEX

1 Viewport 10-9
2 Viewports 10-7
3D Section 7-39

A

Add Component 1-31
Add Detail 1-17
Add Dimension Points 8-14
Add Header 9-10
Add Mass Group 1-48
Add New Material 1-34
Add Railing 6-28
Adjust View 10-8
AEC Content 1-13
AEC Content Wizard 7-12, 7-18
AEC Dimension 1-12, 8-12
AEC Display Resolution 1-11
AEC Editor 1-7
AEC Object Settings 1-10, 6-27
AEC Project Defaults 1-14
Apply 'L' Cleanup 3-9
Apply Tool Properties to Linework 3-4, 5-4, 5-10
Arch 1-26
Area Tags 8-8
Array 6-11, 6-18
Attach Elements 1-49, 1-54
Autodesk Content Browser 10-3, 10-4

B

Block, Insert 7-25
Bottom Rail 6-21
Box 1-44
Brace Trim Planes 6-14
Break 3-7
Break Marks 8-3

C

Camera 10-5
Camera Path 10-10
Cased Opening 3-18
Chases 8-3
Cleanups 3-9
Convert to Block 7-12
Convert to Mass Element 1-53
Convert to Roof Slabs 5-6
Copy 6-10, 7-40
Corner Deceleration 10-11
Create New Folder 7-11
Create Video 10-10
Custom Command 7-13

D

DC Online 1-42
Define Attribute 7-5, 7-6
Design Center 1-42
Desktop Display Manager 1-20
Detail Marks 8-3
Dimensions 8-6
Display Manager 1-20, 1-62
Display Properties 1-35
Door & Window Tags 8-8
Door Schedule 9-15
Door Tag 9-12
Drawing Setup 2-10, 8-1, 8-12

E

Edit Attribute 7-6
Edit Material 1-35
Edit Object Display 7-37
Edit Style 9-2
Elevation Labels 8-5
Elevation Label Modify 2-18
Elevation Marks 8-5
Enable AC Unit Scaling 7-14
Export 9-16

F

Fillet- 0″ 3-8
Fire Rating Lines 8-6
Flat Shaded 1-27

G

Gable 1-46
Generate Member Style 6-5, 6-6
Generate Section 7-35, 7-41

H

Handrail 6-21
Hole, Add 5-7
Hyperlink 7-4

I

Imageframe 7-5
Import Schedule Style 9-15
Insert, Block 7-25, 7-30
Insert, Image 7-4
Isolate Group 5-9, 6-4, 8-11

L

Layer Keys 1-60, 1-61, 7-14
Layer Key Overrides 1-58
Layer Key Standards 1-57
Layer Manager 1-56, 2-7, 2-22
Layer User Group 7-22
Layer Standards 1-57
Leaders 8-5
LY files 1-58

M

Make Block 7-12
Make Linetype 2-3
Mass Element 1-21
Mass Group 1-21, 1-48
Mass Model 1-21
Match Lines 8-6
Mirror 6-10
Model Explorer 1-51
Move UCS 6-25
Mtext 7-3

N

New 1-5
New Filter Group 1-59, 4-18
New Group 6-4
New Layer 1-58, 7-23
New Layout 7-20, 7-32
New Palette 4-5
New Style 1-29, 9-7
New User Group 1-59, 2-22, 7-22
North Arrows 8-7

O

Object Tags 8-8
Opening 3-16
Options 1-7

P

Page Setup 7-27, 7-30
Point Style 2-12
Polygon 7-16
Post Locations 6-22
Presentation Format 1-11
Project Browser 1-15
Property Set Definitions 7-18
Purge 9-7

Q

QNEW 1-6
Quick Select 2-13, 6-15

R

Rail Locations 6-21
Railing 6-19, 6-28
Railing Styles 6-20
Recent Commands 1-51
Reference Docs 9-2
Remove Dimension Points 8-13
Rename Palette 4-6
Reposition Along Wall 3-25
Reverse 3-6, 7-38
Revision Clouds 8-7
RoofAdd 5-1
RoofConvert 5-1
Room & Finish Tags 8-9

S

Scale 7-2
Schedule Table Styles 9-1
Section Marks 8-9
Sections 7-31
Set Current Display Configuration 1-62
Set Image from Selection 3-18
Single Viewport 7-24
Snapshots 1-58, 4-17
Specify Image 1-40
Stair 6-26
Stair Representation 6-27
Straight Leader 7-28
Structual Beam 6-16
Structural Brace 6-12
Structural Column 6-11
Structural Member Catalog 6-5
Structural Member Styles 6-7
Style Manager 1-22, 7-18

T

TableStyle 9-1
Template 1-5
TextStyle 2-5
Title Marks 8-9, 8-11
Toolbars 7-5
Tool Palettes 1-36
Trim Plane 6-14

U

UCS ICON 7-25, 8-11
Units 2-11

V

Viewports 7-12

W

Wall Components 1-31
Wall Styles 1-28
Wall Tags 8-9
Window Schedule 9-13
Window Tag 9-11

About the Author

Elise Moss has worked for the past twenty years as a mechanical designer in Silicon Valley, primarily creating sheet metal designs. She has written articles for Autodesk's Toplines magazine, AUGI's PaperSpace, DigitalCAD.com and Tenlinks.com. She is President of Moss Designs, creating custom applications and designs for corporate clients. She has taught CAD classes at DeAnza College, Silicon Valley College, and for Autodesk resellers. Autodesk has named her as a Faculty of Distinction for the curriculum she has developed for Autodesk products. She holds a baccalaureate degree from San Jose State.

She is married with two sons. Her older son, Benjamin, is and electrical engineer. Her younger son, Daniel, is studying architecture at local community colleges. Her husband, Ari, has a distinguished career in software development.

Elise is a third generation engineer. Her father, Robert Moss, is a metallurgical engineer in the aerospace industry. Her grandfather, Solomon Kupperman, was a civil engineer for the City of Chicago.

She can be contacted via email at elise_moss@mossdesigns.com.

More information about the author and her work can be found on her website at www.mossdesigns.com.

Other books by Elise Moss

Autodesk Inventor R6 Fundamentals: Conquering the Rubicon
AutoCAD 2000i Mechanical Drafting for Beginners
Architectural Desktop R3.3: Laying a Sound Foundation
Revit 5.0 Basics